EXISTENTIAL PERSPECTIVES ON HUMAN ISSUES

D1477108

Also by Emmy van Deurzen:

Existential Psychotherapy and Counselling in Practice
Paradox and Passion in Psychotherapy
Everyday Mysteries

Existential Perspectives on Human Issues

A Handbook for Therapeutic Practice

edited by

Emmy van Deurzen and Claire Arnold-Baker

First published 2005 by
PALGRAVE MACMILLAN
Houndmills, Basingstoke, Hampshire RG21 6XS and
175 Fifth Avenue, New York, N.Y. 10010
Companies and representatives throughout the world

PALGRAVE MACMILLAN is the global academic imprint of the Palgrave Macmillan division of St. Martin's Press, LLC and of Palgrave Macmillan Ltd. Macmillan® is a registered trademark in the United States, United Kingdom and other countries. Palgrave is a registered trademark in the European Union and other countries.

ISBN-13: 978–0–333–98699–8 hardback
ISBN-10: 0–333–98699–7 hardback
ISBN-13: 978–0–333–98700–1 paperback
ISBN-10: 0–333–98700–4 paperback

This book is printed on paper suitable for recycling and made from fully managed and sustained forest sources.
Logging, pulping and manufacturing processes are expected to conform to the environmental regulations of the country of origin.

A catalogue record for this book is available from the British Library.

A catalog record for this book is available from the Library of Congress.

10   9   8   7   6   5   4   3   2
14   13   12   11   10   09   08   07

Printed in China

This book is dedicated to all students, trainees and practitioners of existential psychotherapy and counselling

I must search for being if I want to find my real self. But it is not till I fail in this search for intrinsic being that I begin to philosophize.

Karl Jaspers

Contents

Preface   x

Notes on Contributors   xii

Introduction   xviii
    Emmy van Deurzen and Claire Arnold-Baker

PART I

OVERVIEW   1

1   **Philosophical Background**   3
    Emmy van Deurzen

2   **Therapeutic Background**   15
    Mick Cooper

PART II

PHYSICAL DIMENSION   25

3   **Introduction to the Physical Dimension**   27
    Emmy van Deurzen and Claire Arnold-Baker

4   **Procreation**   31
    Claire Arnold-Baker and Miriam Donaghy

5   **Human Development**   39
    Steve Kirby

6   **The Body and Sexuality**   48
    Paul Smith-Pickard and Richard Swynnerton

7   **Eating Problems**   58
    Kirk J. Schneider and Zoë Fitzgerald-Pool

8   **An Existential Perspective on Addiction**   67
    Simon du Plock and Jonathan Fisher

9   **Death**   78
    Mick Cooper and Martin Adams

PART III

SOCIAL DIMENSION   87

10   Introduction to the Social Dimension   89
      Emmy van Deurzen and Claire Arnold-Baker

11   Language   93
      Michael Harding

12   Dialogue and Communication   100
      Lucia Moja-Strasser

13   Emotions   110
      Emmy van Deurzen

14   Relationships   121
      Digby Tantam and Emmy van Deurzen

15   Families   133
      Naomi and Anthony Stadlen

16   Groups   143
      Digby Tantam

PART IV

PERSONAL DIMENSION   155

17   Introduction to the Personal Dimension   157
      Emmy van Deurzen and Claire Arnold-Baker

18   The Self   160
      Emmy van Deurzen and Claire Arnold-Baker

19   Authenticity and Inauthenticity   171
      John Pollard

20   Anxiety and Engagement   180
      Nick Kirkland-Handley and Diana Mitchell

21   Depression and Apathy   189
      Claire Arnold-Baker

22   Bereavement and Loss   197
      Greg Madison

23   Dreams   207
      Sarah Young

PART V

SPIRITUAL DIMENSION 215

24 Introduction to the Spiritual Dimension 217
Emmy van Deurzen and Claire Arnold-Baker

25 Interpretation: Explanation or Understanding? 221
Hans W. Cohn

26 Time and Purpose 227
Karen Weixel-Dixon and Freddie Strasser

27 Values and Beliefs 236
Bo Jacobsen

28 Political and Ideological Issues 245
Martin Milton

29 Meaning and Transformation 253
Myrtle Heery and James F. T. Bugental

30 A New Ideology 265
Emmy van Deurzen

Conclusion: Therapeutic Work on Four Dimensions 277
Emmy van Deurzen

Bibliography 303

Index 320

Preface

The existential approach to psychotherapy and counselling has now become well-established. It is increasingly recognized and valued for its capacity to throw new light on the old human issues that plague our existence. Rather than analysing or interpreting these, existential therapists approach predictable and unpredictable predicaments by describing them, putting them in context and finding ways to understand the challenges they throw up for us.

This book presents the writing of many of the therapists working at the forefront of the movement of existential therapy at the beginning of the twenty-first century. Most of the contributions are from authors who are based in the UK, many of them connected to the New School of Psychotherapy and Counselling, which is a unique organization, located at Schiller International University on the South Bank of the River Thames in London, just across from Waterloo station. The New School was specifically founded to provide a training institute for existential therapy and it has become a hot spot for the evolution of the approach.

It is very telling, however, that the nationalities of the authors of this book are wide-ranging and include British, American, Canadian, Danish, Dutch, German, Hungarian, Irish and Romanian nationals. In addition, there are two authors based in other European countries and three authors who work in the United States. It will be obvious that all authors have a very personal perspective on what it means to be human, even though most will occasionally refer to some of the standard philosophical texts, such as Heidegger's *Being and Time* and Sartre's *Being and Nothingness*. This diversity and multiplicity of interpretation and method is one of the strengths of the existential approach and it is what makes the appearance of a book of this nature particularly relevant. Allowing for a wide range of views is the only way to oppose the tendency towards dogma that is otherwise inevitable when an approach becomes more established. The objective is to be non-doctrinaire and trans-theoretical and to remain faithful to the personal experiences of individual human beings.

Existential therapy allows for mutuality and reciprocity in the therapeutic relationship and emphasizes the cooperative nature of the work. It provides a space in which prejudice and opinion can be expressed and fairly considered in order that we can sometimes overcome it. Clients are given an opportunity to reflect on their own lives in the way that is most meaningful to them and which allows them to make sense of what may have seemed confusing previously. At the same time, therapists will be aware of some of the parameters of human experience and some of the fundamental structures of living that we all have to take into account. The chapters in this book will sketch out some of these parameters whilst constantly testing them and observing whether it may be possible to extend them and go beyond them.

It is especially when freedom and individuality become such key concepts to an approach that we need to ensure that we do not lose all sense of direction. The existential approach generally tries to find the balance between directiveness and non-directiveness in order to enable clients to find their own direction in a manner that is sure-footed enough to be safe and challenging enough to provide the excitement of adventure.

Trainees and clients alike often experience a sense of liberation and exhilaration on discovering that this approach affords them the freedom to work in their own way whilst giving them the benefit of the insights and wisdom of three millennia of philosophy.

Because of the non-prescriptive nature of existential work, the approach has been notoriously ill-documented and has often been reproached for lacking in theoretical underpinnings, failing to provide a developmental theory or a theory of human nature. This is the logical outcome of a theoretical position that favours open-endedness, but it is no excuse to neglect to reflect on the important human issues that all therapists have to deal with. In this book most of these issues have been addressed and the existential thinking on these topics has been summarized and clarified. Undoubtedly this will lead to further debate and discussion, which will hopefully continue the process of clarification and verification so indispensable to real understanding.

This book will fill some of the gaping holes in the existential approach and provide trainees and therapists with some substantial food for thought. There will be descriptions and ideas to help them to conceptualize their own and their clients' troubles and difficulties with greater accuracy and confidence. All levels of human experience are touched upon, although we are well aware that each would have deserved an entire volume of its own if we could have done justice to the complexity of human existence. Of course there are many other issues that we would have liked to include. We are particularly sad to have had to leave out a chapter on cross-cultural elements of therapy, but incompleteness is a fact of life and hopefully will lead to new explorations at a later stage. We hope that the various facets of human existence that have been highlighted in this book will elucidate new aspects of your daily experience and practice and that they will help you in rekindling your own enthusiasm for living a brighter and more satisfying life.

We would like to thank all the contributors who have made this book so diverse and rich, showing that the existential approach is as varied as the therapists who practise it. The book is truly a team effort and we are grateful for the enthusiastic way in which our colleagues have responded to the challenge we put to them. On a more personal note we would like to thank Digby and Will for their unstinting support and encouragement throughout this project.

Emmy van Deurzen and Claire Arnold-Baker
London, July 2004

Notes on Contributors

The editors

Emmy van Deurzen directs the New School of Psychotherapy and Counselling in London and is Professor in Psychotherapy with Schiller International University. She co-directs the Centre for the Study of Conflict and Reconciliation at the University of Sheffield and is a Director of Dilemma Consultancy in Human Relations. She founded the Society for Existential Analysis in 1988, and is a fellow of the British Association for Counselling and Psychotherapy and of the British Psychological Society. Her books include *Existential Counselling and Psychotherapy in Practice* (2002), *Paradox and Passion in Psychotherapy* (1998) and *Everyday Mysteries* (1997).

Claire Arnold-Baker is a UKCP-registered existential psychotherapist who completed her MA at the New School of Psychotherapy and Counselling. Claire is Course Co-ordinator at the New School, where she also teaches an introductory short course and on the MA programme. Claire is Honorary Treasurer of the Universities Psychotherapy and Counselling Association and Chair of the Society of Psychotherapy.

The contributors

Martin Adams is a psychotherapist in private practice and the National Health Service, and also a sculptor. He has a particular interest in the relationship of therapeutic theory to practice, and the nature and purpose of artistic representation.

James F. T. Bugental is the author of numerous articles and seven books including *Psychotherapy Isn't What You Think*, *The Art of the Psychotherapist* and *The Search For Existential Identity*. He was the first president of Humanistic Psychology, Division 32, the American Psychological Association. His numerous appointments have included Rockefeller Scholar, California Institute of Integral Studies; Visiting Distinguished Professor, California School of Professional Psychology; Emeritus Clinical Faculty, Stanford Medical School; Emeritus Professor, Saybrook Institute; and Faculty in Psychology, University of California, Los Angeles.

Hans W. Cohn (1916–2004) was a therapist in private practice for a great many years. As a tutor and author he attempted to convey his viewpoint to those who wished to become existential therapists. His first book, *Existential Thought and Therapeutic Practice* (1997), is an introduction to existential psychotherapy. More recently, his book *Heidegger and the Roots of Existential Therapy* (2002) explores the role of Heidegger's thought as a basis for therapeutic practice. Hans was on the editorial board of the *Journal of the Society for Existential Analysis* and he was Honorary Visiting Fellow of the School of Psychotherapy and Counselling at Regent's College.

Mick Cooper is Senior Lecturer in Counselling at the University of Strathclyde and a UKCP-registered existential therapist. He is author of *Existential Therapies* (2003), co-editor with John Rowan of *The Plural Self* (1999), and author of several chapters and articles on existential, person-centred and self-pluralistic approaches to counselling and psychotherapy. Mick lives in Glasgow with his partner and three daughters, and can be contacted at mick.cooper@strath.ac.uk.

Miriam Donaghy is a UKCP-registered existential psychotherapist who completed her MA at the New School of Psychotherapy and Counselling. She works as the clinical supervisor of the counselling and group therapy service at Greenwich MIND and co-ordinates the post-natal depression service. She is also in private practice. Miriam has previously published articles in the *CPJ* and *Practical Philosophy* and her research interest is in post-natal depression.

Simon du Plock is Director of the MA course in Counselling Psychology and Post-MA Diploma in Existential Counselling Psychology, and Senior Lecturer in Psychotherapy and Counselling Psychology at the School of Psychotherapy and Counselling, Regent's College, London. He is an associate lecturer on the counselling psychology doctoral programme at the University of Surrey, acts as a clinical supervisor for MIND and works as a psychologist with Employee Assistance Programmes. He also maintains a private practice in existential psychotherapy and clinical supervision. His research interests include the relationship between psychotherapy and literature, and he has edited *Existential Analysis*, the *Journal of the Society for Existential Analysis*, since 1993.

Jonathan Fisher has been working as a counsellor and psychotherapist for the past nine years. He has an MA in Existential Psychotherapy from the New School and a postgraduate diploma in addiction counselling. He has worked in the field of addiction in both residential and day-care settings. He currently works in the Sleep Disorders Centre at St Thomas' Hospital conducting research into the effectiveness of cognitive-behavioural therapy in treating insomnia. He is also in private practice.

Zoë Fitzgerald-Pool is an existential psychotherapist, a trainer and supervisor, with a background in performing arts and education. In the past, Zoë worked as a school counsellor, and in counselling agencies, and has considerable experience working in the field of addiction, and with clients who have eating problems. Zoë is currently the Director of Training and Development of the Central School for Counselling Training. As well as leading the academic team, and writing and delivering courses for CSCT, Zoë has a private practice in Bournemouth.

Michael Harding is an existential psychotherapist, and a faculty member at the School of Psychotherapy and Counselling at Regent's College, London. He is former Chair of the Society for Existential Analysis. His interests include the experience of time and the influence of language on our sense of self, drawing particularly on the work of Heidegger and Wittgenstein. He is particularly interested in links between philosophy, psychoanalysis and the wisdom traditions of older cultures. He has written extensively on the practice and philosophy of astrology, as well as various articles on language and psychotherapy.

Myrtle Heery is an associate professor in the graduate in-depth Psychology Program at Sonoma State University, Rohnert Park, California; Director of the International Institute for Humanistic Studies, Petaluma, California; and a senior teaching associate with James F. T. Bugental. Some of her publications include an excerpt from her doctoral dissertation, *Hearing Voices: A Non-Psychotic Approach* (translated into five languages), *Food for the Soul, A Psychotherapist's Journey Teaching in Russia, Listening to the Listener* and *A Humanistic Perspective on Bereavement*. In addition to her private practice with individuals, couples and groups, she provides trainings in existential-humanistic psychotherapy in Russia, Europe, Mexico, Canada and the United States.

Bo Jacobsen is a research professor at the University of Copenhagen in Denmark. He is also a practising psychologist and existential therapist who trains existential therapists in Denmark. He is a member of the Society of Existential Analysis in London and the International Daseinsanalytic Federation in Zürich and he is the author of a number of books on existential psychology, the existential problems of cancer patients, existential psychotherapy and related subjects.

Steve Kirby is a UKCP-registered and BACP-accredited existential psychotherapist working in private practice. He also works as a substance-misuse practitioner for Ravenswood Road residential rehabilitation centre. He has previously published articles in the *Journal of the Society for Existential Analysis*. He is particularly interested in issues of identity and meaning.

Nick Kirkland-Handley is a chartered clinical psychologist and UKCP-registered psychotherapist. Formerly employed in the NHS, he is now on the visiting faculty of the New School of Psychotherapy and Counselling. He has a private practice in Richmond, Surrey. His interests include considering the implications of existential-phenomenological thought for clinical practice.

Greg Madison is involved in teaching, research, supervision and client work. He is a registered psychotherapist working in university and health settings as well as private practice. He holds a first degree in psychology, an MA in psychotherapeutic studies and an advanced clinical training in existential therapy and focusing. He is currently working on his PhD research, a phenomenological analysis of the existential significance of 'home'.

Martin Milton is Senior Lecturer and Course Director (Practice) of the University of Surrey Practitioner Doctorate in Psychotherapeutic and Counselling Psychology. He is also Consultant Psychologist in Psychotherapy with North East London Mental Health Trust. His research and specialist interests include lesbian and gay affirmative psychology and psychotherapy, HIV-related psychotherapy and existential psychotherapy.

Diana Mitchell is an existential therapist and supervisor. She works for the NHS and has a private practice in Walton on Thames, Surrey. She supervises at the New School of Psychotherapy and Counselling and the School of Psychotherapy and Counselling at Regent's College. She is particularly interested in existential thinking and supervisory practice. Her paper 'Is the Concept of Supervision at Odds with Existential Thinking and Therapeutic Practice?' appeared in the *Journal of the Society for Existential Analysis*: 13(1).

Lucia Moja-Strasser is a founder member of the Society for Existential Analysis, a UKCP-registered psychotherapist and supervisor, working in private practice with individuals and couples. She is also a senior lecturer at the School of Psychotherapy and Counselling at Regent's College, London. Her input at the School consists of lecturing and supervising on the MA and the Advanced Diploma in Existential Psychotherapy. Lucia is Director of the Advanced Diploma in Existential Psychotherapy. In addition to philosophy her interests include music, poetry, yoga and Zen meditation.

John Pollard is a graduate of the philosophy department at the University of Essex and now works as an existential integrative therapist for Tendring Mental Health Support in Clacton-on-Sea, Essex. He has written journal articles and book reviews, taught at the New School of Psychotherapy and Counselling, and is currently co-authoring an alternative self-help book. His current interests include the nature of freedom and responsibility, the importance of meaning and the exploration of therapy as 'ethical' dialogue.

Kirk J. Schneider is a psychologist and widely published author in humanistic and existential psychology. He is the author/editor of four books, *The Paradoxical Self*, *Horror and the Holy*, *The Psychology of Existence* and *The Handbook of Humanistic Psychology*. Recently, he was elected to receive the Rollo May Award for 'outstanding pursuit of new frontiers in humanistic psychology', by the humanistic psychology division of the APA (American Psychological Association).

Paul Smith-Pickard is a UKCP-registered existential psychotherapist working in the NHS and private practice. He is on the visiting faculty of the New School of Psychotherapy and Counselling and the School of Psychotherapy and Counselling at Regent's College. He is currently researching the phenomenology of encounter in psychotherapy. He is present Chair of the Society for Existential Analysis.

Anthony Stadlen has been practising since 1970 as an existential-phenomenological psychotherapist with individuals, couples and families. He teaches and supervises at several London institutes. Since 1977, with the support of the Nuffield Foundation, he has been researching the paradigmatic case studies of Freud, Layard, Fordham, Boss, Laing, Esterson and others. He is a former research fellow of the Freud Museum, London. Since 1996, he has been conducting the Inner Circle Seminars, an ethical, existential, phenomenological search for truth in psychotherapy.

Naomi Stadlen has been practising since 1991 as an existential counsellor and psychotherapist, specialising in work with parents of small children. She is also a breastfeeding counsellor. She teaches and supervises at several London institutes. Her book, *What Mothers Do, Especially When it Looks Like Nothing*, based on her observations of new mothers, and on conversations with them about the experience of becoming a mother, was published by Judy Piatkus in 2004.

Freddie Strasser is a senior lecturer, course leader, accredited supervisor, director of the ADR (mediation) courses and a psychotherapist in private practice. His particular interests are existential time-limited psychotherapy and conflicts in general. His publications include *Existential Time-Limited Therapy*, with A. Strasser (1997); *Emotions* (1999); 'Existential Anxiety from a Personal Perspective' *European Judaism* (29, 1996); and *Mediation: The Tyranny and Award of Conflicts* (2004).

Richard Swynnerton is a psychotherapist and supervisor, working in both the public sector and private practice. He lectures at the New School of Psychotherapy and Counselling where he teaches human sexuality and at the School of Psychotherapy and Counselling at Regent's College. Richard has trained extensively in the existential approach to psychotherapy and finds existential philosophy particularly helpful to furthering his understanding of the human condition.

Digby Tantam is Clinical Professor of Psychotherapy at the University of Sheffield (1995–present) and was previously Professor of Psychotherapy at the University of Warwick (1990–1995). He is a practising psychotherapist, psychiatrist and psychologist. Digby is co-Director of the Centre for the Study of Conflict and Reconciliation in the university and Director of the Mental Health Section. He is a partner in Dilemma Consultancy in Human Relations (www.dilemmas.org). Digby has been Registrar of the European Association of Psychotherapy (1999–2001) and Chair of the United Kingdom Council for Psychotherapy (1995–1998). His book *Psychotherapy and Counselling in Practice: A Narrative Approach* was published in 2002.

Karen Weixel-Dixon is a UKCP-registered existential psychotherapist who also works as a supervisor and trainer. She has recently moved to France where she is developing a new private practice, and she continues to commute to the UK for various projects. She is also a senior lecturer on the Alternative Dispute Resolution Program at Regent's College, London.

Sarah Young originally trained as an orthoptist and worked in the NHS for fifteen years. She is now UKCP-registered and a chartered counselling psychologist working in private practice. For over ten years she trained students at the School of Psychotherapy and Counselling at Regent's College. She is also a visiting lecturer at the New School of Psychotherapy and Counselling, Waterloo, and at Surrey University, Roehampton. As a member of the Executive Committee of the Society for Existential Analysis she was responsible for organizing five of their annual conferences. She was the author of the chapter on Existential Counselling and Psychotherapy in *Introduction to Counselling and Psychotherapy* (2000) edited by Stephen Palmer. She is a volunteer on the helpline at Breast Cancer Care.

Introduction

EMMY VAN DEURZEN AND CLAIRE ARNOLD-BAKER

> You would not find out the boundaries of the soul,
> even by travelling along every path:
> so deep a measure does it have.
>
> Heraclitus, *Aneilla to the Pre-Socratic Philosophers*

The vista of human experience is so vast and diverse that it is impossible to do justice to it. Therefore, in selecting the various chapters for this book we have concentrated on issues that people can relate to in their everyday life. Of course this means that many important and relevant issues have been left out, amongst others the area of mental health. The topics that we did choose to include will nevertheless give an overview of the whole range of human experience and of the way in which the existential approach deals with it.

The book is divided into five parts. The first part provides summaries of existential philosophy and existential practice. The remaining four parts correspond to the four worlds of existence, the Physical, Social, Personal and Spiritual dimensions of human experience. Within each part there is an introductory chapter and six further chapters, each relating to a particular issue on that dimension.

The four worlds of existence offer a framework from which to map out an individual's world or experience. Binswanger (1946) was one of the first practitioners to apply Heidegger's philosophy as a basis for clinical work. Binswanger was interested in Heidegger's concept of being-in-the-world, that individuals are not isolated subjects who inhabit a world, but who rather interconnect with the world. However, he was particularly interested in Heidegger's notion of *Mitsein*,[1] or being-with, as a fundamental aspect of human existence.

Binswanger compared von Uexküll's (1921) biological world-concept with Heidegger's being-in-the-world. Von Uexküll distinguished a perception world and an action world (*Merkwelt* and *Aktionwelt*) in an animal's relationship to its environment (*Umwelt*). Von Uexküll argued that 'one is fully justified in assuming the existence of as many environments (Umwelten) as there are animals' (Uexküll [S.144], quoted in May, 1994). However, Binswanger argued that von Uexküll's model would need to be modified if applied to human beings. Human beings have their own personal world as well as the objective world they share with all. '"World", however, signifies not only world-formation and predesign of world, but – on the basis of the predesign and model-image – also the *how* of being-*in*-the-world and the attitude *toward* world' (Binswanger, 1946: 195).

Binswanger felt that using the concept of being-in-the-world gives human existence a structure, which could be used when working with patients. Rather than looking at the behaviour of a patient, Binswanger shifted the focus to the patient's world, what it was like and how they existed in that world. He wanted to find an alternative to the medical model, which categorized people according to their pathology, and he developed a framework to describe the ways in which people relate to their world instead. The framework was based on Heidegger's concept of being-in-the-world. Binswanger highlighted that there were different ways of being-in-the-world:

> This *materialité* of the world-design, originating from the 'key' (*Gestimmtheit*) of the existence, is by no means confined to the environment, to the world of things, or to the universe in general, but refers equally to the world of one's fellow men (*Mitwelt*) and to the self-world (*Eigenwelt*). (Binswanger, 1946: 212)

Rollo May clarified Binswanger's worldviews. *Umwelt* is seen as the 'world around', which relates to the biological world and the environment. The *Mitwelt* is the world of others, the 'with world', and the *Eigenwelt* represents the world of the self or the 'own world' (May, 1983: 126). The fourth dimension, *Überwelt*, was elucidated by van Deurzen-Smith (1988) and represents the spiritual dimension of human existence, which is also implied in the work of most existential authors.

The *Umwelt* is shared by animals as well as humans and it includes all biological drives and impulses – 'It is the world of natural law and natural cycles of sleep and awakeness, of being born and dying, desire and relief' (May, 1983: 126). It also represents the world that we are *thrown*[2] into, that we have no control over, such as our physical environment and our bodies. It is the world of our senses and awareness of bodily needs. However, this world or dimension also relates to our health, wealth, fitness, relationship to the earth and our body. The *Umwelt* is categorized by adjustment and adaptation – 'I adapt to the cold weather and I adjust to the periodic needs of my body for sleep' (May, 1983: 128).

The *Mitwelt* represents the social dimension of existence; it is the world of relationships with other human beings. This world is not just about relationships with others, it is also about relationships to culture, society and language. This is the public realm of experience, which includes people's relationship to their race, their social class or other reference groups. It also covers a person's attitude to their country, language and cultural history, to their family and work environment and their general attitude towards authority. The *Mitwelt* is categorized by relationship and is regulated by feelings.

The *Eigenwelt* is the world of the self or the personal dimension. It is about intimacy with self and with others and includes feelings, thoughts, character traits and memories. It is the level at which a sense of identity is created. The *Eigenwelt* is where we get a sense of 'me'. It also involves a struggle with one's personal strengths and weaknesses. It is the dimension where personal stability or instability is experienced.

The fourth dimension or *Überwelt* is implied in the work of Kierkegaard (1844), Buber (1923), Jaspers (1951) and Tillich (1952). This dimension represents the world of our values and beliefs, our ideal world 'or the meta-world where all the rest of our experience is put into context' (van Deurzen-Smith, 1997: 123). This world is not just about religion but rather it is where we make sense of our lives. It is where the purpose and meaning of our life are created.

The four-dimensional model is also one which Heidegger (1989) used during the later stages of his career when he wrote about the fourfold (*Geviert*). He described four items, or elements, evolving from the big bang event, which started the world as we know it: world, earth, man and gods. In this description the being that we know is always at the intersection between a physical environment, other people, the human ability to make sense of it and the divine quality of the existence of meaning. These four regions of existence take us beyond Hegel's tripart structures, but Heidegger insists that we keep a playful openness in our movement between these regions (*Spielraum*) instead of analysing them to death. Human beings stand in-between these four worlds and we are able to appropriate them as events (*Ereignis*). 'Man stands like a bridge in the in-between' (Heidegger, 1989: 488). Since this fluidity of the fourfold is at risk of being annihilated by science, we need to guard the freedom of movement between different spheres. The idea of the four dimensions of the world also resonates with the idea of the four worlds in the Kabalah, in the four seasons and in the four elements of earth, water, air and fire.

We could say that existential therapy is about enabling people to regain the freedom to play within the dimensions set out for them; it is a way of helping them to preserve or reappropriate their elbow room, their freedom of movement. The four dimensions are interrelated and we live in all four worlds simultaneously. Clarification of the way in which a person views and experiences their world on each of these levels can help us establish how they are situated in life. Where there are difficulties and limitations, this can help us locate ways in which clients can be enabled to gain a fuller experience of life. The four-world model provides a map of life that can facilitate our understanding of where and how a person is currently moving or held up.

Each dimension of existence contains its paradoxes and contradictions and people often attempt to avoid facing up to one end of the spectrum of their bi-polar human experience. Figure 1 (see page 302) illustrates the complexities of the four dimensions of human existence, their various qualities and characteristics and their polarities. By systematically examining where the client is on each dimension, we can more easily spot those areas of life that are closed off from them. Likewise, areas that are open to clients may be highlighted to enable clients to see how their strengths in one dimension can be brought to bear in other dimensions of their life. The focus is on clarification and greater awareness, which may lead to a new understanding.

The objective of this book is to explore in some detail some specific challenges and human issues that clients struggle with on each of these dimensions, in order to give practitioners and trainees a better insight into how existential thinking is relevant to each of these. While every human being has to find their own way through the complexities of human living, there are enough similarities in the obstacles and opportunities we meet on our road to make it worthwhile to describe them and compare notes on the way in which particular clients were helped to deal with them. This is why each chapter will include a case illustration that will highlight a practical approach to each one of these issues. The concluding chapter brings all four dimensions together in a detailed case study, which systematically examines the client's issues on each of the four dimensions of existence. It should always be borne in mind that both the practitioner's way of working with the issue and the client's predicament are individual instances of universal experiences, which may be dealt with very differently on different occasions. There is no way to clarify human experience without seemingly prescribing a particular point of view or method. This is, however, not our intention and the reader is invited to explore their own perspectives on each of these issues and to keep an open mind about what is going on with each new experience and for each new person. We hope the book will in this way encourage you to freely come to your own conclusions.

Notes

1   'The world of Dasein is a *with-world* [*Mitwelt*]. Being-in is *Being-with* Others. Their Being-in-themselves within-the-world is *Dasein-with* [*Mitdasein* or *Mitsein*]' (Heidegger, 1962: 155).
2   This idea of *thrownness* comes from Heidegger: 'To Being-in-the-world however, belongs the fact that it has been delivered over to itself – that it has in each case already been thrown *into a world*' (Heidegger, 1962: 236).

PART I
OVERVIEW

CHAPTER 1

Philosophical Background

EMMY VAN DEURZEN

> For some it is all darkness; for me too,
> it is dark. But there are hands
> there I can take, voices to hear
> solider than the echoes
> without. And sometimes a strange light
> shines, purer than the moon,
> casting no shadow, that is
> the halo upon the bones
> of the pioneers who died for truth.
>
> Thomas, *Groping, Later Poems: A selection*: 99

Introduction

The existential approach to psychotherapy is unique in its firm location in philosophy. Existential psychotherapy focuses on life rather than on personality. The questions addressed are the questions all human beings ask themselves. What does it mean to be alive? Who am I? What is the purpose of my existence? Why is there anything at all? How should we live? What can I hope to achieve? Is happiness possible? What is expected of me? How should I act and be in relation to other people? Is there fairness in the world? Can I make a change for the better? Is it possible to understand life and get a grip on it? Can I find ways of overcoming my troubles? Is it necessary to suffer this much? How can I live a good life within the constrictions of the world? How can I be a better person? How can I live a worthwhile life?

Existential therapists base their interventions with clients on a careful consideration of human issues and on the clarification of what it means to be alive. They address the ontological level as well as the ontic level of human existence. This will often mean enabling people to ask the right questions, rather than providing them with the answers. Existential work is about understanding and clarifying what is problematic for an individual and enabling clients to tackle their problems in a creative and courageous manner. There is a wide range of philosophical writing available to therapists who work in this way. Not all philosophy is relevant, since some philosophy is based around epistemological, logical or linguistic problems and is more preoccupied with questions about knowledge or language than with human or moral issues. Nevertheless, many of the philosophers that have come to the fore over the past three millennia have made important contributions to the understanding of the human condition and their work deserves to be more widely known amongst counsellors and therapists.

Some people confuse the existential approach to psychotherapy with more narrowly based existentialist or humanistic forms of psychotherapy. This confusion arises because there is a considerable overlap between them as will become evident in the following pages. The continental movement of existentialism which was in vogue in the 1940s, 1950s and 1960s has certainly provided the impetus for a renewed focus on existential issues. It provided the inspiration for humanistic psychology, but it is by no means the only, or the most important, source of existential explorations in philosophy or psychotherapy. In fact, there is a well-established tradition of existential thinking throughout the history of philosophy. Most classical philosophers have written about the human issues and life challenges which psychotherapists and their clients are concerned with and have to deal with.

Existential foundations of psychotherapy

Throughout the history of philosophy numerous roads towards human well-being have been charted. Philosophers, those lovers of wisdom, made it their business to understand the human condition and show people how they could live more resourcefully. Philosophers as varied and widely apart as Heraclitus, Socrates, Plato, Aristotle, Zeno, Marcus Aurelius, Augustine, Spinoza, Kant, Rousseau, Hume, Hegel, Kierkegaard, Nietzsche, Heidegger, Wittgenstein or Sartre can give therapists new insight and encouragement. Some people would add to their list of inspirational works the old religious texts such as the Torah, the Koran, the Bible, the Sutras, the I-Ching, the Vedas or the Upanishads. The advantage of philosophical texts over religious ones is that the former set out to explore the issues rather than to preach about the correct way of dealing with them. Philosophy requires readers to think for themselves rather than to follow a particular doctrine. Psychotherapy and counselling have much to gain from being founded on philosophy rather than on dogma.

Many practitioners breathe a sigh of relief when they realize that their profession has much earlier antecedents and deeper roots than they had originally thought. They soon discover that they have ignored philosophical issues at their peril. Pathologizing clients and their problems in living can turn moral issues into illnesses. These can easily become personalized, internalized and intractable. It is much harder to enable clients to overcome their problems once these have become medicalized. Approaching a client's issue as a problem in living can allow us to open it up and externalize it, putting it back into its situational socio-cultural context. This allows us to make more pragmatic and direct interventions that enable clients to get a grip on their difficulties and find a new direction for themselves. But this is easier said than done. The fact of the matter is that many therapists and counsellors are not trained to explore philosophical questions. The pattern seems to be that therapists gain such perspective only as they become more experienced. When they are confident enough to leave behind a strict adherence to a particular theoretical framework and technique, they begin to think about human issues in a more philosophical way. They may then realize that it was not just with the advent of psychoanalysis or psychology that people became interested in helping each other to live good lives.

Philosophers through the ages have thought of ways in which the human condition can be understood and improved. There is a rich and varied literature on the predictable problems of human existence and how best to deal with them. As our understanding of human living improves through further research and evidence-based practice, this new information will supplement our current picture. Even so we will need a disciplined method of thinking through contradictory bits of information, whilst staying in touch with people's actual experiences rather than get blinded by the science. Keeping track of the history of the evolving human struggle to master life can also be productive in helping individuals realize how they replicate the evolutionary process in their own lives. Philosophy has as much to offer therapists as psychology. Of course not all therapists will want to put such a bold existential emphasis on their therapeutic work. Nevertheless, most practitioners will benefit from widening their perspective to include an existential dimension. So let us define what this entails.

Philosophical themes in psychotherapy

Death and nothingness

The philosophical theme of death is arguably most central when working from an existential perspective. Death is the great leveller. It is the background against which everything else is played out. It is the bottom line of human living. When we face up to our death it brings life back into its wider frame. Heidegger (1927) has written about the essential role of death in human existence. The human condition is such that it only comes to its completion in death and that we are always moving forwards towards this end. Dying is something we do, little by little and on a daily basis. Living is dying. We have to accept our own finality and temporary nature if we are to rise to the challenges of human living. For Sartre (1943) it is not death but nothingness that forms the basis of our existence. We are a fundamental lack and accepting our own emptiness is the sine qua non of becoming real. Much of our days are spent pretending that we are something when actually we are nothing. There can be great relief in seeing crisis situations as an opportunity to come to terms with the death and nothingness that our lives are built on or are attempting to hide.

Anxiety and despair

As we become aware of the importance of limits and of the temporary nature of human existence, the confrontation with the possibility of nothingness brings anxiety. Angst or existential anxiety is the experience of being confronted with the abyss. It is that very peculiar fear we feel in the face of nothing. It is the feeling of disappearing, of being in danger, of being on the edge. It is the possibility of impossibility. Heidegger (1927) claimed that anxiety is what makes us capable of standing alone, aside from other people, and also of coming to terms with our responsibility to live life in our own way. Kierkegaard (1845, 1980b) saw despair as the opposite pole of anxiety. We are either open to the infinite and feel the dizziness of Angst, the challenge of infinite possibility and of impossibility, or we close ourselves off from all of this and become despairing. Somehow in human living we need to find a way to contend with both these sentiments, both states of mind, and learn to live in the tension between them.

Absurdity and meaning

Many people come to a point in life where they question everything. According to Sartre (1943) life is absurd and it is only when we allow ourselves to see this and experience the nausea that comes from facing a meaningless world that we can begin to live for real. Until such time as we open our eyes we make do with fake meanings and falsehoods. Afterwards, and not before we have gone through a phase of despondency, we make the discovery that life has to be chosen in a deliberate way and that meaning has to be created. We realize that we have to opt for significance and happiness and that the creation of these things is worth the effort of living (Camus, 1942). Meaning is created, not found. We have to make a deliberate effort to make life worthwhile.

Alienation and freedom

As long as we do not make this effort to live deliberately, we live by default. Much of human existence is then experienced in an estranged way. People become taken over by others and by situations, by the practicalities and necessities of survival. It is very easy to remain enslaved by the world and by conventions in this way. We reach out for that which is easily available and which can apparently sustain us. It is hard to let go of our illusions and our attachments. Terrific loss is involved in the process of letting go of the things that determine our identity. More often than not we only let go of them when we are forced to do so, through a crisis or by accident. Then we may discover that we are essentially free (essentially nothing) and that we can use this freedom to make new connections, new attachments, form new identities and become more self-determining in the process. Frequently we will become absorbed by the new identities all over again and the same process will start anew.

Authenticity and inauthenticity

Heidegger recognized that our tendency to be fallen with others was a form of inauthenticity or dispossession (*Uneigentlichkeit*). He considered this to be the fundamental mode of human existence, since we do not usually ask too many questions about who we are and how we should and could live. We merely let ourselves be absorbed by circumstances and taken over by others. Yet it is possible to reach, through anxiety and the awareness of our own possibilities and limitations, including our mortality, to a more authentic way of being. Authentic or self-possessed living (*Eigentlichkeit*) consists of owning one's own decisions and being alert to one's own potential for being a self. Like Heidegger, Sartre also thought that bad faith, or inauthenticity, is a necessary evil, since we always have to present ourselves in a particular manner and pretend that we are something when we actually are nothing but consciousness.

Choice and responsibility

It was Sartre too who believed that human beings have to come to terms with the fact that everything we do is in some ways chosen, or rather opted into. We are always at liberty to make a change or abandon whatever lifestyle we have adopted. To put it more extremely – suicide is always an option. This means that we have to become responsible for the choices we make and rather than continue to make them by default start living deliberately, opting for those things that are in line with our original project and with our beliefs. Becoming self-reflective about our intentions and beginning to direct our values, projects and even our emotions more carefully is a real possibility for those who want to take responsibility for themselves. To be responsible is to find our ability to respond to tradition in a reflective and self-possessed way. By becoming answerable to ourselves we take charge of the possibilities of our lives.

Moods and emotions

This also involves becoming aware of our moods. For Sartre emotions are a kind of magic we do to the world in order to transform it. Emotions are the glue between our own worldview and a particular situation. Through our emotions we apprehend problems in the world in a specific way and give our world a particular colouring or flavour (Sartre, 1929; Tantam, 2002). It is, however, possible to become reflective about our own stance and intentionality and thus take charge of it more. We can then become more emotionally effective and more self-aware of the interactions between self and world. For Heidegger, moods were an expression of the close connection between human beings and their world. We feel into the world, resonate with it, respond to it. We are like musical instruments, always attuned to the world in a particular manner. We are always in a mood and can only get out of a mood by getting into another mood. Moods are the constant background to our existence. They express our fundamental bond with the world. Like the weather they are always there and show us many different ways of being in relation. We can suffer them, suppress awareness of them or we can learn to read their messages and face our existential truth.

Truth and self-deception

Truth has become taboo in our post-modern society. We have become aware that truth is often subjective and relative, complex and multi-sided. This has led to deconstructive statements about the non-existence of truth. At the same time, authors such as Heidegger aim for a new, greater truth, which is not partial but whole and which can only be arrived at after careful stripping of self-deceptive and deceptive layers which cover over the actual realities underneath. This search for truth is based on the idea that beyond our partial impressions and errors of interpretation there is an ultimate truth of being. Human beings might be as wrong to assume that nothing is true as to assume that they know what is true. Truth is something that is never acquired or owned once and for all. It has to be continuously searched for. Truth, according to Heidegger, requires us to keep uncovering and exposing what is, rather than covering it up as we all have an inclination to do.

Good and evil

Together with the taboo in relation to truth there is a cultural taboo around moral issues. We have become used to relativizing our thinking about good and evil in an effort to be less judgemental. Politically correct evaluations of ethical problems can stop us making clear judgements about right and wrong. Each person or each situation has to be considered carefully in its own right rather than making Manichean judgements that divide the world into two camps. Enquiring into what lies hidden behind surface appearances, recognizing that things are rarely what they seem or are rarely only one thing, is the beginning of a process of re-evaluation of our values, in line with Nietzsche's recommendation. This process has to be taken to its logical conclusion if we are to escape from moral relativism once and for all. Individuals have the ability to engage with moral questioning on a daily basis. No one is exempt from accounting for his or her opinions and decisions. Clarity of action can only come from clear thinking about right and wrong.

Time and limit situations

Most existential thinkers grapple with issues of time. Heidegger posited that human beings are not just in time, but are themselves time and experience time as an essential dimension of their lives. Our lives are directional and we always move from past through present to future. Awareness of time, of aging and of change all go hand in hand. Such awareness only becomes possible if we face up to the limit situations, which make us aware of the relativity of our experience. Tillich (1952) was particularly vocal about our ultimate concerns,

Jaspers (1969, 1971) spoke of limit situations and both believed that the more we were aware of these ultimates, the more we were alive. Kierkegaard (1844) juxtaposed our capacity for reaching to the infinite with our capacity for dealing with the finite and he believed that both polarities of existence were equally important. Living is to keep a balance between them. To be alive is to allow the inspiration of the infinite and the expiration of finitude in equal measure. We have to breathe in and breathe out, in-spire and ex-spire, live and die.

The theoretical contributions of philosophy

Whilst these existential themes reverberate throughout the history of philosophy, it will be useful to give a brief overview about the philosophical views that provide the cornerstones of western thinking. This bird's eye view can be expanded for those who want to explore this further by turning to other sources (van Deurzen-Smith, 1997; Howard, 2000).

Early Athenian and Roman forerunners

From the pre-Socratics onwards, human issues were the focus of Greek philosophy. But it is particularly Socrates and Plato who established the tradition of systematic thinking about human problems. Their objective was always that of helping people to live the good life (Vlastos, 1991). Socrates' lifestyle and his engagement in dialogue with his pupils and opponents have given us a model for existential therapy. Socratic dialogue is the sort of dialogue where the teacher acts as midwife, enabling pupils to give birth to their own understanding of the world. Socrates believed that there were universal ideas that lay beyond our imperfect grasp of particular situations and experiences. Philosophy, the love of wisdom, was a method for clarifying these ideas. In doing so we can begin to lay the foundations of a just and truthful life in harmony with the principles of the Good.

Nussbaum's book *The Therapy of Desire* (1994) describes some of the other Athenian and Roman contributions to psychotherapy. She shows Aristotelian practice to be particularly therapeutic. Aristotle wanted the philosophy teacher's discourse with the pupil to be cooperative and critical, following the virtues of orderliness, deliberateness and clarity. Teacher (therapist) and pupil are both active and independent, though the teacher is able to offer experienced guidance. The ethical enquiry that they engage in together is seen as a 'winnowing and sifting of people's opinions' (Nussbaum, 1994: 76). Pupils are taught to separate true beliefs from false beliefs and to modify and transform their passions accordingly. The idea that emotion can be educated, rather than ignored, or merely expressed or suppressed, is important. We will find this idea also in the later writings of Spinoza and Sartre. Aristotle's descriptions of the various emotions and what can be done with them are similar to Spinoza's approach in the *Ethics* (1677) where he shows that it is possible to work with emotions in a constructive manner through understanding their meaning and purpose. At the same time, Aristotle's critique of Socrates' teaching that virtue is all and can overcome anything is powerful. For Aristotle the philosophical solution is more pragmatic and less idealistic than for Plato.

The Epicurean answer to dealing with difficulties is different again and consists of removing all corrupting desires and temptations, eliminating pain and disturbance in the process. Epicurean pupils (clients) are taught to adjust their values in order to retain only those that are attainable and may bring them pleasure. This is quite similar to what happens in modern cognitive approaches such as cognitive-behavioural therapy (CBT) or rational emotive behaviour therapy (REBT). Epicureans teach a kind of detachment, which is also not so dissimilar to Buddhist teaching and which encourages people to live in communal settings to help them stick to the right way of life. Epicures also understood something that neither Plato nor Aristotle had fully grasped, that is, that false beliefs are often settled deep in the soul and that they may not be available for argument.

While Epicurean therapy consists of teaching people to adjust their needs downwards so that they can freely pursue realistic pleasures, the Sceptics take the view that the only way to stop anxiety, pain and suffering is to simply not believe or desire anything. So whilst Epicureans try to get rid of false beliefs, the Sceptics want to get rid of all beliefs. So whilst Plato and Aristotle see reason as the answer, Plato in a value-based way and Aristotle in a pragmatic manner, the Epicureans and Sceptics reject reason as a way out of difficulties and they teach people to respectively control desire or eradicate it. The Stoics go another step further and teach people to order the self and the soul. They take the view that we have to tone the muscles of the soul in the same way as we tone the muscles of the body. Stoic therapy can begin anywhere because everything is connected, but different temperaments need different approaches. According to the Stoics there is a critical moment (kairos) for intervention, where a small contribution will make a big difference in a person's life. This view is shared by the Epicureans and referred to by some modern existential authors such as Paul Tillich and Rollo May (May, 1983). The Stoics make a point of finding ways of penetrating deep into the soul and again use storytelling to do so.

The educational aspect of this therapy as of all Greek and Roman therapies is very strong, but this particular one also emphasizes the aspect of self-scrutiny, which includes an understanding of relationships. For the Stoics the goal is for pupils to become their own teacher and learn about life continuously. In this process the soul must be exercised everyday, for instance, by the use of logic and poetry. The objective is wisdom, which is the only ultimate value. This virtue leads to eudaimonia, the flourishing life. The contention is that such wisdom is primarily achieved through detachment and self-control. The Stoics contend that to achieve this we have to extirpate our passions.

Modern forms of existential therapy would on the whole enable a person to expand their capacity for passion at the same time as their ability to manage it, rather than to either get rid of passion (as do the Sceptics), or minimize it (as do the Epicureans) or increase control over it (as do the Stoics). One thing that most ancient philosophies have in common and which existential therapies can benefit from is the recognition that an individual's pursuit of the flourishing life should always benefit the community at large rather than only the individual. This is something that an existential approach, with its emphasis on social, political and cultural context, is firmly committed to.

Renaissance and Enlightenment philosophers

During the centuries that followed and all the way through the middle ages, most of European philosophy was dominated by Christianity. The values that philosophers adhered to were those of the churches. Delivery of help with problems in living was mostly in the clergy's hands. It was only in the seventeenth century that a new wave of thinking was set into motion, in England with Hobbes and Locke, in France with Descartes and Pascal, in Holland with Spinoza and in Germany with Leibniz. Some of the thinking of these philosophers was an attempt to systematize our understanding of the human condition. With Descartes in particular there was an early sketching of the workings of the mind in an attempt to be scientific, famously leading to the split between body and mind. During the Enlightenment period of the eighteenth century these observations became even more systematic and some important philosophical theories were proposed in relation to the inner workings of the human mind. This is the era of Berkeley and Hume in Britain, Rousseau in France and Kant in Germany. These philosophers attempted, each in their own specific way, to create a system of philosophy that would explain human understanding and human interaction with the world in a quasi-scientific way. There is a tremendous amount of insight in their work especially in relation to the workings of the human mind, but the existential angle on the whole is not particularly sharply emphasized.

Philosophers of freedom

In the nineteenth century a new impulse came into philosophy that revolutionized thinking about the human condition once more. In reaction to the increasing dominance of science, some philosophers began to challenge the status quo, proposing a new emphasis on human freedom. Hegel's work set a tone of ideological reflection and his dialectical approach was highly influential. It led to the socio-political thinking and action of Marx and Engels. At the same time there were two other philosophers who showed the way towards clear thinking in human affairs and who both advocated independence of mind and a recovery of human freedom and individuality. They were Søren Kierkegaard in Denmark at the beginning of the century and Friedrich Nietzsche in Germany at the end of the century. Kierkegaard introduced the idea that all human experience was underpinned by paradox. The tension between both polarities is necessary if we are to live life to the full. Kierkegaard's exploration of the possibility of a very individual and passionate engagement with life has been a strong influence on the existential tradition. Nietzsche's bold statement that

'God was dead' and that human beings henceforth had to be their own gods and creators of values continues to be of ground-breaking importance. His recognition of the position of man as spanning between animal and superman led him to advocate a Dionysian and invigorating way of life based on the will to power, providing an interesting counterpart to Kierkegaard's melancholy struggle with anxiety and despair.

Phenomenological and existential thinkers

There were other influences in philosophy during this period, which placed new emphasis on human relations and human understanding. Franz Brentano and Edmund Husserl brought us out of the Cartesian impasse of the body–mind split. Husserl's phenomenology (Husserl, 1925, 1929) was a method intended to replace the exact methods of the natural sciences and it was meant to revolutionize our thinking about the world and in particular about the way in which human beings interact with it. Phenomenology formalizes the possibility of doing qualitative research. It rests on the premise that all human experience is based on intentionality: that is, all human actions, intentions, thoughts and feelings have an object. Human experience is never to be seen in isolation. Everything therefore is situational, contextual, and even subjectively determined. We need to learn how our subjectivity and our particular point of view on the world affect the way in which we see things, rather than aiming for an abstract objectivity, which can always ultimately be questioned or found to fall short.

It was Heidegger, Husserl's pupil, who applied these basic ideas to understanding human beings. His writings about self-possessed or dispossessed modes of living one's life is highly relevant to the quest of psychotherapy and counselling. As we have already seen, this dispossession or disowned form of living (*Uneigentlichkeit*) is referred to as inauthenticity and self-possession or owned living (*Eigentlichkeit*) as authenticity. This is confusing since the word Heidegger uses means something more like actuality or engagement. Heidegger's descriptions of the ways in which human beings are alienated from themselves, because they are essentially connected to the world of things and other people, are very compelling. He proposed a drastic alternative to the classical idea of the self and he also showed the importance of people's existence in time. According to Heidegger we exist outside of ourselves and always in relation to a world. From there on psychotherapy has to become an analysis of existence rather than of the self or the psyche, and of course Boss and Heidegger spoke of Daseinsanalysis (Boss, 1957, 1988), or existential analysis, rather than of psychotherapy. Heidegger also said that human beings always project themselves into a future. We are never complete, always seeking to fulfil our destiny. He proposed that a resolute anticipation of death and a recognition of past, present and future dimensions of our experience was the best way of becoming resolute, engaged and authentic. Even so he showed that we would inevitably continue to fall into forgetfulness of being and disengaged inauthenticity. The moment of vision, which involves the recognition of all that we are, with both strengths and weaknesses, past and future, potential and limitations, is the best we can aim for. It seems a pretty realistic outlook and a good basis for existential psychotherapy.

Sartre (1943) took up some of these ideas, especially those in relation to inauthenticity, which he referred to as self-deception, or bad faith. He argued that people had to create an image of themselves in order to fill the emptiness and nothingness that really exist at the heart of each person. He developed a complex socially based theory about human relations where people are essentially in the business of dominating each other and competing for survival. Later on he recognized that cooperation and generosity could enable people to create a world that was more worth living in, and some of his ideas can also provide interesting guidelines for work from an existential perspective (Sartre, 1960).

There are many other philosophers who have formulated existential principles, for instance Jaspers and Tillich, Merleau Ponty and Camus. Each of them has come up with their own contribution to thinking about the human predicament and they are all worth studying if we want to get more clarity on the issues our clients bring us (van Deurzen-Smith, 1997).

Philosophical principles underlying existential praxis

Not all existential forms of therapy are pinned on the work of these philosophers. They will usually take some of the above-mentioned existential principles into account but not necessarily all of them. So what makes the philosophical difference between an existential approach and a non-existential approach? For an approach to be existential it needs to focus resolutely on life issues in a philosophical manner. This usually means that it emphasizes the search for well-being in relation to an understanding of the human condition. Existential work often means dealing directly with life's inevitable crises and focusing the therapeutic endeavour around a client's struggles with values, purpose and meaning, helping them to find a new direction in their lives.

There are some underlying philosophical factors that all existential approaches have in common.

- The therapeutic work will address questions about life and human living. It will encourage clients to explore their personal understanding of their existence. It will explore the meaning of their particular predicaments, both in terms of their universal significance and their very individual and personal implications.
- There will be an ongoing search for models of living that can improve people's lives, without prescriptive endorsement of any particular model. Clients will usually be encouraged to consider how they are deceiving themselves or hanging on to counterproductive beliefs or illusions.
- There will be openness to individual experience and a considered attempt to resonate with and articulate the life world and worldview of the client.
- There will be considerable emphasis on grasping the cultural, political and social context that defines the client's position and attitudes.

- The therapist will have the philosophical maturity to consider the opposite of any particular idea or experience that is discussed, keeping in mind the wider picture.
- Clients will usually be encouraged to explore the polarities and paradoxes that underpin human living in general and their lives in particular.
- The search for truth that existential therapists engage in with their clients is handled like a philosophical research project that cannot be embarked on lightly and that requires commitment and full engagement on both parts.
- The process will consist in careful description of the client's experience and full exploration of its implications, reasons, purpose and consequences.
- Verification with the client of any interpretations put forward is crucial in this process. It is the client's own narrative that leads the way, not the therapist's theoretical model.
- There has to be an awareness of the importance of dialogue and exchange of views in quiet conversation, where each person is equal and capable of considering what can be learnt from the collaborative exploration.
- There has to be a willingness to test out hypotheses about human living and revise these in the light of new findings. Existential therapy is a form of applied philosophy and needs to comply with rigorous standards of philosophical research and verification as well as with the requirements of direct and reciprocal human interaction and encounter.

Conclusions

The philosophical underpinnings of existential psychotherapy are diverse and complex. People wishing to work in an existential manner do not necessarily need to inform themselves of the rich literature and philosophical heritage that is available. They do, however, have to find some discipline and method in their own philosophical thinking about the world. Existential interventions have to come from informed discussions about life and from deep reflection on what it means to be human. They cannot come from superficially asserted dogmas about living or from over-simplified formulae about therapeutic practice. The next chapter will show the variety of applications that practitioners have come up with over the decades. This will demonstrate how wide-ranging and individually malleable the existential approach is. Its underlying philosophy is that human beings have to keep searching to understand the realities of the human condition and of existence. Life remains the teacher we have to keep attending to. What can be learnt will always surprise us and it can never be fully summarized in books or in prescriptive teachings. We are responsible for our own point of view and our own learning.

CHAPTER 2

Therapeutic Background

MICK COOPER

> The ability truly not to understand what is taken for granted is the beginning
> of scientific or philosophical sagacity.
>
> Laing, Wisdom, Madness and Folly. 45

Introduction

Existential therapy is often thought of as one particular therapeutic approach. In reality, however, there are several different forms of therapeutic practice that orientate themselves around existential questions and concerns, as well as a range of therapeutic approaches that, in part, also draw on existential ideas and principles (for instance, *Gestalt Therapy* (Perls, Hefferline and Goodman, 1951), *Client-Centred Therapy* (Rogers, 1951) and *Psychodrama* (Moreno, 1946)). Of course, to a great extent, every form of therapy contains diversity and difference, but there are reasons why the existential approaches are more diverse than most (Cooper, 2003). First, they have never had a single founder to give them a shared starting point. Second, they are based on a highly diverse set of philosophical assumptions. Third, they are associated with a philosophical outlook that rejects homogenous, unified systems in favour of autonomous and individual forms of practice.

Historically, existential approaches to therapy can be traced back to the first decades of the twentieth century. Here, a number of psychiatrists across the European continent began to draw on the writings of existential and phenomenological philosophers – particularly Husserl and Heidegger – to develop a deeper understanding of psychiatric disorders. First amongst these was the German psychiatrist Karl Jaspers (1883–1969), who went on to become one of the most influential philosophers of existence (see previous chapter). In his *General Psychopathology* (1963), first published in 1913, Jaspers attempted to develop a phenomenology of 'morbid psychic life': cataloguing such phenomena as de-realization and hallucinations in terms of the sufferer's subjectively lived-experiences.

Ludwig Binswanger (1881–1966) was a second psychiatrist to play a major role in the foundation of the existential therapies. Binswanger maintained

15

a close friendship with Sigmund Freud for many years, but felt that Freud's attempts to develop a scientific, causal, a-worldly model of human being had led him to de-humanize the very human beings he was attempting to understand. In contrast, Binswanger drew on the work of such existential philosophers as Martin Heidegger and Martin Buber to develop a 'phenomenological anthropology'. Here, human beings were understood in terms of their relation to their world and to others, and psychological difficulties were conceptualized in terms of a disturbance, disruption or restriction of these relational modes (see Binswanger's case study of Ellen West in May et al., 1958).

Binswanger was one of four members of a phenomenological anthropology 'inner circle', which also included Eugène Minkowski (1885–1972), a French psychiatrist with a particular interest in how people experienced time. For further information about these, and other existential and phenomenological approaches to psychiatry, see Spiegelberg's (1972) detailed study, Halling and Nill's (1995) concise overview or May et al.'s (1958) collection of case studies and commentaries. This chapter, however, focuses primarily on those author-practitioners who have gone on to say something on how existential ideas can be applied to the *practice* of individual therapy, and on those existentially orientated therapies that predominate today.

In discussing these different 'schools' of existential therapy, it should be noted that there is a great deal of homogeneity across, and heterogeneity within, each of the different approaches. However, each of the four existential therapies discussed below has certain core influences, concerns and practices, and these are outlined in the following sections.

Daseinsanalysis

One of the first schools of existential therapy to emerge was that of Daseinsanalysis, which retains a following across Switzerland and Europe today. This school was founded on the work of Ludwig Binswanger, but it was a second Swiss psychiatrist, Medard Boss (1903–1990), who took it beyond a phenomenological anthropology to a systematic form of therapeutic practice. Initially, Boss trained as a psychoanalyst, then as a Jungian, and Daseinsanalytic practice bears many hallmarks of its predecessors, such as the emphasis on dream-work, use of free association and of the couch. In drawing on Heidegger's later teachings as well as South Asian mysticism, however, Boss vigorously critiqued the meta-theoretical assumptions behind Freud's analytical practice, and proposed a radically new set of philosophical assumptions for psychotherapy (Boss, 1963, 1979).

A first part of Freudian meta-theory that Boss (1963, 1979) critiqued was the notion of a thing-like 'psyche', and the hypothesis that different parts existed and interacted within it. Drawing on Heidegger's (1962) notion of being-in-the-world, Boss argued that existence did not reside in a person's head, but between people and their world. Furthermore, he argued that neuroses and psychoses were not a result of intrapsychic dysfunctions, but of a limited, restricted or closed way of relating to one's world. The aim of

Daseinsanalysis, then, was to help clients open themselves up to their world: to be like 'a light which luminates whatever particular being comes into the realm of its rays' (Boss, 1963: 37).

This rejection of intrapsychic parts and dynamics also entailed a rejection of 'the unconscious', and the idea that clients 'transferred' thoughts and feelings from previous figures in their lives onto their therapist. For Boss (1963, 1979), clients were simply closed to some aspects of others' being-in-the-world – such that they did not engage with the full totality of their therapist's being. Hence, Boss rejected the idea that therapists should adopt the role of a blank screen, and instead argued that they should be human and warm, encouraging their clients to ever greater levels of interpersonal openness. Boss's Heideggerian roots also meant that he rejected the causal, deterministic aspects of Freudian thinking. Whilst he did not deny that clients could be influenced by their past, he put greater emphasis on working with a client's present patterns of openness and closedness, and their potentiality for freedom and choice for the future.

Boss's (1963, 1979) Daseinsanalysis, then, is a descriptive rather than explanatory practice, and this is well illustrated in the Daseinsanalytic approach to dream-work. For Boss (1977), dream images and narratives are not symbols for latent, unconscious meaning, but manifestations of the client's spectra of world-openness and world-closedness. A client who only ever dreams of monsters, for instance, would be seen as someone who is primarily open to the fearful and dangerous aspects of their world, whilst closed to the safe and comforting. Daseinsanalytic dream-work, then, consists of helping clients to describe their dreams in increasing levels of detail – through such questions as 'What?', 'Where?' and 'How?' (Condrau, 1998) – such that they can develop a greater insight into their openness and closedness. It also encourages clients to recognize new potentialities for experiencing that may emerge for the first time in dreams (Boss and Kenny, 1987), such that they can consolidate and actualize these world-disclosing possibilities.

Logotherapy

Logotherapy, also termed 'existential analysis', is a therapeutic approach that specifically aims to help clients discover purpose in their lives – 'Logos' being the Greek term for 'meaning' (Frankl, 1984) – and to overcome feelings of meaninglessness and despair. It was developed by the Viennese psychiatrist Viktor Frankl (1905–1997) around 1929 (Klingberg, 1995) – and 'tested out' during his time in the Nazi concentration camps – and continues to flourish today, with logotherapeutic training institutes across continental Europe and America. Whilst logotherapy may be considered a 'supplement, rather than a substitute for psychotherapy' (Frankl, 1986: xii), it has been incorporated into many other forms of interpersonal helping – such as nursing (Starck, 1993) and social work (Guttman, 1996) – and has recently been developed into a more comprehensive form of existential-analytical psychotherapy (Längle, 2001).

Unlike Daseinsanalysis, logotherapy is not based on the teachings of any one existential philosopher, though it has been heavily influenced by the writings of the German phenomenologist Max Scheler (1874–1928). Logotherapy also draws on Adlerian ideas – particularly Adler's notion of a 'final goal' (Tengan, 1999) – and on the Judaic spirituality of its founder.

According to logotherapists, a human being's most fundamental need is to find meaning in his or her life (Frankl, 1984, 1986). Without this, they argue, human beings will experience a deep sense of frustration, emptiness and depression, which can develop into a more serious 'existential', or 'noögenic', neurosis (Frankl, 1986). Here, individuals may turn to such self-destructive patterns as addictions, compulsions or phobias in an attempt to fill their existential void.

At the root of logotherapy, however, is the assumption that every situation a human being encounters – indeed, every human being – holds meanings waiting to be fulfilled, whether through creative activity, an increased receptivity to one's world, or through changing one's attitudes. The aim of logotherapy, then, is to help people find these meanings; and it does so through a range of relatively didactic techniques. At the most directive end of the spectrum is the 'appealing technique' (Lukas, 1979), where logotherapists simply suggest to their clients particular reasons or meanings. A somewhat less didactic technique is termed 'Socratic dialogue' (Lukas, 1979), whereby the logotherapist enters into a dialogue with his or her client, and 'poses questions in such a way that patients become aware of their unconscious decisions, their repressed hopes, and their unadmitted self-knowledge' (Fabry, 1980: 135). A third technique, termed 'paradoxical intention', invites the client to do – or to think about doing – the thing that he or she most fears, on the assumption that a client can take a positive attitude to even the most appalling experiences. Finally, in 'dereflection', the client is encouraged to turn their attention away from their own problems and concerns and instead focus on the world around them.

The existential-humanistic approach

In America, an 'existential-humanistic' approach to therapy has emerged under the tutelage of Rollo May (1909–1994). May originally trained as a minister, and was strongly influenced by the teachings of his mentor, the existential theologian Paul Tillich. In 1958, May co-edited *Existence*, which brought the writings and practices of European existential and phenomenological psychiatrists to America for the first time. Other key figures in the development of the existential-humanistic approach include James Bugental (1915–), Irvin Yalom (1931–) and Kirk Schneider (1956–) – all of whom worked in close collaboration with May. Today, the teaching and practice of existential-humanistic therapy is located primarily on the west coast of the United States, though existential-humanistic practitioners continue to have a major impact on the development of humanistic therapies across the world.

Of all the existential therapies, the existential-humanistic approach tends to place the greatest emphasis on helping clients achieve personal autonomy, independence and subjective self-awareness (May, 1969), though recent years have seen moves towards a more intersubjective standpoint (Schneider, 2003). This individualistic emphasis is partly due to the fact that existential-humanistic psychotherapy has always been closely related to the wider humanistic movement, as developed in the works of such psychologists and psychotherapists as Maslow (1968) and Rogers (1959). This humanistic link – alongside its American heritage – also means that the existential-humanistic approach is the most pragmatic, optimistic and eclectic of the existential therapies, drawing on a range of humanistic strategies, such as focusing (Gendlin, 1996), to help clients 'grow' to realize their true potential (Bugental, 1981).

At the heart of the existential-humanistic enterprise, however, lies an essentially psychodynamic reading of existential – particularly Kierkegaardian and Nietzschean – themes (Cooper, 2003). In particular, it has taken the psychoanalytic formula (based on Yalom, 1980):

DRIVE → ANXIETY → DEFENCE MECHANISM;

and replaced it with

REALITY OF EXISTENCE → EXISTENTIAL ANXIETY → DEFENCE
MECHANISMS.

In other words, it asserts that clients resist an awareness of their true existential condition, pushing this knowledge down into the depths of their unconscious. The fundamental project of existential-humanistic therapy, then, is to help clients identify and overcome their resistances, and to meet the anxiety of existence with an attitude of decisiveness and resolve (May, 1958).

To facilitate this process, one of the most basic existential-humanistic strategies is that of 'inward searching', whereby clients are encouraged to tune their awareness in to their in-the-moment experiencing (Bugental, 1978). Clients, for instance, may be asked to describe whatever concerns them most at the present moment (Bugental, 1978); describe their experiences in as much detail as possible (Yalom and Elkin, 1974); or express how they are feeling at a bodily level (Bugental, 1981). Where resistances to this inner searching process emerge, therapists may attempt to heighten the client's awareness of how they block or limit themselves ('vivification'), and/or confront them to overcome their blocks (Schneider, 2003).

Existential-humanistic therapists also encourage clients to be authentic – or 'present' – to others (Bugental, 1978). Here, clients may be encouraged to articulate how they are feeling in the 'living moment' of the immediate therapeutic encounter, and particularly how they are feeling towards their therapist (Bugental, 1999; Yalom, 2001). Again, resistances to this presence may be vivified and/or confronted. To facilitate this process of increasing presence, Yalom (2001) puts particular emphasis on the importance of *therapists* being present to their clients, and he argues that therapists should be willing to talk about their personal experiences, their views on the mechanisms of therapy, and their feelings towards their clients in the here-and-now.

For Bugental (1981) and Yalom (1980), helping clients face up to their true being also involves helping them come to terms with certain ontological givens. Yalom outlines four such givens – death, freedom, isolation and meaninglessness – and his *Existential Psychotherapy* is a classic exposition of how clients defend themselves against these ultimate concerns, as well as the problems that such defences can evoke, and therapeutic strategies for helping clients overcome such resistances. Bugental, meanwhile, outlines six givens – finiteness, potential to act, choice, awareness, separateness and embodiedness – the last of which bears many similarities to May's (1969) concept of 'the daimonic'.

R. D. Laing and the British school of existential analysis

R. D. Laing (1927–1989), the infamous Scottish psychiatrist, drew on a range of existential and phenomenological teachings to critique the psychiatric assumptions of his – and to a large extent, our – day. In contrast to the 'objective', detached psychiatric standpoint, Laing (1965) argued that psychiatrists needed to enter the phenomenological lived-world of their patients, and that there they would find a far greater sense to the client's 'madness' than they had ever imagined. In his best-known book, *The Divided Self*, Laing attempts to show how a condition as seemingly unintelligible as schizophrenia becomes intelligible and meaningful if one attempts to understand it from the patient's standpoint.

Laing argues that schizoid-predisposed individuals may experience a fundamental sense of 'ontological insecurity' in which they lack a 'firm sense of [their] own and other people's reality and identity' (Laing, 1965: 39). Because of this, Laing argues that they may experience certain fears: of engulfment by others, implosion, or petrification and depersonalization. To defend themselves against these perceived threats to their being, Laing suggests that they may then try to divide themselves in two, leaving an empty and compliant false self and bodily shell on the public plane, whilst retreating to a safer private citadel of their mind. For Laing, however, such a withdrawal may lead the individual towards psychosis, as they become increasingly detached from external reality, and less and less able to experience a dialectical and confirming relationship with others.

For Laing, however, severe forms of mental misery, like schizophrenia, could not just be understood as individual, intrapsychic affairs. Rather, Laing believed that schizophrenia was a particular strategy that individuals develop to try and survive in particular *social* situations (Laing, 1967). In particular, Laing argued that 'madness' was a means of attempting to survive an insane family environment, and in many of his key works (Laing and Esterson, 1964; Laing, 1969, 1971) he outlines the deceptions, double-binds, invalidations and disturbed means of communication that lead people to seek refuge in their own inner world.

Laing wrote little about therapeutic practice, *per se*, but his clients' accounts suggest that he was a highly attentive listener, who ensured that his clients had time to articulate, and connect with, their real experiences (Resnick, 1997). In order to counteract the years of disturbed and deceptive means of communication, Laing could also be brutally honest with his clients (Semyon, 1997), and he had little time for externally imposed boundaries or rules. Rather, at the heart of his practice was a willingness to encounter clients in a spontaneous and un-premeditated way. Indeed, Laing believed that the decisive moments in therapy were often unpredictable, unique, unforgettable, always unrepeatable and often indescribable.

Laing's rejection of therapeutic systems meant that he made no attempt to codify a 'Laingian' approach to therapy. Within the English-speaking world, however, there are many who have followed in his wake, and these practitioners have tended to fall into one of two – relatively overlapping – categories. First are those therapists who have articulated and developed the more psychoanalytic aspects of Laing's thinking, such as Thompson (1994) and members of the Philadelphia Association (Cooper et al., 1989). Second are those therapists who have concentrated primarily on developing the more existential elements of his work.

The second group is sometimes referred to as the British, formerly London, school of existential analysis; and is, according to American existential psychotherapist Groth, 'one of the most hopeful signs of health of existential psychotherapy anywhere in the world' (2000: 7). Emmy van Deurzen (1951–) has been the principal driving force behind the development of this school: developing the first UK-based training course in existential therapy in 1982; establishing the Society for Existential Analysis in 1988; and, in that same year, publishing the first edition of the highly accessible *Existential Counselling in Practice*.

Of all the existential therapies discussed in this chapter, van Deurzen-Smith's approach (1997, 1998, 2002a) is the most explicitly philosophical. She draws on a range of philosophical insights – including those beyond the bounds of existentialism – to help clients address the basic existential question: How can I live a better life? Van Deurzen's starting point is that life is an 'endless struggle where moments of ease and happiness are the exception rather than the rule' (1998: 132); and that problems in living arise when people are reluctant to face the reality of their imperfect, dilemma-ridden and challenging existences. Hence, the aim of existential therapy, for van Deurzen-Smith (1997), is to help clients wake up from self-deception, to face the challenge of living head-on, and to discover their talents and possibilities.

In this process, van Deurzen (2002) likens the role of the existential therapist to that of an art tutor, who helps his or her students gain a sense of perspective and build up an increasingly detailed picture of their world. Like Laing, van Deurzen-Smith (1995) does not suggest particular therapeutic techniques by which this process can take place, but does outline a range of areas that therapists can help their clients to explore. Most notably, she draws on Binswanger and Heidegger to suggest four dimensions of worldly being that clients can be encouraged to investigate (van Deurzen, 2002a): the physical dimension of nature, environment and bodies; the social dimension of interpersonal relationships and socio-cultural environment; the personal dimension of self and psychological processes; and the spiritual dimension of values and meanings. Within these dimensions, she also suggests that there are particular dilemmas, polarities and paradoxes that clients can be encouraged to learn to live with.

For van Deurzen (2002a), this process of exploration is primarily client-led. Like art tutors, however, she argues that therapists must be challenging – even ruthless – with their clients at times: gently but firmly calling them back to the reality of their lives. Furthermore, for van Deurzen, clients' lived difficulties are not only *their* problems, but problems that many other people – including their therapist – may have faced. Hence, van Deurzen argues that there is a place for therapists to bring their philosophical knowledge and personal understandings to bear on their clients' difficulties, to share with them the wisdom of the ages. This is not to point their clients in particular directions, but, like the practice of the philosophical counsellors who have emerged from the British school (for instance, LeBon, 2001), to help them consider a wider range of standpoints than just their own.

Like Laing and van Deurzen, most therapists within the British school of existential analysis adopt a primarily descriptive, non-technique-based approach to therapy, in which clients' difficulties are seen as problems in living rather than pathological modes of functioning (see du Plock, 1997b). The British school, however, can only be considered a school in the loosest sense of the word. As van Deurzen writes: 'The movement has its own history of splitting and fighting and there is a healthy disagreement about what existential work should be' (2002a: x).

One influential figure within the British school who takes a somewhat different approach to van Deurzen is Ernesto Spinelli (1949–), whose writings are particularly influenced by phenomenological and intersubjective ideas. Like Boss, Spinelli (1994, 2001) has critiqued a number of constructs within the psychotherapeutic world – such as the unconscious, transference, the self, and the influence of the past – and proposed alternatives that are more consistent with phenomenologically lived-experience. Following on from this, Spinelli (1997) has suggested that therapists should adopt a stance of 'un-knowing' towards their clients: holding in abeyance fixed beliefs, values and assumptions – including existential ones – such that they can step into their clients' lived worlds and interpretations. Spinelli (1992) also puts particular emphasis on the importance of a genuine, warm and caring relationship between therapist and client; and suggests that it is an exploration of the client's relational worlds – and the interaction between client's and therapist's relational worlds – that gives therapy its particular value (Spinelli, 2001).

Other key voices within the British school of existential analysis include Cohn (1997, 2002), who has developed a particularly Heideggerian approach to therapy; and Freddie Strasser (Strasser and Strasser, 1997), who has devised a time-limited approach to existential therapy. Many more voices can be found in the pages of the British school's journal, *Existential Analysis*, and in the chapters of this book.

Commonalities and polarities

Across the existential therapies, there are a number of commonalities in therapeutic practice (see Cooper, 2003):

- The aim of the therapeutic work is to help clients become more authentic: to acknowledge the reality of their lived existence.
- Therapists tend to work with clients' concrete experiences, rather than abstract hypotheses about these experiences.
- Clients are encouraged to acknowledge, and act on, their freedom and responsibility.
- Clients are encouraged to acknowledge, accept and learn from such discomforting experiences as anxiety, guilt, despair and a sense of tragedy.
- Clients are encouraged to explore their present and future experiences, as well as their past ones.
- Therapists tend to be genuine and direct with their clients.
- Flexibility and adaptibility of practice tend to be emphasized over fixed and immovable boundaries.

At the same time, there are a number of polarities across the existential therapies (see Cooper, 2003):

- emphasis on bracketing assumptions (British school) *versus* orientating the therapeutic work around certain existential assumptions and principles (logotherapy);
- tendency towards directing the therapeutic work (logotherapy) *versus* allowing the client to take the lead (Spinelli, 1997);
- working in a primarily descriptive way (Daseinsanalysis, British school) *versus* adopting a more explanatory approach (existential-humanistic approach);
- exploring psychological experiences and processes (existential-humanistic approach) *versus* undertaking a philosophical exploration (van Deurzen, 2002a);
- individualizing the client's experiences and difficulties (existential-humanistic approach) *versus* locating them within a wider and more trans-personal context (van Deurzen, 2002a);
- pathologizing the client's difficulties (Daseinsanalysis, logotherapy) *versus* de-pathologizing them (Laing and the British school);
- encouraging clients to focus *in* on their subjective experiences (existential-humanistic approach) *versus* encouraging clients to focus *out* on their in-the-worldly being (British school);
- emphasizing the immediacy of the therapeutic encounter (existential-humanistic approach) *versus* placing no great emphasis on the client–therapist relationship (logotherapy);
- engaging the client in a spontaneous and un-premeditated manner (Laing, 1967) *versus* drawing on techniques and therapeutic strategies (logotherapy).

Conclusion

Today, as it has always been, the world of existential therapies is a sprawling, diverse and complex edifice, replete with tensions, dilemmas and contradictions. Indeed, in this chapter, only the predominant existential therapies have been discussed, and there are many other therapeutic approaches – such as Cannon's (1991) Sartrean-based therapy and Hycner's (1991) dialogical psychotherapy – that lie wholly or partly within this field. Few existential therapists, however, would have it any other way, for it is the diversity and difference within the world of existential therapies that gives it such vibrancy, complexity and richness, and ensures that it will remain open to challenges and change in the coming years.

Further reading

Boss, M. *Psychoanalysis and Daseinsanalysis.*
Cooper, M. *Existential Therapies.*
Frankl, V. E. *The Doctor and the Soul: From Psychotherapy to Logotherapy.*
Halling, S. and Nill, J. D. 'A Brief History of Existential-Phenomenological Psychiatry and Psychology', *Journal of Phenomenological Psychology.*
Laing, R. D. *The Divided Self: An Existential Study in Sanity and Madness.*
May, R., Angel, E. and Ellenberger, H. F. (eds) *Existence: A New Dimension in Psychiatry and Psychology.*
Spiegelberg, H. *Phenomenology in Psychology and Psychiatry: A Historical Introduction.*
Spinelli, E. *Tales of Un-Knowing: Therapeutic Encounters from an Existential Perspective.*
van Deurzen, E. *Existential Counselling and Psychotherapy in Practice.*
van Deurzen-Smith, E. *Everyday Mysteries: Existential Dimensions of Psychotherapy.*
Yalom, I. D. *Existential Psychotherapy.*

PART II

PHYSICAL DIMENSION

CHAPTER 3

Introduction to the Physical Dimension

EMMY VAN DEURZEN AND CLAIRE ARNOLD-BAKER

Human beings are first and foremost bodies in a material world. The way in which we are thrown into the world is, in the first instance, physical. We are embodied in an environment (Umwelt) that has existed before we were ever thought of and that will continue long after our bodies have disintegrated. It is well worth paying attention to the interrelationship between our bodies and the things of this world. The way in which we are embodied matters enormously to the quality of life that is accessible to us. Our struggle with life and death is always in the background. The tension between wanting to be healthy yet having to cope with illness and weakness is one expression of this. The same tension is expressed through our pursuit of wealth, which can be seen as a way of ensuring our physical survival, whereas poverty would form an immediate threat to our safety. The tension between the desire for security and the threat of potential insecurity is a powerful element determining our struggle on the physical dimension. But there are many other specific ways in which our being-in-the-world shows up our relationship to our environment and our own body. The arena of the Umwelt is the realm of action. Our doing world is inevitably concerned with matters of concrete objects that need to be dealt with. When we pay attention to this particular dimension of a client's experience, we may want to consider the following:

1. The way the body is experienced: Is it, for instance, long or short, thin or fat, big or small? What effect does this have on a person's actions in the world? All of us as children start with the experience of our inferior physical status. At first we need others to ensure our survival and to gratify our basic needs. As we develop through our lifetime, our changing body constantly confronts us with different demands. Often, our identity and emotional well-being is tied up in how we feel about our bodies.

2. What is a person's experience in relation to their physical autonomy? As growing individuals we only gradually discover our ability to move independently as we become able to crawl, then to walk and later to run. Then more

specific motor skills are added on: we learn to feed ourselves, wash ourselves and deal with our bodily functions. We also learn to heed our need for sleep and for gathering food. We learn to handle the tools that are useful for this purpose. Of course the opposite is true towards the end of life when we lose our ability to move independently or use our bodies autonomously in a gradual way. Through disability, illness or accident this can happen earlier as well and this will usually have profound effects on individuals as they struggle to readjust to their new way of being.

3. This raises the question of how well a person's body works. Is the body fit or unfit, healthy or ill? What is the client's awareness in relation to things going wrong or being dangerous? The process of truly learning to look after ourselves is never ending. We normally learn what is physically good and bad for us from our caretakers. We discover about poisons, sleep deprivation, about what happens when we cannot keep warm, dry, fed and watered: we learn how to guard our safety. But of course our paradoxical nature may continue to challenge the status quo and undermine our own physical balance through various addictions or by pushing our bodies too hard or too little. How do our clients handle themselves physically? Do they for instance strive for 'healthy' lifestyles, that is, by going to the gym, eating a balanced diet and so on; or do they partake in what would be considered unhealthy lifestyles such as smoking, drinking or using drugs? What is the objective and the effect of each of these?

4. How do our clients relate to the bodies of others and handle the way they dominate us? How do they handle their need for physical contact and comfort? What has been their experience of contact with others, in terms of being neglected, ignored, used or abused? Have they been cuddled, comforted, made to feel their body was beautiful? How has this affected their own relation to other people's bodies?

5. Where are our clients in relation to their learning about their own senses; touch, hearing, sight, smell and taste? Which senses do they rely on and which are strong and well developed; which are they not attuned to and take for granted? Our sense of smell, for example, is often neglected, even though it can evoke powerful emotions and memories as the olfactory nerve goes straight to the emotion centre in the brain. Embodiment may become much more fully experienced when missing sensory experience is recovered.

6. These general physical abilities can lead to specific foci for physical experience when our attention is distracted in a particular direction, for instance, in terms of our relationship to food, which is one of the aspects that will be considered specifically in this section. Food is essential for our survival but is often underused, overused or used as an emotional crutch. Our relationship with alcohol and drugs brings up similar issues.

7. The physical qualities of the world around us need to be taken more seriously as well. In the home we try to surround ourselves with comfy beds or easy chairs, good toys, good tools, working heaters, toilets and so on. What happens when they break down? How do people regulate their levels of comfort and discomfort? The level of comfort we are used to and often take for granted may stand in the way of our understanding of what our basic

needs are, whilst appreciating the resources available to us. How is it different for those living in third-world countries, for whom running water would seem a luxury? What happens when a client becomes temporarily deprived, on a foreign trip or in an emergency or through a time of penury?

8. What is the client's attitude towards wealth and poverty? Are they able to afford what they need, more than they need or less than they need? Are they providing for themselves, being provided for or are they providing for others as well? How much effort do they put into their acquisition and ownership of resources? Do they know when they have enough? Are they wealthy people who seem to squander their money or use their money to gain power over others? Are they generous with their resources? Are they individuals living in poverty, or even on the streets, who are trapped in a cycle of deprivation, neglect and abuse? What are the effects of these basic things? What happens to a person when they are not able to get a job as they have no home, and are not able to get a home, as they have no job?

9. We also need to attend to a person's wider physical environment and their response to it. Some people are overwhelmed by deep-seated fear of the dark, for instance, or they may respond negatively to lack of light. Some like the sunshine, some find it disturbing, some are acutely aware of the danger of thunderstorms, ice or snow, whereas others find such challenges exhilarating. Finding out which climate suits them may be very instructive. It is useful even just to establish whether they like the heat or the cold. It can also be helpful to clarify which seasons suit them or affect them, as in the case of Seasonal Affective Disorder (SAD). How do they interact with the natural world, which physical environment do they feel at home in? So do they favour the sea, mountains, countryside or towns? Learning to be in harmony with the natural world can make a big difference to their well-being.

10. This also means asking ourselves what a person's relationship to animals and other forces of nature is. How did they learn to mistrust or trust other creatures? Atavistic fear of snakes and spiders may have become an issue for a person. Liking of dogs, horses and cats can lead to a very different life experience than disliking or avoiding them. There is a lot of mileage in discovering our own talents for getting on with the physical world and the creatures around us.

11. Then we need to ask the next question about the sort of physical skills of dexterity a person has acquired. Do they play any sports, and are they good at them or not? Does this person feel fast or slow, flexible or stiff? Do they feel able to control objects such as bikes or skates or skis? Is this person comfortable being carried by water and swimming? All these things make a difference to how the physical world is experienced. All determine the range and limits to our action in the world.

12. Then we need to address the question that therapists have often reduced a person's physicality to: What about a person's sexuality? What is the state of the libidinal drive that attracts our bodies towards unity with the bodies of others? The whole issue of pleasure and hedonism has become a very important one in our post-Freudian society. What is the person's gender and

how is this experienced? Are they highly sexed or not? Is their preference hetero-, homo-, bi- or auto-sexual? How free is this person in relation to their sexual experience? What are the taboos, the obsessions, the longings, the frustrations, the inhibitions and the pleasures?

13. Procreation is equally important to consider, since it may drive a person to sexual intercourse or may cause them to avoid it. Is this person involved in procreation and parenting or grandparenting, or are they concerned to avoid this possibility? What is their relation to offspring in physical terms? What is the effect of this on their personal physical well-being?

There are of course many other issues worth considering in this area, since the material world is the foundation of any person's existence. The physical dimension is concerned with our relation to many of the 'givens' of life, in other words to those things we cannot change. The material world is the core of our existence and cannot be ciphered away. It centres on the real stuff of life; it is about our survival and safety and about trusting the world. It is about life and death. Those who pretend it does not matter to them may well be deceiving themselves about an aspect of their own nature. Likewise by illuminating our relation to the physical world we can bring greater understanding of our motives, preferences and beliefs.

The chapters that follow in this part are felt to be specifically pertinent to the physical dimension. As our lives begin at birth, and the survival of our species depends on it, it is fitting to start with a chapter on procreation and the issues and implications around pregnancy and birth. The chapter on human development follows, largely as a response to claims that the existential approach does not have a developmental model. This chapter shows that in fact the existential approach has much to say on the issue of development and sees it as a lifelong process. Similarly with human sexuality, little has been written on the subject from an existential perspective and this chapter eluci-dates the main existential thinking on sexuality and puts forward ways in which an existential therapist can approach the issue. The subsequent two chapters are very relevant to everyday life and much has been written on eating problems and addiction from a variety of different perspectives. Addiction and eating problems are centrally based in the physical dimension as they pertain to what we take into our bodies, in what quantities and how it is used. However, these two chapters will show that the issues involved are not just ones in the physical dimension but have implications in the other dimensions as well. As it is appropriate to start this part of the book with birth, it is just as fitting to end this part with death. The final chapter focuses on the issues surrounding death, on which the existential approach has much to say.

CHAPTER 4

Procreation

CLAIRE ARNOLD-BAKER AND MIRIAM DONAGHY

> Ordinarily life is but a condition of existence: in gestation it appears as creative.
>
> de Beauvoir, *The Second Sex*: 514

Introduction

Procreation, 'the bringing into being' (*Oxford Dictionary*, 1984), is essential for the continuation of our species and a 'given' of human existence. Its psychological impact has been considered for centuries; indeed Hippocrates in 400 BC wrote on the subject of mothers experiencing emotional or mental distress postpartum, what might today be thought of as post-natal depression (PND). The universal nature of procreation has meant that it is a subject that has received a great deal of attention from the sociological field, including disciplines such as anthropology and feminism, outlined briefly below, as well as from psychological approaches.

From the sociological perspective, the social significance and personal meaning of having a baby and becoming a parent are considered crucial, as are the context and support mechanisms with which this happens.

Anthropologists use cross-cultural studies to explore the effect of cultural systems on the experience of procreation. Through studying the transition to parenthood in many non-Western societies, and the rituals and customs often entailed in this, they argue that whilst there are similarities from a physiological perspective:

- 'Birth is almost universally treated as a traumatic life crisis event' (Kruckman, 1992: 139).
- Having a baby 'is conceptualized, structured and experienced differently in every culture' (ibid., 138).
- Biological and cultural factors are interdependent in the success or otherwise of the transition to parenthood.

Feminist thinkers have considered many different aspects of procreation, in particular focusing on:

- the bias of biological explanations, and concepts such as 'maternal instinct', seen as a matter of social construction rather than biological inclination;

31

- myths about motherhood and the resultant problems with new mothers' unrealistic expectations;
- 'Mother blaming' theories (Caplan, 1989), which are seen as an inevitable implication of the current research emphasis on the relationship between the welfare of babies and how they are mothered;
- the need for emotional and social support for mothers making the transition into motherhood (Oakley, 1979; Dally, 1982; Rossiter, 1988; Caplan, 1989 and Brown et al., 1994);
- choices or lack of them for women before, during and after having a baby;
- the romanticization of the motherhood role, for which patriarchal power relations and belief systems are held responsible (Nicolson, 1998).

Psychological approaches are broadly interested in the emotional and psychological impact of procreation, in particular, helping parents deal with feelings of vulnerability and potential emotional distress that may be evoked even by the contemplation of having a baby. Psychiatry also has an interest in the emotional distress experienced by new mothers sometimes classified as a mental disorder, as in postpartum mood disorders or PND (American Psychiatric Association, 1997).

Developmental psychologists, who focus on the different stages or phases of life, see the transition to parenthood, as Levinson (1979) would call it, a significant 'marker event' in adult development. For developmentalists, interest centres on:

- how parenthood draws one life phase to a close whilst beginning another;
- the tasks, responsibilities and challenges this new phase brings;
- understanding what may precipitate parenthood for example quest for a viable identity or more negatively, what Sheehy (1976) sees as 'a flight from marital intimacy'.

Psychoanalysis focuses on the inner world of the parents and how their psyches change through the process of having a baby. Some key areas receiving attention include:

- the mother's internal representation of her own mother and how this relates to subsequent mother–child relationships;
- the mental organization of the mother's early attachments and subsequent post-natal attachment (Priel and Besser, 2001).

An existential perspective

> Mothers . . . having given birth, understand exactly how serious life is and how close it is to death, the fear of which is always at the horizon when you have a new born baby in your arms. (van Deurzen, 1998: 33)

Existentialism, with its focus on being and existence, lends itself well to any discussion about procreation. Here we shall explore some of the themes an existential therapist might consider when working with clients who are considering procreation, in the midst of pregnancy, or postpartum. In so doing we hope to elucidate how an existential approach to procreation differs from the approaches outlined above. Before looking at these existential themes, however, it is worth noting that an existential approach to procreation means rejecting objectivity and the search for certain definable knowledge, what Merleau-Ponty referred to as 'high-altitude thinking' (Merleau-Ponty, 1968: 73). What is required instead is a 'return to the world of actual experience' (ibid., 57), where the individual's own experience is central.

Having a baby – indeed, planning to have one – marks the beginning of a transition stage for both parents, affecting all levels of existence. On the physical dimension, the emphasis is on the creation of a human life, the development of the foetus and the resulting bodily changes of the mother. Socially, the expected new arrival is part of, and impacts on, a family unit, extended family and a larger community. On the personal dimension, expectant parents grapple with their expectations, and their hopes and fears of how this new human life will affect them personally, whilst from a spiritual perspective, issues such as what it means to be a parent and what kind of world the child will be brought into are key considerations.

This chapter will have as its focus themes on freedom, responsibility, mortality, anxiety, identity and the body. These themes are all relevant to the existential therapist working with clients facing issues around procreation.

Freedom and responsibility

The developments in birth control in Western societies have introduced a far greater degree of choice and control over reproduction. Although child rearing is still often seen as an expected stage of life, with choice centred on when to conceive, for others the decision is more fundamental, that is, whether or not to have a child. Whilst the availability of terminations in most Western societies means that this choice extends even beyond conception, rising numbers of unwanted pregnancies, particularly amongst teenagers, highlight the limits of this freedom to choose, a point felt keenly too by those couples facing fertility problems.

From an existential perspective, it is often seen as a given of our existence that we are free to choose how we live; however, this also means we have to take responsibility for our choices (Sartre, 1943). With pregnancy, the knowledge that life choices have a direct impact on the foetus means being faced with responsibility for the well-being of the unborn child. Having the freedom to choose does not ensure that all choices will be good or wise ones and the enormity of this responsibility is burdensome, and for some can feel terrifying. This feeling of responsibility increases after the birth where concerns are not just for the physical safety of the infant but also for its emotional development. As Greenberg (1985) suggests, becoming a parent requires the greatest day-to-day responsibility yet encountered.

Responsibility is not just an issue that parents have to accept in relation to their babies; importantly, they are also responsible for themselves. This is often difficult for parents, particularly mothers, who may be faced with sacrificing personal achievements in the public world in order to meet the often competing demands of their offspring. Realizing that we are in charge of our own destiny, in a world that is perceived as random and ambiguous, may involve experiencing the pain of despair, and anxiety. Tillich (1952) calls this moral anxiety, the anxiety of guilt and condemnation, which he describes as arising from a sense that we have not been or achieved all that we might. Such anxiety may be deeply distressing and can be seen in many clients presenting with issues around becoming parents.

Mortality and anxiety

The experience of giving birth brings home the very pragmatic stuff of life – that there is a life cycle that begins with birth and ends with death. Undeniably, this link between birth and death was until recently, and in some 'third world' societies still is, very real, with up to one in seven women dying during labour (Shorter, 1984).[1] In the West although the risks have been greatly reduced, there is still for many an awareness of the possibility of dying and thus for some mothers the birth of their baby means that for the first time, death, or rather her own death, comes clearly into view (Figes, 1998).

This concern with death or the threat of non-being is not confined to childbirth. The sense of one's own mortality is evoked in another less dramatic, but significant, way. With the birth of the baby, the next generation is created and thus, for the parents there is a feeling of moving along in the cycle of life, moving nearer to inevitable death. As de Beauvoir describes the experience of the expectant mother:

> Caught up in the great cycle of the species, she affirms life in the teeth of time and death; in this she glimpses immortality; but in her flesh she feels the truth of Hegel's words; 'The birth of children is the death of parents.' This projection of herself is also for the woman the foreshadowing of her death. (de Beauvoir, 1953: 514)

The supreme responsibility that faces new parents, of caring for a totally dependent baby, gives them a new reason to live, or rather not to die. Even those who have never before worried about dying become increasingly focused on their own mortality and the fear of what will happen to their baby and who will care for it if they die.

It is not just their own death that becomes an issue for new parents. They are also likely to be preoccupied with the possibility of the death of the baby, a possibility that causes concern even before the birth. Throughout the pregnancy, the mother in particular is focused on the survival of her baby, and subject to an increasing number of tests and antenatal checks and cannot help but be aware of her unborn baby's vulnerability.

Feeling unable to control the outcome of pregnancy, described by de Beauvoir as 'a mystery that the mother lends herself to' (ibid., 1953: 514), means experiencing uncertainty. For some women, the sense that they have lost control over the shape of their body means that their previous perception of mastery over their lives is severely shaken. Indeed, 'with the physical changes of pregnancy (or with the process of achieving pregnancy) it becomes apparent that this control may be an illusion' (Dunnewold, 1997: 11).

Thus, in existential terms, procreation means facing the inescapable evidence of thrownness,[2] the impossibility of controlling one's environment or what the future may bring. Being confronted with these 'ultimate concerns' (Jaspers, 1951) often involves an existential crisis (Arnold-Baker, 2000; Donaghy, 2001), which may manifest feelings of anxiety or depression.

Identity and the body

The process of procreation often brings for both parents a new perception of the world, and with it different values which require a reassessment of oneself and one's life. The existential perspective posits that there is no fixed self (Heidegger, 1927; Sartre, 1943; Kierkegaard, 1980b), rather we are a process of becoming and are shaped by our choices and our associations. Thus, the major changes in lifestyle that occur during procreation can mean a fundamental shift in who one believes oneself to be. Indeed, some argue that in becoming a parent a process of transformation and reorganization of self-identity is not only probable, but necessary (Stern, 1995).

For women the challenge to their sense of identity often begins with pregnancy and the physical changes that come with it, such as a change in body image, spatial awareness, diet and physical activity. It is through the body, what Merleau-Ponty calls 'the vehicle through which we experience the world' (Merleau-Ponty, 1962: 167), that we gain an understanding of the world and ourselves, and thus, such dramatic changes to the body impact on how expectant mothers experience themselves.

The bodily changes continue after birth, indeed many women report that their bodies are never the same again (Nicolson, 1998), and thus the transition into motherhood means being faced with a new sense of self, or having to recreate herself anew.

Not all the changes are physical. For both parents, and for the mother in particular, having a baby means altering emotional investments, activities, and reallocating time and energy. Where giving up work is part of this change, there may be a real sense of having lost what previously defined one. For some, such radical transformation may mean a questioning of meaning or purpose, evoking feelings of despair, or what Tillich (1952) calls 'spiritual anxiety'.

Whilst having a baby is usually a joyful experience, this major life transition also involves loss, and requires acknowledgement that there is, along with the joy, also likely to be grieving for one's 'lost self'.

Case illustrations

> Existential psychotherapy does not seek to cure or explain, it merely seeks to explore, describe and clarify in order to try and understand the human predicament. (van Deurzen-Smith, 1977: 3)

Existential psychotherapy offers the opportunity for understanding and normalizing feelings of loss and despair which often arise in the process of procreation and which feel all the more difficult to deal with because they appear contradictory or paradoxical in the light of the 'happy event'. By adopting an open and enquiring attitude, whilst keeping in mind the existential 'givens', existential therapy enables the client to explore their concerns and find the courage to live more authentically in spite of them.

Each of the following three case illustrations centres on one of the themes highlighted above.

Responsibility – Susie (by Claire Arnold-Baker)

Susie was forty-six when she came for counselling. Her presenting issue was the ending of her long-term relationship; however, it soon became apparent that this was not the only loss she was experiencing. Susie had always assumed she would be a mother at some point in her life, but felt it was something she could do later on, once she had established her flourishing career. Realizing she had left it too late led Susie to question her whole life, her values and expectations and the kind of life she would have without children. The focus of the therapy became her need to work through huge feelings of loss and sadness and to come to terms with the realization that she was unlikely to experience motherhood. However, as the therapy progressed and she freed herself from her expectations of a life with a husband and two children, Susie started to fantasize about the different directions her life could now go in. She started to see the other possibilities open to her. Susie's realization that she was responsible for her life and what she made of it gave her the motivation to go forward to find a life for herself that could still be meaningful without having children of her own.

Death – Alan (by Miriam Donaghy)

Alan was thirty when he came for counselling experiencing anxiety and panic attacks. His first baby had died from cot death five years earlier, an event which finally led to the breakdown of his relationship with his wife. Now remarried, his second wife was expecting a child but instead of being happy Alan found himself haunted by the thought that something terrible would happen. Though he had tried to hide his worries from his wife, he was aware that he was keeping a distance, not allowing himself to get too attached. During therapy Alan realized that he had never really faced up to the profound impact the death of his son had on him, nor how the inevitability of 'non-being' and the fragility of life had become for the first time a fact. In the course of the work Alan became more aware of how glimpsing the 'thrownness' of existence in the brutal way he had experienced it had led him to feel out of control. Having the space to experience the full effect of his loss and to struggle with facing his own mortality meant finding the courage to take a risk and allow himself to fully participate in the potential joy of becoming a father again.

Identity – Mariam (by Miriam Donaghy)

A re-evaluation of beliefs and values was central in Mariam's experience of becoming a mother. For Mariam, who came to counselling when her daughter Jade was six months old, having a baby outside of marriage had meant being ostracized by most of her Muslim family. As a consequence, the question of identity, who she was and what was important to her were issues that Mariam struggled with continually during her therapy. Having gained a lot of weight during pregnancy, Mariam felt she no longer recognized herself. With so little time to herself she was also finding the loss of autonomy very difficult. As well as struggling to find who she was in this new role as a mother and facing the losses entailed, the birth of her daughter had also meant revisiting the cultural values of her family, where women were quite literally second-class citizens. It was painful for Mariam to reflect on her own experience of being a girl in a family where girls were not valued, but she was clear that this was not something she was prepared to accept for Jade. Though Mariam was certain that she was no longer willing to abide by her family and cultural expectations, it was nevertheless difficult coming to terms with the consequences of this choice which meant widening the gulf with her family further. However, whilst reassessing her values and beliefs meant more isolation and sadness for what she had lost, it also meant gaining freedom to make choices for herself and her baby.

Critical considerations

The field of procreation is vast and impossible to do justice to in this short space where the focus is on the issues faced by those who experience the transition to parenthood. In approaching procreation as a given of human existence we have elucidated the existential themes that may apply to both sexes. However, we realize that this does not represent a full exploration of the different experiences of men and women during the process of becoming a parent. A more in-depth focus on pregnancy, birth and the immediate post-partum, or the specific experience of becoming a father would deserve further elaboration. Neither has there been space to consider the myriad of problems that can arise during the process of having a baby.

Whilst we realize that other important existential issues in relation to procreation such as meaning, intersubjectivity and relationship have remained unaddressed, those themes chosen give a flavour of some potential crises clients may present with. In illustrating the transition to parenthood as a time of dramatic change for both parents, not just in terms of biology and creating a new life, but also emotionally and spiritually, we have shown it to be a time that requires adaptation and re-evaluation. Having a baby, or even contemplating doing so, can be a wake-up call to life, evoking what Heidegger terms the 'call of consciousness' (Heidegger, 1927).

The potential emotional conflict then that lies within the many aspects of procreation is considerable even when things go well. When problems arise such as for those who experience infertility, miscarriage, termination, or for those who suffer postpartum problems, that is, in the case of neonatal death or disability, or for women who experience PND, it is clear that here lies a positive minefield of worry, distress and suffering. It follows then that the experience of procreation represents an enormous area where psychotherapeutic help might be sought, and in our opinion one where existential psychotherapy has much to offer and positive transformation and re-evaluation of life can be achieved.

Notes

1 'maternal death continued to be high in the early 20th century. In 1918, one mother died for every 264 babies born alive' (Figes, 1998: 65).
2 For Heidegger, *thrownness* is a character of being of Dasein. We are thrown into a world, which is outside Dasein's control, something that Dasein is not responsible for and did not choose (Heidegger, 1927).

Further reading

de Beauvoir, S. *The Second Sex.*
Clulow, C. *To Have and To Hold, Marriage, The First Baby and Preparing Couples for Parenthood.*
Greenberg, M. *The Birth of a Father.*
Nicolson, P. *Postnatal Depression: Psychology, Science and the Transition to Motherhood.*
Raphael-Leff, J. *Pregnancy: The Inside Story.*

CHAPTER 5

Human Development

STEVE KIRBY

'This – is now my way – where is yours?' Thus did I answer those who asked
me 'the way'. For the way – it doth not exist!

Nietzsche, *Thus Spoke Zarathustra*

Introduction

Lifespan or human development theories seek to map the evolving process
of the human life cycle. Early theorists have tended to concentrate upon
infancy, conceiving of this period as laying the foundations for subsequent
development.

Freud (1963) recognized that the newborn infant experiences the world
primarily through its body. His psycho-sexual theory of infant development
comprised of a linear progression through oral, anal, phallic, Oedipal, latency
and genital stages. The negotiation of these, whether successful or problematic,
is held to provide the blueprint for subsequent adult development.

Klein (1988) identified even earlier stages of infant development as the
most significant. According to her theory the pre-verbal infant experiences its
world in very absolute terms; it is either good or bad. The infant projects this
tendency towards splitting outwards upon the world, principally upon the
primary caregiver, resulting in what Klein terms the *paranoid-schizoid position*.
As it matures, the infant begins to recognize gradations of experience and
develops the capacity to integrate the bad and the good. This is known as the
depressive position, so called because of the guilt the infant feels upon realizing
that the bad and the good emanate from a single source.

Recognizing that biological and psychological birth were distinct and
non-synchronous events, Mahler (2000) sought to describe the emergence of
the latter. The first five months of an infant's life are characterized by absolute dependence and a symbiotic merging with the primary caregiver. This
is followed by a gradual process (lasting up to the age of thirty-six months) of
separation and individuation, resulting in the infant's ability to differentiate
between itself and the outside world and the development of a sense of self.

Winnicott (1990) highlighted further the crucial role of the interpersonal. The infant's world is twofold, consisting of its own lived bodily experience and secondly its experience of the mother's care through the provision of food, warmth and touch. He argued that healthy development was dependent upon the infant's learning to trust and depend upon the reliability of the mother's *holding* and her ability to create a secure *holding environment*.

Piaget (1977) focuses upon cognitive development. He proposes that the capacities for *assimilation* and *accommodation* enable the human infant to adapt to the demands of the external environment. Moving through four major developmental stages, the sensory-motor, pre-operational, concrete-operational and formal-operational, the child masters increasingly complex skills such as the ability to use symbols and abstract reasoning.

The contribution of Erikson (1995) looms large in theories of human development. He was the first theorist to extend the concept of stages of human development across the entire lifespan. Moreover, his psycho-social theory encompasses the breadth of developmental processes by bringing together the somatic, ego identity and social context. Building upon Freud's work, Erikson conceived of the human lifespan as punctuated by a series of eight existential challenges or tasks. The first five stages cover childhood and adolescence, the final three adulthood.

According to Erikson the helplessness of the newborn requires the infant to negotiate between a *basic trust* and *mistrust* in getting its needs met. Between the ages of one and three the child's emergent sense of independence brings it into conflict with parental authority. The challenge here is to maintain budding *autonomy* without succumbing to inhibiting *doubt and shame*. Between three and six years, the child is drawn to explore the extent of its own potentiality and the limits of its world. This requires the exercise of *initiative* without giving in to *guilt*. The next phase, *industry versus inferiority*, takes place between the ages of six and eleven and is characterized by the acquisition of socially and culturally relevant skills. Adolescence is dominated by the requirement to forge a sense of self or *identity*. The inability to do so results in *role confusion*.

The first challenge of early adulthood, *intimacy versus isolation*, concerns the search for a close emotional and sexual relationship. Adulthood and middle-age tend to be preoccupied with investment in the future, whether in terms of procreation or developing one's career. The challenge here is one of *generativity versus stagnation*. The final challenge concerns old age and the need to face up to our own mortality with *integrity* and dignity. Regrets about unattained ambitions or opportunities lost may lead us into *despair*.

Each and every individual is required to meet and adapt to the ever-changing physical, psychological and social challenges faced by human beings as they age. Erikson's stages of development are particularly useful for the practitioner in that they both foreground the existential challenges facing the individual and describe the mental health problems associated with failure to achieve the milestones and objectives associated with each stage.

An existential perspective

The central difference between the existential and the more orthodox approaches to human development consists in the shift away from stage- or age-specific tasks towards a more global consideration of the existential challenges facing the individual throughout the course of his/her life. An existential perspective would be characterized by an awareness of the tension between the opposing forces of potentiality and inertia. As a being of conscience and will, mankind battles with the yearning to transcend the givens of his/her existence. Against this are set the inclination towards familiarity and conformism. An existential approach, also questions the implicit determinism found in stage theories of human development. As Briod (1989) points out, the notion of universal stages of human development is a hypothetical abstraction. By contrast, existential-phenomenological approaches to human development seek to capture something of the life world of the developing individual.

Kierkegaard

Kierkegaard (1992) proposes that there are three basic modes of existence: the 'aesthetic', the 'ethical' and the 'religious'. A life lived in the aesthetic mode is characterized by a hedonistic enjoyment of the senses in which desire becomes the motivating force of existence. The aim is simply to maximize pleasure and minimize displeasure or pain. Unlike Freud (2001), who posits the 'pleasure principle' as a universal drive, Kierkegaard views this tendency as merely characteristic of one mode of existence. The aesthetic is the mode of immediacy. This contrasts with the ethical, which is the mode of deferred gratification. To live ethically is to be motivated by that which is good or right and to eschew that which is evil or wrong. Thus, one is required to resist one's immediate desires and make choices on the basis of one's moral code. This necessitates the exercise of will power and commitment. However, adherence to a code also provides certainty and security, to the extent that one is not required to think but simply obey.

The shift from the ethical to the religious mode is enabled by the introduction of doubt. This is the central focus of *Fear & Trembling* (1985). In doubting and questioning the rightness of previously held convictions, I am made aware that certainty and security are not to be found in either ethical codes of conduct or scientific rationalism. In a world of uncertainty and moral ambiguity only faith and a relation to the infinite are adequate to the task of providing solace and direction.

Kierkegaard illustrates the enormity of the transition from the 'ethical' to the 'religious' sphere by drawing upon the biblical account of God's demand for Abraham to kill his son Isaac. Just as Abraham is about to plunge the knife into Isaac's flesh, God intervenes and provides a sacrificial ram instead. In his readiness to honour God's commandment Abraham was prepared to murder his own son, thereby transgressing both ethical and human codes. Viewed from this perspective, his intention is irrational and unacceptable. The point that Kierkegaard seeks to make here is that entry into the 'religious' sphere requires a 'leap of faith' into the unknown, wherein we forego the comfort usually afforded by our reliance upon moral and ethical absolutes.

Kierkegaard's 'stages on life's way' trace a journey from youthful indulgence, through a conservative adherence to established moral/social codes, to arrive finally at a passionate commitment to personal faith and choice.

Nietzsche

Nietzsche conceives of mankind as a process of becoming, a moving away from the animals behind us and a reaching out towards the Superman ahead. Like Kierkegaard, Nietzsche's conception of human development, as outlined in *Thus Spoke Zarathustra* (1961), is tripartite in structure and transformative in nature. By marrying our animalistic drives to our will, we can 'overcome' and transcend ourselves by means of three metamorphoses. At first our spirit is like a camel, resolutely carrying the loads and burdens that life puts before us. Having accepted and borne the givens thrown our way, our spirit needs to become leonine. This necessitates rejecting the demands of duty and taking hold of freedom's possibility in order to 'seize the right to new values' (Nietzsche, 1961: 55). But the creation of new values requires the spirit to undergo a further metamorphosis and become a child. As innocence and forgetfulness, a new beginning and a 'sacred Yes', 'the spirit now wills *its own* will, the spirit sundered from the world now wins *its own* world' (ibid., 55). Nietzsche is hereby advocating the valorization of self-reliance and authenticity in opposition to conformism and inauthenticity.

Merleau-Ponty

The assumption that the newborn infant's world is one of undifferentiated oneness has been seriously challenged by the empirical work of Stern (1985) and others (DeCasper and Fifer, 1980; Rochat and Striano, 2002). Merleau-Ponty (1964a) considers primordial experience to be intersubjective, and in so doing provides the basis of an existential-phenomenological approach to human development. Arguably, his two major contributions were to remind us of our nature as embodied beings and his notion of consciousness as a realm of experience that is both private and public. As well as being the vehicle of my being-in-the-world, the means through which I project myself, the body is also the means and the medium of both perception and intersubjectivity. 'It is through my body that I understand other people, just as it is through my body that I perceive things' (Merleau-Ponty, 1962: 186). Perceptual consciousness is not merely a visual, cognitive or reflective process but is rather practical and immediate.

Unlike my exterior, which is visible to others, my consciousness is not immediately accessible to others. However, it is not my mere visibility that initiates intersubjectivity, but rather the meaningfulness of my behaviour. Because the 'lived body' is visible, the manner in which I live it is accessible to others. 'Consciousness is in the first place not a matter of "I think that" but of "I can"' (ibid., 137). Thus, the nature of consciousness is not to be understood in terms of an isolated subject disinterestedly observing and reflecting upon an external world. Merleau-Ponty posits the 'lived body' as the mediator and communicator of internal states, asserting that the psyche of another is accessible to me through their behaviours or 'conduct'.

> We must abandon the fundamental prejudice according to which the psyche is that which is accessible only to myself and cannot be seen from outside … My consciousness is turned primarily toward the world, turned toward things; it is above all a relation to the world. The other's consciousness as well is chiefly a certain way of comporting himself toward the world. Thus it is in his conduct, in the manner in which the other deals with the world, that I will be able to discover his consciousness. (Merleau-Ponty, 1964: 116)

Merleau-Ponty elaborates Jacques Lacan's (Lacan, 2001) idea that development is centred upon the 'specular' or 'mirror' image. At about eight months of age, the infant comes to recognize itself through its reflection in the mirror. However, in so doing it undergoes an experience of self-objectification. The 'specular I' is born of the image reflected in the mirror. This is distinct from the introceptive, experiential 'lived me'. 'The mirror image itself makes possible a contemplation of self.' Furthermore, 'On this immediately lived *me* there is superimposed a constructed *me*, a *me* that is visible at a distance, an imaginary *me*, which the psychoanalysts call the super-ego' (Merleau-Ponty, 1964a: 136–137).

The 'self-alienation' implicit in the recognition of the specular image creates the conditions for a seismic shift in the child's further cognitive and social development. These include the discovery of other viewpoints and perspectives, and with the acquisition of language, the emergence of self-reflective dialogue. Merleau-Ponty conceives of thought and language as two sides of the same coin; language is a tool that allows us to think, and we think with and through language. Self-evidently, thinking can take place only through the use of such shared social resources, and is thus always potentially intersubjective. 'It shows that thought is an intersubjective action and that there is no private mental world of thoughts behind the world of social coexistence' (Crossley, 1996: 39).

Towards an existential view of human development

Unlike more conventional conceptions of human development, existential views tend to focus upon the implicit meaning of the developmental challenges confronting us as we mature. Kierkegaard and Nietzsche, for example, stress the process of spiritual growth towards increasing self-reliance and authenticity. By contrast, Merleau-Ponty's developmental theory, like Freud's, starts with the body.

An existential approach would resist the temptation towards a simplistic linear conception of human development. Heidegger (1962), for example, has placed the inescapable fact of our death at the centre of our being-in-the-world. To suggest therefore that our mortality is something that only concerns us as we approach old age (as could be implied by Erikson's schema) is untenable. Similarly the challenge of intimacy versus isolation is not confined to our first love, but has to be constantly renegotiated.

Binswanger's (1958) three spheres of existence, Umwelt (physical world), Mitwelt (social world) and Eigenwelt (private world), to which van Deurzen (van Deurzen-Smith, 1984) later added a fourth, Uberwelt (ideal world), provides a framework for exploring human development in all of its dimensions. Thus, for example, the experience of intimacy versus isolation can be explored in both its temporal dimension as it impacts differentially over the course of the lifespan, and also across the breadth of the four worlds.

Case illustration

Amy (not her real name) was a twenty-nine-year-old, single, white female. She was articulate, thoughtful and quietly spoken. Amy began by saying that she felt that she was in a rut and described herself as being depressed, unhappy and lacking in direction. Amy experienced her job as PA to the senior executive of a large city bank as boring and unfulfilling. However, it provided her with financial security and stability and it soon became apparent that these were extremely important values for Amy.

Amy was born and raised on a farm in South Africa. She was one of twelve children, being the eldest girl, with three older brothers. She said that like herself, all of her siblings were shy and lacking in confidence, and linked this to their deeply religious upbringing. As children they were encouraged to 'turn the other cheek', and to 'always put others first'. Amy painted a picture of a childhood characterized by self-denial, conditional love and isolation from an outside world viewed as dangerous and corrupting.

Amy's security needs resulted in her seeking to minimize potential uncertainty by 'playing safe'. She concluded that not taking risks gave her the sense of security she craved, but the downside of this was that there was little by way of stimulation or excitement in her life. Amy shared a flat with a girlfriend and two men. She saw herself as a 'radical thinker', a 'feminist', and as somewhat 'unconventional'. She felt that perhaps these attributes accounted for some of the friction she experienced within the household. However, further exploration revealed that in actuality Amy chose to reign in and play down her feminist and alternative beliefs. She experienced the merest hint of disagreement or challenge as crushing and rejecting. Consequently, in an effort to ameliorate or avoid interpersonal anxiety, Amy hid and censored aspects of herself. This reminds us of Merleau-Ponty's distinction between the felt or experiential self and the objectified self.

Amy viewed the world as a place full of potential dangers, and felt herself to be disadvantaged in her ability to deal with it: 'It's as if I've missed out on some vital lesson.' Additionally, through her body language and barely audible voice Amy practically apologized for her existence. Amy's presence perfectly encapsulated Merleau-Ponty's notion of the 'lived-body' as mediator of internal states. I felt Amy's stagnation and loss of spontaneity to be an expression of her having little sense of being able to realize her possibilities, and saw this as primarily a function of her inability to overcome her fear of rejection and risk being herself.

Seemingly unable to meet the challenge of discovering and choosing her self, Amy was further constrained by the internalized religious values of her parents. Amy described her childhood as being characterized by 'negative reinforcement', 'censorship' and an absence of 'nurturing'. Her parents were not given to overt displays of affection or emotion and held very stereotypical views of gender roles. Thus, practicality, science, rationality and farm work were held in much higher esteem than creativity, nurturing, imagination and domesticity; the latter being precisely those areas in which Amy felt that she excelled. Amy felt her achievements to have gone largely unrecognized. The picture that emerged was of a child desperately trying to conform to strict parental expectations in an effort to secure some tangible signs of love and affection.

In addition to feeling bored, Amy also felt 'put upon' and 'taken advantage of' by work colleagues. Amy was able to link this pattern of behaviour to her unsuccessful attempts to gain the attention and approval of her mother. She came to see how the internalization of the moral construct, 'always put other's needs before your own', in combination with her need to be liked, led her to ignore her felt experience and this resulted in self-alienation. One of the central themes of our work together was Amy's attempt to bridge or narrow the gap between her experiential self and her objectified self.

During a summer break Amy visited Russia where she reconnected with her 'original project',[1] the desire to be creative through writing. She had originally planned to live and write in Russia, earning a living by teaching English. However, Amy's need for security and risk aversion won out over her desire to realize her creative potential. Amy acknowledged that prior to her visit her perception of the difficulty of realizing her ambition had led her to make numerous excuses for her inaction. However, in Russia she had met with Europeans living and working there, and this had helped to make the possibility of doing likewise seem more attainable. She had decided to return to Russia the following summer. However, she now faced the question of what to do in the interim.

Amy felt that she had a very simple and stark choice to make: either to stay in her present job or to try and do something in preparation for her trip to Russia. However, as we began to explore the various options relating to the latter choice, for example taking a formal teaching qualification, seeing a careers counsellor, starting to write and so on, Amy persistently focused upon reasons for not pursuing them, for example, her home environment was unconducive to writing, she was too tired after a hard day at work, the boredom of her job seemed to sap her creativity, she was not inspired right now and so on. Her desire to be creative and industrious was constantly undermined by her sense of inferiority and avoidance of risk.

Amy was a perfectionist and this manifested itself in absolute terms, to be less than the best was to fail. Amy came to realize that her fear of failure and lack of trust in herself fuelled her tendency to procrastination. The anxiety of losing was such that she would rather withdraw into non-participation than take the risk of not winning. We explored how this limited Amy's possibilities and how she might overcome it in an effort to expand her options. With regard to her job, right up until the very end Amy was still unable to decide whether to stay or go. But at least she was now clear about the pros and cons of each choice, and that not choosing was also a choice. Amy's struggle could perhaps be seen in terms of Kierkegaard's ethical and religious ways of being. Her need for acceptance and security, her tendency towards moral absolutes and deferred gratification are all indicative of the ethical mode. If Amy was to realize her possibilities, she needed to make a leap of faith and plunge herself into doubt, uncertainty, self-reliance and ambiguity, all characteristics of the religious mode.

In reviewing our work together Amy concluded that she no longer felt trapped or lost, but had reconnected with her creative ambition. She acknowledged her former tendency to apportion blame for her problems to externals, both others and circumstances. Amy felt that she now had the skills to challenge this predisposition, enabling her to examine her own role in the creation and maintenance of her problems. Amy grew to recognize the similarities between her own way of being and that of her mother. In reaching a better understanding of her mother's coldness the anger she had felt towards her began to diminish. Amy's sedimented patterns of behaviour had evolved primarily as solutions to specific problems encountered in childhood. Whilst they may have helped at the time, these behaviours were now holding her back. However, they had become a part of her way of being-in-the-world and could not be abandoned overnight or without struggle. Amy had achieved her stated goal of finding direction and purpose, but recognized that her continued perfectionism and avoidance of risk prevented her from realizing her possibilities.

Critical considerations

Whilst it might be argued that there is no specific existential theory of human development as such, it could equally be contended that notions of progression and development are implicit in the existential concept of the self as a process of becoming (see Chapter 18). A possible danger here is that in refusing to be tied to a 'stage' conception of development we run the risk of explaining everything and nothing. However, a counter argument is that in bracketing theoretical preconceptions we create the conditions for phenomenological engagement with our client's experience. Existential counsellors and psychotherapists need to steer a course between the latter and the requirement for a better theoretical understanding of human development.

This is a field sorely in need of further study from within the existential-phenomenological framework. One of the challenges of such an approach would be to capture the life world of the developing individual. This suggests an approach that has as much in common with the humanities as the social sciences. Perhaps Sartre's (1963, 1971) biographical portraits of Flaubert and Genet, wherein he sought to trace the unfolding of their original project by exploring their childhood experience, offer us a blueprint of such an approach. Briod (1989) has sought to develop a methodology which brings together phenomenology, biography, narrative and 'intersubjective comparisons' to arrive at a more phenomenological understanding of child development. This provides a basis for further studies and research across the breadth of the human lifespan.

Note

1   Sartre maintained that we all have an 'original project', something important to us that we are seeking to actualize. One may be fully aware of one's project, but equally it may be outside our awareness, more a sense of homing in on something.

Further reading

Briod, M. 'A Phenomenological Approach to Child Development'. In R. S. Valle and S. Halling (eds) *Existential-Phenomenological Perspectives in Psychology*.
Kierkegaard, S. *Either/Or: A Fragment of Life*.
Merleau-Ponty, M. 'The Child's Relations with Others'. In *The Primacy of Perception*.
Nietzsche, N. *Thus Spoke Zarathustra*.
Stern, D. *The Interpersonal World of the Infant*.

CHAPTER 6

The Body and Sexuality

PAUL SMITH-PICKARD AND RICHARD SWYNNERTON

> Behind your thoughts and feelings, my brother, stands a mighty commander, an unknown sage – he is called the Self. He is in your body, he is your body.
>
> Nietzsche, *Thus Spoke Zarathustra*

> There is no explanation of sexuality which reduces it to anything other than itself, for it is already something other than itself, and indeed, if we like, our whole being.
>
> Merleau-Ponty, *The Phenomenology of Perception*

Introduction

Arguably, from an existential perspective, the most adequate and comprehensive ontological exploration of the body and sexuality to date is to be found within the pages of Sartre's *Being and Nothingness* and Merleau-Ponty's *The Phenomenology of Perception*. From their particular perspectives, derived mainly from the works of Husserl, Heidegger, Marcel and Hegel, sexuality is located within embodied perceptual experience in our relations with others. It is, if you like, an embodied intersubjective response to alterity. Even though in these works the neo-Hegelian images of dialectical relationship of master and slave make Sartre and Merleau-Ponty appear to be speaking with one voice, there are significant differences in their phenomenologies and their respective images of embodiment and subjectivity.

Whilst embracing Heidegger's fundamental ontology and Husserl's phenomenology, their departure from Heidegger's thinking was to privilege embodiment as a primary ontological concern, and to reject the Cartesian aspects of Husserlian transcendental phenomenology. Being-in-the-world means being as consciousness incarnate, a body embedded in the shared context of the 'Other' where identity is always intertwined with alterity. We experience sexuality because we are consciousness incarnate caught up in an inevitable involvement and struggle with other embodied sexual beings. We cannot divorce sexuality from our bodies even though we may attempt to divorce our bodies from sexuality.

The significance of the body in existential philosophy is largely attributed to Maurice Merleau-Ponty. Following Gabriel Marcel's image of 'the body I am' rather than 'the body I have', he attempts in his holistic image of the lived body or the 'body-subject' to overcome the Cartesian split of mind from body. The image of the body-subject stands in contradistinction to Sartre's three disjunct but complementary ontological formulations of the body:

- the body-for-itself, or my body for me as I exist, my body in my free subjectivity;
- the body-for-others as used and known by the other as an object or instrument;
- and thirdly, when I exist for myself as a body known by the other, as a body reduced to an object by the look or gaze of the other.

The differences between Merleau-Ponty and Sartre become clearer at the level of the sensing body; specifically with regard to touch and the image of 'double sensation', where according to Sartre:

> we are dealing with two essentially different orders of reality. To touch and to be touched, to feel that one is touching and to feel that one is touched- these are two species of phenomena which it is useless to try to reunite by the term 'double sensation'. In fact they are radically distinct and they exist on two incommunicable levels. (Sartre, 1996: 304)

For Merleau-Ponty, through his insistence on the primacy of perception, the term 'double sensation' means that my body is always ambiguously both subject and object for me. It can alternatingly both touch and be touched, see and be seen, in a mutual and reversible relation to a world, where I co-exist in a world of things and other embodied subjects. This distinction between Sartre and Merleau-Ponty is clear in their respective accounts of one hand touching the other hand and is a metaphor for how they individually regard relationships in general and sexuality in particular. For Merleau-Ponty:

> When I press my two hands together, it is not a matter of two sensations felt together as one perceives two objects placed side by side, but of an ambiguous set-up in which both hands can alternate the roles of 'touching' and 'being touched'. What was meant by . . . 'double sensations' is that, in passing from one role to another, I can identify the hand touched as the same one which will in a moment be touching. (Merleau-Ponty, 1962: 93)

Sartre, however, views this situation as a direct trajectory of intentionality and objectification, where he sees the active grasping hand turning the other hand into a thing: 'the hand which I grasp with my other hand is not apprehended as a hand which is grasping but as an apprehensible object. Thus the nature of *our body for us* entirely escapes us to the extent that we can take upon it the Other's point of view' (Sartre, 1996: 358).

Whilst Sartre's view is focussed more on consciousness and subjectivity and Merleau-Ponty's focussed more on perception and intersubjectivity, they both acknowledge that my sensing body cannot be separated from my existence or my consciousness, an embodied existence that is always already embedded in a world with others. However, for Merleau-Ponty, 'The theory of the body is already a theory of perception' (Merleau-Ponty, 1962: 203), where the body, the site of all perception, is both perceiving and perceivable. 'Our own body', he says, 'is in the world as the heart is in the organism: it keeps the visible spectacle constantly alive, it breathes air into it and sustains it inwardly, and with it forms a system' (ibid., 203).

Merleau-Ponty regards sexuality as the basic way in which we project ourselves into the world and towards others through our bodies. It is a fundamental image of encounter and intersubjectivity. He describes sexuality as the 'mute and permanent question' (ibid., 156) that we pose in our attitude towards being with others and as such is 'always present like an atmosphere' that 'spreads forth like an odour or like a sound' (ibid., 168). Sartre (1996) in turn sees sexuality as the paradigm for other relationships, the 'skeleton' on which all concrete relations with others are hung. He points out that he is not referring to an instinctual 'libido' that slips in everywhere but to a foundation of all human relations, where an understanding of sexuality will provide us with an understanding of how all our relationships are articulated. Merleau-Ponty's and Sartre's images of sexuality extend beyond mere sex or sexual encounter and in this sense sexuality is coextensive with life, beginning at birth and ending in death. However, as Merleau-Ponty warns us, we must be careful not to extend the meaning of sexuality to being synonymous with existence or to make our meaning of it so broad as to be meaningless, rather to understand that 'sexuality permeates existence and vice-versa' (Merleau-Ponty, 1962: 169).

Given the centrality of sexuality in human experience, it is difficult to understand why the phenomenon has barely been explored in existentialism. The question according to Merleau-Ponty is '... not so much whether human life does or does not rest on sexuality, as of knowing what is to be understood by sexuality' (ibid., 158). This is in fact a twofold question. There is the ontological question concerning intersubjectivity that Merleau-Ponty intends, and the second question regarding the ongoing historical, colloquial use of the word as a socio-cultural euphemism for a variety of meanings connected to autonomous images of self-hood and identity.

In ordinary, everyday language, sexuality is often used to indicate predilections and behaviours in various groups and individuals. Here we may find ourselves speaking in terms of one's sexuality as if it was an essential pre-determined quality; a distinguishing feature attached to one's identity, whereby meaning is focussed upon the individual and their acts, where according to Foucault the homosexual become a species. Sexuality thus becomes reified as a defining characteristic of an individual rather than remaining at the level of description of a fundamental aspect of intersubjectivity, as it would be seen from an existential perspective.

Most contemporary existential texts seem to either ignore sexuality or remain unwittingly caught in the echoes of normative biological images, colloquial euphemisms and the facticity of sexual behaviour. There seems to be an uncertainty as to whether sexuality has an ontological dimension or simply ontic manifestations, or both. This has led to confusion and difficulty in describing the phenomenon of sexuality beyond the facticity of sex. If we are to look at the ontic manifestations of sexuality, we must go beyond limiting ourselves to an exploration of sex, because although 'the sexual life is a sector of our life bearing a special relation to the existence of sex' (ibid., 159), sexuality itself is more than an activity focussed on the genital area. 'Is "sex"', asks Foucault, 'really the anchorage point that supports the manifestations of sexuality, or is it not rather a complex idea that was formed inside the deployment of sexuality?' (Foucault, 1990: 152). Foucault, Merleau-Ponty and Sartre all suggest that sex is simply an aspect of sexuality, with sex being the image or instrument of a fundamental sexuality articulated by desire. An ontology of sexuality is dependent on a reflexive phenomenology of sexuality that, in as much as we need to describe how sexuality reveals itself, we also need to describe the embodied manner of its perception. Sexuality has intelligibility and significance that goes beyond an engagement with sex and the deployment of sexuality has an ontological significance. 'It is through sex – in fact an imaginary point determined by the deployment of sexuality – that each individual has to pass in order to have access to his own intelligibility' (ibid., 155).

As we have already indicated, one will find passages in *Being and Nothingness* concerned with freedom and sexuality that could easily be exchanged for similar passages in *The Phenomenology of Perception*. In their adoption of neo-Hegelian images of master and slave to describe how we attempt to capture another's consciousness through sexuality and objectify them as flesh in their own consciousness, both Sartre and Merleau-Ponty come close to sliding into a Cartesian dualism. At this point they both hold a view of human relations articulated through an antagonistic subject/object dichotomy where the other's freedom threatens our freedom. This conceptual objectification of our own or the other's body, where we might regard the body simply as a thing among other things, separates our body from our consciousness rather than seeing embodiment as the foundation of our consciousness. There can be no separation of mind and body, only an incarnation of consciousness. In his later work Merleau-Ponty attempts to dissolve this subject/object dichotomy through the ambiguity of the sentient/sensible body. He shifts his perceptual embodied phenomenology towards ontology and alterity in his elemental image of the *flesh of the world*, which he describes in the following:

> one must see or feel in some way in order to think, (that) every thought known to us occurs to a flesh. . . . the flesh we are speaking of is not matter. It is the coiling over of the visible upon the seeing body, of the tangible upon the touching body, which is attested in particular when the body sees itself, touches itself seeing and touching the things, such that, simultaneously *as* tangible it descends among them, *as* touching it dominates them all. (Merleau-Ponty, 1968: 146)

A fundamental key to understanding sexuality is desire. Sartre comments that most psychologists see sexual desire as an act of consciousness that can only be understood through a study of behaviour connected to our sexual organs and regarded as 'instinct' rather than as being derived from an ontology of consciousness. He also points out that Heidegger makes no allusion to sexuality at all resulting in a *Dasein* that appears completely asexual. It seems likely that Heidegger considered it unnecessary to isolate the phenomenon of sexuality as it would have been grounded similarly to the phenomena that he does identify in *Being and Time*, of *willing, wishing, urge, and addiction*, in the basic ontological phenomenon of 'Care' that he saw as the structural primordial totality that defines Being (Heidegger, 1996: 238). The keys to desire for Sartre are that we are nothingness that always lacks and therefore wants, and as a response to alterity where 'desire and sexuality in general express an original effort of the for-it-self to recover its being which has become estranged through contact with the Other' (Sartre, 1996: 572).

Similarly for Merleau-Ponty, desire places us as embodied subjects in our sexual being in a world with others. Sexuality is always directed towards something as a form of original intentionality, expressed as desire. Prior to the understanding and consideration of any sexual response, pre-reflective comprehension is experienced within the body as desire, which exposes the primordial fact of human existence – that we are always already inextricably caught up in an ambiguous world of embodied heteronomy of which we are both part and which is already ourselves.

The main difference between Sartre's and Merleau-Ponty's images of sexuality can be illustrated through the intentionality of desire. For Sartre it is the intentionality of a reflective consciousness that aims to capture the freedom of the other and invalidate the consciousness of the other in an attempt to maintain our free subjectivity in the face of the other's freedom. For Merleau-Ponty desire is originally primordial, pre-reflective and intersubjective, linking us blindly to the other's body as a fundamental form of intentionality. Sexuality and enchantment meet at the point where the other's consciousness has become identified with their body as flesh, where their free subjectivity has become possessed by their own self-consciousness in their body. I can achieve this incarnation of consciousness through a caress, my gaze, or I can also fascinate the other with my body. 'Desire', says Sartre, 'is expressed by the caress as thought is by language' (Sartre, 1996: 390), and 'is an attempt to strip the body of its movements as of its clothing and make it exist as pure flesh; it is an attempt to *incarnate* the Other's body' (ibid., 389). This project could be seen as self-defeating, however, for, as I attempt to realize the incarnation of the Other's consciousness I also, through desire, bring my own consciousness into my body and I become flesh and an object for the other. However, this is to regard the incarnation of consciousness through the lens of a subject/object dichotomy and there are other interpretations available to us. This concrete image, of flesh as incarnate consciousness, is not to be confused with Merleau-Ponty's later elemental image of the *flesh of the world*, although we can find the origins of the later ontological image in the earlier perceptual phenomenology. It is through an examination of this shift from phenomenology to ontology in his work that we are able to see desire as the moment of self-consciousness that reveals our embodied presence to the world and to ourselves, and that it is primarily through sexuality and its concomitant image of alterity and heteronomy that the truth of being is amplified for us.

If, as Merleau-Ponty and Sartre suggest, sexuality permeates our whole being, then sexuality always has ontological significance. In as much as Being-in-the-world is always Being-in-in-the-world-with-others, it is also Being-in-the-world-sexually, that is, as embodied subjects immersed in a world imbued with sexual significance where sexuality is a primary mode of relatedness. We can therefore say that there is no Being or being without relatedness and that all relatedness and being have sexual significance. We must then acknowledge that a psychotherapeutic encounter inevitably has sexual significance and that willingly or otherwise, both client and therapist are linked together through their bodies and sexuality. As Merleau-Ponty points out, this leads to an ambiguity of relationship:

> Since sexuality is relationship to other persons, and not just to another body, it is going to weave the circular system of projections and introjections, illuminating the unlimited series of reflecting reflections and reflected reflections which are the reasons why I am the other person and he is myself. (Merleau-Ponty, 1968: 230)

It is paradoxical that although I share a consensual world with others, it is not the same perceptual world. I perceive the phenomenal world differently because it is always from the vantage point of my body.

> I do not hear myself as I hear the others ... the sonorous existence of my voice is for me as it were poorly exhibited; I have rather an echo of its articulated existence, it vibrates through my head rather than outside. I am always on the same side of my body; it presents itself to me in one invariable perspective. (Ibid., 148)

We are presented with a vantage point where the sensing self is always situated in some field of sensed phenomena, which it is a part of and involved in. 'I am all that I see', he says, 'I am an intersubjective field, not despite my body and historical situation, but, on the contrary, by being this body and this situation' (Merleau-Ponty, 1962: 452).

But this vantage point is an ambiguous perspective in the realization that my body can be experienced by another, giving rise to the ambiguity of embodied experience and intersubjectivity that lies at the heart of our existential description of sexuality.

Case illustration (by Richard Swynnerton)

The following case illustration highlights a number of points made in this chapter, in particular, the idea that sexuality from an existential perspective is imbued with ontological significance and is more than an activity focussed on the genital area.

When Gerald, a forty-five-year-old recently married man, first came to see me, it was with 'a problem to be solved'. More specifically, Gerald was preoccupied with his inability to sustain an erection during intercourse with his wife Sarah.

A phenomenologically informed therapeutic approach disclosed Gerald's preoccupation with the facticity of his sexual behaviour and only later in the work was this situated within the broader context of an exploration of sexuality as an aspect of his interpersonal relationships.

Gerald's initial focus was very much on what we might refer to as the ontic manifestations of his sexual world. Many of our early sessions were focussed primarily on Gerald's preoccupation with the mechanics of the sexual act and indeed speculative discussions regarding the possibility of underlying physiological difficulties, which might be exacerbating 'the problem'. The fact that Gerald regularly masturbated with no apparent difficulty seemed, however, to somewhat undermine such assumptions. There was also a tacit understanding that this was Gerald's problem, rather than see it as an expression of difficulties, which existed, between the two of them at an interpersonal level.

As the sessions progressed, it became increasingly apparent that Gerald was very much preoccupied with a variety of normative assumptions about sexuality and in particular, the act of sex itself. A long-standing 'fear of sex' coupled with powerful assumptions about how he felt he should conduct himself sexually meant that the couple's sexual encounters had become reduced to the functional act of missionary position intercourse. As Gerald was to later acknowledge, 'we were indeed having sex, but it didn't feel particularly sexy!'

The turning point came when Gerald summoned up the courage to share with Sarah his growing concerns about the somewhat limited nature of their lovemaking. Gerald quickly discovered that talking about sex with Sarah was highly erotic and arousing. More so, in fact, than their previous lovemaking attempts! This was a significant insight for both of them and marked the beginning of a growing awareness of what, from an existential perspective, we might refer to as the ontological aspects of sexuality; in other words, sexuality as an aspect of our interpersonal relationships.

These sexually charged discussions served to throw into sharp relief the blandness and poverty of their lovemaking attempts, which seemed in contrast to be mechanical, predictable and lacking any significant erotic or sensual dimension. They were particularly taken with their ability to conjure up a sexual mood or atmosphere through dialogue, something which had very much been lacking in their sexual life up until this point. They found that once this had become an aspect of their relationship as such, it could readily be imported into their subsequent lovemaking attempts, with the result that Gerald was able to enjoy penetrative sex as an aspect of an altogether more varied and rewarding sexual life.

The more or less successful resolution of Gerald's presenting problem, rather than marking the end of therapy, served as the impetus for a sustained period of therapeutic work. What began as a preoccupation with the mechanics of the sexual act and his inability to successfully 'perform', eventually became a more considered analysis of his lived experience as a sexual being.

On one occasion, Gerald brought a portfolio of photographs, which he had taken over a period of years, for me to view. Although an amateur photographer, many of his pictures had won awards and I was taken aback by how breathtakingly beautiful many of them were. These photographs were organized, in chronological order, in a leather-bound album, with the most recent ones, taken during the period of time in which we had been working together, at the back.

What particularly excited Gerald about his more recent photographs was his conviction that he was somehow managing to capture, in many of his female subjects, a degree of sensuality and eroticism that had been lacking in many of his earlier photos. For Gerald, the women in his more recent photographs seemed more sexually alive. There was a vibrancy and spontaneity about the photos as well as a degree of intimacy and openness not captured in his previous work.

Initially, Gerald attributed this to his improved technical ability with the camera. Nevertheless, as he described the interactions in detail, it became apparent that he was frequently aware, in hindsight, of a sexual atmosphere between himself and his subjects during the process of photography in a way he had not been in the past. Indeed, he often found himself flirting subtly with these women in a way he would not have previously dreamt of doing.

It appeared that the increasingly erotic nature of his discussions and indeed sexual experiences with Sarah meant that Gerald was more comfortable with acknowledging and tuning in to sexuality as an aspect of other interpersonal experiences. This acknowledgement, however, was not initially at a reflective level. During the photographic sessions, Gerald was unaware of any sexual atmosphere. Nevertheless, its presence as an aspect of his interpersonal relationship was captured in his photographs and announced its presence through the bodies of his female subjects in terms of sustained eye contact, smiling and posturing which was evident for all to see.

Through exploring his experience, it became apparent that the element of sexuality, which he was capturing, was not intrinsic to his female subjects but a manifestation of his relatedness to the person he was photographing. In other words the sexual chemistry was clearly something which both of them were importing into the encounter but which ultimately existed between them. Gerald's experience seemed, to me, to exemplify Merleau-Ponty's claim that the conjuring up of a sexual mood is an interpersonal phenomenon born out of our relatedness to each other.

Of equal importance from a therapeutic point of view is a consideration of what the introduction of this rather magnificent volume of photographs into the therapeutic arena meant in terms of my own relationship with Gerald.

Looking back on the encounter, it seems quite possible that what took place between us during the session as he showed me the pictures was not altogether dissimilar from what took place between himself and his female subjects during the photographic sessions. My hunch is that if Gerald had had a camera with him during the session and had been taking pictures of me as I looked at the pictures and discussed them with him, then he would have captured precisely the sort of vibrancy and energy which encapsulated his female subjects.

I was completely 'seduced' by the pictures and felt in awe of Gerald for being capable of such astonishing photographic work. I could clearly tune in to the erotic and sensual element of the pictures: the sustained eye contact, which Gerald was capturing, the smiles and laughter, and seductive posturing – all this was apparent. What I was unaware of at the time, however, was my own increased eye contact with Gerald; the manner in which the energy between the two of us had become more intense, and indeed eroticized through the introduction of the photographic album.

So preoccupied was I with helping Gerald to identify and describe the relational nature of sexuality which he was capturing in his subjects that I was oblivious to the increasingly sexualized mood between the two of us. This, I should stress, is something which I believe existed purely within the ontological realm as an aspect of our interpersonal relationship and was not something which can be reduced to ontic representations, such as a desire to have sex with my client or, indeed, to even any sort of consideration of my client in a sexualized way. I am referring instead, to a particular sexual mood and atmosphere, which the two of us shared and which emerged primarily out of the analysis of the photos.

Sartre's description of how we attempt to capture another's consciousness through sexuality and objectify them as flesh in their own mind seems pertinent here, not only with regard to Gerald's photographing his female subjects but also in terms of his bringing the photos for me to view. Both instances also exemplify Merleau-Ponty's claim that:

> There is interfusion between sexuality and existence, which means that existence permeates sexuality and vice versa, so that it is impossible to determine in a given decision or action, the proportion of sexual to other motivations, impossible to label a decision or act 'sexual' or 'non-sexual'. (Merleau-Ponty, 1962: 169)

For Gerald, engaging more fully with sexuality was characterized by an increase in vitality and potency, which transcended the act of sex, permeating his very existence. What has been most rewarding, however, has been his increasing awareness of his own sexual needs and those of his partner Sarah where sex has become an aspect of the sexuality that is experienced and articulated between them.

Critical considerations

We would suggest that this existential description of the body and sexuality offers a fundamental and radical shift in our perception of ourselves in the world that may be difficult for our clients to enter into with us, and us with them. Will, as Sartre suggests, an existential understanding of sexuality provide us with an understanding of how all our relationships are articulated? And, is it possible to use these ambiguous images of the body and sexuality to develop a radical theory of alterity and encounter that has new relevance for psychotherapy? Certainly the interrelational image of sexuality and how it is articulated between persons may provide an interesting alternative to specialist forms of sex-therapy traditionally used for helping clients presenting with sexual problems. However, the major significance for psychotherapy is undoubtedly the awareness that our work with clients always contains an embodied narrative that links us to the other through our bodies, and runs alongside or independently of any spoken narrative. The key to understanding this embodied narrative is an ontology of sexuality.

Further reading

Abram, D. *The Spell of the Sensuous.*
Mann, D. *Psychotherapy: An Erotic Relationship.*
Steinbeck, J. *The Wayward Bus.*

CHAPTER 7

Eating Problems

KIRK J. SCHNEIDER AND ZOË FITZGERALD-POOL

> Emptiness. The attempt to overcome it by intoxication...intoxication by
> cruelty...intoxication by blind worship. The attempt to submerge oneself...
> in any kind of working routine, any silly little fanaticism; a confusion of all
> means, illness as a result of a general lack of moderation.
>
> Nietzsche, *Will to Power*: 32

Introduction

Amid the patchwork quilt of therapies aimed at 'problem' eating, existential therapy has occupied a virtually imperceptible role. Today, there are a great many 'treatments' targeted at specific beliefs, symptoms, and behaviours of problem eating, but few approaches that venture into the core or depths of those difficulties. Among the standard therapies for eating problems are cognitive-behavioural therapy (CBT), psychopharmacology, nutritional therapy, and exercise (Kaplan, 2002); however, there is an increasing recognition that although 'good short-term results can be reliably produced' from these kinds of strategies, long-term successes can be 'elusive' at best (Wilson and Brownell, 2002: 528) and modest or even 'poor' at the worst end of the spectrum (Stunkard, 1981: 466; Wadden and Stunkard, 1986).

In this chapter, we propose that long-term success with eating problems (which include compulsive eating, anorexia, and bulimia) will not occur until those syndromes are encountered at their personal and interpersonal roots, animated by the immediacy of the moment. While psychoanalytic therapies approach these facilitative benchmarks, they fail, in our view, to push through to their fuller implications, both within the client and between client and therapist. Existential therapy, on the other hand, directly emphasizes depth of exploration as well as immediacy of encounter in the process of that exploration. Existential therapy can be both depth oriented and yet flexible in its moment-to-moment attunement to client concerns (Schneider, 1995, 2003).

An existential perspective
Ellen West

The earliest documented existential case study with an eating disorder was Ellen West, a patient of Binswanger (1946). Her case was written many years after her death. Undoubtedly misdiagnosed as a schizophrenic, the phenomena of her symptoms, bingeing, purging, excessive exercise, and a dread of becoming fat, reflect those of bulimia nervosa. Ellen underwent two unsuccessful periods of psychoanalysis and ultimately committed suicide. The interested reader is referred to 'The Case of Ellen West' in *Existence* (May et al., 1994).

In existential thinking, symptoms express problems with being-in-the-world and have individual significance (ontic response to ontological givens): a disturbance of a total, embodied situation of the individual, where mind and body are simultaneously affected. Embodiment is conceptualized as a personal, yet intersubjective, experience: individuals exist through and in a body, with other people who also exist through and in a body. In existential psychotherapy, assigning the label of 'disorder' or 'illness' to eating behaviours limits how others relate to and understand the individual: labels may obscure as much as they clarify: a person may behave in a similar way to others for very different reasons (Lemma-Wright, 1994).

The body in the world – Umwelt

A client experiencing problems with eating is likely to be living predominantly within the physical dimension at the expense of other dimensions. However, he/she may be disassociated from his/her body, may feel it as a nuisance, needing control, filling, emptying, exercising, purging through vomiting, or with laxatives, or both, or a fortress defending against 'invasion' by others.

The body may express the otherwise inexpressible. Whether through overeating, starving, a combination of the two, or bingeing, vomiting and/or purging with laxatives, the individual is struggling to communicate and relate in the world as best he/she can. From an existential perspective, the psychological and the physical are inseparable – psychological motives and bodily actions overlap and are interrelated, imperceptibly: 'an organic process issues into human behaviour, an instinctive act changes direction and becomes a sentiment, or conversely a human act becomes torpid and is continued absent-mindedly in the form of a reflex' (Merleau-Ponty, 1962: 88).

Substitution for Mitwelt

Eating/not eating may provide escape into comfort, may symbolize longed-for love or supreme control, a reliable 'friend' or ultimate superiority. Existentially, eating/not eating quells a desperate sense of isolation and uncertainty, or is a way of appeasing others' needs and wishes. It is a response to being with others in the world, but paradoxically, the individual becomes trapped in a lonely, destructive cycle (Lemma-Wright, 1994).

Eigenwelt

Without a sense of centredness and with a poor sense of 'I' the individual literally loses his/herself, consuming and being consumed by the food rituals. Alternatively eating/not eating/purging may be experienced as a form of punishment to absolve personal guilt for failure, to expunge the experience of shame. This cycle becomes increasingly self-destructive, as shame over the eating/not eating/purging behaviour leads to more punishment for more failure, an ever-diminishing, inflexible sense of self, and a closing of possibilities.

Uberwelt

The ideal dimension/worldview includes both traditional beliefs and one's ultimate concern – values and ideals are shown through actions, not by what is professed. One can worship, or find an ultimate source of meaning in just about anything, god, career, health, spouse, sex, politics, or alcohol, drugs, and food – eating/not eating (Lemma-Wright, 1994). Pursued blindly, worship provides a 'high', a means of avoiding responsibility for one's own choices and actions, an escape from the reality of being finite and mortal. Eating/not eating may become an easy vehicle for transcendence and temporary liberation from the body, an avoidance of the limitations inherent in life.

Existential worship: a recap and elaboration

'Something is holy to everyone', wrote existential theologian and philosopher Paul Tillich, 'even to those who deny that they have experienced the holy' (Tillich, 1967: 130). Tillich goes on to explain that religion, broadly conceived, refers not just to one's traditional belief (e.g. Judaism) but to one's 'ultimate concern' (ibid., 131) – any of a wide variety of devotions. Other existentially oriented philosophers and psychologists, such as Becker (1973), James (1963), and Rank (1941), have echoed similar positions.

The existential view of worship, therefore, can be understood in *terms* of a wide network of involvements. One can worship a traditional god, one's career, health, spouse, political ideology, or favourite form of recreation. Indeed, as previously mentioned, one can worship or find an ultimate source *of* meaning in just about anything, including alcohol, drugs, and food. The essential question is: 'How adaptive is one's form of worship, how helpful and meaningful is it to one's life?' (Becker, 1973; Schneider, 1999). Or, according to Yalom (1980), who draws partly on May (1958, 1981), 'How well does one's religion manage our deepest anxieties' – the fact that we are limited; the capacity to be free; the risk of isolation; and the burden of responsibility in the face *of* uncertainty? (see also Schneider, 1990, 2003).

Underlying dimensions of food worship

To elaborate, the compulsive ingestion of food exemplifies a maladaptive form of worship – whether the focus of the worship is eating food, rejecting food, or a combination of the two. To some people, food (*or its rejection*) is viewed as central to their psychological as well as physical survival. Clients often describe themselves as 'obsessed' with food and terribly 'deprived' without it. They often have the sense that food 'calls out to them' and 'seduces' them. Existentially, many of these clients use food *to* emphatically allay their anxieties.

Food is seen as a euphoric 'high', similar to the sensation of a drug, orgasm, or religious 'conversion'. Some clients perceive food as an ecstatic, sensual pleasure. It totally changes their lives, they report, at least temporarily. Existentially, such clients often use food to avoid taking responsibility for problems.

Food is perceived as a form of comfort or solace during stressful periods. Many clients equate food with the love or comfort they lacked as children. They describe food in terms of being a balm or a 'friend' that does not 'talk back'. Existentially, these clients often use food to quell a desperate sense of *isolation* and *uncertainty* about their lives.

Food is viewed as a quick, simple vehicle for transcendence. Some clients report feeling 'liberated' from their bodies when they binge. Others feel an inflated sense of control. Existentially, such dieters often use food to avoid the inherent *limitations* in life.

Food is seen as a way of appeasing others' wishes or needs. Several clients feel that they must eat excessively to please others. They either grew up conforming to others' dietary standards or feel they must submit to such standards in their current lives. Existentially, these dieters frequently use food to flee their fear of *isolation*.

Food is experienced as a form of punishment to absolve guilt. Some clients use food as a way to 'get back' at themselves for having engaged in inappropriate behaviour. Often this behaviour leads to the very overeating they eventually use to punish themselves. As a result, they become locked in a cycle of bingeing, guilt and more bingeing. Existentially, these clients often use food to avoid struggling with *responsibility* and *the freedom to choose* (Schneider, 1990).

The wish-world

Symptoms of eating problems also resemble those of addiction. Heidegger (1927) identified addiction as a response to one's thrownness into the world. Addictive behaviour is not inside the person, but takes place *between* individual and world, at the point of interaction. 'The person cuts himself off from possibilities for authentic relatedness, and lives instead in a "wish world"' (Heidegger, 1962: 240) – an illusion of escape from insecurity. Nothing will ever be enough to satisfy this insatiable need. There is a blind hankering after more and more, but this closes off real possibilities, so the individual loses himself/herself further into the addiction. Entering into this closed, unrealistic world, the person seeks omnipotence. When high, the fantasy feels real, anything is possible, and everything is perfect. This evokes Binswanger's description of 'extravagance' (*verstiegenheit*) (Binswanger, 1963: 343) where the individual experiences an 'unquenchable longing' and cannot let things be as they are. Through a hankering for more and more security, friendship and love are denied, and the individual becomes fixated, trapped in an impossible position from which he/she can neither ascend further nor descend. (See Schneider, 1999, on the compulsion to constrict or expand.)

Therapeutic process

The existential therapist explores with the client his/her worldview and relationship with the four dimensions of existence. It will be important to explore the client's inescapable experience of being embodied in a physical world with others (Umwelt); and clarification of the client's assumptions and beliefs about body size and weight, their meaning and significance for them, and how this is connected to their social and intimate relationships with others (Mitwelt).

In addition, an exploration of existential concerns can clarify his/her understanding of himself/herself as an individual (Eigenwelt), and pave the way for changing eating/not eating/purging behaviour. For example, clients can ask, 'How has eating/not eating/purging become a god, a high, a comfort, a form of transcendence, an appeasement, a punisher in my life?' 'How does this behaviour relate to values, goals, aspirations once held or dreamed of?' (Uberwelt). Clients can also explore the feelings, sensations, and images associated with their compulsivity and arrive at an alternative understanding of them, for example, indignance where there once was self-devaluation.

Case illustration (by Zoë Fitzgerald-Pool)

Belle, 24, self-referred because she was trapped in a cycle of bingeing, vomiting/purging after she had lost her job, felt isolated and could not stop crying. She feared that everyone was looking at her and could see she was bulimic. Of average weight, Belle described how her weight rose to 15 stone after her mother died when she was nine.

Belle commented: 'I was teased at school. I told my stepmother how much I hated getting fat, and she fed me huge puddings which I ate. Then I went on a diet and it was war. Me against her. I stopped eating and I think she was jealous of my self-control.'

At sixteen, Belle was raped by her father's younger brother. She said: 'It was my own fault I suppose, I'd started wearing short skirts and flirting – I suppose I was a bit brazen, so triumphant being thin at last. I led him on I suppose – but I didn't want that.'

Belle had never told anyone about the rape, thinking no one would believe her. Belle's weight plummeted to under seven stone, so Belle was admitted to hospital on a behaviour-modification programme to increase her weight. When she failed to gain weight initially, stricter operant conditioning procedures were enforced, and privileges including visitors or TV were forbidden until she gained weight. Belle felt she was being imprisoned and punished. She conformed to the regime, gained the required weight and was released.

Hospital was a nightmare – a feeding prison – that felt like rape.

Belle vowed never to return to hospital, and maintained 'normal' weight. She left home, got a job, and became secretly bulimic.

Belle felt that the hospital therapist had been uninterested in *her* experience of her relationship with the world – either with herself or others. 'Sometimes I feel as if I am dying, or dead, or should be. Sometimes I feel as if I have a dead child inside me, that's why I had to throw up, to get rid of it somehow. People think I'm weird and melodramatic. To the doctors, and my parents I'm just disordered, crazy, manipulative and angry. All they wanted to do was to straighten me out. "Borderline" one doctor said. I am angry, and I felt manipulated. If I am manipulative – I had good teachers. Trouble is, I want something else now, and I don't know how to stop.'

Belle's fear and rage were so intense she needed to tranquillize/anaesthetize herself with eating/not eating, bingeing and purging in order to cope. Fearing engulfment and control by others, she also feared being rejected and abandoned. She feared annihilation. Interaction with others evoked a struggle for survival rather than a potentially enriching experience. She was trapped and isolated in a prison without walls. Her small, rigid sense of self (Eigenwelt) revolved around her struggle with her bulimic symptoms. Sacked from her job, in her Mitwelt she kept people at a distance. She had little comprehension of significance or meaning in her life, other than a struggle to escape her self-made prison. Binswanger stated that once the 'extravagant' individual has climbed so far out of reach of the world, he/she needs help. In a moment of clarity, Belle sought this help.

The therapist adopted a naïve approach towards Belle, wondering how she had managed to organize her life in such a way that had enabled her to carry on, despite her doctor's opinion that her behaviour was so disordered or maladaptive.

Belle was asked what benefit she gained from the behaviour she wanted to change. What might she lose if she were to give up her bingeing/purging? Belle was surprised – she had never considered what she gained, she was used to therapists focusing on strategies for change.

Instead, the work focused on clarifying and re-experiencing how her eating rituals had served her well in the past, how it embodied her 'wish-world'. Her move from overeating to not eating to eating/purging were attempts firstly to comfort herself, then to gain control, to take responsibility for herself, then to hide from the world whilst doing both. Belle identified the vomiting and purging as being the most powerful ritual of all for her, and the most painful. 'I was trying to throw up the anger, the sorrow, the fear, throw up this dead child, the lump inside my belly that wouldn't go away. I threw up till there was nothing there, but I'm the dead child so it was still there.' Belle made the connection with her unresolved anger and sorrow over her mother's death, and after which she had felt very alone. She needed a painkiller, food became the anaesthetic. She herself became the impregnable fortress.

Rather than pathologize her behaviour, the therapist sought to clarify with her its significance: how the various stages of her relationship with eating/not eating/purging reflected her values at the time as well as in the immediacy of the therapeutic moment. Eating after her mother's death gave her comfort, but was bitter-sweet as she began to feel controlled and afraid of her stepmother. So Belle stopped eating in an attempt to establish autonomy and freedom. Feeling in control, her refusal to eat became a weapon against her stepmother as well as a comfort. Being suddenly slim left her vulnerable. First she was raped by her uncle. Then she was forcibly hospitalized, something she experienced as rape by her family and doctors.

Swinging between bingeing and then vomiting/purging was Belle's way of struggling with polarities and contradictions. Her extravagant ritual embodied her increasingly desperate need to sustain herself and cleanse herself of distressing emotions and memories. Eating/vomiting/purging had become an isolated living-death, an expression of distress that she was unable to articulate in other ways. Disturbed by her anger she punished herself further by isolating from others. She was angry with her mother for dying and guilty for feeling angry. She was hungry for needs to be met, but unable to digest anything from outside, unable to hold self-nourishment in, and rejecting of what was within her. Belle was cut off from others and cut off from herself.

Gradually, and through many experiential re-enactments, Belle absorbed the meaning that her eating behaviours held for her, and the values that she was trying to pursue through them. She realized that she was not mad, a victim ravaged by a personality disorder, or with an illness beyond her control. She understood her efforts as resourceful and creative in her quest for identity, autonomy and survival, although they were ultimately self-destructive. Insight facilitated choice leading to small but significant changes in first her purging and then vomiting behaviour. As Belle began to widen her perspectives on her experience, and became open to possibilities that previously she had felt threatened by, the therapeutic focus within sessions included more programmatic, cognitive, and adjunctive support. She then took responsibility for what she ate. Her thinking and behaviour changed. Belle recognized that dominated by the physical realm, she had closed herself off from the other dimensions. Released from the cage of shame and the stricture of perfection, within which her symptoms had trapped her, Belle became more resolutely open to new possibilities, and took steps to re-connect with friends and ultimately family.

Summary

In this case, a focus that validated the client's experience of being-in-the-world, in all its dimensions, facilitated her possibilities for choice, and increased her ability to make sense of contradictions in an uncertain world. Through this process, the client was able to engage with her present existence in a more creative and satisfying way.

Critical considerations

Several approaches use interpretation to facilitate the client's insight into their problems. However, interpretation suggests an assumption that the practitioner 'knows' the client better than he/she knows himself/herself. This may confirm their fear that they are incompetent and out of control, leading them to comply with the therapist's expectations. Directive approaches such as rational emotive behaviour therapy (REBT) or CBT, and even psychoanalytic therapy assume that there is a barometer of normality, and that disordered behaviour indicates dysfunctional and irrational beliefs. As above, these may confirm the client's experience of inadequacy, and they may change behaviour without insight. On the other hand, insight or the motivation to change alone, may not be enough. As illustrated above, an experiential-existential approach *along with* programmatic support may be needed to effect substantive transformation.

Clearly, a client with eating/vomiting/purging behaviour such as described above, was endangering his/her health, possibly his/her life. Severe physical and psychological consequences can result. The client may be unaware of these side effects of his/her behaviour, thus it may be crucial for the therapist to provide (a) information, (b) assistance in changing destructive behaviour patterns. An existential approach in conjunction with cognitive-behavioural strategies can thus be more beneficial than a purely phenomenological approach (Schneider, 1990, 2003).

Conclusion

In considering effectiveness, further research would need to clarify the assumptions, intentions, and expectations of the approach, and should include an exploration of the client's expectations of therapy at the outset, his/her experience of therapy and therapist at the time, the client's subsequent evaluation of the therapeutic experience, and feedback on the long-term outcome. Furthermore, such research should draw upon chiefly qualitative (e.g. phenomenological) rather than strictly quantitative (e.g. experimental) modes of investigation; it is only through such means that clients' whole (intra- and interpersonal) worlds can be assessed, and a fuller understanding can be achieved.

Further reading

Binswanger, L. 'The Existential Analysis School of Thought' and 'The Case of Ellen West'. In R. May et al. (eds) *Existence*.

Kaplan, A. 'Eating Disorder Services'. In C. Fairburn and K. Brownell (eds) *Handbook of Eating Disorders: Theory, Treatment and Research*.

Lemma-Wright, A. *Starving to Live: The Paradox of Anorexia*.

Schneider, K. 'The Worship of Food: An Existential Perspective', *Psychotherapy*.

Schneider, K. 'Guidelines for an Existential-Integrative Approach'. In K. Schneider and R. May (eds) *The Psychology of Existence: An Integrative, Clinical Perspective*.

Schneider, K. *The Paradoxical Self: Toward an Understanding of Our Contradictory Nature.*

Schneider, K. 'Existential-Humanistic Psychotherapies'. In A. Gurman and S. Messer (eds) *Essential Psychotherapies.*

Tillich, P. *The Courage to Be.*

Wilson, G. and Brownell, K. 'Behavioural Treatment and Obesity'. In C. Fairburn and K. Brownell (eds) *Handbook of Eating Disorders: Theory, Treatment and Research.*

CHAPTER 8

An Existential Perspective on Addiction

SIMON DU PLOCK AND JONATHAN FISHER

> Oh, who can tell us the entire history of narcotics? – It is nearly the history of 'culture', our so called higher culture!
>
> Nietzsche, *The Gay Science*: 87

> Those of us who have contributed to the literature about models of drug dependence, have indulged in irrelevancies. We have pushed an abstract scientific course rather than responding to existential needs. We have pro- duced a psycho-bio-social model of drug dependence that excludes the essence of human existence – options, freedom to choose and the centrality of human values.
>
> Drew, *Drug and Alcohol Review*: 210

Introduction

The co-constituted nature of the world and the meanings which we give to our experience of being-in-the-world is a fundamental tenet of the existential-phenomenological approach, whether encountered in its philosophical or therapeutic forms. The with-world, or *Mitwelt*, that we find ourselves thrown into at birth is already suffused with meaning, exists *a priori*, is socially constructed, and lies – as it were – awaiting our adoption. While this co-constituted meaning is a truism of existentialism and phenomenology, its significance is, perhaps, greater with regard to the subject of addiction than it is for any other considered in this text, with the exception of the psychoses. It is not possible to fully comprehend what an existential perspective on addiction might be if we do not understand how the concept arose historically. Equally important, we need to have some sense of how the concept has been employed over time if we are to understand its function not only at the macro-level of society, but also at the micro-level of individuals and the ways in which they recruit the concept in their attempts to create meaning. It might be suggested that the word 'addiction' no more constitutes a 'real' and 'fixed' entity in the world than does the word 'schizophrenia'. Like schizophrenia, addiction refers to a social construct rather than a specific condition located within an individual.

Mood-altering substances, both naturally occurring and more recently synthetic, have played an integral role in the medicinal, spiritual, ceremonial and social life of humanity for at least 13,000 years (Rudgley, 1999). Drug use (generally but not invariably restricted to a priest class) was considered by most early forms of religion to be a way of communicating with the deity(s). Alcohol use is reported as early as 3500 BC in Egypt and has been widely available in most societies since this time.

In the early fourteenth century in London there were 1334 taverns and 354 breweries. Writing in 1773, Dr Johnson made reference to the good old days 'When all the decent people in Lichfield got drunk every night, and were not thought the worse of' (quoted in Ackroyd, 2000). Indeed, excessive alcohol consumption in the West throughout the seventeenth and eighteenth centuries provided the context for the strong reaction to alcohol in the nineteenth.

Gossop (1994) has commented on the way in which drugs now considered harmful and requiring strict regulation have, historically, been considered innocuous or even beneficial. Opium, for example,

> was completely unrestricted in England until 1868, and even after 1868 restrictions were minimal for many years. At this time the drug was sold and used on a considerable scale. It was used in many different preparations, but most commonly in the form of opium pills, or as a tincture of opium in alcohol (laudanum). Vendors often had their own special preparations to be used to quieten children. (Gossop, 1994: 359)

Cocaine too was for many years held in high esteem. It is well known that Freud used cocaine, viewed it as an instrument for therapy and prescribed it widely to family and friends as well as to his patients. So enamoured was he of its strengthening effects that when, in January 1886, Jean-Martin Charcot, the famous Parisian neurologist, invited the young Freud to his house the

> hopeful young doctor was so unsure of himself that he took a dose of cocaine before leaving his rooms. He was relieved when the evening ended. He wrote to his fiancée saying that he had managed, with the help of the cocaine, to get by without making a fool of himself. (Tallis, 1998: 11)

Although the term 'addiction' has been used since the twelfth century, it was the English scientist Dr Benjamin Rush (1745–1813) who first published papers on the concept, and the progressive nature of addiction as a disease, identifying it as a 'disease of the will'. In 1838, the French psychiatrist Esquirol classified alcoholism as a 'monomania' whose principal characteristic was 'an irresistible tendency towards fermented beverages' (In Heather and Robertson, 1989).

It was not until 1934 that addiction was classified as a mental illness by the American Psychiatric Association (APA). Most recently in The diagnostic and statistical manual of mental disorders (DSM IV), substance dependence is indicated as a 'substantial degree of involvement with a psychoactive substance that seriously impairs social functioning' (American Psychiatric Association, 1994).

In 1935, a meeting between William Wilson and Dr Robert Smith in Akron, Ohio, led to the formation of alcoholics anonymous (AA), which constituted a spiritual, non-professional self-help fellowship of alcoholics. AA grew rapidly and the National Council on Alcoholism adopted its philosophy. The self-help principles of AA gradually became incorporated into professional, non-psychiatric treatment and became known as the disease concept of alcoholism. Specialized addiction treatment programmes represent the majority of options currently available to addicts today and twelve-step fellowships, as conceptualized by the founders of AA, now include Narcotics Anonymous, Overeaters Anonymous and Sex and Love Addicts Anonymous, to name but a few.

Cognitive-behavioural therapy has also emerged as a major treatment of choice. The focus of a cognitive-behavioural approach is on surface behaviour in which addiction is seen as social learning and is viewed to be on a continuum, rather than in terms of presence or absence of a disease.

The concept of addiction has in recent years been used by so many people to denote so many different things that it has been in danger of becoming a debased currency. As Jean-Paul Sartre complained of the term 'existentialism' in the 1960s, it has been employed so widely as to have become almost meaning-less. The time is surely due for the concepts of addict and addiction to be reappraised. We live in a post-modernist world and as such we know, at least intellectually, that words do not stand for fixed truths which can be identified 'out there' in the world. Nevertheless, the meaning of addiction seems to be more difficult to pin down than most.

An existential perspective

Is there any reason to suppose that existential psychotherapists are in a position to offer anything new to the debate? Actually, there is, for the existential tradition of philosophy, and its phenomenological reduction, reminds us of the importance of stepping aside from ready-made assumptions and second-hand meanings. This existential mode of enquiry leads us to take as our focus the experience of the person identified as an addict, as distinct from adopting the view of the 'expert' clinician or practitioner.

There is relatively little in the existential-phenomenological literature which specifically addresses working with addiction. This is not surprising given that this approach does not tend to promote specific treatment modalities for fixed client groups. Existential therapists are, typically, concerned to engage with process and with blocks to progress and strive to avoid seeing clients in terms of treatment labels. A notable exception is provided by Fingarette's existential critique of the concept of alcoholism in his book *Heavy Drinking*, published in 1988. Fingarette makes a convincing argument against alcoholism as a disease, and instead looks at the 'alcohol problem' as interrelated with other life problems. This is an inspiring contribution to the literature, but it does not offer a specific way of working existentially with people who have been labelled, or who have labelled themselves, as alcoholics. More recently Wurm has written about his work with clients who use alcohol. He suggests that an existential approach is at least as valid as 'solution focused' therapies. He argues that reminding clients that they are making choices enables them to review how their choices fit with their values. Telling them that they are 'addicted' takes away any sense that they might be able to make a difference (Wurm, 1997).

At the same time, clarification of meaning is central to the existential tradition, and this leads us to ask what we mean when our clients, or we, use the term 'addiction'. Baker (2000) has recently made a convincing argument that the term 'addiction' can be applied to many activities which do not involve the ingestion of a drug. She cites Shaffer's contention that 'anything can be addictive which powerfully and quickly and predictably changes how you feel' (Shaffer, 1994 in Baker, 2000: 10). We might argue then that the 'addict' is one who self-medicates in a compulsive fashion. The addiction can be to a substance or an experience – shopping, gambling or eating (or abstaining from eating) could equally fulfil this definition.

If we think of our clients in private practice, many present either directly or indirectly with problems related to substance abuse. Others may present with issues related to obsessive behaviour such as excessive exercising or using pornography obsessively or sitting at their home computers every moment of their out-of-work time, cruising chat rooms and virtual-reality websites. If we also include those clients who complain that they are caught up in emotional situations in which they experience themselves as determined and unfree, then we are talking about pretty much all of our clients.

Are all these behaviours related to addiction? The degree to which they fit the classical notion of addiction varies, but Walters' definition of addictions as 'the persistent and repetitive enactment of a behavioural pattern' is helpful in this regard. He contends that this pattern is characterized by four ingredients (Walters, 1999: 10):

1. Progression (or increase in severity)
2. Preoccupation with the activity
3. Perceived loss of control
4. Persistence, despite negative long-term consequences.

Perhaps the most facilitative way we can explore issues of addiction with clients is via the concept which Spinelli (1997) and Strasser (1997) have termed the 'self-construct'. The notion of self-construct is important because it directs our attention to the way in which each of us assembles, over time, a set of beliefs, values and aspirations about who we believe ourselves to be. An integral component of this is, of course, that we also make judgements with regard to what we cannot permit ourselves to be. This construction of a self in the face of nothingness, the attempt to create an essence, is not problematic *per se*; rather, it is an inevitable part of human being. As Sartre (1943) famously expressed it, man is a 'useless passion' – since he thought we never could construct a self. In attempting to make ourselves fixed and substantial though, we inevitably deny something of our freedom and human nature. Much of our work as existential therapists focuses on the particular ways clients' unique self-constructs serve both to open up and limit their way-of-being-in-the-world. We engage in this process of clarification with the intention not of 'moving the client on' in some way, but rather in order to enable both client and therapist to 'see what is there'. When the client can truly see the way they have constructed their way-of-being-in-the-world, they may elect to make changes to it. This is not, though, to underestimate how difficult this is likely to be.

It might be objected that the therapist is duty-bound to direct the client towards accepting that their present behaviour is in some way injurious or dysfunctional and that particularly when a client presents seeking to free themselves from an addiction, we must 'do' something to bring this about. We would argue, though, that when the client is in a position to appreciate their role in creating their self-construct they are also in a position to reflect on any changes they may wish to make. The 'lifeboat' approach to therapy may pull the client out of deep water, but does not enable them to reflect on how they are navigating their way through life in order to avoid future perils.

Such an attempt on the part of the therapist to 'be with' rather than 'do to' the client entails a qualitatively different encounter with the client's being, compared with that which is generally the case in working with addiction from the perspective of other orientations, whether cognitive-behavioural or twelve-step. The existential therapist must accept the obvious but discomforting fact that they are a part of the client's relational world. As Spinelli expresses it:

> The therapist's willingness to engage in this way with his or her client provides the latter with the experience of an 'other' (i.e. the therapist) who both represents all others in the client's world and also challenges the client's assumptions about others. But, just as importantly, the same willingness on the part of the therapist offers the client a 'model' with which to 'be with and be for' his or her own way of being-in-the-world. (Spinelli, 1997: 90)

Case illustration

A common-sense approach might urge that a therapist consulted by a client who states that they wish to break out of some 'addictive' pattern should help them to achieve this goal, but a moment's thought – once we put physiological 'cravings' in perspective – will indicate that the client is caught in a tension between, on the one hand, a genuine desire to change their habits and, on the other hand, an equally strong wish not to change, or fear of the consequences should they change. The conflict between these two attitudes keeps them where they are. Clients do not necessarily have to ingest a substance; the 'withdrawal' experienced by a person who attempts to change a sedimented way of being may be as powerful as that experienced by an individual who ceases to use a drug. Self-medication via a substance or an experience, if undertaken in a compulsive fashion, will affect the chemical balance of the brain. While the adrenaline rush of the compulsive gambler, chat-room user or shopper might seem quite distinct from the 'high' experienced by an intravenous drug user, it can be argued to be a difference of degree rather than type. John Booth Davies provides a remarkably clear demystification of the notion of craving and withdrawal symptoms in his work *The Myth of Addiction: An Application of the Physiological Theory of Attribution to Illicit Drug Use*:

> The use of the word 'craving' is an interesting exercise in attribution, and its primary purpose is to convey how we are intended to perceive the addiction process. It refers to the fact that sometimes people feel a strong desire to use, or to use more of, their preferred drug, but it gives the impression of an autonomous force whose power cannot be resisted; hence its attraction. In fact whether people resist the experience depends on whether they have good reasons, or no good reasons, for doing so. People in the dentist's chair have a craving to get up and leave; but by and large they stay put. (Davies, 1997: 50–51)

Is this conflict unconscious? One of the current writers, Simon du Plock, has worked with a number of clients who have argued that they are ruled by their unconscious, but the very detail and passion with which they have put this forward belies a hidden conflict and, rather, suggests their need for self-deception. The alternative reading that, as Sartre argued, the conflict exists at the level of unreflected consciousness is a convincing one. As one set of beliefs becomes increasingly sedimented, the other set of beliefs must be disowned or dissociated. A reaction which is commonly met with is of the following type: 'It wasn't me; it was the addict inside me.' The more we fix and limit our possibilities in order to get by in the world, the more inexplicable our deviations will be to others and ourselves.

A very brief case vignette may serve to indicate how an existential approach might be used when working with a client presenting with issues relating to addiction. We should bear in mind Shaffer's contention that addiction is not limited to substances we commonly refer to as drugs. As Baker says, 'addiction can be to a substance or an experience; shopping, gambling or eating (or abstaining from eating) could equally fulfil this definition' (Baker, 2000: 10), if the individual has learnt to manipulate these behaviours to such an extent as to induce an adrenaline high leading to the release of endorphins that provide security in the face of anxiety which the person comes to crave compulsively.

Simon has worked with a young man – who will be referred to as Paul – who entered therapy with the presenting problem of compulsive shopping. Paul's behaviour as he recounted it included the four key characteristics of addiction identified by Walter (1999) – progression, preoccupation, perceived loss of control and persistence – in his definition of addiction. An appreciation, on the part of the therapist, of the socially-constructed nature of the concept of addiction frees them to focus closely on the specific meaning and function of the behaviour for the individual client (and, in the usual course of events, for the therapist too) so that they can move towards making an informed decision about retaining the behaviour or changing it.

Paul described himself as a 'shopaholic', saying, somewhat shamefacedly, that he thought this was generally a 'woman's addiction' but that he felt it summed up his situation well. He described how, at times of stress, he would go on 'shopping binges', spending far more than he could afford. Like most clients, he had a fair degree of insight into his motivation for this behaviour. Now in his early thirties, he recounted how he began to develop a ritual of gift buying for his family when he had moved from home to attend university. This gift buying became frantic when Christmas loomed.

'I was buying Christmas presents...going into gift shops, toy shops and card shops and by buying these presents I was somehow vouchsafing the future, I was somehow ensuring that my family and I would survive the term, see the end of the tunnel. I was using money that was meant for books etc....because somehow presents meant survival...if I bought someone a present they would be there at Christmas because they would have to receive it. Illogical and irrational as that might seem. And the presents were amassed...I put them away in my room at university and having them there was somehow comforting, a solace'.

He was, then, able to make sense of what might at first seem not just irrational, but meaningless or even 'mad' behaviour, but this gift-buying strategy had not worked in the past, and was not working at the point when he began therapy. During the first few months of therapy it emerged that this distressing behaviour was symptomatic of a more fundamental problem – Paul's anxiety about his ability to grow up and go out into the world to forge his own identity. He painted a picture of an idyllic childhood, which functioned to trap him in his early experience of being loved and nurtured. In contrast, the project of constructing his own life, which necessarily would involve developing relationships of a caring, intimate nature with others outside his immediate family circle, seemed irrelevant.

If he was unable to move away from his parents, and in particular from his mother, he would always remain a child. If he never grew up, he would never have to steer his own course through life, and he would never have to die. As Yalom expresses it:

> an individual may guard himself from the death anxiety inherent in individuation by maintaining a symbolic tie with mother. This defensive strategy may succeed temporarily but, as time passes, it will become a source of secondary anxiety; for example, the reluctance to separate from mother may interfere with attendance at school or the development of social skills; and these tendencies are likely to beget social anxiety and self-contempt which, in turn, may give birth to new defences which temper dysphoria but retard growth and accordingly generate additional layers of anxiety and defence. (Yalom, 1980: 111)

Spinelli describes this idea of death anxiety as an anxiety not so much about death *per se*, as about 'the fragility of human existence'. This death anxiety, which he suggests might more properly be called 'temporal life anxiety',

> seeks to point us to our experience of the fundamental uncertainty of being, such that every step we take, every act we initiate, expresses, at its heart, our inevitable movement towards non-being through unknown and unpredictable life-circumstances.

How each of us deals with death anxiety is likely to be as varied and unique as our experience of being alive. We might, for instance, seek out ways to avoid risk and uncertainty as much as possible and, thereby, cocoon ourselves into a lifestyle bounded by regime and habit, as bereft of novelty and surprise as humanly possible. Equally, we might throw ourselves into a life which seems to require doubt and risk, whose very uncertainty revels in its defiance of security and predictability. (Spinelli, 1997: 10)

It seemed to the therapist, listening to Paul's story, that he had chosen the strategy of closing down his life, of refusing effectively to live his life at all, save in those aspects of it where he was able to create the illusion that he was still a child. The message was a simple one: if I refuse to become an adult, I will maintain myself as a child, and I will never die. Moreover, if my life is arrested, so too are the lives of the family members who are closest to me. Of all the clients the therapist had worked with, Paul's dilemma was the clearest example of the problems which attend on the denial of death. As Yalom has written, '...a life dedicated to the concealment of reality, to the denial of death, restricts experience and will ultimately cave in upon itself' (Yalom, 1980: 210). It was Paul's growing realization that he did not have the power to make his parents, and particularly his mother, safe from the encroachment of time that finally drove him into therapy.

It was tempting to conclude – as Paul concluded – 'that he was a victim of his past'. He stated in the course of therapy that 'the only thing worse than an unhappy childhood was one that was too happy, since everything that follows must be inferior'.

The therapist was curious about this insistence on the past and fear of the future. To accept Paul's evaluation of the situation was to join him in drowning in the tragic aspects of life – its absurdity and ultimate meaninglessness. While finitude is an existential given, our response to it is, necessarily, a choice. Paul's decision to refuse to see anything but the absurdity of life let him off the hook of making his own meaning in life. Moreover, there was something about the way Paul had learned to attune himself to the world, which, far from reflecting a secure and happy childhood, spoke more of a demand for perfection and isolation, and perhaps also for a passive position in which goodness is provided by others. In the light of this it might be suggested that his own attempt to buy things for others might have been an attempt at 'giving something back', the beginning of a generativity that might create a better future.

As therapy continued and Paul took the opportunity to explore and reappraise his childhood and relationship with his family in a safe, if sometimes challenging, environment, he was able to make more active choices about how he wanted to live his life. As he did so, his need to self-medicate via compulsive gift buying reduced. It is important to note that this presenting problem was not replaced by another addiction. We might suggest then that this is because the therapy addressed not only the symptom, but also the anxiety about being-in-the-world, which it expressed.

Critical considerations

This form of challenging engagement, if it is really to be an authentic relationship, demands much, perhaps as much, from the therapist as from the client. This reciprocal encounter with difference must lead the therapist to question their own way of being and their own sedimented beliefs about the world. It is crucial that the therapist monitor their response to this challenge and is open to exploration of the way they attempt to limit or dissociate this challenge. We can make a more radical statement yet: we can say that therapists need, if they are truly to enter the lived world of the client, to accept values and beliefs that they may find wholly alien. Because this is so, and may particularly be so when we meet with behaviour which seems purely negative and destructive, as is often the case when working with addiction, the therapeutic enterprise presents a valuable opportunity for clarification for both parties. The therapist who relinquishes the certainty and distance afforded by an 'expert' role and attempts instead to enter the client's world via the acceptance of such beliefs and values opens themselves to the clarification of their own self-construct in a process which is remarkably similar to that which the client is engaged in.

Our attempts to enter the client's lived world are never, of course, entirely successful, in the sense that they are never complete. It is not possible to experience the experience of the other; that we can never fully know the other is another basic tenet of existentialism and phenomenology – we are thrown into the world alone, we are thrown out of existence alone and we are responsible for our own being in the intervening period. We can attempt, though, however imperfectly, to suspend our judgements and wishes to change the client's way of being in order to hear them and provide more focused challenge. For the challenge to have any meaning to the client, beyond a demand or entreaty or instruction, we would argue it must emerge out of an understanding of the client's unique relational field.

We would suggest that this form of demanding encounter is particularly indicated in the case of clients who present with addiction-related issues, for the simple reason that it provides the possibility for the client to clarify the underlying purpose and meaning of what so often appears to be, or can be 'explained away' as being, either, in the case of substance abuse, a disease accompanied by psychological and physiological 'cravings' or, in the case of obsessional behaviour patterns, repeated 'impulsive' activities that appear uncontrollable.

Such an encounter offers the client the possibility to clarify the meaning of their behaviour – behaviour that they may be all too ready to dismiss as the outcome of a physiological condition over which they have no control. We find ourselves resonating with Spinelli when he states that clients are far more likely to clarify these meanings if the fear that their exposure will trigger demands – however subtle – on the part of the therapist for the client to relinquish the behaviour is removed (Spinelli, 1997: 140). It is as well to remember that any unilateral attempt to alter a client's behaviour is anti-therapeutic since the so-called 'dysfunctional' behaviour is both meaningful and purposeful: it serves to defend against anxiety and cannot, therefore, be discarded until that which is defended against has been addressed.

The existential approach provides a strong challenge to the therapist. It also provides a critique of the status of 'addiction' as a specialized category of client work requiring special techniques, and it raises questions about the characteristics of counsellors working in this field. In the UK and North America it has long been the case that a large proportion of therapists is drawn from the group of 'addicts in recovery'. We might ask whether this recruitment pattern has helped to keep the disease model of addiction at the centre of therapeutic work, despite the relative absence of support for it from academic psychology research. We might also wonder whether addiction itself can become addictive – it may be the case that work as an addiction counsellor provides some individuals with the structure and meaning which was formerly provided by the status of 'addict'. That this might be so for practitioners is not a particularly novel notion – the concept of the 'wounded healer' has been prominent in the therapeutic literature for many years – but it does lead us to ask how a shift in the way we view addiction counselling might impact upon the self-constructs of the therapists themselves.

While we have not provided specific skills and techniques for working with clients presenting with issues relating to addiction, we hope we have been able to indicate some of the ingredients which can contribute to an existential/ phenomenological attitude when working with such problems of living. If we wish to enter the lived world of the 'addict', we need to adopt, preferably embody, an attitude of curiosity and care, just as we attempt to do so with other clients with other presenting problems.

We have suggested that it might be helpful to reconsider what we mean by 'addiction' and whether it applies to the relatively small sub-group of clients, or whether behaviours which are sometimes given the label 'addiction' are not very widespread throughout the population. We feel the concept of self-construct is helpful when considering this possibility.

There is a pressing need for existential-phenomenological research on the nature of addiction and ways of working with people presenting with issues related to addiction to provide a counterbalance to the majority of research carried out to date in which outcomes (and particularly abstinence) play such an important role. Solution-focused therapy provides the context for addiction and the emphasis remains on pathologizing addiction or correcting maladaptive patterns of behaviour. This imbalance may be partly addressed by the publication of detailed client studies which present 'addiction' in the context of the client's struggle to make meaning in their lives.

Structured, abstinence-based interventions should not be forgotten, however, as some clients may be seeking a solution-focused approach and therefore, from an ethical standpoint, should be referred on to an appropriate practitioner.

Phenomenological research has the virtue of requiring the researcher to include themselves in the research project and to view their sample as co-researchers rather than as subjects of objective scrutiny. This form of research reminds us that when we work with addiction we are working with just one more problem of living – albeit at times an intransigent and frightening one. There is no 'them' and 'us', healthy and sick – we all have the propensity to be addicts and few of us will have really lived who have not had the experience of whatever we mean by 'addiction'.

Further reading

Fingarette, H. *Heavy Drinking*.

Flores, P. *Group Psychotherapy with Addictive Populations*.

Heather, N. and Robertson, I. *Problem Drinking*.

Hester, R. and Miller, W. *Handbook of Alcoholism Treatment Approaches*.

May, R., Angel, E. and Ellenberger, H. (eds) 'The Case of Ellen West'. In *Existence: A New Dimension of Psychiatry and Psychology*.

Shaffer, H. J. 'Denial, Ambivalence and Countertransferential Hate'. In J. Levin and R. Weiss (eds) *The Dynamics and Treatment of Alcoholism*.

CHAPTER 9

Death

MICK COOPER AND MARTIN ADAMS

> What does it mean to be a self-conscious animal? The idea is ludicrous, if it is not monstrous. It means to know that one is food for worms. This is the terror: to have emerged from nothing, to have a name, consciousness of self, deep inner feelings, an excruciating yearning for life and self-expression – and with all this yet to die.
>
> Becker, *The Denial of Death*: 87

Introduction

Socrates defined philosophy as 'the pursuit of death', and many other classical thinkers put death to the centre of their philosophical outlook (Gray, 1967). With the emergence of a modernist worldview, however – with its emphasis on scientific analysis, progress through reason, and humankind's ability to control and dominate nature – the question of death became increasingly marginalized within both the philosophical and popular psyche. To a great extent, however, this changed with the emergence of existential thinking in the mid-nineteenth and the twentieth centuries, which once more put the issue of death to the centre of the philosophical agenda. Here, death was not only *a* key philosophical issue, but *the* key philosophical issue that needed to be addressed if people were to live more meaningful and authentic lives. Heidegger (1962), in particular, is credited with having carried out the most detailed study of death and its existential meaning (Macquarrie, 1972): a study that draws on the work of Jaspers (1932), as well as the ideas of the nineteenth century 'father of existentialism', Søren Kierkegaard.

An existential perspective

Heidegger's analysis of death is orientated around a number of key assertions. First, death is an inexorable given of the human condition: a 'boundary condition' or 'limit situation' (Jaspers, 1932) that we cannot escape or evade. Second, death is a 'congealing point of existence' (Jaspers, 1932: 195), in which all our projects and possibilities are drawn to a close, and in which our lives become totalized and finalized. Third, death 'is in every case mine' (Heidegger, 1962: 284): it is the most unsharable, isolated, separate and unrelated of life's possibilities (Gray, 1967), for no one can die for us and no one can save us from this end. Fourth, while we know we will die, we do not know when or how: we are constantly living, therefore, in the face of the possibility of a sudden or abrupt extinction. Fifth, as human beings, we are probably unique in that we know we will die. Sixth, death is not primarily an external event in the way that the death of an other is; but an inward, subjective awareness of being-towards-death. In other words, each of us is aware, from the very beginning of our lives, that we are hurtling towards an unavoidable abyss, and it is this awareness, rather than the event of death itself, that plays a central role in our lives. In this respect, it may be more appropriate to talk of an existential theory of mortality rather than of death (Polt, 1999). Finally, following on from this, we are dying every day: for in every moment we lose something of who we are, and we are no longer what we have been.

From a Heideggerian (1962) perspective, this awareness of life as a hurtling-towards-destruction evokes a great deal of anxiety. 'Proximally and for the most part', then, 'Dasein covers up its ownmost Being-towards-death, fleeing in the face of it' (Heidegger, 1962: 295). Heidegger argues that this fleeing primarily occurs through an immersion in the world of 'the One' (or 'the They'), where death is only spoken about in the third person – as 'one dies' or 'so-and-so died' – rather than *my* death and *my* personal extinction. Subsequent existential philosophers, psychologists and psychotherapists have outlined a number of further strategies by which we may attempt to fend off the anxiety of knowing that we are beings-towards-death, all of which have the purpose of evading and denying the unavoidable fact of dying:

- Assuming that we will have a long life, and that death is many years off (Tillich, 1967).
- Reassuring ourselves with a 'logical' attitude towards death (Jaspers, 1932): for instance, saying to ourselves that when we are dead, we will not know about it, so it does not matter.
- Imagining death as a peaceful and restful sleep, rather than as the complete absence of all being.
- Adopting a belief in spiritual immortality, reincarnation or an afterlife (Baumeister, 1991).
- Striving to achieve 'secular immortality', through producing something that will survive our deaths, such as children, a book or a work of art (Becker, 1973; Baumeister, 1991).
- Adopting, promoting or clinging on to the belief in our own specialness or heroic nature through such practices as workaholism, narcissism, vanity, risk-taking or over-controlling behaviour, in the hope that this will enable us to withstand the natural, universal law of death (Becker, 1973; Yalom, 1980).
- Adopting the belief that some 'ultimate rescuer' – God, a parent, a doctor or even a therapist – will save us from the jaws of infinite non-existence (Yalom, 1980).

- Withdrawing from close emotional or sexual contact with others, to minimize the fear of separation (Firestone, 1994).
- Dissociating from our embodied, sexual being: that part of us that is vulnerable to illness and death (Firestone, 1994).
- Adopting a frivolous, excessively cheerful attitude towards life (May, 1999); or a nonchalant, indifferent attitude (Jaspers, 1932).
- Adopting a depressed, phlegmatic and helpless attitude towards life (Becker, 1973; May, 1999).
- Committing suicide as a way of taking back control from the uncertainty of death (Farber, 2000).
- Immersing ourselves in obsessions, compulsions, pseudo-problems, causes, groups and/or addictions – particularly drugs and alcohol (Firestone, 1994) – to obtain some temporary relief from the anxiety of facing death.

From a Heideggerian standpoint, such defensive strategies may bring a modicum of relief; but, it is argued, they ultimately do more harm than good. Rigid and inflexible defensive strategies require constant shoring-up in the face of reality, with the result that the individual's existential anxieties take on an increasingly neurotic form (Tillich, 2000).

Furthermore, existential philosophers, psychologists and therapists have argued that the acknowledgement of one's mortality can be fundamentally life-enhancing. They have proposed, then, that we should courageously embrace the fact that we are beings-towards-death: resolutely anticipating our radical non-existence (Jaspers, 1932; Heidegger, 1962). The inference here is not that we should brood over our deaths or feel sorry for ourselves, but that we should live every hour in the knowledge of our impending – as well as ongoing – demise. Such a stance, it is argued, can help us in a number of ways.

First, it encourages us to make the most of every moment. Through acknowledging that our lives are finite, we are forced to acknowledge that we cannot postpone living: that our procrastinations, excuses and attention to trivialities eat into the very limited time that we have. Hence, we are motivated to take charge of our lives (Koestenbaum, 1971), and to focus on those things that really matter to us.

Second, and closely related to this, acknowledging the possibility of our non-being throws our present being into sharper relief (Cooper, 1999). It is as if by darkening the background to our lives, the foreground of our present being is brought much more vividly to light (Farber, 2000). Rather than taking existence for granted, then, we are awakened to the wonder of Being (Macquarrie, 1972) (and it is this corollary of acknowledging our being-towards-death that may have led Heidegger to emphasize it so strongly in *Being and Time*). Furthermore, by acknowledging our anxiety in the face of radical non-being, we are alerted to the fact that existence really matters to us: that our basic relationship to the world is one of *care* (Heidegger, 1962). Again, then, we are motivated to grasp hold of our lives, and to make the most of the time that we do have.

Third, through acknowledging our most individual and non-relational possibility – our being-towards-death – we are also brought face to face with our *'ownmost* potentiality-for-Being' (Heidegger, 1962: 294, italics added). That is, when we face the fact that our journeys towards death are ours alone, we also come to realize our separateness and distinctiveness from the One, and with it our unique possibilities and potentialities.

Fourth, through anticipating the totalization and completion of our lives, we can come to grasp our lives as a finite whole (Macquarrie, 1972). It becomes possible, then, to assume a total plan for our lives (Koestenbaum, 1971); rather than considering our lives in a sporadic, fragmented and haphazard way.

From a Heideggerian (1962) perspective, then, an acknowledgement of our being-towards-death can bring sense, meaning and orientation to our lives. Not all existential philosophers, however, agree. For Sartre (1958) and Camus (1955), the arbitrariness of death and the fact that it can cut through our projects without rhyme or reason is final proof of the absurdity of human existence. Sartre forcefully rejects the Heideggerian idea that death is like a resolved chord at the end of a melody – something that gives shape and meaning to the whole – and argues that it threatens to remove all sense completely (though Sartre does posit 'nothingness' as the shadow side of life and the sine qua non of vitality). Furthermore, he suggests that it is simply not possible to anticipate death or to make it a project in life. Death, he argues, is always outside of life, something that can only be experienced from the standpoint of the other. If we attempt to anticipate our deaths, then, all we can anticipate is the victory of being-for-others over being-for-itself. 'The one who tries to grasp the meaning of his future death', writes Sartre, 'must discover himself as the future prey of others' (Sartre, 1958: 543).

Case illustration

Kay was referred to me (Martin Adams) as psychotherapist in a General Practice surgery because of her recent diagnosis of multiple sclerosis. Single and in her early thirties, she worked as a museum curator. I was told this prior to our first meeting and I knew it was especially important to work phenomenologically (Spinelli, 1989; Adams, 2001), so that I did not direct the work either towards, or away from death because of my own assumptions about it. I knew this would be challenging to me. I needed to let her tell her story. I was to see Kay for two and a half years.

In the first session she described the events factually, and when asked how she felt about it she said, 'Obviously it's a bit of a surprise, but I don't know really...I don't think about it much, it's just one of those things.' She said she felt 'a bit fed up' with work but that she 'didn't have much to say' about the illness. She was not sure what she needed to talk about but on balance decided to 'give it a try'.

I was struck by the contrast between the excessively cheerful way (May, 1999) she talked about the diagnosis and the possibility of her sudden and abrupt extinction (Heidegger, 1962). While some anxiety had been evoked – she would not have come to see me otherwise – she seemed to be adopting an indifferent, nonchalant attitude (Jaspers, 1932), although she did admit to being puzzled by this.

She was keen to know from the start what she should talk about. There was a reliance on me as an external authority, a 'they' for her direction (Heidegger, 1962), but I was reluctant to direct her, preferring to stay with her feelings about her everyday life. What preoccupied her most was her work, others' incompetence and the responsibility she took for work that was not hers (Becker, 1973; Yalom, 1980), and her part-time relationship. Always a private person, she was someone who did not take easily to talking about herself. She never had done. She had not told anyone else of her diagnosis. It was a pattern developed over her whole life to withdraw from close emotional contact (Firestone, 1994).

The impact of the multiple sclerosis was hardly referred to in the first year. She would end most sessions with a depressed, phlegmatic and helpless, 'Ah well...never mind...must get on...bye' (Becker, 1973; May, 1999). Through the way she was with me – she never missed a session and always came on time – I became aware of how she balanced her need to talk about what concerned her, which were mostly everyday things, and her need not to talk about her condition. It was as if these issues gave her some temporary relief from the anxiety of facing her death.

Occasionally, I referred to her condition and she wondered why I was interested in it as she did not think about it much. Nevertheless, I was still curious, but challenging her felt intrusive and on more than one occasion I wondered if my own discomfort with death was a contributor to its absence from the sessions. On balance, though, just talking about herself seemed challenging enough and I learnt to respect her defences. By my being able to follow her own thoughts and feelings, Kay increasingly grew to trust me, and simultaneously herself.

Over the first year, she became increasingly dissatisfied with her work and relationship and eventually decided to finish the relationship. She decided that no relationship was better than an unsatisfactory one. In confrontation with her existence she was motivated to take charge (Koestenbaum, 1971). She felt good about this – it was not her usual style – and, as it was the summer break, decided that she did not need to come any more.

In one way I was not surprised at her sudden departure – much of our conversation had been about her relationship – but she was determined, and thanked me for my time. At the same time I was less sure that things were quite as sorted out for her as she thought. She did not agree. I left it that she could get in touch in future if she wished. I felt she would.

When I returned from the break she had already made an appointment to see me. She had had a relapse that had hospitalized her. She was to have another before we finished work. Whereas she used to maintain she had nothing to say about her condition, this time it was different. She talked about how she knew she could not evade or deny it as she usually did with difficult things. She knew she would have to tell people, and through this realized her need for others and also how frightening it had always been to trust. 'It's not easy for me to come here and talk to you about it, you know', she said. I assured her I did know. In addition, she could no longer maintain that she was somehow 'special' because she had no need of others (Becker, 1973; Yalom, 1980). She talked about growing up proud of her self-sufficiency and recalled deciding in childhood that intimate relationships were not for her (Firestone, 1994), whereas now she had to rely on others, on me, on her home help and on her parents, who she had now told about her condition. For the first time, she also wished she had a long-term partner.

Many concerns were coming to the fore, her life pattern of denying feelings, her evasion of the reality of her condition that she would die before her parents, and her avoidance of close relationships. She acknowledged that our relationship had been one of these. She started to use a walking stick when necessary and got a disabled sticker for her car. These were not easy things to do but as she said, 'I just need them, that's all there is to it'. She talked about maybe having to give up her job, the one life project that she felt was in her power to achieve and which she had struggled so hard to get. She had immersed herself in her career because she had found relationships too difficult, and now she could lose her career.

She talked about her fear of another possibly fatal relapse. All these feelings came over her like waves and shocked her with their emotional force. She talked about leaving the therapy again because, 'Whenever I come here I feel worse...but I know it's not going to go away...' She had realized that although her choices to avoid things had previously brought some relief (Heidegger, 1962), her life had been reduced as a result, and valuable qualities such as independence and responsibility had become neurotic and self-destructive. She realized the way she had become was the result of decisions taken earlier in her life and that needed to be changed.

During this period of therapy, she was coming face to face with her condition and prospects which meant that she reconsider her present (Cooper, 1999). Gradually she began to take responsibility for her condition and her future. She became less afraid of her own and others' feelings and became more uncompromising in her stance towards others. When she needed something, she asked for it, and when she was unhappy about something, she said so. As she said, 'It's now I've got to live, not later'. Her existence was becoming her own, rather than attributing it to others, the 'they' (Heidegger, 1962). She became less frustrated by work, although the conditions had not changed. She talked to her parents about their will, what would happen to her learning-disabled brother when they died, and about her own will, and what it would mean if she died first. She had realized how much they mattered to each other.

My work with Kay raised many important issues for me as a therapist. Not least the conflict between encouraging her to talk about death and not wanting to direct her, especially as she was so keen to have direction from me. I decided to periodically remind her that I had not forgotten about the reason for her referral, even if she was not ready to talk about death. Events, the givens, her relapses provided the prompting she needed to explore the issue. These, combined with my ability to hear what she was working out for herself in confrontation with her condition, enabled the work to reach a conclusion in which she was more engaged with her own life choices and the people who mattered to her (Heidegger, 1962). The possibility of non-being threw her present way of being into sharper relief (Cooper, 1999).

In confronting her own death, she had discovered that her life was hers to live rather than to avoid, and that, through her life possibilities being reduced, she was more determined than she had ever been to make the most of the time she had left.

Critical considerations

When faced with the problem of translating existential philosophical insights regarding death into clinical practice, a number of points should be borne in mind.

First, it should not be underestimated how difficult it may be for clients to talk about death, and the extent to which clients may be unwilling to engage with this subject. It is important, therefore, to acknowledge and respect clients' defences, as well as being willing to challenge them.

Second, since it may be so difficult for clients to talk about death, the subject may give rise to extremely strong and disorientating feelings. These may appear in therapy as content – for instance, clients may talk about suicide; or as process – for instance, clients may want to end the therapeutic work. Defensive strategies already familiar to a client – for instance, addictions or compulsive behaviour – may also be brought more strongly to the fore.

Third, a client's reluctance to talk about death may be due to their therapist's own reluctance to engage with it. In other words, the therapist's own thanatophobia may obstruct the therapeutic process. Therapists have a responsibility, therefore, to be familiar with their own death-related issues. At the same time, therapists need to be wary of imposing their own death-related anxieties, experiences and values on the client: their philosophy must be regarded as a map and not mistaken as the territory.

Fourth, life and death are equal aspects of existence and dwelling excessively on death in therapy can sometimes be unproductive, and be used as a way of evading the responsibilities and the possibilities of the brightness of life.

Fifth, death and loss often go together: for loss is of another person, and death is about oneself. Of the two, loss tends to be easier to talk about and therefore may be addressed in preference to – and to the exclusion of – the more difficult issue of death.

From a critical standpoint, it would also seem important that existential philosophers, psychologists and therapists provide a more adequate level of evidence in support of their hypotheses regarding death. Neimeyer and Van Brunt (1997: 52), for instance, report that 'direct evidence for the ubiquitous denial of death anxiety is remarkably sparse'. There is also little direct evidence that individuals who acknowledge their beingness-towards-death, in all its existential anxiety, experience lower levels of neurotic anxiety. Indeed, studies tend to suggest that the more individuals experience death anxiety, the *more* they also tend to experience neurotic anxiety, low self-esteem and a sense of purposelessness in life (see Neimeyer and Van Brunt, 1997). Such findings may emerge because of the multidimensionality of death-anxiety measures, but it would seem important for existential researchers to find a means of directly assessing – either quantitatively or qualitatively – an individual's willingness to face up to their own demise, as Wong et al.'s (1994) measures of 'neutral acceptance of death' and 'death avoidance' have begun to do. It would then be possible to test whether individuals scoring highly on such measures – or who score increasingly highly as a result of existential therapy – also:

- experience life more intensely;
- have a greater sense of their own individuality and unique potential;
- experience a lower level of neurotic anxiety; and
- have a more complete, and less fragmented, sense of their own identity.

Further reading

Becker, E. *The Denial of Death.*
Edwards, P. *Heidegger on Death: A Critical Evaluation.*
Farber, L. H. 'O Death, Where is Thy Sting-a-ling-ling?'. In *The Ways of the Will.*
Heidegger, M. *Being and Time.*
Jaspers, K. 'Boundary Situations'. In *Philosophy* (Vol. 2).
Yalom, I. D. *Existential Psychotherapy.*

PART III
SOCIAL DIMENSION

CHAPTER 10

Introduction to the Social Dimension

EMMY VAN DEURZEN AND CLAIRE ARNOLD-BAKER

If the physical world is that of our bodily actions in relation to objects, the social world is that of our emotional relations to other people. We are always thrown together with other people in a with-world (Mitwelt) and many of the activities we undertake at a physical level also lead to interaction with others. Others define us long before we define ourselves. We start off by observing others and comparing what we are to what they are and to what they seem to expect of us. Through being what we imagine others want us to be or think we are, we get a sense of who we are. Heidegger's notion of Being-with-others is just as central as his notion of Being-in-the-world. We are with others on so many different levels, in a public way and in a private way. As Sartre pointed out, we can either be with others in a competitive way or in a cooperative way. When we consider different aspects of our clients' social world we will note, amongst other things, the following:

1. The way we find ourselves in a world with others varies from moment-to-moment and from person to person. How do different clients deal with the existence of others in their lives? Who are these other people in their lives and how do clients deal with them? Are there many others in their lives or only a few? Are they dominant or submissive in relation to these others? Are they competitive or cooperative, active or passive, engaged or withdrawn? Of course, the enquiry will often start with clients' relationship to their parents or carers. More often than not these figures are seen as an extension of oneself until we feel wronged by them and come to realize they are different.

2. We need to face up to the strangeness of love: What does it mean to be loved and protected by parents and other family members? Can outsiders love us? There usually is a marked difference between those who have experienced life in an extended family and those who have not. There may be interesting investigations to be done in relation to the way in which people have experienced other family members, friends or neighbours. Were these others also part of the

network of care and could they be trusted? Or were they unreliable or even dangerous and abusive?

3. The whole issue of people's relationship to their siblings and the dangers of rivalry, competition or abuse needs to be faced. There is much to be understood about the way in which people have come to expect to be oppressed or to be able to oppress others without adults noticing. It is even more interesting to trace the way in which these dynamics can be continued into adult life and become entrenched. Of course, being an only child has other implications for the way in which we relate to others.

4. It can also be educational to explore how a person has discovered the differences between the generations. We all find out that our relationships vary according to the group of others we relate to. Ancestors and grandparents are different to parents, are different to siblings, different to peers, different to outsiders, other family members, teachers and then strangers or famous people: Where do they all fit in? How varied or restricted have our relationships been? How have we handled each of these different types of relating?

5. Furthermore, all of these layers of relationships are regulated by our emotions. Discovering how feelings tell us about our relationships to other people and how each emotion betrays our particular connection to the others in our world can open up our own understanding of our distance or closeness to these others. It is almost always useful for clients to learn about desire, anger, fear, jealousy, envy, admiration and learn to be more cognizant of and at ease with their feelings.

6. This will also allow us to become more active in regulating the secret rules of distance and proximity. We can now decide with more deliberation who we can allow to be close, fairly close or even intimate or who we should keep at bay or stay away from altogether. Practising strategies to recognize who is who and how to achieve the correct distance with each can be helpful.

7. Of course much of the work on the social dimension is about learning to be capable of holding one's own in relation to others. The very first task is not to be dominated or bullied by others, but keep them in their place and take up our own rightful place amongst all the others in the world. The second task is to not take up too much space and learn to be respectful of the needs of others. This is about not being domineering and overbearing with others but learning to be empathic and understanding and compassionate as well.

8. Eventually all this leads to finding a comfortable place of one's own in relation to others. We as well as our clients learn about different relationships: we distinguish between friendship and commitment, liking and loving, fighting and challenging. This also means to learn about what it means to make and break promises and why and how it is important to *be loyal or* still be free to change one's mind.

9. Underlying the obvious social structures of our world are deeper social structures that also help to determine our experience. Understanding the

culture or society we are born into or live in is important. This can extend into understanding the social laws, prejudices, roles and assumptions that govern us. Sometimes it will be useful to ask ourselves how these things differ or compare in other cultures. The more personal question of how we are in relation to people from our own culture and from other cultures may also arise.

10. Throughout all of these social issues is the important fact of communication. How did our clients learn to communicate with others? What is their use of language, actions and emotions in relation to the world of others?

The paradoxical poles of this dimension are isolation and inclusion, wanting to feel part of a group and at the same time wanting to be alone. An understanding of this dimension will make it easier to discover the different ways we can be in different groups, our family group, work group, groups of friends and so on. We may even learn which people make us feel good about ourselves and why and how and which people upset us. We may then make considered decisions about which contacts to develop and which to avoid. Of course, therapists may be able to show that such decisions often need to be challenged, as doing what is easiest is not always the best strategy.

The chapters in this part of the book focus on various aspects of our social relationships. The first topic to be considered is language (Chapter 11), which is an important aspect of human existence and its implication is that human beings are incomplete without others (Macquarrie, 1972). Language enables us to communicate and be intimate with others; without language we would be separate and distinct entities unable to come together and share our lives and ourselves with others. This chapter takes a philosophical view of language and looks at the importance of language in the therapeutic relationship.

Chapter 12 deals with a similar but quite distinct issue of dialogue and communication. Of course, language plays a part in this, but there are other ways and levels at which we communicate with others. Often this is an area of particular difficulty for clients – the ability to communicate their desires, wishes, ideas, fears and longings with other people. This chapter will elucidate the existential perspective and stress the importance of dialogue.

Equally important as our ability to listen to others and to communicate effectively with them is our ability to listen to ourselves, and it is our emotions which guide us through our social relationships. The chapter on emotions (Chapter 13) shows how emotions can act like a compass and enable us to gain a bearing on how we feel about other people and the effect they have on us. This chapter will highlight how clients can become more aware of, and in tune with, their emotions through existential psychotherapy.

The chapter on relationships (Chapter 14) is central to this part of the book and focuses on the different ways in which we relate to others and indeed how clients and therapists relate to each other in the therapy room.

Of course, our adult relationships are coloured by our experience of growing up in a particular family environment. The chapter on families (Chapter 15) puts this aspect of our relationships into perspective, by taking an existential view of families and family life and their implications.

All of us are part of many groups; whether it is a family group, work group, community or cultural group. Groups are an essential part of human existence. The chapter on groups (Chapter 16) elucidates an existential way of thinking about and working with groups.

CHAPTER 11

Language

MICHAEL HARDING

> For, strictly speaking, it is language that speaks. Man speaks when, and only when, he responds to language by listening to its appeal.
>
> Heidegger, *Poetry, Language and Thought*: 216

Introduction

In nature nothing is true or false. As physical objects, the tree, the stone and the fox exist as unnamed 'things' that we encounter, but when we name them we draw them into our own concerns and possibilities, and argue endlessly as to the truth or falsity of what we perceive them, and ourselves, to be.

An existential perspective

This search for 'the truth of things' often drives us to philosophy or therapy. In the modern world it was Nietzsche (1968: 280) who first questioned our motives for this endeavour. Our search may sound noble, but might stem from baser needs. Knowledge can give us a spurious power; our certainties may have nothing to do with a quest for truth, but stem from a need to keep anxieties at bay by creating seeming 'certainties'. In short, 'truth' may be any convenient fiction that suits the needs of individuals and societies. Writing as a psychologist, Nietzsche pre-empts Freud by asking us what purpose our noble motives serve. Often 'truth' stands revealed as nothing more than a grand label stuck on shoddy merchandise.

Nietzsche's deconstruction of 'truth' pointed to a world where language lay revealed as plastic and unquantifiable. The gods were dead, and our world was all that we had. We could no longer hope that our words signified exterior powers and eternal virtues. From now on they could lead us only to other words and other reasons. Silent for centuries, the subject of language erupted into philosophy in the early years of the twentieth century, heralding the post-modern 'age of anxiety'. If language was no longer the simple vehicle of verbal exchange, what else might it show us? Was it a vastly complex mechanism in which human desires and wishes were entangled – even produced – or were other paths to its understanding also possible?

In a technological age the 'scientific' approach is seductive, but frequently flawed. Chomsky suggests that the following takes place when the infant is first exposed to the 'data' of language:

> The child approaches the data with the presumption that they are drawn from a language of certain antecedently well-defined type, his problem being to determine which of the (humanly) possible languages is that of the community in which he is placed. Language learning would be impossible unless this were the case. (Chomsky, 1968: 25)

As Malcolm (1995: 71f.) has observed, the pre-verbal infant has been granted prodigious abilities. It recognizes the structure of the language into which it has been born, selects the correct one and happily chortles its way into words. The infant is supposed to have at its disposal a 'universal theory of grammar' and uses this to make logical choices to determine which language it is expected to speak, prior to the acquisition of the one factor that makes logic possible: language. It may be more true to claim that language learning would be impossible if this *were* the case.

Heidegger rejects such approaches to our understanding of language. In *Being and Time* he defines language – discourse – '*as equiprimordial with attunement and understanding*' (Heidegger, 1996: 150f.). Language is fundamental and 'worldly'; the nature of our thrownness and our embodiment in the world is the essential quality of language (a point equally made by Wittgenstein). For Heidegger, 'the totality of significations of intelligibility is put into words. Words accrue to signification . . . Discourse . . . constitutes the disclosedness of being-in-the-world'. In our words we reveal the nature of our experience, which is inextricably bound up with our sense of all that surrounds us. In language something is always 'ahead of us' and world-disclosing: the questions we raise, even if we do not at first understand them, reveal our unconsidered sense of things that thinking can bring to light.

How different is this from Freud's general claim that our words reveal a hidden truth about ourselves? Freud gives language a biological root. It emerged from primitive, sexual origins (Freud, 1917: 167), and the images that our words might reveal can be codified according to an assumed primal register. We return to a specific system of 'natural' signs whose 'laws' can be de-coded by the psychoanalyst using such technical concepts as condensation, combination and so on: a mechanism is said to be at work. Heidegger is not concerned with 'human nature' but with human being, and instead considers the ebb and flow of culture. In different ages we are concerned with different questions, different ways of framing our sense of things. But culture does not progress in the linear patterns suggested by Hegel and Marx: change takes place, apparently randomly, when language is listened to, and a new truth emerges. In his later work Heidegger's focus on language becomes central and challenging. Consider the following statements:

- We do not speak: we are spoken (Heidegger, 1982: 57f.).
- What is spoken is never, and in no language, what is said (Heidegger, 1971: 11).
- We human beings remain committed to, and within, the being of language, and can never step out of it and look at it from somewhere else. Thus we always see the nature of language only to the extent to which language itself has us in view, has appropriated us to itself (Heidegger, 1982: 134).
- Everything depends on whether language gives or withholds the appropriate word (Heidegger, 1971: 59).

While we appear to be given a picture of the human being at the mercy of language, such confusions as we may have do not arise from quasi-technical 'processes', but emerge from our relationship with language itself. In *Being and Time* Heidegger describes *discourse* as the 'articulation of intelligibility' (Heidegger, 1996: 150). Discourse is the primordial manner in which we disclose the world. Our grasp of being-in-the-world is expressed as discourse, and the manner in which discourse is expressed *is* language. Later he declares that, ultimately, language is not a system of words that we use to express ourselves. *In its essence, language is neither expression nor an activity of man. Language speaks* (Heidegger, 1971: 197). Language is ultimately *worldly* (Heidegger, 1966: 150). In *What Is Called Thinking* Heidegger says:

> Language admits of two things: One, that be reduced to a mere system of signs, uniformly available to everybody...and two, that language at one great moment says one unique thing, for one time only, which remains inexhaustible because it is always originary...Customary speech vacillates between the two possible ways in which language speaks. It gets caught halfway. (Heidegger, 1982: 191)

If language is always caught in this way, can it ever describe the truth of things?

In his reinterpretation of Anaximander, Heidegger suggests that 'truth', *aletheia*, does not mean 'true' (as in not-false) but rather a 'revealing and a hiding'. Thought can reveal something to us, but it will simultaneously hide something – hence his challenging claim that 'truth is an un-truth' (Heidegger, 1971: 60). Here we can use the image of a light which draws our attention to one aspect of the world, but leaves the rest in darkness. In his critique of technology Heidegger again charges Western philosophy with its failure to address the nature of Being itself – the Being that is hinted at by the act of unconcealment: '...man does not have control over unconcealment itself, in which at any time the real shows itself or withdraws...The thinker only responded to what addressed itself to him...But unconcealment itself, within which ordering unfolds, is never a human handiwork' (Heidegger, 1977b: 18).

In other words, when something is revealed – in this case to a philosopher – the philosopher is captivated by the possibilities of ordering that are shown. A potential system is revealed, such as Plato's vision of hierarchical principles, but however coherent they seem there are always other possibilities. As Safranski has commented, '...every design of Being produces, materially and spiritually, a world interpreted and organized in a definite way' (Safranski, 1988: 219). Heidegger's point here is that the thinker will focus exclusively on what has been revealed, and not on the fact that the world is such that this *can happen*. The central issue – the fact of Being itself – has been ignored at the moment of its showing, obscured by a 'truth' that is always partial.

This dual revealing/concealing nature of being has its echo within us all. As it is ontological, so at the everyday, ontic level we reveal and conceal ourselves. There is no 'psychic mechanism' at work; such ways of thinking stem from our current entrapment within a technological worldview (Heidegger, 1977b). This possibility was foreseen by Parmenides, who outlined his fears that a need to systemize experience would lead to a fragmented sense of the world (Pictet, 2001). We are constantly tempted to look for causes, at the expense of experience, and thus risk living in a theoretical world which is disconnected from immediacy. For the psychotherapist, who is increasingly enmeshed in models of the person-as-object, Heidegger's thought has particular power. On the one hand, we can be described by innumerable psycho-biological theories, with their inherent contradictions; on the other, we are let loose in a post-modern world to find meaning where we can, but none with any authority. Where should we look for a real, embodied sense of ourselves, and how should we compare one view of the world with another?

When Galileo declared that the sun, and not the earth, was the centre of our solar system, this flew in the face of all current reason. How different is this from someone diagnosed as 'delusional' who claims that he is the rightful King of England, or that the CIA plans to steal her soul by bugging her television? Are these just two equal opinions about 'how things are'? In the first case Galileo can point to language itself. Spherical trigonometry is no less of a language than any other (Wittgenstein, 1922). But here proof is not self-referential: it lies open to the common gaze, and emerges from a common practice. In the second case the reasons invariably find their support in the exclusive interpretation of the experiencer. This is not to suggest that strange worldviews or behaviour should be dismissed. These, too, lock into the nature of a world where power is routinely misused, people are denied their free expression, where guilt and dirt are commonly viewed as similar by many religions, and where such images as being turned into stone abound – all common themes in the cannons of psychopathology. The manner in which we make sense of our world demands attention, but the act of 'making sense' does not occur in a vacuum, and our attempts at understanding should also include the manner in which we carry out this task. If I make a quasi-Cartesian claim that I, alone, have an exclusive, interior knowledge of truth and am the final arbiter of meaning, then *this* is my delusion, not the particular form of words that I use. Our intuitive grasp of life may often aid us, but it is the nature of the world itself, and our shared language, that confirms or denies the correctness of our insights. Sometimes, such insights show themselves in ways that may surprise us.

Eugene Gendlin draws on the work of Heidegger and Wittgenstein in his psychotherapeutic approach. For Gendlin, language is often 'ahead of us' in our bodily sensations. He draws our attention to the physical discomfort that often accompanies an inability to find the right word. When the word finally comes to us, the discomfort dissolves and this shift confirms the rightness of our choice. Gendlin (1988: 43f.) reminds us of Heidegger's concept of *Befindlichkeit*, often translated as 'mood', 'attunement' or 'state-of-mind', but perhaps more literally 'how-you-are-ness'. We *find* ourselves to be in such-and-such a state. But where does this finding take place? Often in the body. Here *Befindlichkeit* 'always already has its own understanding'. This is not to be understood in the terms of bio-dynamic therapies (Reich, Lowen, etc.), with their concepts of body memory and energy dynamics, but as a showing of how we are at a particular moment. Gendlin's claim is that 'the feeling knows how to speak and demands just the right words. The feeling, more exactly, is sufficient to bring the words to the person's speech'. These are words we must heed, for 'without going after what the mood discloses, we cannot be authentic. Authenticity is fundamentally grounded in Befindlichkeit, and requires bringing oneself before how one is disclosed in the mood' (Gendlin, 1988: 57). But, of course, inauthenticity may be similarly grounded. While Wittgenstein (1997: 182f.) observes that if the word 'if' has an 'if' feeling to it, then this feeling cannot be separated from the word, Gendlin charges the therapist to work with what is shown as our sensations reveal their linguistic equivalents.

Case illustrations

Debbie consulted me because she was faced with a particular problem involving the need for her to make a choice. She was convinced that only three roads were open to her, and each one was unacceptable. After some while spent following her down these paths I began to challenge her claim to know the certainty of what others involved would do, and thus what the future might bring. These tentative explorations were met with considerable hostility. One day, when the 'problem' was again before us, and Debbie said once more that I had failed to understand her, I replied that what I failed to understand was her certainty that this kind of problem had only three solutions. Debbie was furious, and rising from her chair she said, 'There are only three ways out. Can't you see that?' She held out her hand, with fingers raised, waving it in front of my face. She was holding up, not three, but *four* fingers. Following my gaze, Debbie looked at what her body had just shown us. She sat back in her chair and burst out laughing. We then began to discuss her problem, as if for the first time. Here, as both Heidegger and Gendlin suggest, her embodied understanding was 'ahead' of her.

Gerald was a patient in a psychiatric day hospital. He had been admitted following an unfortunate experience with hashish, in a state of confusion and paranoia. At an art therapy session he had painted a picture of some men. The therapist made the comment that they were a striking colour, a 'coral pink'. On hearing this Gerald stormed out of the room. I followed him, but it was not for some time until he told me the reasons for his anger. He complained that the therapist was accusing him of homosexual tendencies, and of being regressed. The reasons were this: the art therapist had used the word 'coral'. For Gerald this was heard as c-oral. In other words, *see oral.* The painting was of men. Hence *see men* (semen). He felt that the group had been told that he had a wish to suck a penis. Our relationship with the world discloses differing possibilities. These qualities are not owned exclusively by us, but are inherent in language. In different frames of mind we might see beyond the apparent, everyday seamlessness of speech: language holds many messages. Its essential 'otherness', its arbitrary, fragmented structure can break through, and our familiar world can fall apart. Creative writers, such as Joyce (1992), have made much of this. Sartre's hero in *Nausea* (1964a) panics when words dissolve and raw nature erupts in their place. In a not dissimilar state Gerald (who had experienced psychoanalysis) picked out elements of pathology in a casual statement, elements found not in the everyday meaning but more in the shape and sound of words, and the complexity of their roots. We do not need an 'unconscious mechanism' to rearrange that which might describe us anymore than artists such as Picasso need it to see that two toy cars, glued together, ape the head of a monkey. We draw on our sense of the world, and what might be shown and seen at differing moments.

Of course, the therapist is no less caught when language erupts. James informed me, for the tenth time that day, that he was Jesus Christ. His manner, as ever, was sonorous and patronizing. Caught off-guard, and in the midst of trying to clear up the day room, I responded by saying, 'How can that be? I thought the real Jesus Christ was locked up somewhere else.' James burst out laughing. His whole body relaxed, for a moment all his physical rigidity dissolved. He touched my arm and said, 'That's a good one. I like it.' Instead of his usual middle-distance gaze, his eyes held mine directly. Then he froze again, and took a step back. 'That's blasphemy. You will be damned.' Then he marched off in carefully measured paces. But we had met for a moment, both of us had been caught by the unexpected, and I never found him irritating again.

Critical considerations

Considering the enormous impact Heidegger's work on language has had on continental philosophy and critical theory in general, it is surprising that relatively little attention has been paid to it by existential psychotherapists. His influence is far stronger in much current psychoanalysis, albeit in a psycholo-gized form and, in the case of Lacan, allied to quasi-mathematical models and developmentally determined categories of symbolization. In *Being and Time* Heidegger warns against 'word mysticism' (Heidegger, 1996: 202), and yet has been accused of this by Adorno (2002) onwards. Is Heidegger's use of such words as 'language' and 'Being' an attempt to reintroduce some concept of God back into a post-Nietzsche world? (Pattison, 2000: 187f.). The existential approach claims to be open to such possibilities, but does it engage with them? Much is made of the human being as 'meaning creating', but the 'otherness' and mystery of language itself, and the implications of Heidegger's claim that 'the real shows itself or withdraws', are less addressed – as is the subject of the 'real' itself. Similarly, the fact that we are 'sexed-bodies' (Irigary, 1994) existing in a pre-described world too often slides by. Again, a reluctance to engage with sexuality (Spinelli, 1996) and biology (Cooper, 2001) can further extend a tendency towards a solipsism that Adorno criticized in existential thought.

While existential therapists cannot be accused of failing to address the ontological nature of guilt and anxiety, and thus the inevitability of their showing within the life of the individual, this discussion on our essential qualities remains partial. The 'essence' of the human being, which for Heidegger refers to 'the way in which something pursues its course, the way it remains through time as it is' (Heidegger, 1996: 3), is unlikely to emerge as a consequence of methodology (itself 'merely the run-off of a great hidden stream which moves all things' – Heidegger, 1982: 92). It is engagement with the moment of language itself, when something 'concerns us, carries us away, oppresses or encourages us' that language may have 'distantly and fleetingly touched us with its essential being' (Heidegger, 1971: 59).

Further reading

Heidegger, M. *The Way to Language.*

Levin, D. M. (ed.) *Language Beyond Postmodernism: Saying and Thinking in Gendlin's Philosophy.*

Pattison, G. *The Later Heidegger.*

Polt, R. *Heidegger: An Introduction.*

Wilson, B. *Wittgenstein's Philosophical Investigations: A Guide.*

CHAPTER 12

Dialogue and Communication

LUCIA MOJA-STRASSER

> existential psychotherapy ... is similar to the Socratic method.
> van Deurzen, *Existential Counselling and Psychotherapy in Practice*: 131

Introduction

Metaphorically, it could be said that, at the beginning being and nothingness entered into a dialogue and the outcome was the creation of the universe. These opposites, being and nothingness, are present in all living creatures and they are in an eternal dialogue with each other. Heraclitus describes this poetically: 'That which is in opposition is in concert and from things that differ comes the most beautiful harmony' (Heraclitus, 1962: 25).

'Dialogue' originates from the Greek word 'dialogos'. 'Dia' means through; 'logo' as a verb means to gather, to collect, as a noun it means word or saying. The simplest translation is: 'through the word' or 'through speaking'. Sometimes 'dialogue' is also translated as to 'converse'. It can be argued that any form of speech or writing is a form of dialogue. Every dialogue has an element of conversation in it. Not every conversation, however, is a dialogue. Both conversation and dialogue presuppose language.

Socrates emphasized the importance of dialogue as a means for teaching the practice of philosophy. Dialogue is a powerful method for learning and teaching philosophy. It involves several elements: a speaker, a listener (or respondent), the relationship between the two and the topic of the dialogue. In this chapter it will become clear that dialogue is at the heart of working with clients.

For Socrates dialogue was a way of life, as it was for all free Athenians. Socratic dialogues need to be approached in the spirit of their original intention, that is, as conversation. Intriguingly, in spite of this, there is a tendency to transform Socrates' philosophy into a technique. Socrates wanted to make people think for themselves and whilst practising philosophy gain in self-knowledge. These philosophical conversations were spontaneous with no particular outcome in view.

Socrates had no doctrine or method for his dialogues. He was challenging, questioning, disapproving and attempted to free his interlocutors from 'pseudo-knowledge'. Through his questioning Socrates was not pursuing a specific answer, but rather like all philosophers, he was in a search of truth and believed that an individual can only attain truth through dialogue with another individual. What Socrates did was to pave the way to 'wisdom' as it is discovered in relationship.

His sceptical spirit subjected all claims of knowledge to a rigorous scrutiny. This involved a process of questioning people's position. The answers to his questions would expose the contradictions within people's claims and prompt them to reconsider their position. His way of asking questions usually led the other to an admission that they knew nothing on the subject. This is often referred to as 'radical negativity' – the knowledge of not knowing. He was not trying to argue his interlocutors down, but rather he wished to examine the weight of their opinion. In this way he was testing them not in order to expose the weakness of what was said but to bring out its real strength: 'in this process what is said is continually transformed into the utmost possibilities of its rightness and truth' (Gadamer, 2000: 367).

To be able to converse as Socrates did is an art – the art of thinking. Likewise, when we read his dialogues it is difficult, if not impossible, not to become part of the lively philosophical enquiry. We are forced to think for ourselves.

There is a difference between the way Socrates asked questions and interrogation. The latter is seeking a specific answer, usually content-related, and is about acquiring more information in order to complete the picture. When Socrates asked a question, he himself did not have the answer. However, Socrates' interlocutors often believed that he really knew the answer to the question he posed but was deliberately withholding it. Thinking that he was being treacherous, they named this withholding 'ironia'. The truth was that he did not have the answer.

This attitude has many echoes within the world of psychotherapy. One example is the parallel that can be drawn with Lacan, who was familiar with Socrates' dialogues. Lacan talks about patients coming to therapy believing the therapist has the knowledge and the remedy for their problems. He based his notion of the so-called 'transference' on this assumption: '. . . it is insofar as he is "supposed to know" – however incorrect this is, of course – that the analyst becomes the support of the transference' (Lacan, 1989: 72).

Socrates was intimately associated with irony. If we read his dialogues too literally, we miss the most important message, a message that could not be communicated directly. The ability to use humour about a very serious subject was one of the ways in which Socrates used irony. This often disoriented his interlocutors. He frequently said one thing and meant its opposite. In irony there is always a contradiction between what is said and what is meant. The literal meaning of the speech is the opposite of what it appears to mean. The conversation has statements that can be taken in many different ways and it is the hearer's responsibility to choose the meaning.

Socrates never committed the dialogues to paper. The knowledge we have of Socrates himself and of his way of philosophizing is indirect, mainly through Plato. We know him through the various influences he had on his contemporaries, some of whom were his disciples.

The lasting influence of his style of thinking was partly due to his personal qualities such as modesty and nobility of soul as well as the force of his intellect. He did not belong to any school of philosophy. He was profoundly interested in human beings irrespective of whether they were engaged in the arts or trade. He was able to learn from anyone with whom he engaged in conversation. In some ways he was a simple man who knew what he under-stood and what he did not understand. Above all, Socrates was aware of the breadth of his ignorance. Socrates lived his philosophy and to the end of his life remained faithful to his most cherished values: living for truth was as important to him as dying for it.

Let us now consider the relevance of dialogue for existential therapy.

An existential perspective

Van Deurzen (2002a) has pointed out the connection between existential psychotherapy and the Socratic method. This is not to be taken lightly. Although Socrates' humility and insight is an example for any psychotherapist, the link between existential therapy and Socratic dialogue cannot be learned and applied as a technique – rather it needs to be taken seriously and grappled with by each individual existential therapist. I hope this chapter will encourage the reader to consider the divergences as well as the similarities between Socratic dialogue and existential therapy.

Dialogue is an inductive approach to acquiring insight. The individual is being thrown back unto themselves and truth opens up to them. In the context of existential psychotherapy, dialogue is fundamental to the process of therapy. The communication is always intended to reach the other, and only this other who is listening. In the process of dialogue, qualities emerge that are specific to that particular relationship.

Frequently, the therapeutic relationship starts as a monologue (hopefully the client's!). Depending on the therapist's patience, quality of listening and way of being, the space and time offered to accommodate this monologue will form the basis upon which the dialogue emerges. I cannot will to have a dialogue, but I can firmly intend to be open to having one. Dialogue is something that will occur when both client and therapist have established trust as well as the desire to reveal themselves to each other. Dialogue becomes the medium through which their respective beings come to light. The therapist cannot hide behind his/her role – he or she needs to be truly themselves.

Existential therapy, which is a philosophical practice, is a relationship between two human beings. It is happening in the moment and is experienced directly. The directness is made possible by the immediacy of the relation between the client and the therapist. The attention is focussed on the possibilities of the phenomena presented; asking clients pertinent questions is an invitation for them to become mindful, to examine and reflect on what concerns them.

Being a philosophical practice, existential psychotherapy is a lifelong project on the part of the therapist. The therapist's active engagement with philosophy is ongoing. The nature of philosophy is dialogue. Dialogue with the philosophical text enhances our understanding of ourselves, affects our way of being and consequently the quality of listening we are giving to our clients.

Listening to the client is the existential way of being open to what is present. 'Being-open to what is present is the fundamental characteristic of being human' (Heidegger, 2001: 73). It is simple, immediate but 'one can continuously overlook it in favour of contrived psychological theories' (ibid., 74). When we truly listen, we are absorbed in the shared world with our clients and 'only then, communication is possible' (ibid., 161).

Can we listen to the client's story philosophically? We can listen to our clients' life stories as if reading a book – a book with which we are intimately concerned. We are concerned about what sense their life makes to them and how they construct its narrative. Speed-reading philosophy is a contradiction in terms. Equally, with our clients we need to give our attention and time, and give as long as it takes. This is a process that cannot be rushed.

In the therapeutic relationship we are in a side-by-side dialogue, which is based on interrelatedness and interconnectedness as well as on difference. I am attending to a human being, and by necessity this will involve tension. If I would have an agenda that aims to solve their problems, this would interfere with how I would listen and could prevent me from hearing and noticing things which are familiar and usually overlooked. Having an agenda could also make me look too far ahead and miss what is right there, in front of my eyes.

When I listen to my clients, I need to give them my full attention. In practical terms, through dialogue I listen to the client's intonation, the tempo of their discourse, in essence to their way of being. If I listen only to the words, I might miss the essential – that which cannot be said but is often implied.

The client's narratives point towards their way of being, show the sacred or the spiritual aspects of their being and demonstrate what is valued and meaningful in their lives. When listening to and hearing these stories, the client and the therapist together try to make sense of them. Bringing these values and meanings to an explicit and understandable level often needs interpretation. The hermeneutic type of interpretation does exactly that: it makes the implicit explicit.

My presence with my client includes being thoughtful, patient and willing to listen. All this contributes to gaining a deeper understanding of what the problems are and what can be learned from them. In order for this to happen, I as a therapist need to have some insight and clarity about my own place in the world.

Our particular relationship and the way in which we are with each other can touch us very deeply. The strange thing that cannot be explained is why this is happening, why we are moved, and more often than not it has nothing to do with what is said. When I listen and hear my client, most of the time, I am able to tune in to their experience and resonate with it – rather like the piano and the violin tuning into each other in order to be able to play together harmoniously.

'Being-with' develops during dialogue. The role of dialogue is to communicate meaning through the process of question and answer. The asking of questions implies that both client and therapist are interested in wanting to gain insight. Similar to the Socratic dialogue neither has the answer to the question beforehand. There is no particular method of asking questions. As a therapist, if I am unable to suspend my assumptions and opinions, this will prevent me from asking appropriate questions and from facilitating the emergence of truth: 'the art of questioning is not the art of resisting the pressure of opinion; it already presupposes this freedom' (Gadamer, 2000: 366).

In dialogue, my client and I belong-together and are held by something that is encompassing both of us. Our communication stimulates thought and has a creative element to it that has the power to transform. It affects us both. The truth that unfolds does not belong to either of us and transcends us both. Gadamer refers to this as the 'fusion of horizons' (ibid., 388): '... what emerges in its truth is the logos, which is neither mine nor yours and hence transcends the interlocutor's subjective opinions that even the person leading the conversation knows he does not know' (ibid., 368). Dialogue is not something that can be sustained over long periods but rather it occurs for brief moments bringing us insights and putting us in touch with the mystery of Being. This is very similar to Buber's (1970) notion of I and Thou.

With regard to therapy, a dialogue can happen only when both therapist and client are able to recognize each other, when they are willing and able to engage with one another, by opening themselves to each other and becoming absorbed into each other's being and what concerns them at the moment. This is a process that is not entirely dependent on what is being communicated but is more dependent on the quality of being. It involves an openness towards the other as well as towards oneself. 'Openness by necessity, involves the ability to think for oneself. To think means to see possibilities and to be open to other ways of thinking and being' (Moja-Strasser, 2001: 36). Being and letting be are fundamental to this process.

However, the therapist can enhance the possibility for dialogue to occur. The ability to stand back and suspend judgement not only of the client's values and assumptions but also of his or her own is the first step. This requires from the therapist self-awareness and a sense of wonder; abstaining from rejecting or accepting the other's opinion; letting go of the desire to lead the client in a particular direction; stopping, waiting and trusting that something will happen; listening and being open to the other; submitting oneself to what one hears, being touched by it and eventually responding to it. Without openness no true connection can be made. But the response is preceded by silence: '... in speaking we have men as teachers, but in keeping silence we have Gods, and we receive from them this lesson of silence at initiations into the Mysteries' (Plutarch, 1967: 417). Listening and speaking belong to language. Before verbally articulating our thoughts in speech, we formulate them first in silence. The ground of speech is silence. Silence and language are intrinsically linked and are important for both speaker and listener.

Indeed, keeping silent is not the same as restraining from speaking. It is not a doing but a being quality. It involves giving space and time for the other, developing an understanding of the phenomena presented. This can only occur by keeping silent. Paradoxically, only someone who has something to say will be able to keep silent (Heidegger, 1962).

The aim of dialogue in therapy is to gain insight for both client and therapist. The questions we ask as therapists help to clarify the meaning of what is said and go beyond that. It is more difficult to ask questions than to answer them. The dialectic of questioning can enhance understanding and insight for both client and therapist. Socrates held that self-knowledge is more important than any other knowledge, 'an unexamined life is not worth living' (Plato, 1938: 40, section 38).

Case illustration

This case illustration is an attempt to demonstrate the process of dialogue: how the client's monologue will open up to become dialogue given sufficient time, space and attention from the therapist.

Ann came to see me because her husband believed that she needed therapy. The first meeting was mainly spent in looking at how she believed that she could do justice to herself in coming to therapy. Initially she did not feel that she could benefit from it, but came just to be obedient to her husband's demands. At a later stage our conversation brought to light that, even if the initial push had come from her husband, she had now come to recognize the possibility of using this time for her own benefit. She admitted that there were some aspects of her life that seemed obscure and that were puzzling her.

Ann originated from Jamaica though she was brought to Britain when she was two years old. Soon after the family arrived in Britain her mother suddenly died. Her father remarried and Ann was brought up by her step-mother. She hinted on several occasions that her stepmother was very fair but extremely cold and could not bear physical closeness with Ann. She described her relationship with her father as warm and loving. Ann was a very good student and achieved excellent results in school. Eventually she went on to study law at university. Ann was a beautiful woman and was always smartly dressed.

She gave up practising law in order to look after her six-year-old twins whom she felt needed her total attention and devotion. We agreed to meet once a week for an open-ended period, with the possibility of terminating our agreement at any time but with the proviso that there should be an ending session, when we could say goodbye to each other.

Ann was never late or missed a session. However, in the first four sessions she only reported how she spent her week, and there was little attempt to engage in any meaningful reflection. She did not feel to have any real sense of what she wanted to gain from therapy.

To my surprise, the following dialogue took place in the fifth session:

Ann: You've never asked me why my husband sent me to therapy?
Luci: What if I did not? What did you make of that?

In the context of this relationship whilst the intervention may sound rather challenging, I believed trust had been established and that Ann could tolerate these questions.

Ann: To tell you the truth I thought you were not interested.
Luci: Whatever your husband had in mind when he suggested that you should go to therapy only becomes relevant here with me if you consider it important enough to make it the focus of our discussion.

Here I emphasized that my concern was with how Ann saw her predicament. Ann looked at me, bemused. She became quiet and I could see that she was struggling over whether to make her thoughts explicit or to remain silent. She chose to remain silent for several minutes during which time her face became very red and she was obviously fighting back tears. Her body language was speaking loudly, her fidgeting betrayed that something needed to be expressed and could not be postponed any longer. I felt very touched by her struggle and had no difficulty in resonating with it. I felt a deep sadness and that the pregnant silence was enveloping both of us. Something had changed between us and it was tangible. Ann took a deep breath and with a composed and clear voice carried on.

Ann: It is about my father. I wanted to go with my children to visit my parents. They live in Brighton now. My husband argued with me, saying that my children are not safe.

Another long silence followed. The silence gave Ann the opportunity to articulate her thoughts and by me remaining silent I contributed to that process. I strongly felt that we were in dialogue during the silence. Ann looked straight into my eyes and it seemed as if she was wondering: 'can she take what is about to come?' I nodded, meaning 'yes, I can'. She smiled and continued.

Ann: After my father remarried, he and I became very close. The thing that I did not know then but found out later was that as a Caribbean man, my father needed a woman who was warm and affectionate. My stepmother, who is English, although she was a very correct woman was lacking warmth. So I suppose I took my stepmother's place.
Luci: How could you?

I had great difficulty in suspending judgement on what I was hearing, but I succeeded in letting go of my desire to take her in a particular direction.

Ann: My father was very physical with me and he often touched my intimate parts but never had penetrative sex with me. I felt good about what we had together but nevertheless eventually I asked him not to do this to me ever again. This happened when I was nine years old and it coincided with my first period. I know that many people talk about this as child abuse.

Luci: How did you experience that?

Ann: I did not experience it as such. He never hurt me and was always very gentle with me. I have read many books on child abuse and I disagree with many things that psychologists write about it. I have a very good sexual life. I never had any problems in that area.

Luci: What were you looking for? What made you read all those books on sexual abuse?

This question was too challenging and also the timing was much too early.

Ann: I suppose because of my husband. He was the first person I told about this. He pushed me to confront my father about the 'abuse' in the presence of him and my stepmother. My father did admit that we were very close but denied that he abused me sexually. Since then the relationship between my parents and my husband has become very distant. I can live with that, provided that he does not prevent me and my children from visiting my parents. My husband is paying for my therapy sessions and he is hoping that you will convince me to take my father to court. My husband is very rich and he can afford this, but with all the money in the world he cannot force me to do such a thing. It is utterly wrong to expect that.

Luci: What are you hoping to get from therapy, for yourself?

I encouraged Ann to consider her own expectations of being in therapy and I felt that this was the first time the question could have been asked.

Ann: My problem is of a very different nature. What I struggle with is that I have these feelings of love for my father, my children, my husband, my stepmother, myself and they seem to be in conflict with each other.

After a moment of reflection she asked:

Ann: What is love?

I avoided engaging with this question and asked:

Luci: Can I just clarify this: Are you talking about all these people you say you love being in conflict with each other, or are you saying that the feelings of love you have for them are conflicting?

Although this intervention appears to be solely for my benefit, it also served to give Ann the opportunity to further clarify her own issue. However, the way I formulated it was not very helpful. After reflecting for a few moments, Ann carried on.

Ann: This is an interesting question. Initially I meant the latter but now I think they are both true. We do seem to be in conflict, especially my husband and I. You see, I do love my father dearly. He is the one who was always there for me and helped me to make important decisions in my life, without ever trying to tell me what was best for me but instead allowing me to find out for myself. As adults we have a loving and trusting relationship. My husband is very jealous of this. I love and adore my children and I would die for them. They are getting on very well with each other and they love both Graham and myself. My love for Graham, I suppose, is the most problematic. I love him but he wants me to be different and do things his way without considering what I want for myself.

Luci: When you say you love Graham what do you really mean?

This is a difficult question to fully answer. Nevertheless, I was inviting Ann to clarify for herself in what way her love for Graham was problematic.

Ann: When you put it this way, I don't really know.

A moment of silence followed.

Luci: Let me put it differently. What do you love about Graham and how do you demonstrate it?

I did break the silence as I felt my previous question was too broad, wide open and rather abstract. I considered this last question as being more specific and easier for Ann to engage with.

Ann started to search for something in her handbag while tears began to fall down her cheeks. She cried silently for a while.

Ann: I do not think I do demonstrate often that I love him. We do often argue and generally he loses the argument and storms out of the house. I suppose he is rather immature in that respect. I do love that about him. It is almost like having another child. He is strong and very good at his job. Everyone admires and respects him including myself.

At that moment a big storm started, with thunder and spectacular lightning. After a brief pause Ann continued.

Ann: This storm is like my marriage. Things seem to be fine and then suddenly we are having a 'stormy' argument. Like yesterday; we were talking about going to the park together with the children when out of the blue Graham accused me of not loving my children, because he says if I loved them I would not even contemplate exposing them to the danger of being near my father. I found this offensive on two accounts: one, that he dares to say that I do not love my children and second, to think that my father could in any way put them in danger. I hate him in moments like this.

Luci: You love your children and your father. You also love your husband, but sometimes you hate him. Maybe it is an impossible task for you to find a single answer to your question as to what love is!? It seems from what you have described that it is more important to live, or demonstrate love rather than conceptualize it. Your experience demonstrates that love is many different things depending upon whom it is felt towards, and it can also turn into its opposite at times.

This intervention is a hermeneutic type of interpretation that aimed to highlight the ambiguity of Ann's feelings, to acknowledge the love she experiences for different people. Also it highlights how difficult it is to define what love is.

After this nothing else was said. The session came to an end.

Critical considerations

What this chapter demonstrates is how much easier it is to conceptualize what dialogue entails as opposed to putting it into practice. During the session described above I think we had a glimpse of dialogue whilst we were in silence. It was something other than words, something implied in the quality of the engagement that allowed for this powerful communication. It demonstrated that communication starts before using words and begins when people actively engage with each other and the questions they want to consider. Dialogue takes place on many different levels.

Our dialogue disclosed and revealed: it revealed to me again that there is no possibility for dialogue in therapy without loving my clients. Love in this sense is directed towards the being of the client and goes beyond the particulars of their character, personality or how they present themselves (Lacan, 1989). This kind of love cannot be explained but it could easily be judged when misinterpreted. Whatever type of therapy, the quality of the relationship is what clients seem to appreciate most. Dialogue is much more than what is said. It is the meeting of two worlds, two horizons and two different styles of being-in-the-world.

When working existentially the emphasis is on being with the client and the way in which they experience their way of being-in-the-world, as opposed to trying to fit their experience into a theoretical framework. Dialogue can be highly beneficial when working this way; however, it can become extremely threatening or even counterproductive when the client is unable or unwilling to be self-reflective, take up challenges or question themselves.

Nobody can predict what the outcome of a dialogue will be. In dialogue we are not aiming for some certainty, some outcome or evidence that can be demonstrated. Dialogue involves us in an intersubjective process. This process cannot be quantified and its form of communication is often indirect. 'While objective thought translates everything into results, and helps mankind to cheat by copying these off and reciting them by rote, subjective thought puts everything in process and omits the result' (Kierkegaard, 1968: 68).

Further reading

Buber, M. *Between Man and Man.*
Buber, M. *I and Thou.*
Kierkegaard, S. *The Concept of Irony.*
Szlezak, T. A. *Reading Plato.*

CHAPTER 13

Emotions

EMMY VAN DEURZEN

When we master a mood, we do so by way of a counter-mood; we are never free of moods.

Heidegger, Being and Time: 136

Introduction

Emotions are an intrinsic part of human experience. We are not fully human unless we feel. Our emotions are a movement through which we e-mote, which literally means that we move out of ourselves. This movement always takes place in relation to the world. Emotion is movement from us towards the world. This movement takes place primarily in relation to others and to the values they represent for us. Emotions are not experienced in a vacuum. They always have an implied object. Emotions are therefore an important aspect of our connection with the world and others. They are a direct indication of how we feel about others and ourselves in our present situation. They allow us to gauge the quality and magnitude of our attachments and of our level of care. Emotions then, from an existential perspective, are the experience of our resonance with the world and with others. The objective is not to suppress or merely express them, but to understand and integrate them into our lives.

A cognitive model

This is not the way in which emotions generally have been viewed or studied by psychologists or psychotherapists. Many orthodox theories consider emotions to be a pathological side effect of human actions and interactions. The theories of cognitive-behaviour therapists such as Beck and Ellis (Beck, 1991; Ellis, 2001) are examples of this. They take the view that bad feelings are the by-product of bad cognitions and irrational beliefs. Their objective is to minimize such negative emotions by detaching human experience from catastrophic thinking. In this they are not dissimilar from the epicureans or the sceptics who pursued ways in which they could reduce human unhappiness by respectively reducing their level of emotionality or relativizing experiences leading to it.

A psychodynamic model

Interestingly, psychodynamic theories are equally negative about emotions, since they often regard emotion to be a symptom of unconscious conflict and an expression of pathology. Psychoanalytic or psychodynamic therapies aim to interpret the conflicts in question so as to relieve the person of unnecessary anxiety. Emotion is transformed into something more rational and is sublimated.

A humanistic model

The humanistic model of emotion, based to a large extent on early psychoanalytic thinking, has taken the Reichian view that blocked instinctual energies need to be accessed, but not in order to normalize and sublimate them but in order to encourage emotional expression. The notion of catharsis or purification is at the core of humanistic dealings with emotion and cathartic methods assume that the more emotion is expressed, the better it is, because somehow the natural balance of energy will be re-established in the process. This is, however, not necessarily the case and it has since been shown that the encouragement of abreaction and emotional expression may amount to a rehearsal of that emotion, leading to teach a person to feel such emotion more readily next time.

Psychological models

Psychological studies on emotion have thrown further light on the complexity of feelings and affects. After the innovative work of people such as William James (James, 1950) many new models of emotion have been developed. Some of these are compatible with an existential perspective, such as for instance Oatley's contribution (Oatley, 1992) and in particular De Rivera's structural model (De Rivera, 1977) and Frijda's action model (Frijda, 1986). Most of these models make useful distinctions between affects, feelings, moods and emotions (Izard, 1977; Ekman and Davidson, 1994) and they systematically study the differences between these. Detailed analyses of each separate emotion or affect are proposed by such authors. The simple distinction between feeling and emotion as defined by Damasio (1999) can also be useful in making sense of increasing levels of conscious knowing about our own emotional experiencing.

An existential perspective

Against the background of all this psychological and psychotherapeutic theorizing about emotions, it is important to note that philosophers have long been concerned with emotions. As has been mentioned earlier, Martha

Nussbaum's contribution to our understanding of the Athenian dealings with emotionality is enlightening in this respect (Nussbaum, 1994, 2003). Athenians clearly did not like too much emotion. Later philosophers such as Spinoza developed models of ethics, which also included an understanding of emotion. He described emotion as a gauge of the likelihood of us achieving our values. Spinoza's view was that some emotions indicate a reaching-out to what is desirable and others an aversion towards what is undesirable (Spinoza, 1677).

Kierkegaard

Kierkegaard (1844, 1980b) recognized that there were some basic emotions that dominated human existence and that we would find ourselves inevitably either experiencing dread, or Angst, when being open to existence and its challenges or despair, the sickness unto death, when attempting to forget about the reality of life, pretending not to be ourselves. These two fundamental emotional states, for him, span the two poles of existence. Thus for the first time emotion is described as an important and inevitable depth of human existence.

Nietzsche

Nietzsche went beyond Kierkegaard in this sense by positively welcoming and celebrating passion and all forms of emotion that are part of a person being truly alive. He reclaimed the importance of living a passionate life rather than allowing yourself to become too rational and trying to stay in control of life (Nietzsche, 1882). Nietzsche's notion that human beings ought to cultivate the Dionysian aspects of experience introduced the possibility of valuing the emotional spectrum rather than reading it as pathological or trying to reduce or even eliminate it.

Heidegger

Heidegger's understanding of human experience is also crucial. His description of the fundamental existential of *Befindlichkeit*, which is variously translated as attunement, disposition or state of mind, shows that human beings always find themselves disposed or attuned to the world in a particular way. Heidegger was the first to argue that emotion was far from an occasional or extreme event. It was instead an ontological given. Human existence is essentially attuned existence. This means that in an ontic fashion every moment of our experience will be coloured by a particular tonality, or mood (*Stimmung*). For Heidegger emotion is one aspect of the three-part movement of disposition, understanding and discourse. We feel into the world, make sense of our world and then learn to speak about it. Gendlin's application of Heidegger's insights led to his development of the technique of focusing (Gendlin, 1996), which works with the emotional dimension from an existential perspective.

Sartre

Sartre's description of emotion as action rather than merely as passion is also significant. In his book *Sketch for a Theory of the Emotions* (1939) he elaborated the idea that emotionality is a kind of magic, a way of transforming the world when we are confronted with difficulties. The main practitioners of existential psychotherapy have all paid particular attention to working with clients' emotional states, following Heidegger's and Sartre's lead. Feelings are considered to be an important source of information of where and how the client is.

Binswanger and Boss

Binswanger showed the importance of taking clients' feelings seriously and uncovering the source of the emotion rather than treating emotions as manifestations of pathology. His case studies of Ellen West and Lola Voss are good illustrations of this (May et al., 1958).

Medard Boss took the teaching of Heidegger on the importance of the emotional, attuned dimension of existence extremely seriously and he placed considerable emphasis on such experiences as those of existential anxiety and existential guilt (Boss, 1957, 1962).

More recent existential contributions

Similarly Rollo May wrote much about the importance of addressing existential anxiety as something that is fundamental to human existence instead of treating anxiety as something that we need to get rid of. Tillich's notion of existential courage is very similar to Heidegger's descriptions of resolute living. It means that we affirm our essential nature, which includes our mortality and our doubts and fears, and allow ourselves to see emotionality as a function of our vitality. Courage is the affirmation of being in spite of the threat of non-being (Tillich, 1952).

Yalom's acceptance of anxiety as a response to the threat of non-being is mostly in line with May and Tillich's work. In Britain, Laing's work on onto-logical insecurity clarified the experience of schizophrenia and the feelings of implosion, engulfment and petrification that go with it (Laing, 1960). This somewhat obscured the original existential idea that anxiety is a fundamental part of the human condition (van Deurzen, 1998). The emotional cycle model first published in *Existential Counselling in Practice* (van Deurzen-Smith, 1988) was based on Spinoza's and Sartre's insights into emotion. It sketched out a systematic way of working with emotion from an existential perspective. It shows how each emotion can be experienced as positive or negative. Some emotions move us away from our value and downwards towards loss and depression; others move us towards our value and upwards towards anxiety. Each tonality of emotion is a specific and meaningful way of relating to the world and to others and has a role to play. Such a model provides a clear framework for therapeutic work (van Deurzen-Smith, 1997, 2002a) since it shows the phenomenological significance of each emotional position in relation to the world. It is compatible with Tantam's (2002) narrative-existential model of emotions, where emotions are described as flavours of experience.

Case illustration

Penny was a bundle of human misery when I first saw her. Her doctor had referred her to me after diagnosing her with acute clinical depression. She gave the impression of being so overwhelmed by contradictory emotions that she just wanted to hide in her despair. She seemed to keep herself as low as she could in order not to be touched or moved by anything or anyone. She sat very still and looked like a frightened deer, hardly able to meet my gaze, trembling whenever I spoke. She pleaded with moist eyes as she briefly glanced at me before looking away again, as if she were beseeching me not to hurt her any further because she could not take anymore.

Penny was in her forties. She was slightly built and she looked fragile. She had pale skin and mousy blond, greying hair, which she kept tied in a tight bun. Her features were delicate but careworn. Her wide, startled eyes gave her an almost theatrical appearance, like a character in a silent movie. Penny's world had fallen apart when she had discovered that her husband had betrayed her by conducting an affair with her cousin Janet. Not only had her marriage failed, leaving her bereft and distressed, but she had also lost trust in her cousin, who, apart from her children and husband, had been her only remaining family. She used to be quite close to Janet and she could not understand why she had misjudged her so. Penny had become so upset upon discovering the affair that she had had to stay home from her work in the local library where she had been an employee for over twenty years without a single day of absence. Penny had been off sick for several weeks by the time she came to see me and she had hardly moved or spoken during this time. Her husband had driven her to the session. She was on a high dose of anti-depressants and had a strong nervous cough, nervous tremors around her eyes and mouth and very shaky hands. Her posture was stooped and her gaze was averted. Insecurity was written all over her. She seemed cut off and in pain. At first she withheld from communication as much as possible, speaking in monosyllables. As she began to trust that I would help her, she was able to move into more active expression of distress and she wept softly and continuously as she told me her story.

After a brief account of what her husband had done to her and how it was affecting her, she said that the situation reminded her of what she had experienced as a teenager when she had suddenly lost both her parents. Being an only child of overprotective parents, their death had left her feeling bereft and confused. No one had been able to support her during this early phase of mourning, since she had at first lived with a grandfather who was rather forlorn himself. She had become a problem child in school for a while, refusing to do any work and often playing truant. Her aunt and uncle had then taken her in and she had formed a close relationship with her cousin Janet, who was their only daughter. For many years she had been afraid to start living alone and she had only begun to enjoy life and achieve some independence when she had started going out with Geoff, her husband-to-be, who had been introduced to her by her uncle and aunt. Geoff was ten years older than her and he had been a childhood friend of Janet's. He had just finished his training as a doctor when they met. He had been previously married and his first wife had left him for someone else. He had adored Penny and courted her vigorously, making her feel special, secure and wanted. She had married him within a year of meeting him and she had never looked back, even though she felt there was something missing in the relationship.

After the birth of her children she had just become a devoted mother to her two sons, both of whom were now grown up and had professional careers. It had been a disappointment to Geoff that neither son had gone into medicine. Penny believed that her sons had opted for careers that were different to Geoff's because they feared him and would not compete with him. She herself had always looked up to Geoff and she deferred to him and his family. It had been essential for her to work in the library to keep her sanity and she had always done so, even when her children were young. What she had not done was to keep track of the relationship with her husband. She had left him pretty much to his career and to his relationship with his own parents, which was very intense and which she resented. She did not get on with her in-laws and had not been too bereft when they had died soon after each other four years ago. Geoff had been heartbroken, however, especially after his mother died, and he had sought comfort in his relationship with Janet, who, together with her husband John, was a good friend to the couple, living next door to them. Penny who thought of Janet as a sister had been rather pleased that Geoff got on with her so well and that Janet could now comfort him in his grief. She had not paid much attention to the signs of Geoff's growing affection for Janet and had not considered Janet to be a potential threat.

With hindsight that was a big mistake, since the affair must have started as soon as he began spending time next door, after the death of his mother. Clearly Janet had been able to fill the gap that was left by his mother's death in a way Penny herself had not been able or willing to do. Janet, Penny said bitterly, was the motherly type. She was quite a few years older than Penny, more like Geoff's age, had four children and three grandchildren. Janet had long been frustrated with John's regular travel for his work. She was often alone for weeks on end. Penny had ignored the dangers of letting another woman get so close to her husband and she had been shocked to discover that they were lovers. She was furious with Janet and outraged at Geoff's bad taste, for she had never considered Janet to be at all attractive, with her middle-age spread and over-large breasts. When she spoke about Janet in this rather venomous manner, she seemed to briefly emerge from her depression. It became immediately clear that underneath her depression there were lots of other intense and complex feelings. She expressed disdain, jealousy and envy as well as murderous rage with Janet for betraying their friendship. There was also a fair amount of surprise and disbelief at Geoff's behaviour and disappointment and even disgust with her own naivety. There was in addition a large dose of regret over having lost her husband so recklessly by being too trusting. She was coming to the conclusion that she had really not known him at all. She could not understand his sudden passion and deeply resented him feeling it for someone other than herself.

There had been little or no emotional expression in the marriage for many years and although she and Geoff occasionally still had sexual intercourse, there was no real ardour. Penny came to understand during the therapy that she had not allowed herself to feel much about anything since the death of her parents nearly forty years ago. She had settled for safety and contentment with her family and had more or less given up on experiencing anything extremely positive or extremely negative. Penny had kept her emotions under control and she had been uncomplaining about her husband's absence from the family. Geoff was a successful surgeon and was away for long hours. He believed in keeping himself to himself and had always dealt with adversity through the stiff upper lip method. She had learnt to live around him rather than with him and had not expected very much from him. They had colluded in keeping the emotional challenges to a minimum.

Now all that was changed. Suddenly it had turned out that he desired another woman in a very intense manner. He was prepared to divorce Penny and marry Janet. John, Janet's husband, had moved out without further ado and Janet was waiting for Geoff to leave Penny in turn. Penny refused to speak to her or meet her. Geoff continued to spend large amounts of time next door. It drove Penny insane with jealousy to see him going through Janet's front door. She would stand by the window for hours observing Janet's house and wondering what was going on inside. She had bought a stethoscope, which she would put against the wall, to listen to the sounds she could hear them making. She felt fury and maddening frustration when doing so, but could not help herself. The intensity of her feelings had taken her by surprise. She did not know that people could feel so strongly.

Her jealousy had built up gradually over a period of a year as she had become increasingly suspicious of Geoff and had started to suspect his unfaithfulness. She had started noticing how odd it was that Janet regularly went on holiday when Geoff had to attend conferences and she had then snooped on Geoff, discovering that he was in the habit of making daily and numerous phone calls to Janet's home. She became obsessed with his every move and had followed him around, checking up on him and going through his pockets, his briefcase, his computer and his wallet. As she had gathered more and more evidence, she had drawn the obvious conclusion that they were having an affair and she had felt a sense of utter abandonment and total rejection. Yet, instead of confronting them, she had started spying on Geoff and Janet. During this period she had frequently thought that she was going insane and must be making it all up.

Eventually she had followed them to a hotel in a nearby town where they were to spend a weekend together and she had interrupted them in their hotel room when they were just about to start making love. Even then Geoff and Janet had tried to deny what was going on and had claimed their meeting to be innocent. Penny had ended up believing that she was going insane and she had even consulted her GP to ask for medication to stop her paranoid feelings and her irrational jealousy. He prescribed anti-depressants. It was only when John came home early from a business trip and caught the pair making love that the affair exploded into the open.

From then on Penny had felt numb with terror at the thought that she might lose Geoff. She was also plagued by all these other intense emotions, but somehow managed to squash them down, hiding in the protective shell of her depression instead. She accepted that she was using the same strategy as she had when her parents had died: she was trying to hide and cope. But the more she withheld her distress, the worse her symptoms became. She described herself as a nervous wreck, unable to go out or have social interaction. Her ticks were quite bad and she also used alcohol in a very self-destructive manner, for it released some of her inhibitions and enabled her to shout at Geoff occasionally. She had tried hitting him a couple of times, but she had settled for biting her own arms instead whenever she felt the rage rise in her. She would do this till she bled and she would show her arms to Geoff to punish him. This gave her some cruel satisfaction. I pointed out to her how even when she was punishing Geoff she still did it by victimizing herself. It was essential for her to stop describing the situation to herself as one in which she had been done to. She had to start waking up from her trance and start facing facts, taking some responsibility for her own predicament. When she said she did not know how to do this, I proposed that she could let her feelings guide her in the right direction. When she complained that she was 'just depressed', I countered that she was actually outraged and sad and angry and upset and regretful and jealous and disappointed and lots of other things that we could make sense of together, as long as she was willing to take charge of the process of her recovery.

In the initial phase of our work I encouraged Penny to just go over the facts as she saw them, retelling the story in an increasingly more active manner and making new connections each time. I also invited her to explore the whole range of her complex feelings, naming them and understanding what they told her about her relationship with other people and with herself. She needed a lot of help in learning to articulate and make sense of her reactions and was inclined to dismiss and suppress her state of mind. When she said: 'I am insanely jealous of Geoff. I cannot stand to let him out of my sight at all, I think I must be mad, perhaps I should be hospitalized', I would enable her to find out where the jealousy came from and what it meant. 'Of course you are having to be vigilant and cautious now.' I might say, 'you have realized that you can lose him and you have discovered that he is precious to you'. Once reassured that her feelings were acceptable and perhaps even understandable, nay wise, Penny could trace their origin and meaning with me. 'What is it exactly that you would lose, if he left?', I might ask and she would then slowly follow the path of her feelings and discover where they led. Feelings were not frightening or insane anymore, but helpful cues about where she was at in life. She learnt that they were not as dangerous as she had feared and that they were even eminently comprehensible.

She became capable of seeing the logic of the events that had taken place and began to recognize and respect her own reactions, whilst understanding where she had gone wrong. Instead of focusing on Geoff and Janet's bad behaviour and seeing herself as a victim of events, she began to understand her own role in her relationships and she was waking up to a universe where she could again have some grasp of what was happening. She stopped talking about being depressed, whilst recognizing her fear and her sadness together with all the other emotions she was experiencing. In emerging from her depression she could allow herself to let things matter to her again. She stopped trying not to care. I would point out these progressive steps to her as she was taking them and every time her progress was named she was able to retain it and refer to it next time. She realized how afraid she had been to love and be loved and how, too, she had feared her own feelings and desires. She had played it safe and thus inevitably courted danger. Now she wanted to open herself up to what was happening in her life. She could see the relationship between her childhood terror of being left alone and the avoidance of closeness and her fear of love. She could also see that this state of emotional coldness had kept her separate from her husband in a profound way. It had been enough for him while his mother was alive, but then he had started craving for love and found it in Janet's arms. It was ironic that Janet had played the same part with Geoff as she had previously played in Penny's own life: she had provided warmth and understanding for each after their parents died. While these kinds of recognitions did not lessen Penny's outrage at her rival, they made her think and respond to the situation in a much more active and assertive manner.

Not surprisingly Penny's depression began to make way for anxiety at this stage. It was as if the veil had been lifted. Somehow she became able to see that something needed to be done and that this was not the end of her life or even necessarily of her love, but rather a new beginning. She did not want to remain a victim. She wanted to survive, understand, reach out to the world and make things better. I stimulated her engagement with her new desire for life, and reassured her that anxiety was a positive sign of her waking-up out of her depression. The anxiety was quite overwhelming at first and it soon led to her feeling dreadful envy of Janet for being so self-confident, for rivalling so effectively with her for the affection of Geoff and for having the temerity to get what she wanted. At first she tried to suppress these feelings. She went as far as gagging herself to make herself vomit. She also tried cutting herself a couple of times, as if to punish herself for wanting things. We would talk through the emotions underlying these false attempts at autonomy and self-affirmation and it was not long before she saw that she was only keeping herself victimized and incapable of overcoming her troubles if she gave in to such gestures. She soon agreed there must be other, better, ways to reassert herself. We came to a point where she acknowledged that she was hesitant to move on because she feared that if she stopped being a victim, Geoff would immediately leave. He had promised he would stay until she was out of her depression.

So we worked with her fear of loss and we had to go back to the terrifying loss of her parents in childhood. We found that there had been lots of other emotions around that time and that they were similar to what she was feeling at the moment. Shame was an important part of this. She had felt shame at living with her grandpa and not having a 'proper family', as she felt shame now at having allowed her husband to stray. She felt shame also about her husband's preference of her much older and less attractive cousin to herself. Somehow the affair had proven that her life had been based on illusion and that she was worthless. She felt a complete failure as a person and as a woman and soon acknowledged that this is exactly what she set out to cover over by marrying Geoff in the first place. If he left her now that would prove that she was without any value whatsoever. She accepted that she had to find a way to get out of this impasse and recover her self-esteem, or perhaps establish it for the first time. At last there was something to fight for now and she could feel her energy returning as she realized this was an opportunity to tackle the problems of her adolescence and become a person in her own right at last. Finally we were getting somewhere and Penny allowed the depression to be lifted officially, making room for new ambitions and new emotions. She decided to gradually come off her anti-depressants.

This led to a whole new phase in our work together, which included understanding her anger with cousin Janet for treating her like a second-rate person. It was important to help her harness this anger in a constructive way. This meant helping her discover that she wanted, more than anything, to move away from next door to Janet, either with or without Geoff. The situation of physical closeness to Janet was sapping her self-confidence and her sense of freedom. The anger was largely territorial. Once it became focused on finding a new home, it became useful. This also became the way in which her relationship with Geoff took on a much more fair and realistic turn. She stopped accusing him of so many things and started enlisting him in helping her sort the situation out. For a long time it was not clear whether Geoff was humouring her, planning to move with her, or determined to move in with Janet, but at least they were working towards some resolution.

By the end of the therapy Geoff had actually decided to move to a new town with Penny and to stop seeing Janet. This was achieved by Penny facing up to having to look after herself and retrieving the desire to be a joyful person who might discover how to live with others and love a lot better than she had in the past. The therapy was often about helping Penny uncover new moods and feelings in herself, understand them and put them to good use rather than become overwhelmed by them. Penny had to learn to thrive on the energy of her emotions and use it to move forward in her life. She gathered more and more self-esteem as she appreciated her own achievement in overcoming her depression and in getting better at understanding her situation. Then she learnt to translate her new learning into an ability to talk things through with Geoff in a way that had seemed impossible before. Geoff found her assertiveness quite attractive, but sometimes a bit overwhelming, for instance when he finally proposed that they should try to save the marriage and Penny objected and affirmed that they had to build a new marriage instead of saving the old one. It said a lot about her new vitality. Penny herself was quite proud of her confidence and she felt that her life was only really starting now that she was no longer afraid to lose Geoff or frightened to live. Being in touch with her emotions and what they told her about her values was the key to her discovery of a better way to be.

Critical considerations

Emotions can be overrated as well as understated in psychotherapy. It would have been easy to let Penny drown me in her initially overwhelming feelings of despair and depression. Empathy is often overused in these situations as people are asked to expand on their feelings without any offer of new direction or reconstructive action in relation to their emotions. On the other hand, it would have been possible to address Penny's problems by ignoring her feelings or help her remove them, appealing to her rationality and her will to overcome her sadness. I believe that neither of these strategies would have achieved the desired result: that of enabling Penny to reclaim her own passionate experience of life in all the fullness and complexity of her emotionality without being afraid of it. Feelings, emotions and moods are the driving forces of our everyday experience and we need to become more competent at recognizing them, allowing them to develop and managing their energy in a positive fashion. This is often what therapy is about: teaching a person to be at ease with the world-disclosing states of mind, feel them, articulate them and understand them. By talking through emotions we can harness their energy in order to generate new events and actions in our lives. We need to be clear about the power of feelings and be equal to that power without flinching or fear, but also without provocation and machismo. To live in harmony with one's emotions is a goal well worth achieving. Therapists can always learn a lot more about how to do this for themselves and for others.

Further reading

Damasio, A. *The Feeling of What Happens: Body, Emotion and the Making of Consciousness.*
Kierkegaard, S. *The Concept of Dread.*
May, R. *Love and Will.*
Nussbaum, M. C. *Upheavals of Thought: The Intelligence of Emotions.*
Sartre, J. P. *Sketch for a Theory of the Emotions.*

CHAPTER 14

Relationships

DIGBY TANTAM AND EMMY VAN DEURZEN

> True, I knew the glory of friendship (in common studies, in the cordial atmosphere of home or countryside). But then came the moments of strangeness, as if human beings lived in different worlds. Steadily the consciousness of loneliness grew upon me in my youth, yet nothing seemed more pernicious to me than loneliness, especially the loneliness in the midst of social intercourse that deceives itself in a multitude of friendships.
>
> Jaspers, *On My Philosophy*: 146

Introduction

Human beings define themselves in relation to others, whether they live in close contact with others or not. In the same way in which a person could not exist without a physical environment, we cannot call ourselves human unless we see ourselves in the context of our being-with-others. There are human relationships of all different sorts. Relationships can be public or private, friendly or adversarial, supportive or undermining, cooperative or competitive. They can be freely chosen or they can be forced upon us by necessity or circumstances.

Baumeister and Leary (1995) suggest that the foundation of all relationships is the 'need to belong', which they describe as 'a powerful, fundamental, and extremely pervasive motivation'. But what does this common sentiment towards belonging mean?

It is a given of our existence that we come into being situated in a social world. Heidegger's formulation of 'Dasein' as being-in-the-world and being-with-others encapsulates his idea that there is never a stage of being when we are waiting to discover the world: we come into being from within the world. We are always part of the world, interrelated. In the womb, we experience the emotions of our mothers. We emerge from the birth canal to be held by human hands, smiled at by human faces, talked to by human voices. Babies are not insensitive to this, but from birth look referentially at human faces and imitate the expressions of other humans. By the time infants begin to develop self-awareness, sometime during the third year of life, they are already established in relationships.

121

These relationships are likely to be both cooperative and competitive. Infants by the end of their first year of life have normally also developed a healthy fear of strangers and a sense of security when close to adults to whom they are attached. Before social awareness has fully emerged, infants have developed a capacity for emotional contagion, the ability to be ashamed if they do something that is socially undesirable, and some degree of solicitude for others.

Melanie Klein, Margaret Mahler and other psychoanalysts had a profound influence on theories about social relationships, primarily by focussing on these early years of life. Although many of their formulations now seem dated, scientific developmental psychology and psychotherapy theory have continued to find common ground and their fundamental assertion, that adult relationships continue to be linked to the patterns of these very early relationships, remains sound. We choose the term 'linked' because it allows for various kinds of coupling. Infants who are confident are more likely to make friends easily, and to be popular, which maintains their confidence and allows them to make more friends easily later in childhood. Confident children are able to make more careful choices about relationships. Confident, emotionally secure girls are less likely, for example, to have teenage pregnancies and therefore less likely to be hurried into relationships that might not turn out to be the best for them, or into careers that may take them away from what they really want. However, none of these steps is fully determined; each can be affected by contingency. For instance, a girl who loses her mother in childhood loses some of her security and is more likely, later on, to get trapped into the wrong kind of relationship.

This object relations approach is, and will continue to be, a powerful influence on understanding human relationships, based as it is on a modern version of the nineteenth century notion of the unconscious. From this perspective, instead of perceiving a region of our mind as formulating its own wishes or impulses and constantly battling to get those ends met, unconscious functioning is seen as a process that influences our decisions and our actions, tipping them in one direction or another by preferences or aversions of which we may not be aware, with provenances which we may never discover.

Current research suggests that this story is more right than wrong, but incomplete. It leaves out what consequences self-awareness has for relationships. It leaves out what Heidegger called the ontological givens.

Ontic versus Ontological

For Heidegger, ontology was not simply an extension of philosophical enquiry into human nature, as it had been for Aristotle, but an experience of one's own being, free of its embeddedness in the lived world. Reading Heidegger, it is sometimes difficult to appreciate that he was describing quite common, ordinary experiences, albeit experiences that are also strange, disturbing and, as Heidegger himself recognized, full of anxiety since they seem constantly to threaten to make life arbitrary or meaningless.

Heidegger's phenomenological approach to ontology also throws into relief what it is to belong, to use a term mentioned previously. The ontic refers to the way we experience the everyday world. Many of our actions and reactions are unthinking, influenced by the emotional tendencies and previous experiences that we have described above. When it comes to some relationships, we are also influenced by behavioural considerations dictated, to use a contemporary term, by our selfish genes (Dawkins, 1989). Women are attracted to partners who have different histo-compatibility antigens to their own (proteins on the surface of every cell that are often the target for an immune reaction) and this is thought to increase the chances of their children having effective immune systems, capable of fighting off infections. Fathers are more protective of their children than stepfathers, perhaps because genetic similarity increases liking.

The everyday world itself provides its own unspoken influences; there is, to use Jung's term, a collective unconscious, or rather a collective influence on the individual. This is particularly clear when it comes to relationships. Most languages contain many words for relationships – uncle, friend, lover, acquaintance, partner, stepmother, cousin, sister, boss and employee are just a few – and each of these words carries with it a set of rules or expectations about how these relationships are supposed to be carried through.

Self-awareness develops at the same time, and at the same rate, as the awareness of others as separate beings (an awareness that is frequently called the 'theory of mind'). We use this other awareness to reflect on, and deepen, our ontic experience. For example, many of us have friends before we know exactly what a friend is, and we behave towards our friends, as we have already described, with dispositions to react with hostility or submission, or to be secure or insecure. There comes a time, however, when we begin to reflect on what a friend is. Girls, especially, may spend hours debating whether one girl or another is a 'true friend', what friends should and should not do, how much reliance one can put on friends and so on. These discussions shape our conception of friendship, just as similar discussions shape our conception of what it is to be a good son, or how to be a parent, or what duties, if any, are owed to a cousin. These discussions may sometimes go public, with referral to tribunals, which define the duties of an employer or an employee for instance.

Heidegger's point was that we often discuss such issues, as philosophers have done, without fully applying our self-awareness to the question: 'Who am I if I do not belong to the world?' Such questions are important and do occur to us. Many of us will remember, or will observe in our children, pre-occupations about solipsism, asking questions such as: 'How do I know that anyone else is real? You could all be figments of my imagination.' These preoccupations occur at about the same time as children become fearful of death (Gullone, 2000), and it is of interest, therefore, that Heidegger linked ontological awareness – authenticity – so closely to the awareness of the inevitability of one's own death. Later childhood is when ontological questions first occur to children and this is also the time when children become aware of being rejected or accepted by other children, of choosing or being chosen to be one child's friend, and not that of another.

There is the beginning of the sense that we choose our relationships, and that the relationships that we choose define us. Following this thought through, as Heidegger did, means imagining what it is to be the chooser before the choice is made, rather than just perceiving ourselves as at the receiving end of other people's choices. In reality, we never do transcend our relationships. They tie us to the here and now. Even if we are living on a desert island, we relate to our memories of parents, children, friends, lovers and many others who have shaped our emotional lives. But, by an effort of imagination, we can set aside our perception of ourselves as reactors and think of ourselves as actors. We can grasp, or nearly grasp, how we seem to others and how we help shape the world.

An existential perspective

The existential perspective can be summarized in this way. The acquisition of self-awareness is not an all or nothing phenomenon, but an accumulation of awareness, beginning first in bodily awareness, then in the different ways that others relate to us, then in the awareness of our own personality as others experience it and then in the awareness of our own finitude. Perhaps there are more 'thens' that we have yet to experience. This self-awareness makes it possible to imagine ourselves as authentic beings who transcend the matrix of social interaction in which we are always situated, and who are free to choose with whom to relate, and how to relate.

This formulation is different to the positive humanism that is often taken to be the existential stance. Park summarizes this naïve formulation neatly when he writes, 'We were all initially creatures of culture, but if we exercise our freedom, we can reshape ourselves into the persons we want to be' (Park, 2002: 32). Sartre is often claimed to be the originator of such ideas. He famously claimed that, for man, existence precedes essence:

> What do we mean by saying that existence precedes essence? We mean that man first of all exists, encounters himself, surges up in the world – and defines himself afterwards. If man as the existentialist sees him is not definable, it is because to begin with he is nothing. He will not be anything until later, and then he will be what he makes of himself. Thus, there is no human nature, because there is no God to have a conception of it. Man simply is. Not that he is simply what he conceives himself to be, but he is what he wills, and as he conceives himself after already existing – as he wills to be after that leap towards existence. Man is nothing else but that which he makes of himself. (Sartre, 1948b: 28)

Sartre, as this quotation shows, was addressing conventional ontology. He was interested in what human nature was. That existence precedes essences is an inference of the assumption that if there is no God and no creator, there can be no idea of human nature, no blue print for a human being, before the creation of a particular human being. We must therefore define ourselves once we are created. Were 'self-awareness' not such a well-established and widely used term, it would be better to call it something like 'self-creation'.

Sartre is not taking seriously Heidegger's conception of Dasein as an inter-related entity, and at this time had a very unsophisticated theory of relationships. His remarks do apply to some aspects of our developing identity. Some of our identity is ascribed to us, sometimes arbitrarily and sometimes because of our fate to be born at a particular time, in a particular place, or to particular parents. Such identities may have little relation to any intrinsic qualities in us, and Sartre and Park are right to state that we can supersede and alter them.

However, as we have seen, it is quite absurd to deny that each of us has an individual nature, an essence, long before we become aware of it. This need not imply a designer, only a blueprint. What we can make of ourselves in imagination may be limited only by the scope of our capacity to imagine our potential, but in practice we are also firmly grounded in the world. Sartre's later writings take account of his re-discovery, through Marxism, of the importance of human relationships and of the constraints that they place on our nature:

> I believe that a man can always make something out of what is made of him. This is the limit I would today accord to freedom: the small movement which makes of a totally conditioned social being someone who does not render back completely what his conditioning has given him, which makes of Genet a poet when he had been rigorously conditioned to be a thief. (Sartre, 1974: 33–34)

Both Sartre and Heidegger presumed that we are always in a state of becoming and that it is only at the point of death that we are fully determined, since we have by then completed what we are. Sartre (1943) wrote of the nothingness of being, and the nausea we experience when we accept this nothingness. Heidegger (1927) described this same feeling as that of Unheimlichkeit, a feeling of being homeless, unsettled. Heidegger suggested that we remain fallen with others as an avoidance of the anxiety we experience when facing our separateness in the world. If we can somehow tolerate that anxiety sufficiently, we can find new, more authentic ways of relating. This formulation is entirely consistent with both attachment theory and temperament theory. Both give an important place to anxiety, and suggest that many of our difficulties in relationship arise because we react to anxiety and not to the reality of the relationship. Heidegger, however, considers anxiety to be what allows us to experience our individuality and sees anxiety as a major factor in us achieving separateness and authenticity.

Anxiety is subjectively indistinguishable from fear. Kierkegaard's (1844) distinction between the two is based on the object of the two emotions: anxiety is fear of the future, of freedom or boundlessness, in other words fear of nothing, whereas fear is always the fear of something concrete. Fear may tell us in a relationship that it will turn out ill for us if we pursue it further, and we should certainly heed such instincts. Anxiety, too, may be an indication that however much we want to be close to another person, we may not at that moment be able to stand the refashioning of identity that would be required. If we are to sideline anxiety or fear as indicators of when to withdraw from relationship or when it is safe to get closer, what guide do we have?

Many existential writers suggest that there is no guide, and that it is best to cultivate self-sufficiency and only tackle relationships when one is safe from the perturbations they may cause. Kierkegaard formulated this as being resistant to being absorbed in the crowd. He wrote: 'A crowd . . . in its very concept is the untruth, by reason of the fact that it renders the individual completely impenitent and irresponsible, or at least weakens his sense of responsibility by reducing it to a fraction' (Kierkegaard, 1851: 112).

First, Kierkegaard thought, one had to become an individual in one's own subjectivity, capable of standing firmly between the poles of infinity and finitude and take full responsibility for one's own existence, before relating to others from such a strong foothold in reality. There are, he wrote: 'The Two Ways. One is to suffer; the other is to become a professor of the fact that another suffered' (Kierkegaard, 2003: 150).

Sartre's notion of the 'look' is similarly negative. It led him to the infamous dictum that 'hell is other people', demonstrated so poignantly in his play *No Exit* (Sartre, 1943). Sartre's theory of human relations posits that we are always threatened by the presence of the other, since the other tries to capture our being in the same way in which we try to capture the other's being. Others are our potential jailors and we, according to Sartre, are in a constant battle to either oppress or be oppressed. Like Nietzsche the other solution Sartre saw was that of withdrawal from relationships all together. His three levels of relation are therefore sadism, masochism and indifference. This is a rather grim list, which effectively deals with what we have called competitive relationships, or the power dimension of relationships.

Marxism also assumes that human relations are dominated by the oppression of the proletariat by the owners of capital, but does not attribute this to human nature but to the competition of scarce resources. Marx (1848) considered that the historical inevitability of oppression can be interrupted by a political process, the 'dictatorship of the proletariat' which would distribute resources equally between all and lead to a new basis of cooperative relationships between people. Sartre turned to Marxism in his later life, and his bleak emphasis on power as the basis of all human relationships in *Being and Nothingness* (Sartre, 1943) became tempered by the additional possibility of human relations of cooperation. This led to him discussing the importance of generosity, mutuality and reciprocity in human relationships that are to function in a positive way. Even so there is not a lot of room in his descriptions for the old fashioned notion of love.

An alternative view

All of the existential authors whose works have been discussed in the previous section were men. De Beauvoir takes men to task for being obsessed with a project, a project that seeks to take something or someone in the world as an object (Beauvoir, 1989). This is, according to de Beauvoir, what makes men experience themselves as a self, as we might now say an agent. But since the object of the male project is often another person, and usually a woman, it also makes others into 'the Other' whose identity is fixed in, and limited by, the project (ibid.). Although de Beauvoir was writing particularly about what men did to women, her formulation applies to any one-sided relationship. Its epistemological origins lie in Hegel's (1979) master–slave dialectic and also in Buber's (1923) writings on relationship.

Buber made the well-known but not always understood distinction between I–It and I–Thou relationships. I–It relationships are those where 'I' behaves towards another person according to the use that 'I' can put the other person to. They are a relationship based in the same asymmetry of relationship as the master–slave relationship. Buber notes that by treating the other as an object I become an object myself.

I–Thou relationships, as Buber described them, are not driven by any project other than to experience the other as an 'I'. We may change or develop as a result of such relationships, since treating the other as 'I' creates a different relationship which makes room for myself as a 'Thou' to the other's 'I'. The way we change is therefore based on the interaction, rather than being determined by any project we have for ourselves. Buber's characterization of the I–Thou relationship is very similar to Binswanger's formulation of the dual mode of relating (Binswanger, 1963) or to some of Hegel's descriptions of intersubjectivity. Ultimately, if enough people could relate as I–Thou, Buber thought that relationships would extend into what he called 'community', which is a sense of collaborative unity in which all human beings gain a greater sense of purpose and of reality. For Buber this is only possible because the Thou that we address is always God and by relating in an I–Thou way we become ourselves related to God.

Kierkegaard spoke of love in exactly the same way, especially in his book *Works of Love* (Kierkegaard, 1847), where he argues that we have to love God and the universal before we can love another. He discusses the need for understanding before love can become a reality. He is aware of the confusion of definitions of love that are given by different people, since, as he puts it, love covers a multitude of sins. The humanistic/existential authors Fromm and May have both written books to discuss the complexities of love. Clients in psychotherapy still find *The Art of Loving* (Fromm, 2000) and *Love and Will* (May, 1969) useful books to read when they want to understand their relationships. Both authors make the distinction between different sorts of love. They list Libido, or sexual love, Eros, defined as the love that leads to procreation and creation, Agape, which is the love of the welfare of others, and Philia, which is friendship or brotherly love. Fromm, in particular, insists that giving is an essential part of any form of love. He also argues that it always needs to include elements of care, responsibility, respect and knowledge as well (Fromm, 2000: 28). May saw the necessity for will and determination to be combined with love if love were to have any real power and benefit.

Tillich's writing about love was the inspiration for their work and he argued that love was the drive towards the reunion of the separated (Tillich, 1954), which is essentially a Platonic view. For Tillich it was most important that the three principles of Love, Power and Justice were united in a personal relationship.

He considered that creative justice in relationship requires people to be capable of three elements, namely listening, giving and forgiving (ibid., 84).

Jaspers struggled with the actuality of love and commitment in a very direct and exemplary way. Although he was not Jewish himself, his wife, Gertrud, was. They had the misfortune to be living in Nazi Germany and Jaspers was dismissed from the university for his mixed marriage. He responded with calm and suffered the dangers together with her. Most people ostracized them and Jaspers recognized that this response was a typical reaction of lack of responsibility-taking for what was happening to him and other people at that time. Jaspers recognized the tragic dimension of much of human relating in this and wrote about it in his diary as follows: 'One cannot blame the individual person for this. It is a basic component of our existence that can only be broken through by exceptional people' (Erhlich et al., 1986: 536). When in their despair Gertrud offered to leave him so that he would no longer be persecuted, Jaspers discovered that the relationship between them was worth far more than freedom or his career and that this special way of being committed to loving another is a precious thing indeed.

> Everything would lose its substance if a separation such as what Gertrud proposes were to be ascertained by me as reasonable, permissible, possible. Then indeed, there would be nothing serious left in the world. A person is human only if he, at some point, stands up for something at the risk of his whole life. (Ibid., 541)

Heidegger's distinction between authentic and inauthentic ways of being and relating seem to pale into insignificance by comparison. Heidegger (1927) shows how Dasein, amongst other things, is always in relation to others. This Mitsein, or being-with-others, starts out as a state of fallenness with other people. This means that we are inclined to relate to ourselves and to others in an anonymous fashion. We are inauthentically in the mode of the 'They–self'; we act with self and others as we imagine others would act. In this state of anonymous relating we will tend to hide in gossip, curiosity and ambiguity. In relation to others we will tend to jump in for others and make decisions for them, rather than jumping ahead of the other and revealing the whole of the possibilities available and rendering Being back to the other in a kind of non-intrusive generosity. It is often forgotten that Heidegger took the view that the inauthentic way of being with others was a precursor to an authentic way and that it remained connected to it. This obviously raises questions about the potential for lasting authenticity in relationship. '*Authentic Being-one's Self* does not rest upon an exceptional condition of the subject, a condition that has been detached from the "they"; *it is rather an existentiell modification of the "they" – of the "they" as an essential existentiale*' (Heidegger, 1927: 130). In other words, we are so fundamentally in relation that our authentic being is in fact always an expression of the way in which we relate to others.

Levinas (1987) went even beyond this view by proposing that the other should become the centre point of our existence. The primacy of the other is illustrated by the fact that the other will always in some way continue to be a stranger for me. Our ethical relationship to the other is therefore paramount.

'Access to the face is straightaway ethical' (Levinas, 1987: 85). Perhaps this is most relevant to the therapeutic relationship, which is of course also an ethical relationship, with a relative stranger to whom as therapists we have to accord primacy. The quality of the therapeutic relationship is an important determinant of psychotherapy outcome, but it has proved surprisingly difficult to identify exactly what it is about the therapeutic relationship that matters. In particular, it does not seem that positive feelings alone are enough. In fact, the application of relationship theory to psychotherapy has been surprisingly disappointing (Derlega et al., 1992). As existential psychotherapists, we might argue that this is because enough attention has not been given to intersubjectivity. There is some empirical evidence for this. In fact it appears that therapists who 'approve' of their clients have better outcomes than therapists who do not.

Case illustration

Bob and Ellen are a couple who are both in their early forties. They come to see the therapist (Emmy van Deurzen) for joint therapy because their relationship is floundering and they are unable to get as much from each other as they need. They have two teenage children, who are both in secondary school and are doing relatively well. Bob and Ellen are both aware that the children would rather spend time with their friends, playing games on their computers or watching music television than to contribute to the family life in an active manner. They know that these young people are almost self-sufficient and will fly the nest in a few years time. Bob resents his children's freedom of movement and often refers to what he calls their 'state of blissful ignorance of the pressures of real life'. Ellen admits to envying her daughter for 'entering the best years of her life', whilst she perceives herself as having come to the end of her own reproductive life and therefore, in her mind, the end of her life as a woman.

Ellen is quite preoccupied with her appearance and works as a beautician. Bob is an IT department manager in a large company and often travels for his work. On these occasions Ellen arranges to go out with her girlfriends, whom she has known since she was seventeen. They like to go to clubs, where younger men chat them up and they 'have a good laugh'. Ellen is keen to maintain this youthful commitment to partying, but feels that she is increasingly pushing it, since she has passed the forty mark. Bob does not like her going out with her girlfriends and there have been a number of occasions where Ellen has received unwelcome phone calls from young admirers, which has driven Bob into a rage and has led to explosive fighting. Ellen claims that Bob goes out on his travels and that he chats up women in bars occasionally. Bob denies this and says that even if it were so that would not make Ellen's behaviour all right. The level of communication between the couple is primarily that of fighting and point scoring. Each is clearly frustrated about the other's behaviour, but instead of communicating about this and admitting their needs and expectations of each other their frustration comes out as reproach and embattled competitiveness. There is a definite 'anything you can do I can do better' feel about the relationship. The couple's project at best seems to outwit each other and if possible to control the other, or at worst to annihilate each other. When this is pointed out to them they are momentarily stunned and lost for words. Suddenly they realize they have a common problem and that there is something fundamentally wrong with the relationship between them. They discover that the only times they agree with each other is when they are both exasperated about their children's irresponsibility. They use discussions about the children to come closer, but unfortunately this is almost inevitably done at the expense of the children, who become the object of disapproval. They can both see that this is gradually undermining their relationship with the children as well.

Some of the initial sessions are spent on working out these basic strategic facts about the couple's interactions, mainly to draw their attention to the way in which they operate rather than trying to make them change anything about it. Then there is some focus on their negative interactions with the children and from here it becomes fairly easy to get them to work as a team in considering what the joint objectives are in relation to the children's further education. This leads to lots of disagreements and more expression of bitterness about their own waning youth, but it also begins to open up the ontological considerations they have thus far studiously avoided.

There are moments of severe confrontation and disagreement about whether or not the goal in life is to have as much 'fun' as possible. Ellen at first believes that this is her perspective on life, but soon realizes that she fears it is Bob's and that her outings with her girlfriends are very much about competing with his male freedom and his unattached status when he is on his journeys. It turns out that she resents his trips and is highly suspicious of what he might get up to, but has preferred to rival with him and beat him at his own game, rather than become a homebound, grudging and nagging wife. Bob continues to deny that he does anything that Ellen would disapprove of if she were there with him and eventually his bluff is called and they decide that Ellen should come with him on some of his trips, since the children can very well stand to be alone and she only works part-time anyway. She claims that if she could feel that he wants her there and they could chat together in the car and go out together in the evenings then she would no longer feel the need to get dressed provocatively (mutton dressed as lamb, says Bob sneeringly) and go clubbing with the girls.

What transpires from this experiment is that Bob and Ellen are surprisingly happy together when they can stop fearing the other's desertion. They realize that they need each other and that they want more rather than less from each other. They also realize they actually really enjoy each other's company. They begin to articulate their previous way of relating as 'having been lost in chasing their youth'. They work out a fundamental agreement on the following points.

1. They have been competing with the children and each other to try and retain their youth.
2. They have lost track of what they really wanted for themselves and with each other.

3. They value closeness and commitment more than they had dare think for themselves or expect from the other.
4. It is a relief to be able to openly admit to each other that they have been afraid of losing out in the relentless competition with the other.
5. It is a wonderful experience to feel that they might be able to have a cooperative relationship in which they actually enable and support each other.
6. They discover that there are many things they value above and beyond their previous pursuit of youth and enjoyment.
7. They make a new commitment to each other and discover that being engaged with each other in a more real way makes them feel renewed as individuals as well.
8. On the strength of their new discoveries they change their tack with the children from being slightly rivalrous and controlling to being much more cooperative and supportive.
9. The atmosphere in the home changes in many unexpected positive ways, which reinforces their sense that they are on the right track.

In the final analysis it is by reconsidering the values they live by and their experience of their interpersonal reality that Bob and Ellen are able to come to new decisions about themselves and their joint way of life.

Comment

Working with Bob and Ellen could have focussed on their needs in relationship, taught them to make more positive and fewer negative comments, or considered the systemic strains of their changing family structure. What the therapist did, however, was to ask Bob and Ellen to reformulate what kind of life each of them wanted for themselves and with each other. They had increasingly fallen into defining themselves in reaction to their perception of the other person so that this took them some time to do. But the therapist was confident that there was truth in the existential presumption that each of us is able to lift ourselves out of the push and shove of everyday relationships and think about what kind of person we want to be. Bob, as it turned out, did not want to have the lifestyle of the predator that Ellen thought that businessmen aspired to, and Ellen did not want to be a flirt, although Bob had assumed that she got a lot of satisfaction from knowing that she could still 'pull'. Each of them had increasingly lived the life that the other feared that they wanted. They had each fallen into an inauthentic way of being driven by their fear of ridicule or lack of understanding if they should articulate what they really wanted.

Critical considerations

Existential work with relationships has not been developed or written about very much and much needs to be done to clarify this kind of joint existential investigation. In many ways existential work with groups or relationships is an obvious application of the philosophical ideas. If human existence is always in relation, then it follows that relationships are a privileged arena for existential work. There is here a huge need for more evidence and a tremendous lack of resources currently available. Much of our own work is with couples and families and aims at understanding the way in which individuals relate to themselves through each other. Such work needs to be documented more carefully. Research needs to be carried out on how personal and interpersonal disposition, mood and decision-making interact with people's values and beliefs. We need to come to a better understanding of people's concrete ontic interactions and relate them to their ontological conceptions and their sense of meaning and purpose. We also need to understand better how different modes of relating affect individual freedom and success of relationships. There needs to be research comparing existential work with couples to other forms of couple therapy.

Further reading

Buber, M. *Between Man and Man.*
Laing, R. D. *Self and Others.*
May, R. *Love and Will.*
Sartre, J. P. *No Exit.*
van Deurzen, E. *Paradox and Passion in Psychotherapy: Existential Perspectives on Therapy and Counselling.*

CHAPTER 15

Families

NAOMI AND ANTHONY STADLEN

> Till This Moment, I Never Knew Myself
>
> Jane Austen, *Pride and Prejudice*: 285

Introduction

Existential thinking on families has a fine tradition to build on. Insight into family relationships is not new. Stories from many different cultures record a wealth of such insight, existential in all but name. For example, many stories describe what happens when parents favour (or disfavour) one of their children above the rest. In *Genesis* (25.28), Isaac and Rebecca have twin sons: 'Now Isaac loved Esau, because he did eat of his venison; and Rebecca loved Jacob.' A complex story unfolds from this. Shakespeare shows in *Richard III* how Richard was a disfavoured son, a trouble to his mother, as she tells him (Act 4, Scene 4), from birth onwards, presumably unlike his brothers. In *Pride and Prejudice*, Austen (1990 [1813]) points out that Elizabeth Bennet is her father's favourite, while Lydia is her mother's. In *Jane Eyre*, Brontë (n.d. [1847]) introduces Jane as an orphan, who was frequently compared unfavourably with her cousins, with whom she lived, like a sibling. In each story, the adults try to impose on the child their own, sometimes contradictory, views of who the child is, or should become. However, the child gradually discovers the moral and existential imperative to seek to transcend this constriction of his or her being. As Elizabeth Bennet cried (Austen, 1990 [1813]: 285[1]): 'Till this moment, I never knew myself.'

This rich tradition takes it as self-evident that the individual is indebted to his/her family but has the task of moving beyond it. Family influence is not seen as 'linear causality'. Rather, traditional stories imply that an individual encounters crises, which offer a challenge to transcend the family heritage.

Psychotherapy has drawn from this tradition. Freud acknowledged the great novelists and playwrights as his precursors. He revered the book *Moderne Geister* by the Danish literary critic Brandes (1923 [1882]); and, as it

133

contains various references to Kierkegaard, Freud probably read Kierkegaard himself. Freud wrote his case histories, he said, 'like novellas' (*SE* 2: 160),[2] to illumine 'the relation between *Leidensgeschichte* and *Leiden*' (*SE* 2: 138). *Leiden* ('suffering') was the patient's complaint, the 'symptoms'. *Leidensgeschichte* ('suffering history') was the existential 'passion narrative' that the 'symptoms' concealed and the 'talking cure' revealed (Freud, *SE* 2: 30, 40), like a deeper 'archaeological' layer (*SE* 2: 139), but still phenomenological, 'beneath' the 'banal' known history (*SE* 2: 144). Kierkegaard (1988 [1845]: 185) used the equivalent Danish word *Lidelseshistorie* as subtitle of the section ' "Guilty?"/ "Not Guilty?" ' in *Stages on Life's Way*. This 'passion narrative' centred on the patient's family relationships, from childhood on. For example, Freud's early 'Katharina' case (*SE* 2: 125–134) is *his* narrative of how, starting from Katharina's complaint of headaches and breathlessness, he helped her tell *her* 'passion narrative': she had discovered her father having sexual intercourse with her cousin, and had herself been sexually molested by her father. Freud claimed Elisabeth von R.'s leg pains hid her 'repressed' love for her dead sister's husband (*SE* 2: 135–181), and Dora's hoarseness, *hers* for her father's friend, Herr K., who had sexually molested her with the tacit permission of her father in exchange for sexual favours from Herr K.'s wife (Freud, *SE* 7: 1–122; Stadlen, 1989 [1985]). Freud's search for the 'passion narrative' was in principle existential and phenomenological (Stadlen, 2000); but sometimes the narrative, and perhaps the passion, was more his than his patient's. He opened up the phenomenological study both of families and of 'unconscious phantasy', but tended to discount his perception of family interactions, replacing it with merely 'assumed' 'unconscious phantasies' he attributed to his patients. Freud thus effected an opening and a closure (Stadlen, 1989 [1985], 2003a). Both have had a profound influence.

Jung (*CW* 5: 274–305) wrote of 'The battle for deliverance from the mother'. The Jungian analyst Layard (1944) sought to help a teenage girl by facilitating change in her whole family through analysing her mother's dreams.

Other psychotherapists studied whole families, and tried to 'treat' the 'illness' of the individual by so-called 'family therapy' of their family. They made valuable findings (Haley and Hoffmann, 1967; Handel, 1968; Jackson, 1968a, b; Framo, 1972). But the family was described as a 'system' (Haley, 1967; Sonne, 1967; Jackson, 1968a [1957]; Minuchin, 1974; Weichert, 1975), or as an 'organism' (Bowen, 1960: 346), with its own 'family pathology' (Whitaker, 1958: 208; Bell, 1967; Haley, 1967; Jackson et al., 1968 [1961]: 233; Fleck, 1976: 211; Sander, 1979: 82). Szasz (1961), however, insisted that 'mental illness' is a 'myth'. And Laing (1962: 13) wrote: '*Family pathology* is an even more corrupt concept than individual *psycho*-pathology. It simply extends the unintelligibility of individual behaviour to the unintelligibility of the group.'

An existential perspective

Understanding families is not an optional extra for existential psychotherapists or for those who consult them. The quest to understand how one has responded to one's family of origin, and to transcend it, is at the heart of any existential search for self-knowledge.

Ludwig Binswanger is regarded as the 'father' of 'existential psychiatry'. Psychiatry has always used compulsory intervention. But we understand by 'psychotherapy' a voluntary, contractual relationship between consenting adults, as defined by Szasz (1965). Binswanger threw some light on the relevance of families, but introduced some confusion. He wrote phenomenological analyses of his 'schizophrenic' patients' 'worlds'. He described Jürg Zünd's 'upstairs world' (with his parents), 'downstairs world' (with his grandfather, aunt and uncle) and 'street world' (Binswanger, 1957a [1946–47]; Sadler, 1969: 300–312; Sonnemann, 1999 [1954]: 223–228). But Binswanger (1958 [1944–1945]) made next to nothing of his own data showing Ellen West's family's interference with her personal relationships. As Laing (1982: 55) points out, 'it is not clear whether [Binswanger] ever puts two and two together' to ask if her experience of the 'swamp-world', 'grave-world' and 'ethereal world' might be her despairing response to her family's invalidation of her, which she perhaps lacked the insight or courage to transcend.

Binswanger himself divided human being-in-the-world in general into three 'worlds': *Mitwelt* ('with-world'), *Umwelt* ('around-world'), and what he called *Eigenwelt* ('own world') (Binswanger, 1942: 428). But he appears to have misunderstood Heidegger's term, *Mitwelt. Mitwelt* is not just one 'world', or 'dimension', among others. As Heidegger says (1962 [1927]: 155; our translation and brackets): 'The world of Da-sein is *with-world* [*Mitwelt*]'. We are always already in the world with others. *Mitwelt* needs no supplementing with *Umwelt, Eigenwelt, Überwelt* ('overworld', to make room for spirit) or *Unterwelt* ('underworld', to allow for Freud's and Jung's findings) for the simple reason that it includes them. Even 'private' modalities of experience, such as dream, imagination, sexual desire, 'unconscious phantasy', memory, transcendental experience, are modalities of our being-in-the-world-with-others. Being-in-the-world with others is not one 'dimension' of being human. It is what being human *is*.

Max Scheler, an early pupil of Husserl, wrote (1954: 247): 'Imbued as [the child] is with "family feeling", his own life is at first almost completely hidden from him.' Heidegger said (2001 [1987]: 163; our translation; the American translation omits the second sentence altogether): 'The child is absorbed in the comportment of the mother. It is absorbed in the ways of being-in-the-world of the mother. It is exactly the opposite of having introjected the mother.'

Medard Boss and Gion Condrau, who studied with Heidegger, acknowledged in their case studies the relevance of family 'upbringing' (Boss, 1963 [1957], 1983 [1971]; Condrau, 1998). Boss wrote (1983 [1971]: 236; our translation): '. . . with no single patient can one speak of his being schizophrenic *per se*. Rather, one must always ask: schizophrenic under the excessive demands of what pattern of human relationships?' But this still begs the question of what 'schizophrenic' means.

Heidegger liked talking with 'schizophrenics', and doubted that they were medically 'ill' (Wiesenhütter, 1979: 158; Stadlen, 2003b: 173–175). He revered the poetry of the allegedly 'mentally ill' Hölderlin (Heidegger, 2000 [1981]) and Trakl (Heidegger, 1971a [1959], 1982b [1959]). However, in a 1965 Zollikon seminar, while discussing critically a case study of a 'schizophrenic' by Franz Fischer (1930), Heidegger (2001 [1987]: 51–54) was silent on Fischer's report (1930: 249–252) of an 'unexpected' visit to the 'hospitalized' patient by his father (see also Stadlen, 2002: 169; 2003b: 173–175; 2003c). The patient says:

> I don't know you. Are you the father? ... He looks like my father, but false and not real, perhaps made of mist or painted air, a great deception against me ... How long have I been here? ... Perhaps I've already been here longer than my father is actually old ... (Fischer, 1930: 249–250; our translation)

Fischer analyses the patient's alleged 'disturbance' of 'thought' and 'space–time structure', but does not consider the possibility that the patient might be stating accurately what he feels about his father. Fischer mentions the patient's 'internment' in the 'institution', but not the father's necessary role in this. He does not say how the father related to his son, or what *he* said to *him*. Heidegger, Boss (1983 [1971]: 228–231), Stern (1983: xix–xx) and the 'phenomenological' psychiatrist Minkowski (1970 [1933]: 288–289) all discuss this case of Fischer's at length without mentioning the father or the son's 'internment'. This is the standard psychiatric tradition.

Yet Sartre had already published *Saint Genet*, a lengthy existential analysis of the writer Jean Genet, in which he sought to discover Genet's 'original project', the fundamental existential choice he had made in childhood as a way to live his family situation (Laing and Cooper, 1964: 65–90; Sartre, 1964b [1952]). Sartre had discussed the principles of existential analysis of the 'project', anticipating his later work on Flaubert, in *Search for a Method* (Laing and Cooper, 1964: 49–64; Sartre, 1968 [1960]: 85–166).

Moreover, Bateson et al. (1956) had hypothesized that the interactions in families of individuals diagnosed as 'schizophrenic' would be characterized by the 'double bind', which they defined as an incongruity between a communication and a metacommunication. The hypothesis was derived from observation of individuals, *not* of their families, but subsequent family studies tended to confirm the prediction (see also Jackson, 1968b; Berger, 1978).

As Laing wrote (1969 [1961]: 129), the work of Bateson et al. '*revolutionized* the concept of what is meant by "environment"'. But Laing anticipated Scheflen's 1977 criticism (Berger, 1978: 97) that Russell's (1956 [1908]) theory of logical types was 'not the best language' in which to describe the 'double bind', to which Bateson responded, 'Maybe not...' (Berger, 1978: 97). Laing himself (1969 [1961]: 145–153) analysed how Raskolnikov, in Dostoevsky's *Crime and Punishment*, is driven frantic by contradictory attributions and injunctions in a letter from his mother, the day before he commits his murders.

Almost all family studies still presupposed the existence of 'schizophrenia'. It was regarded as an 'illness', to whose 'aetiology' family interaction was a possible contributing factor (Lidz et al., 1965). The family itself was often described as 'sick' (Jackson and Satir, 1961: 265). The one exception was *Sanity, Madness and the Family*, by Laing and Esterson (1970 [1964]). This book built on the work of the Bateson group and other American family studies, but was also informed by the existential tradition, including Sartre's *Critique of Dialectical Reason* (1976 [1960]), and Szasz's *The Myth of Mental Illness* (1961). It reported the findings of Esterson's research on the families of eleven 'schizophrenic' women. He pioneered the method of phenomenological study of all subsets of each family. The case studies, containing extracts from his tape-recorded interviews, make ordinary human sense of the women's experience and behaviour. The book reveals as each woman's *praxis* (Laing and Cooper, 1964; Sartre, 1976 [1960]) her intentional, intelligible activity, what the psychiatrists saw as 'signs' and 'symptoms' of an unintelligible *process*, a medical-type 'illness', 'schizophrenia', 'inside' the person.

For example, one of the women, Mary Irwin, aged twenty, explained (Laing and Esterson, 1970 [1964]: 211–214) that her mother would 'just go on and on'. 'She seemed to stop me from thinking.' 'Tell you what I do, I sort of go rigid so nobody can get at me.' What the psychiatrists saw as her 'catatonic' behaviour, the outcome of a meaningless 'schizophrenic' process, was simply Mary's intelligible, intentional act of self-protection, her understandable, purposeful praxis. Mary's sister confirmed this, both in the book (Laing and Esterson, 1970 [1964]: 214–215) and to us four decades later (interview with A. Stadlen, 1 August 2001) after Mary's death (see also Esterson, 1976).

In *The Leaves of Spring* (1970), Esterson studied in-depth one of the families, the Danzigs, shifting the focus from the daughter, Sarah, to the family itself. He showed that the Danzigs saw Sarah as 'sick' for seeking autonomy rather than 'ontic security' and 'alterated identity' (concepts derived from Heidegger and Sartre, respectively). Their family 'harmony' was an appearance of harmony, their 'religion' a search for respectability. They saw Sarah's 'thinking' and serious reading of the Bible as caused by the 'illness' they thought she had.

These existential-phenomenological case studies by Laing and Esterson show in straightforward detail who is saying and doing what to whom. The families' use of language to define the being-in-the-world of the 'patient', by invalidation, mystification and subtle ambiguity, is made crystal clear (see also Hopkins, 1967; Laing, 1971).

This is a fundamental advance on the vague, stereotypical summaries of patients' families in Boss's case studies, for example. It is curious that, despite Heidegger's dictum that language is 'the house of Being' (1982a [1959]: 5, 21–28; 1998a [1947]: 239), the Daseinsanalysts have neglected this field.

There is a noble philosophical tradition of thinking on the so-called 'intersubjectivity', better called 'being-with' (Heidegger, 2001 [1987]: 111) or 'Thou–Thou relationships' (Heidegger, 2001 [1987]: 210): Kierkegaard, Feuerbach, Husserl, Scheler, Stein, von Hildebrand, Heidegger, Ebner, Rosenstock, Rosenzweig, Buber, Marcel, Sartre, Merleau-Ponty, Macmurray and

Levinas. But this is not enough. The fine detail revealed by Laing and Esterson attunes psychotherapists to aspects of an individual's *Leidensgeschichte* that Freud, Jung, Binswanger and Boss did not focus on.

This is *the* proper field of study for existential psychotherapists. It goes to the heart of how an individual can adopt a false or untenable existential position in relation to others under the influence of some of those others.

Claire Church was diagnosed as a chronic, institutionalized, 'paranoid schizophrenic'. Laing and Esterson's complex analysis of the interaction between her and her mother is no academic exercise (1970 [1964]: 83–89). Claire told us four decades later (interview with A. Stadlen, 3 January 2001) that her discussions with Esterson, individually and with her mother, had enabled her to leave hospital and pursue a satisfying career.

Recent writing (Goldstein and Doane, 1985; Tompkins, 1995; Alanen, 1997) offers a bland, 'interdisciplinary' approach to 'schizophrenia' and the family, endorsed by many 'existential' psychotherapists, for example, Yalom (1995a). This approach sees 'schizophrenia' as an 'illness', and 'family therapy' as a 'technique', ancillary to compulsory clinical psychiatry, to 'improve the course of the disease' (Tompkins, 1995: 334). Such writing either ignores Laing and Esterson's work or implies that it has long been assimilated and surpassed. In our view, Laing and Esterson's work has not been understood. The chronologically later writing is, existentially, a retrogression.

Most clients who seek psychotherapy are explicitly struggling to make sense of their family relationships, past and present. Some clients are at first preoccupied with other relationships; but their own attempts at understanding usually lead them spontaneously to start reconsidering their family relationships from earliest childhood on. It is the responsibility and privilege of existential psychotherapists to develop a discipline to help clients in this quest.

The case study that follows illustrates the way we work, which is informed by these principles. The study has been intentionally written in everyday English, which is a language overflowing with existential and phenomenological insight. Although we have not used the terms we have just been discussing, such as 'praxis', 'process', '*Mitwelt*' or '*Leidensgeschichte*', we hope the reader will have no difficulty in seeing how these are exemplified in the case.

Case illustration (by Naomi Stadlen)

Lucy, aged thirty-two, sought counselling because she could not decide whether to let her small son continue breastfeeding at night. She said that her head 'told her' that a boy of eighteen months should be weaned and made to sleep in his own bed, whereas her heart disagreed. But she did not trust herself to decide because, she said, 'I keep feeling that something deep down is terribly wrong with me. It's a very familiar feeling'. All kinds of everyday situations would evoke this feeling. Lucy would feel distressed until the feeling wore off.

At first, it sounded as though Lucy's difficulties related entirely to the present. The task of counselling seemed to be to help Lucy explore the conflicting logic of 'head' versus 'heart'. Yet this seemed premature. Lucy preferred to talk about weekly events that troubled her. Nor was it helpful to encourage Lucy to experience the full anguish of feeling 'terribly wrong'. She seemed oddly relaxed in her distress. It might therefore have been possible to challenge her calm as a form of resistance, which prevented her from engaging more fully in life and in her counselling. Was Lucy in bad faith, going through the motions of having counselling while remaining untouched? The evidence did not support such an interpretation. Lucy always came on time, and usually wanted to discuss a current problem. She seemed to be 'voting with her feet', and for some time that seemed to be all she could manage.

Like most clients, Lucy talked spontaneously about her parents and her childhood. At one session, Lucy said she had 'nothing to say'. 'Really nothing?', I asked. She replied: 'I feel I've said everything already.' I asked: 'When did you say it?' She explained that her mother had been visiting, and had followed her in and out of rooms, talking constantly. 'Is that when you said everything?', I asked. Lucy suddenly realized that she herself had hardly said anything. Her *mother* had done the talking. 'When she talks, she never stops, and I can't hear my own voice', she said. She was shocked to realize this and wondered whether she really had any voice of her own. 'I never have my own opinions', she said. 'When something new happens, I have to ask other people what *they* think. I haven't got an opinion of my own.' She was in despair and could not imagine speaking with her own voice.

To reach this realization took more than a year. Most of what I did was to listen, remember and ask questions to help her to explain what she meant. So that, even while she said that she seemed to have no voice of her own, she was struggling to voice her difficulty. Talking to me like this was a new venture for her, and her 'heart' felt it was right, while her 'head' accused her of 'navel-gazing' and fruitless introspection.

Even so, she needed a long time before she felt ready to say any more about her statement that 'there must be something terribly wrong with me'. What seemed to make this so difficult was the corollary it implied: that if there were not something wrong with her, then there would have to be something wrong about her parents, and therefore about her entire perception of life which she had based on theirs. Lucy said that her parents presented family life to her as 'a beautiful picture'. 'I bought their picture', Lucy said. At first, the idea of radically questioning this picture was so far-reaching that Lucy preferred to doubt herself, even if this meant devaluing countless contradictory feelings and observations of her own.

Lucy described her parents as a highly educated and cultured couple, so she could find plenty of evidence to confirm the 'beautiful picture'. In her childhood home, anything that did not fit into this picture was simply never acknowledged. For example, she told me: 'I was expected to be good at school'. Yet, even in the first class, because her parents only acknowledged some perceptions but not others, Lucy, when five years old, felt a nameless and terrifying confusion about what she was 'supposed' to perceive. She was afraid to learn, she was terrified that this meant there was something wrong with her, she was puzzled that other children were apparently so at ease, and she felt in despair at failing her academic parents. She settled for pretending, and created the impression of an intelligent and well-adjusted child, as good a match as she could manage to the parental picture.

Dramatic events occurred in the family story. However, Lucy's difficulty lay in finding the words to substantiate her continual sense that something was 'terribly wrong', even in her most ordinary and everyday interactions. As her family did not talk about conflict and difficulties, Lucy had no vocabulary that she could use to help hold on to her feelings.

She would often describe her small son's 'difficult' behaviour. However, when we discussed how he might feel, his 'difficult' behaviour made sense. This led her to compare his childhood with hers. Her parents had not listened to her feelings in her childhood or even thought that she had any. Now she started to reconsider some of her own previously devalued childhood observations and feelings. I used to suggest possible reasons why she might have felt as she did, and then she, with integrity, would separate what 'feels absolutely right' from what, as she politely put it, '*might* be right'. Slowly, her own feelings and observations began to connect together as crucial parts of her whole coherent story. This gave her a completely different picture of herself. Slowly she started to rethink everything, her entire 'picture'. She also wanted to make sense of her parents, and their parents, in this new way. She was fascinated that so much made sense, but was shocked at how much the parental picture had left out. Often, the 'beautiful picture' would seem so much more attractive than the untidiness of her own honest feelings and observations, and she would succumb to the seductive pull of thinking that, after all, there must be something terribly wrong with herself.

However, connecting together her honest feelings enabled her to feel more whole. Even her failures of memory made sense. 'I suppose there's a lot I don't remember because it didn't feel like me', she observed. Once she saw how she had settled for pretending, as a child, to be someone she was not, she kept noticing how much she was still living that pretence as an adult. But, because she had started to value her real feelings and observations, the old pretence felt intolerable. Connecting with her past gave her the understanding to face difficult moments when she chose to transgress an unspoken parental prohibition, and to take responsibility for her own perceptions. This gave her a voice that was distinct from her mother's. However, her voice had no language. She wanted to voice ideas that she had been taught to overlook as a child. It was her lack of vocabulary that made it so easy to think that 'there was something terribly wrong with me'. She felt she had a vacuum where everyone else seemed so articulate. Slowly, she began to use simple words to address interpersonal difficulties that arose with her husband and children. The question of 'head' versus 'heart' seems to have resolved imperceptibly, as she began to respond as a more whole person. Her husband (whose childhood family she described as having its own methods of avoiding confrontation) overheard Lucy having an honest dialogue with their son, and commented to Lucy: 'I like the way you talk.'

Critical considerations

Family interactions are complex. Yet, once a client starts to understand them, details fall into place, and the client is freed to decide how to use this new understanding.

'Existential' psychotherapists often do not understand what understanding is. They see their clients' attempts to understand as a search for 'linear causality'. They disdain questioning and attending to detail. Yet Heidegger said (1977a [1954]: 35; our translation): 'Questioning is the piety of thinking.' And (1961 [1953]: 172): 'To know how to question means to know how to wait, even a whole lifetime.' Therapist and client need patience and perseverance to question, until the detail reveals its existential meaning. This cannot be learned from books or taught in modules. Trainees need to explore, through truly existential psychotherapy, their own family experience. Few 'existential' training therapists or supervisors have attempted this themselves.

It can be a shock to examine one's interactions, and to see, as both Elizabeth Bennet and Darcy recognized, how one's apparently clear perceptions may be utterly warped by the restrictions of one's family outlook. Both Elizabeth and Darcy felt ashamed when they first took moral responsibility for their actions. Both despaired of one another's love, because of their new understanding of their earlier actions. Jane Austen shows that their love for one another depends on their new self-knowledge.

'The novel', wrote D. H. Lawrence (quoted by Leavis, 1965–1966: 7), 'is the highest form of subtle inter-relatedness that man has discovered'. Will the insights of existential psychotherapists into family relationships ever be good enough to challenge this claim?

Acknowledgement

We are grateful to Professor Thomas S. Szasz for his constructive comments.

Notes

1 In Volume 2, Chapter 13; or, in some editions, Chapter 36.
2 We give references to standard English translations where available, but the translations we give are our own.

Further reading

Note: Readers may be surprised that most of our recommended reading stems from the 1960s and 1970s. Present-day writing ignores or patronizes these works without, in our view, understanding them. As we stated at the end of the section 'An existential perspective', the chronologically later works are, in existential terms, a retrogression.

Anon. 'Toward the Differentiation of a Self in One's Own Family'. In J. L. Framo (ed.)
    Family Interaction: A Dialogue between Family Researchers and Family Therapists.
Hopkins, J. *Talking to a Stranger: Four Television Plays.*
Laing, R. D. and Esterson, A. *Sanity, Madness and the Family: Families of Schizophrenics.*
Olsen, T. *Tell Me a Riddle.*
Tolstoy, L. *Anna Karenina* (especially Part 2, Chapters 1–3).

CHAPTER 16

Groups

DIGBY TANTAM

> I live alone, entirely alone. I never speak to anyone, never; I receive nothing,
> I give nothing...When you live alone you no longer know what it is to tell
> something: the plausible disappears at the same time as the friends. You let
> events flow past; suddenly you see people pop up who speak and who go
> away, you plunge into stories without beginning or end: you make a terrible
> witness. But in compensation, one misses nothing, no improbability or, story
> too tall to be believed in cafés.
>
> Sartre, *Nausea*: 14–15

Introduction

People from time immemorial have come together in groups at moments of
change or existential crisis; for funerals, for weddings, for rites of passage
and for exorcisms. These groups are formalized by a prescribed ceremonial
or ritual, and the participants have prescribed places as officiants or witnesses.
There is no doubt that powerful emotions are released on these occasions,
and social changes are initiated that may have profound and long-lasting effects.
Healing rituals exist in many cultures, and have usually been assimilated into
the prevailing religion that derives the healing power from divine authority
and provides a ceremonial that structures the group process.

The modern therapeutic group differs from such healing ceremonies in
that it is autochthonous. Its power comes from inside the group, not from
outside, and its structure is fluid and newly created. Mesmer (1733–1815)
may be credited with inventing the modern therapeutic group. Mesmer often
treated patients in groups. The group members would be sitting in a circle, each
holding a cord joining them to a central apparatus, the 'baquet'. The effectiveness of this treatment, it can now be seen, was not due to 'animal magnetism'
as Mesmer thought, but to the group situation itself, which created a state of
suggestibility in the members of the group and gave Mesmer a particularly
strong influence over them. In its most extreme form this state continues to
be known by the term that Braid, an early exponent of the medical use of
Mesmerism, coined: 'hypnotic' or 'hypnoid' state. Two things about the hypnotic

state were clear from the beginning: that people in this state could be influenced to do or feel things that they would not normally do or feel, and that the hypnotist therefore had power over them whilst they were in a trance.

Participation in groups may lead to a suggestible state similar to hypnosis, and group participation, like hypnosis, can lead to self-destructive behaviour and open group members up to exploitation by an unethical group leader. Janis invented the term 'groupthink' in the 1970s to apply to the failure of rational decision-making in groups (Esser, 1998) due, as he saw it, to the subjugation of individual judgement by the group. This term refers only to the cognitive consequences of group immersion, but it has an immediacy that alternative terms lack. Leadership that taps into the powerful influences that Mesmer described has been variously termed 'charismatic' or 'transformational' in recent literature, and compared to 'transactional' leadership in which there is a rational contract between leader and led (Bass, 1997). Charismatic leadership was the term that Lieberman, Yalom and Miles gave to a particularly leader-centred style in encounter groups (Lieberman et al., 1973).

The same concerns that have been felt about charisma in the setting of hypnosis have also been felt about the charismatic group leader. The evil hypnotist is a stock villain in films and thrillers, but so is the crime boss or provocateur who incites the mob or the crowd. Unscrupulous charismatic leaders present a danger to authority, and to the established order. Even worse than the orchestrated mob is the rabble, the crowd that has no authority and no leader. Canetti in his masterwork, *Crowds and Power* (Canetti, 1981), argued that the French Revolution introduced this modern kind of crowd, which was no longer brought together for a religious purpose, but so that its members could 'experience for itself [it=the crowd] the strongest possible feeling of its own animal force and passion and, as means to this end, it [it=the crowd] will use whatever social pretexts and demands offer themselves' (ibid., 22).

An existential perspective

Kierkegaard shared Canetti's dislike of crowds, even extending the scope of the word to include what we would nowadays call the general public and the press. He wrote,

> There is a view of life which conceives that where the crowd is, there is also the truth, and that in truth itself there is need of having the crowd on its side. There is another view of life which conceives that wherever there is a crowd there is untruth, so that (to consider for a moment the extreme case), even if every individual, each for himself in private, were to be in possession of the truth, yet in case they were all to get together in a crowd – a crowd to which any decisive significance is attributed, a voting, noisy, audible crowd – untruth would at once be in evidence. (Kierkegaard, 1846: Dedication)

Nietzsche had a similar view of truth:

> We still do not know where the urge for truth comes from; for as yet we have heard only of the obligation imposed by society that it should exist: to be truthful means

using the customary metaphors – in moral terms, the obligation to lie according to fixed convention, to lie herd-like in a style obligatory for all. (Nietzsche, 1954: 47)

What Kierkegaard and Nietzsche object to in groups is their capacity for being the supports and proselytizers of a unified authority. Because of groupthink and the influence of a charismatic leader, group participation ensures that the members of the group have the same attitudes and opinions as the leader. Groups – or rather social institutions – support that authority and uphold its views as truth. Kierkegaard's suspicion of authorities or majorities, which claim to determine what is, or is not, true, finds an echo in modern philosophers. D'Agustino writes, for example:

> Perhaps the Foucauldians and post-modernists are right in claiming that notions of legitimacy are inherently and inescapably themselves instruments of power, rather than 'rational' alternatives to force. Certainly, if there is no public conception of public justification, any regime is 'legitimate' only given a conception of legitimacy that is itself controversial, and hence can be imposed only by force – not by the inducements of 'reason' (in this context it is worth noting that Sartre's later work – Critique of Dialectical Reason – speaks of cooperation and the need for groups to overcome the seriality of relationships). (d'Agustino, 1997)

The rabbles of which Canetti wrote are inimical to authority, and the authorities are also the enemies of rabbles, but rabbles can be as tyrannical to individuals as can social institutions. In a rabble, as in an authoritarian society, someone wanting to go a different way either has to carry the group with him or her, or run the risk of being excluded, shamed, pilloried, or even attacked. However, in a society there are checks to the extent to which an outcast is punished. These checks do not exist in a rabble.

Given these dangers, why should people want to form groups at all? Some groups are no more than task-orientated associations. People join these to undertake tasks that require the pooling of resources, and as soon as the task is achieved the group can dissolve. They require little sacrifice of autonomy, and what loss they do demand is easily recompensed by the task. However, joining more permanent social institutions – even becoming a member of society – does require a greater loss of autonomy. Both Heidegger and Sartre thought that group members were repaid emotionally for this sacrifice. For Heidegger, society offers a seductive anonymity and averageness, which can be absorbing. Heidegger (1998) wrote of this 'absorption in . . .' that it has mostly the character of 'Being-lost in the public-ness of the "they"'. Dasein, being-there, is exposed to the anxieties of choice, of responsibility for the consequences of past actions, and of contingency. Falling into the world takes away these anxieties because a person who is absorbed in the world feels herself or himself to have no choice, but to be going along with the crowd. For Sartre, society offers spurious identities that, like theatrical costumes, we can put on and play at being a character. This is attractive because we can never fully realize who we are, and living in such a way as to fully realize this freedom, and in such a way as to fully accept our responsibility for being who we are is disturbing.

Although Sartre's language and his starting point are different from Heidegger's, their conclusions about socialization are similar. Being someone only because one exists for someone else, becoming an en-soi, is very similar to what Heidegger calls living as Das Man. It is to turn away from what one might have been and adopt a more limited kind of being, a kind of existence that Sartre calls living in bad faith and Heidegger, living inauthentically. And it is the siren call of the group that makes both bad faith and inauthenticity so alluring.

Sartre's and Heidegger's viewpoints are, perhaps, extreme. Van Deurzen argues that there should be a balance between authenticity and inauthenticity and that what matters is that one can move between them (van Deurzen, 2002b). Nietzsche also had another viewpoint on the group. He argued that it was held together by ressentiment of what was noble and individual (Nietzsche, 1998). There are many strands in Nietzsche's argument, some of which we would now consider 'elitist'. His main point that groups may deliberately restrict themselves to stave off envious feelings is, however, an important one. The cost is that anyone who is outside the group is denigrated and humiliated. If the outcast accepts this judgement of the group, they become shamed and hide, so ensuring that they no longer threaten the members of the group.

The caricature of existentialism is that as groups are bad for us, we should do without them. According to this caricature, existentialism is an individualistic philosophy in which each person must ignore what others expect of them, and make decisions and choices for themselves, willingly accepting the anxiety that follows and considering it not as a danger signal but as an intimation of freedom. In fact, the history of existential philosophy demonstrates that living one's life in this way is not easy, and past examples are not encouraging. Kierkegaard rejected the social station that had been prepared for him. He turned against organized religion so fully that his followers disrupted his funeral service because it was being conducted by a pastor. Their action became so notorious that Søren was an infamous name in Denmark for many years. Laing who, with Cooper, introduced existential thinking into psychiatry in the UK similarly broke free of the normal social expectations placed on a psychiatrist and psychoanalyst. His spectacular rise to fame led, as Kierkegaard's had, to an equally profound eclipse associated with exclusion from the very groups that had lionized him previously. Neither Nietzsche nor Heidegger fared much better.

Building blocks for an understanding of groups

There is clear recognition in existentialism of the power of groups, and particularly of their emotional power. There is a strong assertion that group participation demands a price in independent thinking, consistent with what Janis called groupthink. Existentialism emphasizes the importance of each person's recognition of their fundamental autonomy, and few existentialists have therefore addressed either groups or leadership. Yalom has done so, but his approach to groups is Sullivanian rather than existential. Sartre also did so, in the *Critique of Dialectical Reason*, which has the subtitle (in the English translation): the theory of practical groups.

Sartre started from the observation that all of us treat groupings of people – he called them 'ensembles' – as a reality in ordinary life. We know where to stand to show we are in a bus queue, and when we glance at a street, we recognize people who are queuing, people who are chatting, people who have just left the cinema and so on. Sartre also supposed that we have an unreflective capacity to recognize what Durkheim called 'solidarity' and contemporary group theorists might call 'cohesion'. The least cohesive ensembles were composed of strangers, like the bus queue. Their ruling principle was 'alterity': the creation of barriers that served to show that whilst one was with others, one was not of them. Sartre called this ensemble a series. Getting together with people with whom one has a relationship is different. Then one works not to create a barrier but to maintain the relationship, a principle that Sartre called 'reciprocity'. Gatherings are a series in which one or two people have a relationship of reciprocity to every other member of the group, and can therefore act as leaders. However, the other group members remain as alters to each other. Gatherings may, however, fuse into groups, as each group member establishes some reciprocity with the other. Once a group is fused, or formed, it may give itself a pledge, and this often requires some sort of division of labour. The pledge also introduces the notion of group commitment since members' actions can be judged against whether or not they have worked as they have pledged to do. Pledged groups may fold as they fulfil their pledge or they may find other pledges, and work towards maintaining themselves to fulfil a series of pledges by creating a self-sustaining organization. At first, these pledges may have no relationship to each other, but once a relationship between them develops – for example, that each pledge is just a manifestation of representing a profession or a trade – then a social institution is formed. The members of this institution may now be a series, because it is the reciprocal relations between the pledges of the institution that turn it into an autonomous group.

Sartre's classification was designed to lead up to a definition of class, the 'ensemble of ensembles', the totalization of all the constituent series, groups and institutions. This definition is perhaps of less importance for us than Sartre's concept of the reciprocity that forms a glue between members in a group. The principles of reciprocity are:

> (1) that the Other be a means to the exact degree that I am a means myself...(2) that I recognize the Other as praxis...(3) that I recognize his movement toward his own ends in the very movement by which I project myself toward mine; and (4) that I discover myself as an object and instrument of his ends by the same act which makes him an object and instrument of mine. (Flynn, 1984: 112)

None of Sartre's principles touch on the emotional consequences of group membership, although these emotional consequences seem at least as fundamental as Sartre's principles of alterity and reciprocity. David Hume observed that

No quality of human nature is more remarkable, both in itself and in its consequences, than that propensity we have to sympathize with others, and to receive by communication their inclinations and sentiments, however different from, or even contrary to our own . . . A good-natur'd man finds himself in an instant of the same humour with his company; and even the proudest and most surly take a tincture from their countrymen and acquaintance. A cheerful countenance infuses a sensible complacency and serenity into my mind; as an angry or sorrowful one throws a sudden dump upon me. Hatred, resentment, esteem, love, courage, mirth and melancholy; all these passions I feel more from communication than from my own natural temper and disposition. (Hume, 1978: 316)

Royzman and Kumar (2001) quote a later passage from this same section with approval, stating that recent social psychological research has supported it in two particulars: that we are more empathic to those who we consider to be in our own groups and we are more empathic about immediate occurrences. Foulkes (1964) termed the capacity of groups to share the same emotional experience or theme 'resonance', and Bion (1961) called the states of shared feeling into which groups might fall 'basic assumptions'.

Emotional contagion may occur in all ensembles, including queues or, as we saw in an earlier section, in crowds. However, for ensembles to function effectively on tasks, there must be some means of limiting the impact of emotional contagion, otherwise the group would, like the crowd, be dominated by the most basic emotions.

Boundaries

At their very simplest, ensembles are recognizable because they have boundaries: an edge or spatial boundary and a stability of membership or temporal boundary. Establishing where the boundary is may be one of our first questions to the group, as when we ask someone 'Are you in the queue?' Once an ensemble has developed a boundary, emotional contagion may occur within it even if the relationship between ensemble members is one of alterity. The buzz that passes down a queue if the doors have been closed or the bus is full is evidence of that. However, if the buzz makes some people angry and others disappointed, the ensemble fractionates along these lines. The disappointed people turn away, and perhaps commiserate with each other. The angry storm the door, shouting and trying to get in. Divisions between opposing basic emotions like these create internal boundaries, and therefore sub-groups. Conversely, other factors that create internal boundaries lead to emotional divisions that amplify the internal boundaries. Perhaps one of the best, and most infamous, demonstration of this is the boys' camp experiment conducted by the Sherifs, in which boys at a camp were artificially divided into two groups, and loyal adherence to these groups was created by fomenting hostility between them (Sherif, 2001).

Sartre, as we have already noted, considered that group formation required the development of relations of reciprocity, but we have also noted that groups must also have some means of limiting emotional contagion. This requires that emotional responses to other ensemble members are 'differentiated'. If, for example, one member comes to a group distressed about having discovered a lump in her breast, other members must find some middle way between having no emotional reaction at all – a possible reaction only if the group has ceased to exist – or being taken over by the same death anxiety of the woman with the lump. In a well-functioning group, each group member will experience their own emotional response to the woman's experience, an emotional response that says something about themselves but is also congruent with the emotions of each other. The result will be that the group's emotional response is more complex, containing more emotional colour than the response of any one member, but still recognizably an integral emotional response.

Leadership

Sartre indicated that the leader is critical to group development because he or she is the first to establish reciprocal relations with other group members. However, leadership may also be necessary to make it possible for group members to have their own individual emotions without imperilling the integrity of the group itself. Emotional leaders may do this by finding common emotional ground, linking individual emotional experiences (Pescosolido, 2002).

Reciprocal relations can be established on a basis of mutual self-interest. Leaders of groups of this type – sometimes called 'transactional leaders' – derive their authority from an explicit or implicit contract that defines the contribution expected of each group member, and determines the rewards that each should receive for that contribution.

Transactional leaders may obtain their authority on forged credentials. They may, for example, deceive group members about the value of their contribution or the resources available to pay out rewards. However, they do not exert emotional control over those they lead. Transactional leaders are not, therefore, good models for leaders of therapy groups which aim at emotional change through relationship. Leaders of such groups are as much emotional as transactional leaders. They are therefore, in the language of management studies, transformational or charismatic leaders.

Transformational leaders become leaders because they are able to contain the emotions of the group, and make them safe. They may do that by sorting out the relationships between group members and ensuring that each respects and can work with the emotional reactions of the others. Or they may do that by manipulating the boundaries of the group, for example by expelling members who do not fit into the group 'ethos', or who are not 'good team players'.

At their best, transformational leaders aim to motivate those they lead not just to do the job, but to achieve their own full potential (Popper and Mayseless, 2003). At their worst, they can use their power to destroy other members of the group in pursuit of their own self-interest.

Popper and Mayseless (2003) take an attachment theory perspective to transformational leadership, but Bass and Steidlmeier (1999) apply existential criteria, arguing that transformational leadership that is in the interests of the followers as well as the leader is 'authentic'. Authentic transformational leadership, according to Bass and Steidlmeier, comes about if the leader is guided by the right values: a respect for individual freedom, for diversity, and for honesty rather than deception.

Towards an existential approach to group therapy

Sartre considered what happens in ensembles involving generic people, whose differing temperaments and personal experience were not taken into account. But people in reality are individual. They may resist the influence of ensembles. They may want to treat others as others, and not reciprocate. They may experience emotions that they are unwilling to share. Being unable to reciprocate or unwilling to share prevents a person from being able to make or to maintain satisfying emotional relationships with others. So these are the problems that bring people to group therapy, and because of these problems, people in group therapy resist becoming part members of a group at all.

Many group therapists consider that the single most important reason that people do not have 'goodwill' towards groups is that they fear them.

Anxiety

It is an empirical fact that anxiety sometimes creates what Whitaker calls 'restrictive solutions' in groups. However, psychotherapists of all persuasions also consider that too little anxiety allows groups to continue in pre-existing, restrictive solutions. This kind of formulation fits with early psychological experiments on task performance that show that performance is best when there is some anxiety, but not too much, about outcome (Yerkes and Dodson, 1908). Heidegger distinguishes a type of anxiety that he terms 'unheimlichkeit', 'homelessness'. This is the anxiety that comes from not taking a place in the world for granted. Experiencing umheimlichkeit is an indication that a person has cut themselves off from the comfort that comes from custom and prejudice (and therefore feels 'ill at ease'). It is an indication in a group that a person is observing or experiencing the group in a new way, and thus a possible indicator of the potentiality of change.

Dialogue

Buber, like Heidegger and Sartre, believed that there were two ways of being-in-the-world and his characterization of them is comparable to theirs. However, there is one important difference. Buber did not problematize Dasein, or le soi (the self). He simply referred to 'I'. What concerned him was how 'I' related to another person, which could be as an 'It' or as a 'Thou'.

> To man the world is twofold in accordance with his twofold attitude. The attitude of man is twofold in accordance with the twofold nature of the primary words which he

speaks. The primary words are not isolated words, but combined words. The one primary word is the combination I–Thou. The other primary word is the combination I–It wherein, without a change in the primary word, one of the words He and She can replace it. (Buber, 2003: 53)

The relationship of I–It does not necessarily involve objectification. Its hallmark is that It is experienced as a possible means to an end of I, and not in itself. But 'The human being to whom I say You I do not experience. But I stand in relation to him, in the sacred basic word. Only when I step out of this do I experience him again. Experience is remoteness from you' (ibid., 54).

Arnett (1986) suggests that dialogue has three characteristics: its participants are committed to being true to their own values rather than seeking advantage; it tries to establish common ground, however limited, where participants can meet without conflict; and it is about meaning and mutual understanding.

Buber saw dialogue as a means of creating community, and of resolving disputes or conflicts. His vision has been carried on in numerous dialogue groups and conferences, many of them developing from the work of the theoretical physicist Bohm (1990). Bohm, like Buber and Foulkes the inventor of group analysis, was meliorist. He believed, like them, that true dialogue would dissipate conflict as each person truly saw the value of the other's viewpoint, and gave up the need to use the other for personal ends. Conflict results, according to this view, with a dualistic approach to life: that the environment is other and should be treated as a means but not as an end. Bohm worked on gas plasmas at the University of Berkeley whilst a graduate student and observed mass movements of electrons that are now termed Bohm-diffusion. These movements were more orderly than expected as if, Bohm said, the sea of electrons was alive. The notion that there was an underlying orderliness to processes and that this could be discovered once they became sufficiently energetic was one that Bohm also applied to human groups. Dialogue worked because individuals naturally gather together, like electrons, into higher order collectivities when exposed to sufficient intensity. There was an implicate order in nature that, for Bohm, made it holy.

Bohm did not put himself forward as a leader whose will could be imposed on the group, nor did he believe that any established group had a monopoly of the truth. Indeed one of the groups carrying on his work has charmingly called itself the 'School of Ignorance'. Bohm's position is similar to that of group psychotherapists. Bion, for example, was once asked why he spoke so little in groups (one of the sources of his considerable impact on them). He said that if he knew what to say he would say it (Bion, 1961). Foulkes, too, writes of the group conductor needing to be the servant of the group, and not the master. Heidegger, too, seems to have come to a similar conclusion at the end of his life, although he uses a pastoral metaphor which harks back to his youthful Jesuistic training. He writes in his *Letter on Humanism*:

Man is not the lord of beings. Man is the shepherd of Being. Man loses nothing in this 'less'; rather, he gains in that he attains the truth of Being. He gains the essential poverty of the shepherd, whose dignity consists in being called by Being itself into the preservation of Being's truth. (Heidegger, 1998)

Bohm's personal experience must have given him little faith in established groups. He lost his tenure at Princeton because he refused to testify against J. Robert Oppenheimer, the leader of the team who developed the atom bomb, when Oppenheimer was investigated by the McCarthy Committee on Unamerican Activities, despite being championed by Einstein. As a result, Bohm was never to work in his native US again. For most of this career, Bohm worked in the UK, firstly at Bristol and then at Birkbeck college in the University of London, where he worked until the day of his death.

It was dialogue itself that Bohm considered had the power to heal, and this power seemed somehow holy, as indeed it had to Buber and other religious leaders before him. This confidence in dialogue itself has its parallel in contemporary group psychotherapy, too. Group analysts place considerable emphasis on 'free communication', a phenomenon that Foulkes originally described as the group equivalent of free association (Foulkes, 1964). However, it is far from saying the first thing that comes into one's head. Free communication is free of strategic concealment or deception.

One derivative of group analysis, the median group developed by Pat de Mare, has become homologous with dialogue groups. The emphasis is not on therapy but on citizenship or, as de Mare says, the focus is on the relations of participants with society and not their relation to their families (de Mare, 1991).

Conducting dialogues in practice raises issues that are familiar to everyone working in groups. Not the least of these is speaking-time allocation. Is someone silent because they are participating best as a listener, or because others are hogging the group's attention? Do a minority get most of the speaking time because they have the most to say, or because they are socially or personally dominant? One way of dealing with this is to give each person in a dialogue a certain number of units that they can spend by speaking. Each person may transfer these units, too, if they wish. A person may, for example, give his or her units to an especially good speaker if the person agrees with what the speaker says (Judge, 1994).

Each person generally starts out with the same number of units because each person is assumed to be equal to every other. This democratic assumption averts any discussion of inequality and therefore averts conflict. But inequality is fundamental to human groups, especially family groups. And where there is inequality, issues of legitimacy and authority arise. These issues are not by-products of inauthenticity or I–It thinking. They are structural, and, as Rousseau noted, they inevitably lead to conflict in the absence of an absolute or divine authority that confers legitimacy on particular social solutions. It is important to note that conflict is not just an unfortunate aspect of groups, but a valuable one, for it creates the barriers that are necessary for differentiation to take place.

Case illustration

Delia was a new member of the group. She was a bit more glamorous than many other members, and obviously well off in an understated way. Whilst she was always friendly and her responses to other group members thoughtful, they were not welcomed. In one group David said that he thought that she said things out of social graciousness and not out of real feeling. The group members had tried to find out more about Delia, but to no avail. She mentioned having a daughter who was at RADA, and having a country cottage, but nothing about her feelings. Over a period of time, Delia became more and more silent and fewer and fewer group members wanted to rescue her. Then there were two weeks when Delia had to cancel at the last minute because of 'pressing engagements'. The group leader thought that Delia's prediction, made at her original interview for a place in the group seven months before, was coming true. She would not find a place in the group, just as she had failed to fit in anywhere except at the most superficial level. The conductor even knew why this was. Delia's father had murdered her mother. This terrible secret was known to very few people, and was a source of constant shame and horror to Delia.

A day came in the group when everyone was discussing a particularly gripping and particularly horrible television programme about a man who had shot himself after he had killed his whole family. Only Delia said nothing. Although the conductor could see that she had tears in her eyes, no one else seemed to notice. The group expressed the deepest horror at the crime, and utter loathing of its perpetrator. Until one member, himself almost as isolated normally as Delia, said that he believed that the man was depressed. One could only commit a crime like that in the deepest despair, he said. He deserved the group's pity, not its execration. Someone said, 'Where would we be if we all took this same attitude? I know evil when I see it, and I detest anyone who could hurt women or children like that.' But the mood of the group had changed, and deepened. Other people said that they had known people who had been violent through a similar kind of despair. Then Jack said that his father had once suffered a serious depression, and had driven the family car, with the whole family in it, into a tree. Jack knew this was deliberate, even though it was put-down to a loss of concentration. But he had forgiven his father, who had been full of remorse for years after. Delia's crying had turned to sobbing, and the conductor asked her what she was thinking about. Through the sobs, she told her own story.

The group was silent, almost overwhelmed. But then one by one each person started talking, mainly of living with a secret or a shame. Delia's hidden emotions had finally become assimilated into the emotional life of the group.

How does this illustration link with the theory outlined in this chapter? The group when it begins behaves like the orderly society that Kierkegaard hated. Perhaps it offered a secure home to its members so long as none of them wanted to try to think for herself or himself. Perhaps its members construed group membership as group uniformity, unreflectingly thinking that this was one way of dealing with the envy that members of the group often felt for people who did not have the psychological problems that they did. Delia was superior in a certain way, and was aware of the group's resentment. However, she interpreted it in her own way, as a consequence of the shame she felt about her mother's murder. Her glamour and her upper-crust manner were her way of protecting herself, but sooner or later she knew that her secret would be out and then she was sure that the group would reject her. Although her secret did come out, it was in the context of suffering leading to violence. The group members did distance themselves from the violence that they saw around them, but the raison d'etre of the group was suffering and so it was not possible to simply reject violent men if their depression was due to violence. Having made this step, group members were willing to scrutinize angry, negative and hateful feelings resulting from depression, and even admit to having experienced such feelings within their own families. Delia was able to tell her story without being rejected as a result. Rather than being an outcast, she was a sister in adversity.

Critical considerations

Most theories of psychotherapy are not really theories at all, but speculations. The material in this chapter is no exception. However, there is clear scope for the study of group formation and maintenance from the point of view of emotional expression and using discourse analysis as a method of analysing the importance of reciprocity.

Further reading

Foulkes, S. J. *Group-Analytic Psychotherapy: Methods and Principles*.
Yalom, I. D. *The Theory and Practice of Group Psychotherapy*.

PART IV

PERSONAL DIMENSION

CHAPTER 17

Introduction to the Personal Dimension

EMMY VAN DEURZEN AND CLAIRE ARNOLD-BAKER

While the physical and social dimensions are pretty much given from the outset, the personal dimension has to be acquired by each individual. A person's sense of self develops over the years in a number of ways, through the capacities we discover in ourselves, through the things that we do, through the effect we have on others and on the world and through the things people tell us about ourselves. Some people have a much more fluid sense of self than others. Some people have a positive self image, others a non-existent or even negative self image. From a theoretical perspective existential authors contend that there is no such thing as a self, at least not a solid self. Nevertheless Heidegger spoke of the importance of being our own and of accepting our ownmost potentiality for being ourselves. Our world experience always includes a sense of mineness. We experience the world always in a specific internally felt manner that is different to the way in which anyone else experiences the world. There is a tension between affirming our own identity or letting ourselves be taken over by our relationships. There is undoubtedly a realm that we create which is private to ourselves, a world of our own (Eigenwelt), which is regulated by a sense of ownership, individuality and integrity. Heidegger distinguished sharply between inauthentic modes of existing in which we allow the world to decide for us and authentic modes of existence where we affirm our own way of being. Whilst he declared both to be equally important and necessary, he also showed the authentic mode of existing to be only gradually achieved with much effort and insight. Clients move through various levels of self-awareness. It is important to observe where each client is at.

1. First we discover simply that we are. This can be surprising. Am I really me and not somebody else?

2. Then we discover that we are who we are. We discover that we are separate and different to everyone else, while noting that although we may share qualities with others, we are at the same time different. This discovery is a pleasant

one if the qualities we come to claim as our own are positive, but it may be less pleasant if we feel like disowning what is attributed to us.

3. What we experience is a particular and personal experience. We are alone and no one will ever quite feel the same way we do. This is the mystery of recognizing our individuality. Siblings growing up in the same family environment will have different experiences of the same events.

4. People can only learn to accept the things that define them when they begin to reflect upon them. Thus they can learn about their nationality, language, family name and first name. They begin to formulate their own evaluation of what is important to them and why.

5. What people say to us about our character and our personality does have a bearing on how we come to identify ourselves. Gradually we find out, reading between the lines, that we have some good and some not so good characteristics. With further reflection and understanding this may lead to our finding out about perfectibility and duty, while acknowledging that perfection is an unreachable goal. It may also lead to our questioning whether we want to take on board all these identities bestowed on us, or perhaps claim some others, so far withheld from us, but achievable perhaps through our own efforts.

6. In this process we discover the boundaries of our freedom. Wanting to assert our own wishes we find we have to deal with other people's needs. We may also realize we fear freedom and prefer to carry on with set routines or copy others not wanting to be individuals.

7. Experiencing the anxiety that comes with standing out as a person in our own right can be hard. It can be a tall order to be seen and heard without flinching and without shame. Finding our own mind and our own voice is another challenge. Even then it is never certain that this identity and this voice are any more real than the identities and voices we have not chosen or been allotted. Through all these personal explorations we soon find out how we hide ourselves and how we avoid the situations we feel vulnerable in.

8. Therapists may need to help clients to strike a balance between being able to assert themselves and efface themselves, between claiming their selfhood and merging with others or with the world. They may also help clients in formulating strengths and weaknesses and in making the most of both.

9. Coming to terms with this dimension will also lead to understanding the dependency, independence, counter dependence and rebellion people experience in relation to others. Sorting out our own position in the world clarifies our stance. Interdependence might be the most realistic option for being oneself with others.

10. This often means we have to discover the experience of loneliness and isolation as well as the positive side of aloneness, since coming to terms with ourselves requires a bit of solitude. Of course if a person is inclined to be in solitude most of the time, this may need to be balanced by a more outgoing position.

11. As we gain more ease on the personal or psychological dimension, we learn to value what is good and positive about us and put it into context with

the drawbacks of our personality. Finding a sense of direction and selfhood that can be affirmed for the good of those around us as well as for ourselves is not a bad objective for therapy.

12. Meanwhile, the existential questioning of the idea of selfhood will continue to provide fuel for the potential changes in identity that can be effected through reflection and over time. People can change completely according to where they live, what they do, who they keep company with and what they aspire to. There are, however, other aspects of a person that appear to become more established and less open to change as time goes by. These are usually related to the physical givens of the person's bodily existence.

13. To be flexible in our experience of ourselves as we change and mature over the years and kind to ourselves in our fallibility and limitations is probably another worthwhile goal for work on this level.

This part of the book focuses on the personal dimension and it is with a chapter on an existential view of self (Chapter 18) that we begin this part. Existential philosophy has a particular view of the self, that it is fluid and flexible, and this view is explored in the chapter and put into the context of everyday living.

There follows a chapter on authenticity (Chapter 19); an important concept for existential philosophers but equally important for everyday living as it is often thought of as a goal, something to strive for, to become who we want to be and how we want to live our lives.

However, striving for authentic living will undoubtedly mean experiencing anxiety, which is as much part of human existence as the air that we breathe. The chapter on anxiety and engagement (Chapter 20) will show the importance of anxiety to existential thinkers and demonstrate a way in which clients can be helped to face their anxieties and use them creatively.

Depression is also as much a part of everyday existence as anxiety, both of which can be experienced in varying degrees. Therefore the chapter on depression and apathy (Chapter 21) will elucidate an existential perspective and way of working with depressed clients.

Bereavement (Chapter 22) is a crucial chapter in this section as it deals with an issue we all have to face at some point, the loss of a loved one whether by death or rejection. How we deal with this loss and the loss of self it inevitably involves will impact on the way we feel about ourselves and the way we conduct our future relationships.

For existential practitioners the dreaming life is as important as our waking existence and therefore we can gain a deeper understanding of ourselves and the way we live our lives through examining our dreams. The chapter on the phenomenology of dreams (Chapter 23) will put forward the existential approach to dream work and its application to clinical practice.

CHAPTER 18

The Self

EMMY VAN DEURZEN AND CLAIRE ARNOLD-BAKER

> What's a man's first duty? The answer is brief: to be himself.
>
> Ibsen, *Peer Gynt*, IV–1

Introduction

Traditionally the self has been defined 'in the sense of the *personality* or *ego*, regarded as an agent, conscious of his own continuing identity' (*Penguin Dictionary of Psychology*, 1978: 262). The existential view of self is significantly different to this. From an existential perspective there is no such thing as a substantial or solid self. What we experience as our self or our identity is always a process of becoming and transformation. Selfhood might be best defined as the dynamic and ever-changing experience of being at the narrative centre of gravity of one's particular world experience.

The self has been conceptualized in a number of different ways by different authors but outside the existential domain it is usually seen as something substantial and enduring, something that is active in the world. The biological view of the self emphasizes the role of genetics and evolution and suggests that an individual's personality is tied to the body and inherited through our genetic make-up.

The psychoanalytic perspective proposes that the self is a dynamic process made up of three components, the id, ego and superego. The way in which these processes interact to form the self is determined by developmental experiences in early childhood, which allow us to transit through the psychosexual stages. The way in which the child confronts the conflicts at each stage will affect its ability to resolve conflicts later in life.

Carl Jung, although influenced by Freud, felt that human experience consisted of polarities, which together made up ego functioning or the self. The dominant polarity of introversion/extraversion determines an individual's experience, according to Jung. However, Jung thought that the polarities thinking/feeling and sensing/intuiting were also important.

Object relations theorists like Melanie Klein emphasize the importance of early relationships with others in developing a sense of self. The two assumptions that underlie this theory are that a person's way of relating is determined by interactions in early childhood and that these patterns are fixed and reoccur throughout a person's life.

Erik Erikson's psychosocial perspective sees the self as developing through eight distinct stages each involving a crisis to be overcome, either positively or negatively. At each stage the individual acquires attitudes and skills to make them an active member of society. The stages, which cover the lifespan from birth to old age, put challenges to the individual and require him or her to resolve specific conflicts at each step of the way. Many of the established personality theories include elements of existential struggle, yet they tend to assume that the self as it evolves becomes a fairly solid entity.

An existential perspective

With the existential approach a whole new idea of selfhood emerges. The dictum 'existence precedes essence' (Heidegger, 1927; Sartre, 1943) introduces the notion that people have to live first and discover who they become out of what they have created for themselves later. Because of this, most existential authors share in common the assumption that selfhood is something that cannot be taken for granted and that it is always in transformation and question. Their description of selfhood takes different forms and there is a definite evolution towards a less-and-less defined sense of self from author to author.

Kierkegaard

Kierkegaard's conception is that the self is a relation and a synthesis of opposing tendencies. 'Man is a synthesis of the infinite and the finite, of the temporal and eternal, of . . . [possibility] and necessity, in short it is a synthesis. A synthesis is a relation between two factors. So regarded, man is not yet a self' (Kierkegaard, 1980b: 146).

The self is created through living with these tensions of life. Human life is a struggle between seeing things in new ways, in relation to the infinite, while at the same time respecting the facts, the finite. It also involves holding together the many possible versions of 'me' that are conceived by the imagination and which are based on what I am now. The future 'me' will be a result of the relationship between the imagination or possibility on the one hand and necessity on the other hand. This process of definition of selfhood evolves over time. Kierkegaard calls the changing self that gets older and has experiences, which colour it, the 'temporal aspect'. The eternal element on the other hand represents not only the constancy of the self, my continuity, but also my true self.

Within these paradoxes of life there is an unavoidable tension. This tension, which is what we experience as anxiety, stems from the fact that man is a free being. However, it is through the activity of living with these tensions and paradoxes that a self is eventually created. The refusal to accept this challenge leads to the opposite of anxiety, namely despair.

By standing up to ourselves and facing our own challenges we are able to be true to our self, that is, not to avoid being our-self nor trying to create a self different to what we are. Kierkegaard believes that fundamentally there is an aspect of unity that does not change; however, there is also a pluralistic aspect of human nature, which allows for an inner dialogue and ultimately a dialogue with God. Kierkegaard's definition of self is as follows:

> the conscious synthesis of infinitude and finitude that relates itself to itself, whose task is to become itself, which can be done only through the relationship to God. To become oneself is to become concrete. But to become concrete is neither to become finite nor to become infinite, for that which is to become concrete is indeed a synthesis. Consequently the progress of becoming must be an infinite coming back to itself in the finitising process. (Ibid., 29–30)

For Kierkegaard then the self is a constant process of creation in the tension of opposites and with the potential threat of not succeeding in this self-creation of what we truly are.

> Yet every moment that a self exists, it is in a process of becoming, for the self κατα δυναμιν (in potentiality) does not actually exist, but is simply that which ought to come into existence. In sofar, then, as the self does not become itself, it is not itself; but not to be itself is precisely despair. (Ibid., 30)

In other words, the endless struggle with the paradoxical aspects of selfhood has to be endured if we are not to succumb to a bottomless pit of despair. The self will always continue to be in movement, since it is a tension between opposing tendencies and an equilibrium that has to be rebalanced over and over again. Kierkegaard recognizes a number of stages on life's way that we can progress through or resist (see also Chapter 5). He saw people as being nothing but vegetative creatures to start with, only to discover an aesthetic way to be alive, mostly in a hedonistic fashion, following our senses. This is followed by an ethical way of being a self, which is essentially to adjust our selfhood to the requirements of society and some higher authority. After this we may achieve the capacity to think for ourselves when doubt sets in. This doubt leads eventually to an experience of abandonment and this can only be overcome through taking the leap of faith into a spiritual way of being. In a spiritual mode of existing, people's selves become truly individual as they engage fully with the realities of life and the infinite possibilities that God holds. Thus we make ourselves real by living in the tension between finite and infinite.

Nietzsche

Nietzsche shares Kierkegaard's view that self is a process and a creation. He believes that this process is an active part of living, but for him this process is one that involves power and assertion rather than the balancing act that Kierkegaard described: '*Will a self.* – Active, successful natures act, not according to the dictum "know thyself", but as if there hovered before them the commandment: *will* a self and thou shalt *become* a self' (Nietzsche, 1977: 232).

For Nietzsche then, somehow people have a will to power and an ability to assert themselves long before they create a self. Rather than building his understanding of human beings on the notion that they are balancing mechanisms, his idea is that freedom and power are the decisive factors in what human beings achieve for themselves. How is this possible? It is quite simply because Nietzsche puts the emphasis back on the power of the human body, which generates the will to power that he describes. In this, Nietzsche is the forerunner of psychodynamic instinct theories, although he overcomes the divisions of personality that such theories create by firmly positing the oneness of mind, body and soul:

> The Self is always listening and seeking: it compares, subdues, conquers, destroys. It rules and is also the Ego's ruler. Behind your thoughts and feelings, my brother, stands a mighty commander, an unknown sage – he is called Self. He lives in your body, he is your body. (Nietzsche, 1961: 62)

Heidegger

Heidegger takes a rather different view, approaching human existence from an ontological rather than an ontic perspective. He was interested in describing the essential givens of human existence. Heidegger rejects the concept of self. He speaks instead of Dasein[1], or human being and sees this as an entity, which is always in relation to others and to the world. Neither existence nor human being is ever fixed. Human beings are always open to change, always open to possibilities. They are in fact defined as openness and possibility and therefore also as care.

> Understanding of the world, as understanding of Dasein, is self-understanding. Self and world belong together in one being, Dasein. Self and world are not two beings, as subject and object, also not as I and you, but self and world are – in the unity of the structure of Being-in-the-world – the fundamental determination of Dasein itself. (Zimmerman, 1981: 27)

Heidegger describes a number of ontological characteristics of Dasein that determine it to some extent. First, there is *mineness*: the fact that the world that I experience is always mine and not anyone else's. More importantly there is the central concept of *care*, the fact that Dasein is always concerned about its relationships with others and the world. The world matters to Dasein, because it is intrinsically connected to it. Dasein is not a substance but a potentiality that projects itself into the future and onto the world. Heidegger argues that I am not a self just because I am able to reflect on myself. For Heidegger, my self is revealed when I reflect on my interaction with beings in the world, 'I learn about what it means to be human from the very activity of being human' (ibid., 29).

Dasein can exist in either an authentic or inauthentic mode of being, which will affect its openness to life and experience. The way in which we understand ourselves in the average everyday mode of existence is as 'they-self'; we look at ourselves in relation to other people and in doing so we look for the similarities and differences between us. We become nothing more than one of them.

> The Self of everyday Dasein is the *they-self*, which we distinguish from the *authentic Self* – that is, from the self which has been taken hold of in its own way . . . As they-self, the particular Dasein has been *dispersed* into the 'they', and must first find itself. (Heidegger, 1927: 167)

One way in which Dasein finds itself is through the experience of Angst or anxiety. Anxiety makes us feel unsettled and we are not able to keep our minds on the activities we use to cover up our mortal freedom. Anxiety can either make us flee into inauthenticity by distracting activities and entertainment or it can help Dasein become more authentic.

> And because Dasein is in each case essentially its own possibility it *can*, in its very Being, 'choose' itself and win itself; it can also lose itself and never win itself; or only 'seem' to do so. But only in so far as it is essentially something which can be authentic – that is, something of its own – can it have lost itself and not yet won itself. (Ibid., 42)

Heidegger's description shows selfhood to be elusive and something that cannot be thought of in essentialistic terms. Dasein needs to be ready to be free for its ownmost potentiality for being, which is something that includes its mortality, its limitations and its death and this will inevitably bring anxiety: 'Being free *for* one's ownmost potentiality-for-Being, and therewith for the possibility of authenticity and inauthenticity is shown with a primordial elemental concreteness in anxiety' (ibid., 191). This anxiety is crucial for Dasein to come into its own, away from the sway of the They. It is only when this process of authentication or rather of ownership begins to happen that we may begin to think of Dasein as becoming authentically and resolutely capable of being ready for its potentiality of being. This potentiality of being is, however, still not to be thought of as a self, but rather as a constant moving forwards into the future with an awareness of past and present as well. This process also makes Dasein aware of its position in relation to the world of things, or the ready-to-hand and the existence of others. Therefore Dasein, when authentic, is a process of relation to the world it finds itself thrown into.

> Resoluteness, as authentic Being-one's-Self does not detach Dasein from its world, nor does it isolate it so that it becomes a free-floating 'I'. And how should it, when resoluteness as authentic disclosedness, is *authentically* nothing else than *Being-in-the-world*? Resoluteness brings the Self right into its current concernful Being-alongside what is ready-to-hand, and pushes it into solicitous Being with Others. (Ibid., 298)

Sartre

Sartre's starting point is that existence precedes essence and that fundamentally we are nothingness and pre-reflective consciousness. What Sartre means by this is that we are not concrete selves in the same way that objects are. He makes radical distinctions between things that are beings-in-themselves and consciousness, which is being-for-itself. In other words there is a big difference between objects that are solidly determined to be what they are on the one hand and people who are self-determining freedom on the other hand. Sartre posits that we can only exist in the moment and that we are in a constant process of change. We cannot take our selves for granted and have to create ourselves anew every day. We are not the person we were ten years ago, nor are we the same person that we will be ten years from now. As we move into the present we transcend our past self and it becomes an object of our consciousness in the same way as material objects are. This is possible because there is a gap between the past self and the present self and also between the present self and future self. It is this idea that nothing stands between the present self and the future self that causes anguish. 'The anguish *is me* since by the very fact of taking my position in existence as consciousness of being, I make myself *not to be* the past of good resolutions *which I am*' (Sartre, 1943: 33).

Sartre introduces the idea of human agency and asserts that people are free to choose and this freedom obliges us to create and re-create ourselves and to be responsible for our choices. Hazel Barnes (Barnes, 1990) has distinguished four stages in Sartre's self as it develops in action. First, there is the pre-reflective cogito of pure intentionality, when we merely act in the world without any reflection upon what we are or even that we are. Secondly, there is the self as ego, which develops out of the feedback others give us about our actions in the world. Thirdly, there is the self as value, when we begin to shape our selfhood in the way that we choose and want to be. Finally, there is the embodied consciousness of the person who lives wholeheartedly, fully bodily immersed in the world and yet wholly aware of his or her own existence and actions. Sartre believes that we deny our possibilities for becoming fully embodied consciousness by acts of bad faith, with which we pretend to be more or less than we actually are. What we actually are is a nothing trying to be a something. Therefore we are constantly changing and continually in a state of flux. 'in fact the *self* cannot be apprehended as a real existent; the subject can not *be* self, for coincidence with self, as we have seen, causes the self to disappear' (Sartre, 1943: 76).

Buber

Buber's notion of a self, which only exists in a relational context, is highly compatible with existential thinking. For Buber (1970), I only become myself as I relate to the other. There is never purely an I on its own. There is only ever the 'I' of the I–Thou or the 'I' of the I–It. The hyphen between us is crucial. Everything takes place in relationship and encounter. The 'I' is in the in-between that people create and therefore the way in which I relate to the world ultimately determines who I am. Although Buber favours the I–Thou relationship as one where the other is fully seen and related to rather than merely used, ultimately the I needs to define itself both in relation to an It and in relation to a Thou. Without the I–It I cannot live, but without the I–You I am not fully human.

Laing

Laing's notion of the divided self (1960, 1961) was instrumental in making people rethink the established notions of self. Laing's work was inspired by a Sartrian perspective and showed how in some circumstances people can manipulate their sense of selfhood in relation to others in order to acquire greater safety. His concept of the false self is very similar to Sartre's idea of bad faith: it is a mask behind which I hide. Laing's observation that in such circumstances there were three main anxieties, that is, the fear of engulfment, implosion and petrification, showed that it was possible for a person to be taken over by others to the extent of experiencing a complete annihilation of self. Although Laing applied these categories to schizophrenia, it was clear that he intended to show that people in general can experience a kind of death of self in this manner. In this he prefigured an existential understanding of the relativity of selfhood, which is now fundamental to existential psychotherapy.

Towards an existential view of self

In summary then existential philosophers reject the idea that the self is solidly constructed. Rather we are temporal beings. We are a process of becoming, rather than objects in the world. Kierkegaard speaks of self as a synthesis of paradoxical tensions. Heidegger believes that there is no self but only a continual connection to the world, being-in-the-world. Tillich similarly argues that in order to become a self we need the 'Courage to be' (Tillich, 1952), whereas Jaspers sees individuals as existing in existential communication, existing as freedom, 'I am responsible for myself and yet only in being free do I discover who I am' (Friedman, 1996: 151).

However, while rejecting the notion of a fixed concept of self, these existential authors do recognize that it is difficult for individuals to live authentically or in good faith. Primarily, because the responsibility of our own freedom causes us too much anxiety, there is also an aspect of being human which wants to confirm itself and have others confirm it too, this is often most easily achieved by conforming to the norm or other people's expectations. As Friedman states, no one can really escape from playing a role and at some point there is: 'the sense of incongruity that comes when one part of oneself is consciously "role-playing" while another part looks on and asks whether one can, in all good faith, identify oneself with this role' (ibid., 169).

There are ways in which individuals overcome the anxiety of their freedom. Van Deurzen comments on how individuals try to create continuity by recommitting 'themselves daily to the same sort of things, ideas, people, notions, concepts, beliefs, memories, as the day before' (van Deurzen, 1998: 39). However, van Deurzen highlights the paradoxical nature of this daily process of connecting with others, the world, ideas and so on; on the one hand it is 'indispensable to our survival' (ibid., 39) and yet at the same time causes 'an unnecessary encumbrance which complicates our lives' (ibid., 39). Therefore the very things that give us our identity are also the things that prevent us from seeing our own freedom. The very things that make us secure may stop us continuing to be alive in the tension of opposites out of which we have to construct an ever-changing selfhood.

Case illustration (by Emmy van Deurzen)

Parisa's experience illustrates the struggles with selfhood well. Parisa is a young Iranian woman who comes to therapy because she is unable to cope with the demands of her children and the tensions of her marriage to a British man. She is very anxious and often incapable of even leaving her house to go shopping or pick the children up from school. Although she is in her early thirties she says she feels she has hardly had a chance to grow up and is still a child at heart. She thinks she has never found out who she really is, because too many people have pressurized her into being what they thought she should be. She says she only feels like a real person when she plays with her two daughters. When she plays with her little girls and their dolls she can just do what feels right to her and she does not have to hide the emptiness inside. She complains of having no satisfactory sense of herself at all and she cries as if she is heart-broken by this state of affairs.

She has been in the UK for many years and has adopted a British way of life. She says this with a kind of pride even though she contradicts the statement by adding that she has never really found herself in the culture. In fact it has been hard to raise her children the British way, because she has no role model of how a British woman is supposed to raise her kids. She feels rejected by her in-laws and experiences her husband as treating her with disdain. She claims that he considers her to be a nuisance and that he takes no interest in her emotional pain. She is afraid that he is having affairs with other women, seeing her as an acquired asset and wanting her to stay at home and raise the two girls without making a fuss about anything. She just cannot do this anymore. This, she thinks, is because she feels too humiliated by the way in which her husband treats her.

When the therapist remarks that Parisa must have a good sense of who she is and how she deserves to be treated by others if she feels humiliated by her husband, Parisa begins to speak of her pride in being a liberated woman. Indeed she had to do battle with her own parents and brother to liberate herself from many of the cultural restrictions of Iranian culture before integrating into the UK culture and marrying a British husband. She felt very strongly about wanting to do so, and modelled herself on her London school friends, who came from a variety of different cultural backgrounds and who formed a strong group around her. During her teenage years and early twenties she felt very much alive and knew what she wanted: to be a free woman and live an emancipated life in Britain. Ironically after having achieved what she wanted and having become the free woman she had aspired to be, she now feels enslaved. Parisa dissolves into sobs when she recognizes the contradictions in her situation. Somehow the point of maximum pain and anxiety has been touched. She has put her finger on the crux of the contradictions in her life. It is not difficult from here to help her express her experience of the struggle for freedom and remind her of her deepest aspirations. She discovers that her daughters have replaced the friends who used to make her feel supported and who confirmed her identity as a rebel and freedom fighter. It is only with them that she feels safe. Somehow her husband's attitude towards her has robbed her of the belief in herself and in her right to be who she feels she is capable of being. He has no idea of what is required of a husband, she remarks. As an Iranian woman she has been raised to serve men, but also to expect a certain respect in return. Since she is not really appreciated for her subservience, nor given the respect she feels she is owed, she has become confused about who she is, should be or wants to be.

She can easily see how her own confusion is played out in her contradictory expectations that she should both be 'liberated and western' and yet subservient and respected. Perhaps she has condoned her husband's behaviour, because she had continued to expect to be put back into 'her place'? Though Parisa is at first shocked at being asked to wonder about her actions and responsibilities in relation to what she experiences as a kind of victimhood, it is in accepting her part in creating her present situation that Parisa is reminded of her own strength, her ability to affirm and recover a sense of self.

The therapeutic work focuses on helping her to articulate the values she aspires to rather than becoming paralysed by the identity she feels she has become entrapped in. This is enabling her, in Sartre's model, to move from a self that is determined by others, to a self that is seen as a value and therefore as something that can be realized in the future. Parisa acknowledges that she is confused about her identity and about who she wants to be rather than having no sense of self at all. She also recognizes that she has let herself fall back on the role of mother and wife that she learnt in her childhood. She has actually given up being the 'liberated' person she briefly was as a student. She is afraid of the freedom she once had and finds it hard to accommodate the past freedom with her present sense of duty and devotion to her family. There are so many contradictions for her. On the one hand, she still considers men to be the bearers of authority and she implicitly allows her husband to determine who she is, or indeed gives him the power to make her less than she is capable of being. On the other hand, somewhere at the core of herself she feels a strong desire to soar above the life that she has settled for and wants to reclaim the liberated and emancipated person she knows she is capable of being.

Over the first weeks of therapy this sense of aspiring selfhood becomes increasingly obvious as the therapist encourages her to articulate her frustrations and rediscover the blueprint of a better future that Parisa has conceived of silently behind her tears and her despair. She has a complex and sometimes contradictory image of womanhood and it is quite a challenge to help her make sense of the tensions and paradoxes at work. There is a constant temptation for Parisa to hide behind the expectations of her culture of origin or those of her husband.

The therapy is about helping her to keep addressing her need to let herself feel safe and hide at times, yet at other times to formulate a future for herself in which she is more self-determining and active. She takes small steps in confronting her own submissiveness with her husband. She gradually discovers that it is possible to establish a calm and composed but self-possessed (eigentlich) attitude towards her husband. It is in discovering that it is possible to opt for different ways of being and therefore become a different person that Parisa's identity gets stronger. This is not about just becoming more assertive, but about letting herself think about life and her position in relation to it. It is about creatively finding her way through apparent opposites. Thus Parisa eventually emerges from her confusion and finds a clear and satisfactory direction of her own, which takes account of both sets of experiences and values. The process of therapy consists of encouraging Parisa to keep clarifying and conceptualizing, problematizing and understanding her own way of engaging with the world. She is never treated as if she has a character or personality problem. The objective is to help her claim her own liberation through reflection on the philosophical problem that is her life.

Critical considerations

Existential views of self can be unsettling and confusing. Some people in the humanistic camp criticize it from their position of belief in the idea of a core self. The humanist notion of a powerful 'real' self, which has a particular potential, which should be allowed to develop to the full is as diametrically opposed to the existential view as it is possible to get. On the other end of the spectrum there are the post-modern authors, who consider selfhood to be an illusion, and who question the very possibility of selfhood and thus relativize all subjective experience. This could however easily undermine a client's already weak sense of identity and jeopardize their ability to take themselves seriously. The flexible view of self that comes with an existential perspective can be extremely empowering. We no longer have to think that clients are condemned to a weak ego, or perceive their personality as pathological or their character as tragically set and determined by circumstances. The existential perspective allows for a broader outlook on selfhood and identity, which shows how we are always in transformation and capable of altering the direction we take. As people alter their perceptions and actions their sense of self also changes, for their centre of gravity is moved to a different place. This is highlighted in times of crisis, such as redundancy, when individuals are confronted with a re-evaluation not just of their values and beliefs but of their whole being. The objective of existential work at those times is not to impose a new order on confused experience but to allow the person to rediscover a sense of their own authority and authorship. Sartre's case studies of Genet and Flaubert (Sartre, 1952, 1960) illustrated in detail what a gradual process this is. It led him to a formulation that is highly appropriate for existential therapy.

I believe that a man can always make something out of what is made of him. This is the limit I would today accord to freedom: the small movement which makes of a totally conditioned social being someone who does not render back completely what his conditioning has given him. Which makes of Genet a poet when he had been rigorously conditioned to be a thief. (Sartre, 1974: 33–34)

Note

1   Dasein literally means 'being-there' (Heidegger, 1927).

Further reading

Kierkegaard, S. *The Sickness unto Death.*
Laing, R. D. *Self and Others.*
Laing, R. D. *The Divided Self.*
Nietzsche, F. *Thus Spoke Zarathustra.*
Zimmerman, M. E. *Eclipse of the Self: The Development of Heidegger's Concept of Authenticity.*

CHAPTER 19

Authenticity and Inauthenticity

JOHN POLLARD

> Nothing is more problematic in existential philosophy than the question of authenticity – and nothing is more important.
> Macann, *Who is Dasein? Towards an Ethics of Authenticity.* 225

Introduction

Existential Authenticity is a paradoxical and controversial concept among philosophers and therapists – even those who describe themselves as 'existential' psychotherapists or counsellors. For example, there could be an objection to its *prescriptive* nature – telling people how to live, 'be authentic', does not sound very 'therapeutic'. However, although authenticity does have a prescriptive element, it is more accurate to describe it as an anti-prescriptive prescriptivism – the paradoxical prescription being that each individual should choose, for themselves, how to live.

The second problem relates to the answer to the first. If authenticity seems to defy an objective explanation, as it has to be reached by the individual who seeks it, how can anyone communicate anything of importance regarding its definition? These are genuine problems, although a description of existential authenticity and inauthenticity can attempt to answer the question – 'what does it *mean* to live one's own life?'

Authenticity embraces paradox, both by believing something *universal* about living an 'authentic' *individual* life and, with particular relevance for therapy, the paradox of *helping others* towards a way of being that they have to ultimately *decide* for *themselves*.

An existential perspective
Freedom and responsibility

One of the generally agreed foundations of existential philosophy and therapy is that there is no *essential human nature*. Our 'existence comes before essence' (Sartre, 1948a: 26) or, the '"essence" of Dasein lies in its existence'

(Heidegger, 1927: 382). We are, first and foremost, existing beings constantly in a state of movement and becoming. The existential philosopher believes something different about the well-known exhortation to 'be true to yourself'. Rather than equate authenticity with a 'real self', the existential approach sees the self, not as a fixed and static entity whose nature is pre-determined, but rather as an ever-changing, creative process marked by freedom and responsibility.

Sartre illustrates this by comparing human being ('for-itself') with the being of objects ('in-itself'). Sartre's early philosophy focused on the conscious aspect of being human, seeing consciousness as a kind of pure, spontaneous creativity. He describes the way we have a tendency to treat ourselves and others as though we were objects, thereby avoiding our freedom and responsibility, and resulting in what he describes as 'bad faith' (Sartre, 1943: 43).

Sartre's early definition of freedom and responsibility as 'being the incontestable author of an event or of an object' (ibid., 553) is a useful one, although freedom is always freedom in a particular situation – this will involve elements we do not directly control. Sartre's view of authenticity is explicitly linked with the freedom, responsibility and 'anguish' of consciousness, while Heidegger starts with the question of Being and the being who addresses this question – human being or 'Dasein'. Heidegger emphasizes those aspects of human existence we do not control, by using terms such as 'falling' and 'thrownness', which gives more credence to the power and importance of our past heritage. These relate to the limitations on our freedom in the world in which we find ourselves embedded. But Heidegger also states clearly that we can choose how to respond to our situation – our cultural heritage for instance – by choosing that which we embrace or reject.

Anxiety and the 'they'

Existential anxiety relates to human *Being* and is differentiated from fear, which is always a fear of some thing or another. We can try to flee this anxiety or we can attempt to understand its message and significance. Understanding the positive aspect of anxiety is manifested for an individual in 'it's *Being towards* its ownmost potentiality-for-Being that is, its *Being-free for* the freedom of choosing itself and taking hold of itself' (Heidegger, 1927: 232).

The immersion into the everyday world of the 'they' involves the possibility of fleeing our anxiety and disowning our freedom. One way that this fleeing takes form is the views on life and the roles that we unquestioningly adopt. One does what the anonymous 'they' do, says the sorts of things 'they' say, believes the sorts of things 'they' believe and so on. The 'they' is an impersonal construct but becomes part of one's own Being in the mode of the 'they self' (ibid., 167).

We all have tendencies to go along with the 'they' or, to use other existential terms, the 'one', the 'crowd', the 'public' or the 'herd'. If one resists the 'they' there is a risk of rejection, isolation and an anxious confrontation with one's freedom. So we attempt to relieve ourselves of choosing our own possibilities and play it safe – this lessens our anxiety by bringing us 'a tranquillity, for which everything is "in the best of order"' (ibid., 222). However, we remain largely ignorant of our own freedom and detached from our own possibilities. This process of inauthenticity can be reversed only if an individual 'specifically brings itself back to itself from its lostness in the "they"' (ibid., 312). The state of inauthentic tranquillity is a fragile one and the possibility for authenticity remains close at hand.

To complicate matters, inauthenticity is not always a negative or dysfunctional mode of being, as we share aspects of our humanity and a common cultural heritage that involve everyday ways of existing. This necessary immersion into the everyday world of the 'they' means we cannot continually reflect on our freedom and responsibility and whether we are acting in accordance with our own choices or the prescriptions of others. Of course, we can do many of these things differently from the 'they', but it would be undesirable, impractical and impossible to resist *constantly* the way that the world and human beings function. However, because we are embedded, distracted and preoccupied in this social world (being-with-others), we often forget that we do have the possibility of questioning ourselves more frequently and embracing personal change. What is important is whether an individual has some reflective awareness of when, how and why they act inauthentically.

Death

Our own identity is open to question and never complete until the end of our life. As our death is not an event that we live through, our relation to it is either through the death of others or in terms of our own status as a 'being-towards-death'. The possibility of our demise is ever present, yet we often sanitize and impersonalize death by thinking it is somewhere 'out there' in the distant future. With this view, we again fall into the grip of the 'they', fleeing our being-towards-death and the meaning it has for our life. If death is an ever-present possibility then all our possibilities and choices have an existential relationship to it. We have the potential to resolutely affirm our own temporal, finite existence in an authentic way, in what Heidegger terms 'an impassioned *freedom towards death* – a freedom which has been released from the Illusions of the "they", and which is factical, certain of itself, and anxious' (ibid., 311).

Guilt and the 'call of conscience'

The personal nature of authenticity entails a dramatic change within the individual, a conversion of some kind. Heidegger describes this movement as the 'call of conscience'. The message one receives is a calling back to oneself that relates to our potential, although it does not dictate the particular concrete choices we should make in our life, but simply the choice to resolutely affirm our freedom and resist our tendency to fall into the 'they'. The call of conscience disrupts one's state of tranquillization and emanates both from and beyond me. As authenticity involves possibility, the *beyondness* of the call relates to the future – it confronts me with the question of who I am to become and my responsibility for answering this call or not.

Conscience involves the acceptance of our existential guilt, which does not relate directly to transgressions against others, but rather against our very *Being*. One way of seeing guilt is in our failure to have acted in the past in a way that we feel we should have. But, with reference to our Being, it also refers to an ever-present guilt that is related to the fact that we have no solid and objective ground to make our choices from, and yet we find ourselves thrown into a world where we cannot avoid the responsibility of choosing. Human existence is a continual tension between aspects of our existence we cannot change (our 'facticity') and those we can. The existential state of becoming means that until we try out new ways of being-in-the-world we will never be sure how achievable, or desirable, our present possibilities really are.

Values

If affirming anxiety and uncertainty, freedom and responsibility, and the groundlessness of being human is a radically anxious way to be, where might we obtain a sense of security? The importance of our values, including our own ethical principles, may indicate an answer to this question, as our existence is wrapped up in what we value. Accordingly, for Sartre, human beings should will 'freedom as the foundation of all values' (Sartre, 1948a: 51). If authenticity and inauthenticity permeate throughout all aspects of our lives, they can be seen as the foundation of not only our values, but our own identity. This question of whether authenticity can be an ethical, or regulative, principle is still subject to ongoing debate, although I believe authenticity does have an intrinsic 'ethical' dimension.

The importance of values is significant to psychotherapy and counselling, which largely consist of an ethical dialogue and exploration where the client and the therapist explore 'better' ways to be. The question for any counsellor or therapist is how to engage with ethical issues while affirming the autonomy of their clients. Existential authenticity helps us with this problem, as it illuminates the *way* we come to believe in our values and the attitude we have towards them.

The call of conscience involves the *care* that is essential to being human. The question then becomes one of what we care (and do not care) about and how this relates to our identity and to the choices we make. Authenticity can provide an ethical grounding that can underlie all our other values. If values are chosen in an authentic way then there is a sense that one can succeed or fail in being true to one's self. That is, we can act or fail to act in accordance with the values we have authentically chosen.

Others

Although authenticity stems from the individual, one always remains as a 'being-with-others' and this necessitates a standpoint towards other persons – Heidegger terms this 'solicitude'. Just as with other existential concerns, we can be authentic or inauthentic with respect to our concerns with, and for, others. Authentic being-with-others entails a way of relating that helps the other in their own search for authenticity and, in my opinion, is essential for a therapy calling itself 'existential'. If we 'leap in' for the other we risk disburdening them of the responsibility for their choices, while inauthentically elevating our own status. Such inauthentic relating to others can result in the other becoming 'dominated and dependent, even if this domination is a tacit one and remains hidden from him' (Heidegger, 1927: 158). In this way we implicitly affirm to the other a way of being that is not their own, appealing to their desire (and perhaps our own) for a 'safe' but inauthentic life.

The authentic position involves a desire for the other to be open to their own chosen possibilities. This embodies a 'leap ahead' of the other, 'not in order to take away his "care" but rather to give it back to him authentically' (ibid., 159). Although it is impossible to 'give' this to another person – they have to come to this interpretation themselves – one can certainly play a positive and enabling role in this process. If one acts with the other's authenticity in mind then it is true that we can help, but certainly not *cause*, 'the Other to become transparent to himself in his care and to become free for it' (ibid., 159).

We can view our status as being-with-others as compromising our own individuality to the extent of radically separating ourselves from other people. But this would involve inauthentically fleeing our being-with-others and our potential for meaningful relationships. Authenticity embraces both our individualism and our social being in an intersubjectivity that can be described as a positive, and ethical, *being 'alone-with-others'* (Batchelor, 1983).

Case illustration

This case study concerns my counselling with Zoë, referred by her GP, which took place at the mental health charity where I work that offers free counselling. The counselling lasted for twelve sessions with three 'monthly' follow-up appointments.

Zoë was twenty-five, married with two young children, and experienced depression, anxiety and panic attacks. She was frightened about leaving her home and was scared about her own safety and that of her children. Zoë's parents had separated when she was eight and her father had 'disappeared' from her life six years ago, his present whereabouts unknown. She was angry and upset with her father for abandoning her and felt disappointment with her mother, who had become dependent on her for emotional support.

Zoë thought deeply about issues and wanted to be open with her feelings while her husband James did not. They were both confused about whether their relationship could work. Zoë loved her children and felt guilty about resenting them for restricting her life.

In the early sessions we focused on Zoë's anxiety and panic attacks, although she tended to focus on the possible reasons for her anxiety rather than on the panic attacks themselves. I asked her how she felt about 'uncertainty' and whether this could be related to her anxiety and panic attacks. I believe that this intervention was appropriate, 'uncertainty' being one of my fundamental assumptions regarding the human condition, and also for Zoë, as her concrete fears revolved around the genuine possibility (although exaggerated) of 'bad' things happening.

In the fourth session Zoë showed me a letter she had received 'out of the blue' that week which was from her father and contained apologies about his past behaviour and a request to meet with her. She was in conflict about whether she wanted to meet him and it now seemed that a great deal of her well-being rested on how he would be. She was tearful as she talked about the 'big hole' that he had left in her life – the 'support, unconditional love and advice' that a father should provide. She believed that if her father had been present throughout her life she 'wouldn't be in this state'. This illustrated the power of the hole she experienced, where a 'good' father should have been. Although this was a genuine 'hole' in her life, it seemed to me that it had become a divergence from the emptiness in her general existence and her own identity.

I offered my concerns to Zoë that her future well-being, from her perspective, seemed to rest on how her father would turn out, and that I thought it 'nigh on impossible' for him to be the person that she required him to be. It seemed that no one other than Zoë herself could fill this hole. Could she address this predicament by assuming responsibility for her situation rather than seeing her father as the cause of most of her present problems?

The power that Zoë 'gave' her father lessened over the next few sessions, as she realized she may have to accept that her father could never be what she wanted him to be, or provide the fulfilment she wanted so much. This coincided with Zoë raising concerns that went beyond her father, mother and husband, and towards issues of meaning, values and her future. She spoke about her 'fear of being sixty and looking back on my life thinking I'd missed out, hadn't achieved things'. She went on to ask, 'what am I meant to do? What was I put on this earth for? I have ideals that the world doesn't live up to.' This reinforced for me that Zoë's values were crucial to her, and that she felt very isolated. I encouraged her to take positive meaning from her own values and we explored how she could create more meaningful life projects and relationships with others.

We revisited the problem of uncertainty towards the end of the counselling when I raised the positive consequences from embracing its existence. If the future is not determined then good things can happen, as well as bad. I still felt that when Zoë affirmed her own freedom and attended to her own desires and goals, she would have more confidence to deal with the uncertainties that related to her problems. 'Perhaps', she said, 'I could hide from these uncertainties.' I replied, 'yes, you could', affirming this possibility. 'No', she calmly stated, 'it would be shallow to hide from them.'

When Zoë was finally ready to meet her father, the importance of him living up to her expectations had lessened – she had become more accepting of the past while embracing her present/future possibilities and her own capabilities. This helped her deal with the fact that her father did not turn out to be the demon that caused all her problems, or the powerful entity that could save her from the difficulties of living.

Zoë decided to act on these recently discovered/created strengths and pursue a degree in the Humanities. She had missed out on her education when a rebellious teenager and was now determined to learn more about the world, as well as herself. She had already found a part-time job, which she enjoyed, and this seemed to be another part of her reclaiming her own (authentic) space. In terms of her marriage she was still open about whether her relationship would work or not. She was 'trying' but was not prepared to wait 'years for it to work'.

At the end of the counselling Zoë reflected on the changes she had gone through in the previous five months. She had come to accept more of life's uncertainties as well as realizing that her obsession with, rather than acknowledgement of, the possibility of tragic events may have been an attempt to look away from her own personal issues. She began to accept more of the flaws in her parents and her relationship with them. She came to a better understanding about her own feelings towards her children, including her guilt, and her relationship with them had noticeably improved. Zoë's panic attacks had greatly reduced through the period of counselling, although we had spent very little time directly talking about them. This seemed to me to be in keeping with her greater acceptance of uncertainty and a new-found confidence in herself.

When reflecting on the reasons for change in therapy it is always difficult to pinpoint what part the actual therapy, or therapist, has played. I think it is important for a therapist to open up possibilities for clients, including the underlying possibilities connected with authenticity. 'Socratic questioning' is a therapeutic tool that can help clients to confront their own conflicts and contradictory views. This does not suggest that one view is necessarily more valid than another, but it can illuminate and clarify the nature of such conflicts.

In this case study one could say that Zoë had become more 'authentic', although the term is a crude 'label' for many different human values and concerns. Zoë had the courage to take more responsibility for her life and embrace her own freedom to create a self that was more open to change. This is an often isolating and anxious process but Zoë no longer wanted to accept her life as it had been. Zoë had made positive changes and these could be described as a shift towards a more authentic way of living.

Critical considerations

The therapist as 'ironist'

Authenticity is an antidote for the tendency to exaggerate the power of psychotherapy and counselling. It is common to hear from the therapeutic literature that it is 'the relationship that heals' and it is implicit in the culture of therapy that it *causes* positive change. I believe this gives too much power to therapy, and the therapist, and does a disservice to our clients' potential. While the individual qualities of the therapist and the nature of the therapeutic relationship are crucial, authenticity demystifies the power of therapy and the therapist. In a profound sense clients heal themselves and are responsible for their own growth. While therapists do bear a heavy moral responsibility, it is 'to' their clients and not 'for' them. One of the most important of these responsibilities is to help clients prepare for their life beyond formal therapy – clients are encouraged to build on their own resources and become their own therapist.

A therapist who advocates this type of authentic standpoint can be termed an '*Ironist*' (Kierkegaard, 1965). The ironist believes passionately in a certain type of authentic selfhood that he or she thinks others would benefit from embracing. Yet the ironist knows that others have to come to this decision themselves. If another person tries to embrace authenticity to please the therapist, or because the therapist is the expert and has recommended that this is a way they should be, both have failed with regard to authenticity. Ironically, once it is accepted that one's power lies in changing the client's *world* but not the client, one can actually increase the positive influence therapy has.

It would be inaccurate to say that a therapist can simply *use* the notion of authenticity in their practice. Authenticity is not a technique, it is a way of *Being*, and can become an integral part of being a therapist. Whether therapy explores bereavement, sexuality, eating disorders, and so on, the question of authenticity will play a crucial part in such explorations. Talking about the concepts relating to authenticity 'explicitly' may well be part of the process, but these concepts will be hinted at, and implied, throughout the therapeutic process.

The most obvious danger of authenticity would be an attempt to zealously 'push' clients in its direction. This would be unethical and contradicts authenticity's meaning. It is important to appreciate how our clients relate to the issues of authenticity and when to challenge, when to encourage and when to 'let be'. 'Using' the concepts of authenticity involves an ability to sense when, and how, to open up issues such as responsibility, freedom, uncertainty and values.

The literature on authenticity is often impenetrable, ambiguous and exclusive. Yet a person can embody the values of authenticity without having a great in-depth *academic philosophical* understanding. Accordingly, another person may have a theoretical understanding and yet fail to act authentically – these diametric positions should not be surprising as authentic selfhood has to be expressed through *action*. It could be argued that Heidegger's involvement in National Socialism is a powerful example of this latter way of losing one's self, falling into the grip of the 'they' and failing to put one's ideas into action (Collins, 2000).

Conclusion

Therapists cannot hide from what they value or believe – a 'non-directive' therapist would not be a therapist at all. Therefore, if we cherish both our own values and the self-determination of others, I would contend that the paradoxical quality of existential authenticity best illuminates this conundrum.

Although authenticity involves contemplation, it also entails the courage to take risks and act in the world, to try out new ways of existing. As Jacob Golomb suggests in his thought-provoking book, 'the very search for authenticity constitutes its meaning and discloses the seeker's authenticity' (Golomb, 1995: 59). Therefore, authenticity has a distinctly active nature – you will not arrive at the definition of authenticity by 'reading', or 'listening' to, other people's views on the subject.

Exploring what authenticity may mean is an ongoing process and has no final completion. Due to our temporal nature and the possibilities of human existence, authenticity and its concerns, in fact our very existence, remains open to question and change as long as we live.

Acknowledgement

I would like to thank Lawrence Quill and Al Mahrer for their helpful criticisms and suggestions.

Further reading

Golomb, J. *In Search of Authenticity: From Kierkegaard to Camus*.
Guignon, C. B. 'Authenticity, Moral Values, and Psychotherapy'. In C. B. Guignon (ed.) *The Cambridge Companion to Heidegger*.
Keenan, B. *An Evil Cradling*.
Macann, C. 'Who is Dasein? Towards an Ethics of Authenticity'. In C. Macann (ed.) *Martin Heidegger: Critical Assessments, Volume IV Reverberations*.
van Deurzen, E. *Paradox and Passion in Psychotherapy: An Existential Approach to Therapy and Counselling*.

CHAPTER 20

Anxiety and Engagement

NICK KIRKLAND-HANDLEY AND DIANA MITCHELL

> Anxiety turns us towards courage, because the other alternative is despair.
> Courage resists despair by taking anxiety into itself.
>
> Tillich, The Courage to Be

Introduction

Etymologically, 'anxiety' is derived from the Latin 'angere' which means to squeeze or strangle. The German word 'angst' has the stem 'ang', which means narrow or tight (Cohn, 1997). May notes in this etymology a reference to birth trauma as the metaphorical prototype for anxiety (May, 1958: 52). Though the shades of meaning covered by 'anxiety' and 'angst' overlap, the terms are not co-terminous. Macquarrie (1972) suggests that angst implies 'uneasiness' and 'malaise', while Rycroft (1968) argues that 'angst' has a meaning closer to 'anguish'. What is clear is that anxiety is manifested physically as well as emotionally. Indeed, from an existential viewpoint: 'palpitations, sweaty hands and giddiness are not *caused* by anxiety, they are part of a total anxious state which manifests itself both physically and...as a characteristic feeling...[called] anxiety' (Cohn, 1997: 63).

The predominant view of anxiety in our culture is to see it as a disorder.[1] As such it became, and remains, the province of medicine, especially psychiatry and the cognate professions of clinical psychology and psychiatric nursing. Thus people troubled by anxiety may be treated with anxiolytic drugs or hypnotherapy, or managed by relaxation training, breathing exercises, stress management or cognitive-behavioural techniques to control, if not eliminate, the symptoms. What is rarely considered is that this same anxiety might be recognized as a reliable source of information pointing the subject to a life situation which needs to be addressed and thus, potentially, to a more authentic way of living.

Smail (1984) is highly critical of this dualistic, alienated view we take of ourselves as faulty machines:

> Far from being a mechanical fault,...the experience of anxiety constitutes an assertion of the real nature of our subjective engagement with the world. To fall prey to anxiety is, at least in part, to fall out of self-deception...(Smail, 1984: 82)

He adds that the 'symptoms' of anxiety may be speaking a language both more succinct and more eloquent than conventional words (Smail, 1984: 94). In the exploration of the meaning of the phenomenon of anxiety, two schools of thought predominate: the psychoanalytic and the existential. Emmanuel (2000) offers an interesting overview of the psychoanalytical approach; this chapter focuses on the existential.

An existential perspective

An existential-phenomenological view sees anxiety 'not as a result of psychological mechanisms, but as an inevitable aspect of existence itself' (Cohn, 1997: 70). In this perspective, anxiety is not the result of individual (ontic) development, but is an ontological aspect of Dasein. Though an early and continuing experience of intense threat and insecurity may give an anxious 'tuning' to our experience, this is not seen as the direct effect of an earlier anxiety-provoking event but rather as an experientially rooted inclination to respond to life anxiously (ibid.).

Cohn describes the threefold ground for the inevitability of anxiety: it is rooted in

1. our thrownness into a world we did not choose;
2. the necessity to make choices, the outcomes of which are never certain and which always imply the rejection of alternatives; and
3. the realization that life inevitably moves towards death.

Heidegger's view of anxiety is also connected to our fallenness with other people – our being taken over by 'the They' until we experience 'unheimleichkeit', 'ill-at-easeness', and discover we stand alone; this anxiety is linked to authenticity. Moreover, anxiety is not just a *response* to the fact of finding ourselves thrown into the world – it is through anxiety that we become aware of this thrownness.

According to Kierkegaard, anxiety is 'the giddiness of freedom'; it makes us aware of our possibilities and can be considered as the price we pay for freedom. In 'Begrebet Angest' (1844) he establishes the ontological nature of anxiety and links it to freedom and choice (very strongly), but also to guilt and responsibility. Kierkegaard points to the possibility of embracing anxiety in order to actualize one's possibilities. This little book, written more than half a century before Freud, inspired many later thinkers, including Heidegger, May and Tillich.

For Heidegger, anxiety is 'Grundbefindlichkeit', the basic way in which one finds oneself in the world (Heidegger, 1927). Like Kierkegaard, he acknowledged the paradoxical nature of existence as disclosed in anxiety. In Heidegger, the emphasis shifts from the possibility to the finitude of existence: anxiety discloses man's existence as possibility thrown into the world (Macquarrie, 1975: 66). These accounts are complementary rather than contradictory.

Heidegger shows that in anxiety we are jerked out of the pseudo-securities with which we surround ourselves, we are made to feel 'unheimlich'. 'Uncanniness (unheimlichkeit) declares those moments in which anxiety confronts Dasein with the tremendous freedom to choose being or non-being, to dwell in inauthenticity or to strive for self-possession' (Steiner, 1992: 100). Indeed anxiety (like conscience) may be considered a privilege – a saving grace.

This implies that fears are secondary to anxiety and serve a defensive function. According to Dreyfus (1991: 180), were one able to embrace the anxiety inherent in the human condition, one would be fearless. Anxiety has the power to shake us from our illusions. It confronts the individual with his or her responsibility and summons him or her out of forgetfulness of being.

Rollo May, who did a great deal to bring existential ideas to an English-speaking audience, defines anxiety as 'the experience of being affirming itself against non-being' (May, 1977: xxi). He emphasizes that anxiety is always a threat to the centre of my existence: it is the experience of the threat of imminent non-being (May, 1983: 109). May's original contribution to the understanding of the nature of anxiety links the idea to the concept of *value*: 'Anxiety is the apprehension cued off by a threat to some value that the individual holds essential to his existence' (May, 1977: 186).

It strikes at the basis of the psychological structure wherein the perception of oneself occurs. In contrast to fear, anxiety tends to be experienced as over-whelming because it attacks the foundations of who I think I am (ibid., 191).[2] We may avoid anxiety only at the price of apathy or numbing of our sensibilities and our imagination (ibid., 329).

May was greatly influenced by the existential theologian Paul Tillich, who included an account of the ontology of anxiety in a series of lectures which he gave on courage (1962). Tillich sees anxiety and courage as interdependent, and he describes anxiety as 'finitude experienced as one's own finitude'. While contrasting anxiety with fear, he argues that they cannot be separated: they have the same ontological root and they are immanent in one another. According to Tillich, it is the anxiety of not being able to preserve one's being which underlines every fear. Anxiety strives to become fear, as fear can be met by courage. But ultimately the attempt to transform fear into anxiety is futile: the anxiety of a finite being about non-being cannot be eliminated (Tillich, 1962: 47–48). Tillich's major contribution is to distinguish three types of anxiety according to the three directions in non-being which threaten being. These create anxieties of death, meaninglessness and condemnation.

> Non-being threatens man's *ontic* self-affirmation relatively in terms of fate and absolutely in terms of death; it threatens his *spiritual* self-affirmation relatively in terms of emptiness and absolutely in terms of meaninglessness; and it threatens his *moral* self-affirmation relatively in terms of guilt and absolutely in terms of condemnation. (Tillich, 1962: 49)

These three types of anxiety are immanent in one another. According to Tillich, the authentic response to existential anxiety is that of courageously taking the anxiety into oneself; he states that we shall have more being as we can take more anxiety of non-being into our stride. He also acknowledges that people who are particularly sensitive to non-being and who suffer from profound anxiety may be unable to do so.

Summary: Characteristics of an existential approach

- Anxiety is 'Being's awareness of the possibility of non-being' (Tillich, 1962).
- Anxiety is inevitable and cannot be eliminated.
- Anxiety is our fundamental response to the situation in which we find ourselves: we are thrown into the world and are confronted by facticity, the characteristics of our being and the circumstances of our life which we cannot change, yet which have no ultimate necessity.
- We are required to choose and are responsible for our choices, though we have to make them on the basis of inadequate information.
- We are free within limits and subject to contingency.
- We know we must die, but we do not know the hour of our death.
- Anxiety discloses to us the paradoxical nature of existence; it reveals the unresolved tension between freedom and its possibilities, finitude and its constraints and the ever-present possibility of annihilation.
- Anxiety involves conflict – not least because it reveals that we also desire that which we dread (Kierkegaard, 1980a; May, 1977).
- Anxiety is oriented towards the future.
- Anxiety lies behind every fear and provides the fearful element in it.
- Anxiety is educative: if we embrace it, we are freed to actualize our possibilities.
- Anxiety has the power to jerk us out of the pseudo-securities with which we surround ourselves and summons us to a more authentic existence.

Implications for therapy

An existential perspective offers a model for understanding anxiety, which is fundamentally different from those which dominate clinical practice, and an application of this perspective has profound implications for therapy. For example, if it is the case that fears are an attempt to contain and manage anxiety, then to treat them as autonomous 'symptoms', which we can seek to eradicate without regard to their function, may be seen as counter-productive or even dangerous. In doing so the therapist is missing the opportunity to help the client set his/her fears in a context of meaning and is also foregoing the possibility of aiding him/her in uncovering the existential anxiety, which lies beneath his/her fears.

When anxiety is properly and deeply understood, it is seen that far from being a problem to be eradicated, it is the chief ally of the therapeutic couple in the endeavour to wake the client up from his or her illusions and to spur him or her into living life more authentically.

Case illustration (by Diana Mitchell)

The purpose of a case study is to show how something is done. As an existential therapist I was faced with a dilemma: I do not have a strategy or a general way of working with people who are suffering from panic attacks or anxiety. My particular way of thinking about and understanding of anxiety will of course be expressed in what I do and do not do within the therapeutic relationship. This case example has been created from a unique therapeutic encounter. It cannot be used in order to show how an existential therapist 'works with anxiety' as such, and possibly reveals as much about me as it does about my client. However, it does show what happened when a particular client and a particular therapist joined forces in order to assist the client in her struggle to reach a clearer understanding of her possibilities and limitations. This in turn was influenced by the context (i.e. writing for this particular book) in which this case illustration was created. At the same time it must be remembered that the examples I have chosen have been taken out of the context in which they occurred, that is, our therapeutic relationship (Cohn, 2002).

Throughout this case study I have used italics in order to show how Jane's experience and her way of being could be linked to the existential way of understanding anxiety in 'An Existential Perspective'. But it must be stressed that these observations are not intended to be explanations or interpretations that I would pass on to my client.

Jane was a single woman in her early thirties who came to see me for ten weeks via an employee assistance scheme. When I opened my front door I was faced with two anxious-looking women. After establishing that the second woman was Jane's sister who had given her a lift, I explained that Jane would be seeing me on her own for about fifty minutes.

Jane told me how she had never been to a therapist and that she had no idea what to expect. She was very confused and frightened about what was happening to her, but she added that this was 'worth a try'. Jane told me that she had been off work for almost three weeks, 'ever since I collapsed with a massive panic attack after work'. She described how she suddenly felt a tight gripping pain in her chest and had difficulty breathing; 'after that I just broke down and couldn't stop crying, I've never had anything like that happen before'. *Here was an example of how the physical expression of anxiety was part of her total anxious state (Cohn, 1997).*

She continued to have panic attacks that had, until recently, prevented her from leaving her house. She experienced these 'attacks' as 'coming from out of nowhere, even when I'm just sitting at home, relaxing and not worrying about anything...this is not like me at all'. *How Jane felt about herself and what was happening to her reminded me of May's (1977) belief that anxiety can be experienced as so overwhelming, because it attacks the foundations of who I think I am.*

She was shaking and perspiring as she told me how she normally 'just gets on with things' and how she rarely talked to anyone about her problems. She could not understand what was happening to her, but the one thing that she was very clear about was that she was determined to 'find a way through this'.

Jane looked very tense and distressed. It must have taken a lot out of her to leave her familiar area, something she had up until now been too frightened to attempt, in spite of the help of her sister. I was struck by the way she seemed to convey anxiety and courage in equal measure. *This reminded me of how Tillich (1962) links anxiety and courage, showing us how interdependent anxiety and courage are.*

Having lost her previous job through redundancy, Jane went on to tell me how much she put into her job. It was important for her to succeed and to give a good impression at work. Her experience of being made redundant had left her feeling very insecure and fearful that this might suddenly happen to her again. This led her to wonder if the state she was in had something to do with her work. *Tillich (1962) shows us how anxiety and fear have the 'same ontological root'; Jane's fear of being made redundant again could be seen as her personal and individual (ontic) response to those inescapable aspects of existence that we have no control over (ontological).*

I asked her to tell me more about what happened on that last day at work. She recalled that on the day of her 'breakdown' her manager had told her that there were going to be some changes in the company. This meant that she would be working with a different manager in the near future. She told me that she had felt fine all day at work, but the moment she got home she collapsed. I wondered if her 'just getting on with things' was her way of coping with this potentially 'anxiety provoking' situation. On that day she seemed unable to engage with what her manager was telling her and what the implications for her future might be. Was she suddenly faced with the prospect of change and an unknown future that she had no control over? *From what Jane had told me, her job seemed very important to her: according to May (1977), anxiety indicates 'a threat to some value the individual holds essential to his existence'.*

Jane managed to stay with me for half an hour and then indicated to me that she wanted to leave. It was an understatement to say that she looked relieved when I told her that was fine and that I would see her next week.

Over the following weeks Jane found it difficult to talk at any length about aspects of her life that made her anxious. It was when she started to talk about her relationship with her manager and how she approached her job that her particular response to her situation started to emerge. One way she said she stayed 'on top of the situation' was to make sure that her 'in tray' was always empty at the end of every working day. Part of her strategy was to 'keep her head down' and never let on that she might have trouble coping with the assignments she was given. She told me with some pride how she never left any work unfinished. When we talked about how it would be for her to leave work unfinished it emerged that this would make her feel very insecure, unsafe and not in control of her situation. Being judged well by others, particularly her manager, also made her feel safe. *She seemed to go to great lengths in order to feel safe and secure. Heidegger refers to the 'pseudo-securities with which we surround ourselves' (Steiner, 1992).*

Together we looked more closely at her response to the news that there would be changes at work and a new manager. It emerged that she was very anxious about being thrown into a new situation, without knowing what lay in store for her, hating any kind of unexpected change that she had no say in or control over. 'I'm afraid that my new manager will expect me to do more work on top of what I'm already struggling to do. I've been working through my lunch hour and taking work home with me as it is . . . I really can't see a way through this now.'

Was it her assumption that with a lot of hard work on her part she should be able to find a way to control the situation she found herself in and to prevent the unexpected from happening? *Throughout our time together Jane showed how worried she was about her future: one of the characteristics of anxiety is that it is future-orientated.*

I asked her if she had discussed the difficulties she had experienced with her manager. She admitted that she never told (or showed) her manager that she was having difficulties coping with her workload, and realized that he could not know that she was not coping, when she 'presented' herself as a kind of superwoman to him (and to herself). We both laughed at how paradoxical the situation was. She was now for the first time starting to see that she, too, played a part in what happened and did not happen to her. This was our first playful and light-hearted moment together. There was now a different kind of openness between us.

Between our sessions Jane seemed to be engaging with others and her life in a more open way. For instance, she joined a gym, signed up for driving lessons, started to share her difficulties with her sister and became more 'visible' and stylish in the way she dressed! It was as if she was starting to grasp her own freedom and to realize the different possibilities that were, after all, open to her.

Another specific example of her change in attitude was that for the first time she had told her manager and a few colleagues how she really felt and what her difficulties were. She was amazed how understanding and supportive they were. I wondered if Jane was also starting to be more open to the idea that, no matter how hard she tried, there were certain aspects of her life that she could not foresee or control.

We now had two more sessions to go and I was starting to feel a bit uneasy because everything seemed to be going too well. She was gaining in confidence, but I wondered how she would react when she found herself faced with those aspects of life that she had no control over. All her new 'adventures' had worked out well and I wondered if she had been lulled into believing that she was once again in control of her life.

She arrived for our eighth session looking anxious, flustered and angry. It appeared that she had just had a phone call from her manager, who had just 'sprung' it on her that the date for the changes had been moved forward. Her new manager and a new system would be in place before she returned to work, 'how could he do this ... he promised me that the changes would not take place until after I had started back at work!'.

Once again her anxiety overwhelmed her when the certainty she wanted to believe was out there was replaced by uncertainty. Her immediate reaction was to see this as a setback. Part of the setback was her returning fears about 'something being done to her' that was out of her control and her fear that she would not be able to cope.

This faded away when we looked more closely at was happening and how differently she responded to this new (and to her) unexpected situation. Rather than being paralyzed by her anxiety she found herself already expressing, engaging and 'listening' to her anxiety in a new and more open way. *This reminded me of Heidegger's view that anxiety can 'shake us from our illusions', in doing so, the individual is confronted with his responsibility (Dreyfus, 1991).*

Towards the end of our time together she went as far as to say that she was grateful for what had happened to her, describing the whole experience as 'my wake-up call'.

She was able to phone her manager, who reassured her that he would still be around if she wanted his support. She admitted that she was still anxious about returning to work, but at the same time she was aware that her attitude had changed and with that a new-found freedom. *It could be said that she had found a way to 'embrace anxiety in order to actualize her possibilities' (Kierkegaard, 1980a).*

It appeared to me that whatever happened between us impacted in some way on other aspects of her life and in turn, what happened 'out there' was part of what happened (and did not happen) between us. I also believe that the courage and determination Jane showed in pushing herself to seek help in the first place suggested that her 'new way' of engaging and being with her anxiety had begun before we met. This is not to say that I did not play a part in helping her to articulate and reflect on her relationship with others and the expectations she had of herself. She was now starting to see that she played her part in creating the predicament she found herself trapped in, while at the same time acknowledging that there would always be aspects of life that she had no control over.

Critical considerations

There can be a temptation on the part of an existential therapist to understand the client's anxiety in terms of ontological or existential anxiety. This interpretation could so easily close down, rather than open up, the client's personal understanding and possibilities. To do this would be to forget that neither the therapist nor the client is in possession of 'the truth'. Each will have a different worldview. It is ultimately the client's understanding that the therapist is concerned with. It could be said that the existential approach is potentially at risk of relativizing people's problems (Diana Mitchell).

While an existential perspective will for some clients offer a welcome opportunity to embrace their life situation with courage and thus move towards more authentic ways of being, this is not true for all. As Tillich (1962) observed, there are those – whether 'particularly sensitive to non-being', 'suffering more profound anxiety' or for whom this approach is philosophically alien – for whom the uncovering of existential anxiety is not appropriate. For these people, the more conventional approaches referred to above may be seen as more helpful; the existential therapist in this situation may do well to be more 'containing' – that is, to learn from the other approaches. In addition, there are many clients who, though willing to re-construe the significance of their anxiety, find it more useful to do so in ontic terms, such as those offered by psychoanalytic views on child development and the necessary conditions for a young person to thrive emotionally. In the experience of one of the authors, Bion's (1963) idea of anxiety as a premonition of the emergence into awareness of powerful emotion, which is perceived as threatening and which has hitherto been outside consciousness, is in many cases particularly helpful in understanding the experience of panic. This is not incompatible with an existential perspective (Nick Kirkland-Handley).

Anxiety has already been and continues to be extensively documented from a philosophical, psychoanalytical and psychological perspective. The existential view is that we are who and how we are in response to others and to the situation we already find ourselves in. This particular way of understanding the human predicament implies that an awareness of context and relatedness will in some way be part of the therapeutic encounter. This way of thinking will colour the therapist's response to his or her client's struggle with anxiety. Any 'research' of anxiety from an existential perspective would have to take the researcher's experience and understanding of anxiety into account. It seems to me that an ongoing open-mindedness to different ways of experiencing and making sense of anxiety is important. Maybe the existential therapist's task is to try to be less sure about his or her understanding of anxiety in order to learn more about anxiety (Diana Mitchell).

Notes

1   Indeed DSM IV (APA, 1994) distinguishes no less than *twelve* anxiety disorders.
2   May quotes Goldstein: one *has* fear, but one *is* anxious.

Further reading

Cohn, H. W. *Existential Thought and Therapeutic Practice: An Introduction to Existential Psychotherapy.*
Cohn, H. W. *Heidegger and the Roots of Existential Therapy.*
Heidegger, M. *Being and Time.* Trans. J. Macquarrie and E. S. Robinson.
Kierkegaard, S. *The Concept of Anxiety.*
Smail, S. *Illusion and Reality: The Language of Anxiety.*
Tillich, P. *The Courage to Be.*

CHAPTER 21

Depression and Apathy

CLAIRE ARNOLD-BAKER

> Patients fall into despair as a result of a confrontation with harsh facts of the
> human condition – the 'givens' of existence.
>
> Yalom, *The Gift of Therapy*. xvi

Introduction

Life is harsh. It is a struggle. It involves suffering, feelings of guilt and anxiety
and is subject to chance (Jaspers, 1951). Confronted with the true nature of
our life as human beings it is no wonder that we fall into despair, as Yalom
puts it, or have feelings of depression, at some point in our lives. Depression
affects those who feel they cannot cope with what is happening in their lives,
either as a result of a build up of things or one major event that knocks them
off balance. As Brown et al. (1973, 1978) discovered, how one perceives and
reacts to life events is dependent on how much social support is available and
on the individual's ability, or inability, to cope with these events due to earlier
experience or simultaneous difficulty.

Epidemiological research has shown that young adults tend to be more at
risk from depression. It is also more likely to be found in women than men,
as women tend to have a 'ruminative' response to the onset of a depressed
mood, rather than a 'distracting' style of response (Nolen-Hoeksema, 1990).
However, men are more likely to become alcohol or drug abusers which is
seen as '"self-medication" for depressive symptoms' (Lemma, 1996: 77).
Differences due to culture will be manifest in the differences in experience and
there is evidence that depression is more prevalent in working-class people.
Twin studies have shown that genetic factors influence the onset of depression,
especially if linked to stressful life events. Epidemiology gives a flavour of
how depression affects the general population; however, these can only ever be
generalized statements and do not apply to all individuals or their personal
experiences.

Depression is not a modern-day phenomenon and much has been written
on the subject from a variety of perspectives. Kraepelin, a German psychiatrist,
reclassified melancholia, the term for depression in the pre-nineteenth century,

as a neurosis in 1899. But modern-day psychiatry classifies depression under the category of mood disorders. In the current diagnostic and statistical manual of mental disorders (DSM IV) there are two forms of depression – depressive disorders and bipolar or manic depressive disorders. This chapter will focus on the former, the symptoms of which include depressed mood, loss of interest, loss of pleasure, change in weight, insomnia or hypersomnia, fatigue, feelings of worthlessness, excessive or inappropriate guilt and recurrent thoughts of death, recurrent suicidal ideation or attempt (American Psychiatric Association, 1994: 162).

An existential perspective

The existential approach offers an alternative perspective to the medical model and does not look at the individual in terms of traits that can be separated and studied or treated in isolation; instead the person and their world are seen as interconnected. This was highlighted by Karl Jaspers, who conceived an alternative understanding of psychiatry in 1913 in his book *General Psychopathology* (Jaspers, 1913). Jaspers proposed the use of a phenomenological method when examining mental disorders as he felt the medical model was too limited. Jaspers' phenomenological method emphasized the human being as a whole. He argued that by allowing the individual to communicate their experience, the psychiatrist would be able to go beyond the restrictive method of defining and categorizing mental disorders.

Similarly, Laing (1960) used existential phenomenology to understand the phenomena presented in his patients, 'to articulate what the other's "world" is and his way of being in it' (Laing, 1960: 25). Laing argued for not only the mind of a person to be considered but the wider picture too, the body, others and the world. Szasz shared this view, 'psychiatrists are not concerned with mental illness and their treatments. In actual practice they deal with personal, social and ethical problems in living' (Szasz, 1974: 262).

Therefore the existential approach to depression takes a more holistic stance. It does not focus only on negative or faulty thoughts, as is the case for cognitive therapies. Nor does it only consider issues of loss and rejection as expounded by the psychoanalytic approach. The existential approach seeks to enable clients to look at every aspect of their life and how it impacts on their feelings of depression. Clients are encouraged to examine, question and confront how they live their lives as well as helped to come to terms with events that have occurred. Through this examination, clients will be in a better position to move forward into a future that they have determined for themselves.

Depression could be viewed as being in a particular mood and indeed it is under the title of mood disorders that depression is placed in the medical model. Heidegger believed that moods are an intrinsic part of living; the mood that we are in will affect how we relate to the world and others (see Chapter 13). Heidegger posits that we are always positioned in the world in a particular way and our moods represent our attunement or expression of that position; therefore we are always in a certain mood, where one mood is replaced by another, different mood (Heidegger, 1962).

Heidegger uses the term *Befindlichkeit* to express the way we are disposed to or positioned in the world, 'which means roughly "how one finds oneself", "how one is to be found" or "how one is doing"' (Inwood, 1997: 36). This term is also linked to Heidegger's idea of *thrownness*, that we are in a particular world, as Being-in-the-world, and this world will determine the possibilities available. *Befindlichkeit* therefore is how we find ourselves in this specific and particular world and this reveals the possibilities of the situation and it is our moods, or *Stimmung*, which express our attunement to that situation. Therefore, according to Heidegger, moods can tell an individual a lot about themselves, and what matters to them, because it is through moods that 'Dasein is always brought before itself, and has always found itself, not in the sense of coming across itself by perceiving itself, but in the sense of finding itself in the mood that it has' (Heidegger, 1962: 174).

It is through experiencing the world through their moods, that is, when for instance all things are drab, boring and depressing, that an individual can realize that their mood is depressed and in this process gain some insight into themselves. Heidegger believed that moods do not come about from something within ourselves, or from external sources, rather they emerge out of our interactions with the world, our Being-in-the-world. He went on to say that our moods cannot help us to reflect on ourselves as they have a disclosing character; instead, they show us something about our interactions in the world.

> A mood assails us. It comes neither from 'outside' nor from 'inside', but arises out of Being-in-the-world, as a way of such Being. . . . The mood has already disclosed, in every case, Being-in-the-world as a whole, and makes it possible first of all to direct oneself towards something. (Ibid., 136)

Therefore in the case of depression, the depressed mood cannot be changed by reflecting on what is going on inside, as it arises out of our interactions with the world. It follows, then, that an individual can only come out of a depressed mood by being and interacting differently in the world, which in turn will allow them to enter into a new mood. Moods can therefore give individuals knowledge about themselves and their world. They can also show us what matters to us. Heidegger asserted that part of our basic state is to care about the world and ourselves. However, depression may be a time when an individual lacks this care, as Inwood explains: 'In extreme depression or anxiety, the closest that we come in our waking state to lacking care, we find it hard to will or to wish for anything, even for release from our condition' (Inwood, 1997: 52).

Similarly, Boss believed that moods are an innate potential of being: 'They are particular modes in which human existential attunement is fulfilled' (Boss, 1994: 110). Attunement can be seen as the way in which a person is open to, or receptive to, the world and their perceptions. For someone suffering from depression their perception of the world is very narrow and closed off. They withdraw and become disconnected from the world, which restricts what is available to them.

Boss therefore sees mental disorders as impairment: 'What is actually impaired in a given illness is the ill person's ability to engage in carrying out these particular potentialities as free behaviour toward what he encounters in his world' (ibid., 199). For Boss, depression is an impairment of the basic existential traits of spatiality and temporality in relating to the phenomena of the world, that is, space and time: 'Of the three temporal existential extensions of past, present, and future, the first and third are nearly totally covered up in such patients, so much so that their existence is practically reduced to the present' (ibid., 213).

These ideas were based on Eugene Minkowski's description of the experience of time when working with someone with schizophrenic depression. He noted that for his client 'each day life began anew, like a solitary island in a gray sea of passing time' (Minkowski, 1994: 133). Minkowski concluded that for this client the future was blocked by fear that a destructive event would occur, brought on by guilt of perceived wrongdoings in his past.

Therefore the depressed person can see no future, and is confronted with a guilty past and a meaningless present. Boss believed that time has stopped for them and they are unable to fulfil their inborn possibilities. They perceive the world around them in a particular way, as it is related directly to them: 'The melancholic sees in himself nothing but emptiness, inferiority, worthlessness, and culpability. Anything that may remain open to his limited perception is experienced as an accusation and a proof of his worthlessness' (Boss, 1994: 219).

The guilt that is experienced by depressed clients is existential guilt, and occurs when one does not live up to one's own possibilities and potentialities. Existential guilt represents a lack in one's self, a failing to live up to what one could be. However, rather than it being about falling short of some ideal and unrealistic notion of one's self, which is what is experienced by most depressed clients, the failing is more to do with not accepting who we are and our own potentials in life. As Jaspers states, depression is a *disturbance of vital events*: '"disturbance in becoming a person", an "elementary obstruction on becoming", an inhibition "of one's own inner timing", an "inhibition of the personally moulded urge to become", . . . a "standstill in the flow of personal becoming"' (Jaspers, 1997: 540).

The guilt can also be experienced as neurotic guilt, which represents a loss of something that is valued. This may be in terms of the loss of someone, or the loss of identity, some ideal or value.

Binswanger sees depression as a clinging to a guilt-ridden past, a fear of punishment in the future and where the present has no place: 'Everything that is possible has already happened. Life is ruled by the shadow of loss – a loss which is not just anticipated but is already fact' (Cohn, 1997: 110). Binswanger believed that depression is not brought on by a life event, it is more fundamental than that; Binswanger contended that these individuals have a specific world-design – 'the break-up of the experience of time's continuous flow' (ibid., 111). Accordingly, Binswanger believed that 'the goal of psychotherapy is to bring the patient safely back 'down to earth' from his extravagance. Only from this point is any new departure and ascent possible' (ibid., 112).

Boss had a similar view to Binswanger in that he suggested that to be effective, therapy must not focus totally on the past, as the client is correct in their feelings of guilt. Those suffering from depression often single out some minor offence which becomes the source of their unhappiness and guilt feelings. Boss saw those suffering from depression as constantly denying their selfhood, 'afraid to risk losing the favourable regard of others, practicing this lifelong self-annihilation on a scale far exceeding that of the self-violation shown in people suffering from hysterical or compulsive illness' (Boss, 1994: 220). This self-annihilation that Boss talked of leads inevitably to an extreme, that is, to the desire to end their own life. Depression can be seen as a loss of freedom of attunement and death is often the last act of free will, which can overcome the numbness.

May (1983) stated that when working with either depressed or anxious clients he tried to help the client to focus on a point outside the depression, allowing the client to gain a more objective view of their situation and also gain the possibility of hope. Cohn believes that the focus with depressed or withdrawn clients should be on the client's total situation 'exploring the world he or she has created, focusing on the important "themes" as they emerge' (Cohn, 1997: 114).

The depressed client becomes 'stuck' in this mood; their feelings of sorrow, loss or guilt seem so overwhelming that nothing feels possible and there is no hope of a future. The fact that there is no future means that life has lost all meaning; Strasser notes, 'When clients lose their meaning, depression ensues. Meaning is interconnected with our values, our aspirations, and our strategies for survival' (Strasser, 1999: 16). Frankl concurs that for some people meaning must be found in their suffering if they are to move forward (Frankl, 1955). Frankl sees depression, or melancholia, as existential anxiety brought about by the tension between what the person is and what he or she ought to be. Rather than experiencing this tension between reality and the ideal as a gap, the melancholic experiences the gap as an abyss that can never be breached. 'It becomes clear that the melancholic's anxiety of conscience arises out of an intrinsically human experience: that of heightened tension between the need and the possibility of fulfilment' (ibid., 1955: 191). When a person's goal becomes unattainable because of the perceived abyss, he or she loses a sense of future and this brings about feelings of insufficiency, worthlessness and meaninglessness of both the self and the world due to guilt.

The task of the client is to find some meaning or hope in life, which will pull them forward towards the future. As Tillich (1952) states, the objective is *to have the courage to be*, to become a person in the face of non-being. However, this is not as easy as it sounds as the depression consumes the whole of the person and often people do not realize that they are depressed until they start coming out of it.

Case illustration

> Depression is a prison where you are both the suffering prisoner and the cruel jailer.
> (Rowe, 1996)

Neisha was depressed and unable to cope both emotionally and financially when she first came to therapy. She was originally from India before settling in England with her family. Neisha's main concern was for her children. She wanted them to gain a good education and get good jobs. She had lived her life for them but felt she had let them down by being a bad mother because she could not control her anger and argued with her children. Her children were reaching an age when they would be leaving home and although Neisha did not want them to leave, as her own life would be empty without them, she realized that her actions were actually driving them away.

Neisha reported that she found it difficult to concentrate as she suffered headaches and felt that she wanted to die. 'I wish God would take me', she said. She felt completely without support and her children did not seem to notice that she needed their support; instead they claimed that she was mad, which added to her problems. Neisha felt stuck, 'not going forward but not going backwards either, just stuck'.

Through our work together it emerged that Neisha had led a life filled with sadness and, somewhat due to her naivety, missed opportunities. There was much that she felt guilty about. Her father had died suddenly and Neisha had not had a chance to say sorry to him for the argument they had had when she left India. This guilt had stopped Neisha grieving properly for her father. Neisha also felt guilty that she had wanted to abort both her pregnancies as she had been pressurized into having children she did not want, but now had two sensitive and intelligent daughters. The fact that Neisha had stayed with her husband for so long even though the marriage had ended many years ago also made her feel guilty since she had lost all her pride. She also felt guilty for the effect this had had on her children who had witnessed some violent arguments during this time. Even the thought of taking her own life made her feel guilty because she would be letting her children down.

Despite the fact that Neisha felt stuck, as a result of the work we did together she was able to formulate the idea that she did want to get an education, since getting a job was important to her. It seemed like a big hurdle she had to cross.

Therapist: 'You are at a point where you have to make a choice, do something for yourself, probably for the first time in your life.'

Neisha: 'Yes, I know, but it is frightening. I have always done what was expected of me, but now there are no expectations, only my own ...'

Therapist: 'and this is what is frightening?'

Neisha: 'yes, what are my expectations for myself?'

Neisha was soon to be on her own and would have to take full responsibility for herself. All her life Neisha had done what was expected of her, being a good daughter and wife; looking after others, cooking and cleaning in both her family's home and then in her husband's family. Since her arrival in the UK Neisha had seen her life in terms of looking after her children and had not put any time or thought into what she herself wanted to achieve. With her children's imminent departure from home, Neisha was faced with the fact that she would be alone and with this came a loss of identity and role in life.

In the therapy Neisha was able to explore the events of her life and by doing this put them into some perspective. She also found qualities in herself that she was proud of, especially her belief in equal opportunities for men and women particularly in education, which was frowned on in her culture. Neisha was able to gain clarity on her situation and her life, and actually put her suffering and experiences into some context. She started a women's group, for Asian women, and invited a number of guest speakers to come and talk about issues related to their lives. Neisha saw the importance of knowledge and how it can help people to make choices about their lives and how her life would have been different if she had known about contraceptives or post-natal depression. Through this process Neisha was able to find meaning in her experiences and this helped her to move forward into the future and discard her feelings of guilt. When the therapy ended Neisha was a lot more positive about her life and busy with the courses she had started as well as with her women's group. She did not fear the fact that her children would soon be leaving home and this allowed her to try and understand them better.

Conclusion

It often seems that depression stems from a fear of the future. However, it is really a fear of being able to live life fully in the present and the risks that this entails, which keeps people depressed. It is ironic that depressed people are able to take the risk to end their life rather than risk living their life. The aim of psychotherapy for these clients is to help them to live and relate in a different way, lifting them out of the gloom or that particular mood and replace it with another mood. Sometimes it is only by feeling that you have reached the bottom, the lowest of the low, that some meaning or insight can be found and an upward ascent is possible.

Critical considerations

The existential approach focuses on exploring the client's worldview and their particular slant on life so as to avoid generalizations and assumptions that may come from the therapist's understanding of what 'depression' is. However, this does not stop existential psychotherapists from having an existential bias on what they are hearing. Therapists need to constantly monitor themselves to ensure that they are enabling their clients to gain an understanding of what *their* depression is like and to find a way forward together.

Recent research has suggested that exercise or physical activity can be helpful for depression (Artal and Sherman, 1998). Not only will this increase the level of serotonin in the body but will stimulate the body's endorphins or feelings of pleasure. However, physical activity has another role in that it allows the person to become reconnected to the world again in a new way. Reconnected through their bodies rather than through social relationships or through their personal thoughts and feelings. This new interaction with the world breaks the stasis that has been their life, and can allow a shift to occur. However, physical activity is not always possible particularly for those depressed clients who also suffer from some physical disability; for some their depression actually stems from their bodily difficulties.

Further investigation of the role of physical activity in the treatment of depression is warranted, as is the role of despair in depression and how existential guilt and anxiety create particular blockages in depressed clients.

Further reading

Boss, M. *Existential Foundations of Medicine and Psychology*.

Cohn, H. W. *Existential Thought and Therapeutic Practice: An Introduction to Existential Psychotherapy*.

May, R. *The Discovery of Being: Writings in Existential Psychology*.

Minkowski, E. 'Findings in a Case of Schizophrenic Depression'. In R. May, E. Angel and H. Ellenberger (eds) *Existence*.

Rowe, D. *Depression: The Way Out of Your Prison*.

CHAPTER 22

Bereavement and Loss

GREG MADISON

> After her death
> at last
> the strong face broke
> through the blurred mask.
>
> Now perhaps
> (if she could see it)
> she would also accept the tree again
> in front of the window.

Cohn, With All Five Senses

Introduction

The forerunner of our modern word 'bereavement' was the old English word *bereafian*, which included the definitions 'to be robbed' or 'deprived of something valuable' (Chambers Dictionary, 1995). In contemporary society *bereavement* most commonly refers to our response to the death of a significant person. Bereavement can be expressed in culturally specific acts of *mourning* – funeral rites, or ritualized withdrawal from public activities, for example. *Grieving* refers to the psychological component of bereavement, the feelings evoked by a significant loss, especially the suffering entailed when a loved person dies.

Since Freud, grieving and mourning have been conceived as the processes whereby the bereaved person adjusts to the reality of their loss, enabling them to disengage from the deceased and reinvest in new relationships (see Klass et al., 1996: 3–16). John Bowlby's attachment theory (1969–1980) and Colin Murray Parkes' psycho-social elaborations (1972) offer psychological models of bereavement, allowing predictions regarding the outcome of an individual's bereavement process (Parkes, 1993). Bowlby believed that our emotional bonds 'arise out of deep seated innate mechanisms which have evolved in order to ensure survival' (ibid., 246). Bowlby argued that infants of many species have physical features and behaviours, which call forth care and protection

197

from older group members. Infants also possess a motivational 'attachment system' 'designed by natural selection to regulate and maintain proximity between infants and their caregivers' (Fraley and Shaver, 1999: 736). The theory implies a cause–effect relationship between early attachment patterns and later reactions to bereavement, arguing that 'whether an individual exhibits a healthy or problematic pattern of grief following separation depends on the way his or her attachment system has become organized over the course of development' (ibid., 740). While accepting Bowlby's theory, Parkes also emphasizes the importance of the psycho-social transitions required after bereavement (see Parkes, 1993: 241–247).

Since the publication of Elisabeth Kubler-Ross's seminal book *On Death and Dying* in 1969, stage models of grief and coming to terms with death have also predominated. Kubler-Ross suggests five distinct phases: denial and isolation, anger, bargaining, depression, and finally, acceptance (Kubler-Ross, 1969). Any person who is bereaved, facing his or her own death, or dealing with loss, should move through these phases sequentially. Potentially a person could get 'stuck' at any stage, impeding their movement to the next stage and thus obstructing 'resolution' of their grieving process.

These various understandings of bereavement allow that each person can have individualized features to their response to loss, but that the process of 'resolving' their bereavement is based upon a predictable template, observable by mental health professionals. Thus we have expectations and theoretical concepts of what is considered 'normal' regarding bereavement, giving rise to 'risk factors' that predict a greater likelihood of 'complicated bereavement' and even diagnoses of 'pathological, unresolved, grief'. An example of this practice is the tendency to pathologize as 'denial' or 'separation anxiety' reports by the bereaved that the deceased may be seen, heard, or conferred with, despite indications that these occurrences may in fact be very common, as well as comforting and reassuring for the bereaved.

The orthodox theories of Parkes (1972, 1983), Bowlby (1969–1980), Worden (1991), and Kubler-Ross (1969) are now being challenged and modified according to a more generally post-modern (and in some respects, existential) approach to understanding in the human sciences and in psychotherapy. In this critique, modernist clinical assumptions regarding healthy outcomes are relativized as one possibility among many and not to be prioritized or imposed universally upon the experience of bereaved people.

In their introductory chapter to *Continuing Bonds*, Klass et al. (1996: 3–27) argue that the prevailing model of bereavement emphasizes our separateness from each other, putting a positive value on autonomy and individuation while devaluing interdependence (ibid., 14–15). Klass et al. do not see bereavement or grieving as ever fully resolved, culminating in 'closure' or 'recovery'. They propose that 'rather than emphasising letting go, the emphasis should be on negotiating and renegotiating the meaning of the loss over time. While the death is permanent and unchanging, the process is not' (ibid., 18–19). The work of grieving and mourning in this view is to maintain the presence of the deceased in the web of family and social relationships by establishing a continuing role for them within the lives of the bereaved. For example, bereaved parents may indicate the deceased child's ongoing presence in the family with statements such as, 'We've got three children, one of whom has died' (Walter, 1996: 10).

Bowlby-enthusiasts dispute that these recent challenges, emphasizing continuing bonds to the deceased rather than breaking bonds to develop new relationships, contradict attachment theory. As the controversy continues, it is at least apparent that *Continuing Bonds* challenges theories that had become sedimented as fact while reclaiming as possibilities reactions that were previously pathologized. These reclaimed possibilities may have constituted the norm in other cultures or at other times, for example with various rituals of ancestor worship or communicating with the dead. An existential-phenomenological stance offers an opportunity to augment these views while offering a less directive approach to bereavement counselling.

An existential perspective

Bereavement epitomizes a linked confrontation of two fundamental existential givens: death and relatedness. How do we remain open to others, form bonds with them, seek their company, fall in love, knowing the day will come...? In the words of Eric Klinger, 'The essence of tragedy is that humans are the playthings of the gods: that people's lives are vehicles for the expression of cosmic forces, that people's fortunes must often submit to forces beyond their control' (Klinger, 1977: 137).

The discussion will emphasize the following themes:

- an intersubjective and interactional view of human existence as opposed to the individualism of other approaches;
- questioning the ethological underpinning for bereavement theories;
- the impact that the death of another can have on our awareness of personal mortality; and
- a note on bereavement counselling and working phenomenologically.

Intersubjectivity

In *Being and Time* (1927) Heidegger describes how human beings are absorbed in the world, inextricably responsive to it, and concerned with it, since fundamentally our being is an *opening onto existence*. We are not complete sealed-off subjects separated from an outside by the skin of our bodies.[1] Each human existence *essentially is* interaction with the world and with other people. 'Heidegger's name for this communal dimension of my own Being-in-the-world is *Being-with*' (Polt, 1999: 60). 'Being-with' challenges the concept of separate subjects needing to form 'attachments' across their isolation in order to survive. Heidegger fundamentally questions the idea of individuals having 'inner worlds' pointed at 'outer' objects. Before we can have an 'attachment theory' we have to presuppose a 'separation theory', which from an existential-phenomenological stance is not sustainable. Even the choice to be alone is – within the context of relationships – a comment on it. We are inescapably *with-beings*, thrown into and responding to specific social and cultural worlds.

The French existential philosopher Merleau-Ponty refers to society as a 'between-world' (cf. Madison, 2001: 4). He attributes this to the intersubjective aspect of our early childhood experiences in which we live in a sort of anonymous collectivity and this continues to function in, and remains the ground of, our later adult relationships (Merleau-Ponty, 1964a). We remain forever associated in a nexus which exceeds our understanding, and our 'emotional ties with others are possible only because we continue to live primarily in the other's gestures and responses' (Diamond, 1996: 129).

Eugene Gendlin, an American existential philosopher and psychologist, furthers this phenomenological tradition by prioritizing bodily 'interaction'. He points out that we usually separate a relationship into the 'individuals' involved and focus on them. According to Gendlin our being-in-the-world is fundamental: 'It's not that the interaction affects the individual and then makes him different. In the very ongoing of that interaction, he is already different' (Gendlin, 1966: 216–217). Interaction is first, so that *how we live* our situations (and relationships) is not merely an inner, subjective or hidden variable of objective space. Gendlin points us back to how our bodies live 'opened up to' situations, especially other humans – the two people are *derived from* their specific situational relationship – so what happens when one person is no longer there?

The bereaved person not only metaphorically but also literally has lost a part of their world. The bereaved body will continue to 'imply' the deceased in order to fill in that co-created interaction, that relationship within which they both lived. Widows[2] describe poignantly their spontaneous imaginings of the dead husband about to return home, ready to share the day's events together as always, his place set at the table, a whole world re-created before the unfulfilled interaction reveals his absence, the 'mourned-for' again falls out from the assumed environment. Such moments can lead to heartfelt grief and once again, even years after the death, a world fails to materialize because he is not there. For some, an approximate 'filling-in' of this implying can be found in *socially supported* continuing bonds to the deceased. For others, it may be that eventually the need for the lost relationship is addressed when a new relationship allows the implied interaction to reoccur in some way. Still others will choose to withdraw from the world of relationship and carry their loss along unchanged. Each choice reveals aspects of the person's way of being and this can be disclosed and explored in counselling without presuming which choice is preferable.

While writing this chapter I experienced the bereavement of a favourite tutor and mentor. I had visited him once in hospital and was planning to visit him again the morning I was told of his death. I had seen him infrequently the months before he died but since his death he has at times become almost physically present for me. His absence is now 'present' in a compelling way. In certain settings, like the training college where we both taught, I can 'recognize him' whenever I see a stout old man with white hair across the park. Immediately I feel a warmth and sadness rise in my chest. It is as if something in me implies his existence and his meaning for me. If I stay with that feeling I find in it a tragic sense related to the circumstances of his dying, something of my own mortality and how unexpected it might be, and a distinct feeling of 'something more' that is not easily thought.

Human being and animal behaviour

As well as questioning the individualism of attachment theory, an existential stance challenges the appropriateness of the theory's underlying ethology. Are humans so similar to other species that the scientific study of animal behaviour can form the basis of an understanding of complex human experiences like bereavement? Can a duck use relationships to bolster self-esteem, express love, deny death and fulfil its future?[3] According to Heidegger, 'Da-sein is a being that does not simply occur among other beings. Rather it is ontically distinguished by the fact that in its being this being is concerned *about* its very being' (Heidegger, 1996: 10). Da-sein, human being, is unique in that we 'care' about our existence (it matters to us). Significant aspects of our 'care' would include an awareness of our interrelatedness and the anxiety concerning our own mortality. The death of someone significant is a powerful reminder of one's own impotence, vulnerable openness and impending demise. Bereavement simultaneously calls forth an awareness of personal mortality imbued with the experience of an implied interaction which cannot be fulfilled, an incompleteness frozen in the face of the end of all possibilities. Of course not all bereavements imply such 'lack' and mourning, but even this variation in possibilities further highlights that Dasein's distinctive mode of being necessitates a distinctively human understanding of our response to death and loss.

Bereavement and mortality

In *Existential Psychotherapy* (1980), Irvin Yalom proposes that the uniqueness of the existential approach is that it does not assume 'suppressed instincts' or 'internalized parental conflicts', but rather seeks to explore the 'conflict that flows from the individual's confrontation with the givens of existence' (Yalom, 1980: 8). In working with the bereaved, Yalom has found,

> The death of someone close will, if the therapist persists, always lead to an increased death awareness. There are many components to grief – the sheer loss, the ambivalence and guilt, the disruption of a life plan – and all need to be thoroughly dealt with in treatment. But, ... the death of another also brings one closer to facing one's own death; and this part of grief work is commonly omitted. Some psychotherapists may feel that the bereaved is already too overwhelmed to accept the added task of dealing with his or her own finiteness. I think, however, that assumption is often an error: some individuals can grow enormously as a result of personal tragedy. (Ibid., 167–168)

Yalom's view is that loss and bereavement can cause a rip in the fabric of our assumed world, through which unwelcome existential realities may be glimpsed. Bereavement, therefore, could be an 'existential opportunity' though a painful or even overwhelming one. The edifices we construct around a 'self', our reputations, self-esteem, relationships, values, and possessions, can be exposed as folly in the face of death. At the very least, it highlights how death can interrupt life unexpectedly, making a mockery of our well-laid plans. In the words of Victor Frankl, 'As a finite being, man never perfectly completes his life task. When he is willing and able to shoulder the burden of this incompleteness, he is acknowledging this finiteness' (Frankl, 1967: 54). As stated above, the tension of bereavement can highlight the primordial human paradox of being fundamentally intersubjective, while inexorably retaining the formidable 'mine' of existence, my death.

Bereavement counselling

From an existential perspective, it would be more accurate to say 'counselling instigated by a bereavement' rather than 'bereavement counselling'. This is an important distinction because it acknowledges the impossibility of separating out from a person's world one issue and providing counselling for just that. Clients do not experience their world in such a compartmentalized way and rarely do they stick to discussing only their bereavement, even in 'bereavement counselling'. In the words of one client, 'I'm not looking for a bereavement counsellor . . . I want to look at myself, at my whole life. I want to find out what it is all about' (Jonathan, 1997: 128).

Bereavement often initiates intensive self-reflection regarding life in general. Rather than cause–effect interpretations based upon the client's earliest attachments, the existential therapist explores the client's own interpretations of the meaning of their choices, as well as unfulfilled potentials, future intentions, personal values, and their response to the limits inherent in life. The therapist gives up the pretence of knowing in advance and does not predict appropriate outcomes for the client, but rather remains democratic, descriptive and exploratory. Counselling sessions seek to increase the client's awareness of what remains implicit in their responses and actions and to explore shared human experiences as they are revealed within the therapeutic dyad. This means that the counsellor does not remain distant and impersonal, but enters fully into a mutual dialogue concerning the client's experience. Gendlin's concept of 'interaction first' (1997: 22) reminds us that there cannot be a purely 'professional relationship'. What the client is feeling and thinking will be what-the-client-is-like-*with-this-therapist* but also vice versa. It opens up the possible range of interventions to include relationship variables: asking how the client is feeling talking to the therapist, therapist disclosure of what the interaction feels like from their side, and therapist self-disclosure about their own life and bereavements. Anything that moves and deepens the therapeutic relationship will also imply change in the client because there is no *separated-off* client.

Most people do not seek, or need, counselling after bereavement. In *A New Model of Grief: Bereavement and Biography*, Walter (1996) suggests that grief is not an individual process best responded to in counselling sessions, but rather a social process.[4] His own experience of bereavement was that 'this was not social support for an intrinsically personal grief process, but an intrinsically social process in which we negotiated and re-negotiated who Corina was, how she had died and what she meant to us' (Walter, 1996: 13). If we accept that the preferred response to bereavement is social dialogue, incorporating the network of people who knew the deceased, what is the role of the so-called 'bereavement counselling'?

Contrary to Walter's description, bereaved people can be made to feel there is something wrong with continuing to locate the deceased in their ongoing lives. It is not uncommon for the bereaved to enter counselling precisely because the people around them are no longer interested in discussing the deceased. On the other hand, some clients may seek counselling because they, unlike their friends and family, cannot talk about the deceased. And there are also instances when the social world does not recognize the legitimacy of the required discourse, so that the bereaved cannot locate and process the new roles and reality impinging upon them.[5] Perhaps the role of counselling is to offer a relationship that allows the bereaved to re-enter a world of discourse, to approximate the social world when, for whatever reason, it has receded from their daily lives.

Case illustration: when he died I could finally grieve for myself

While a hospital inpatient, Mrs N learned that her husband had also fallen ill and been admitted to a different ward in the same hospital. Mrs N was too ill to visit her husband and two days later he died – they had been married forty-nine years. A counsellor agreed to meet with Mrs N and to sit with her while the rest of the family attended the funeral in a few days time.

Mrs N quickly warmed to the idea of counselling and asked the counsellor to call her Antonia. She was a polite seventy-two-year-old native Austrian who presented as quite self-conscious and reserved. She felt ashamed of not crying or acting upset at her husband's death and explained this away as 'shock'. She made it clear from the outset that she wanted to concentrate on what had been 'good' in her relationship with her husband, implying that some things had not been so good between them. Antonia and the counsellor agreed to meet weekly for what turned out to be the duration of her hospital stay, six months.

The story of Mrs N's life gradually unfolded over the ensuing weeks. She had grown up as an only child in a small town in Austria during the Nazi occupation. Her parents were cold and abusive towards her. She thought of herself as weak and easily frightened, though she gradually questioned this as she recalled situations in which she acted with extreme courage. For example, Antonia described her efforts to feed a Jewish family in hiding near her childhood home. She would bring them bread when possible until she was exposed and spent a terrifying afternoon undergoing Gestapo interrogation. When the allies liberated her town she met a young British soldier who promptly asked her to marry him and she soon left for London against the advice of her parents and friends.

Early in the counselling, Mrs N alluded to how her husband's behaviour became violent when she arrived in London, but she maintained that he 'was a good man, difficult, but good'. It emerged that he regularly attacked her and gave her black eyes and bruises. She felt too ashamed and too proud to admit the relationship was a mistake and leave him. Antonia had never confessed these things to anyone else. Although her children were aware of the abuse, they never spoke of it, nor was Antonia allowed to talk to them about her past. Her children were left with only a cursory idea of who their mother was.

Although the original counselling issue was bereavement, the sessions quickly broadened out to include Mrs N's whole way of living as it was expressed in her past decisions, her relationship with her husband and children, her present relationship with the counsellor, and her hopes for the future. Telling her story for the first time to the counsellor allowed Antonia to feel a growing self-respect for her ability to stand up to tyrants. She had been suffering from terrifying night visions of her husband's corpse standing in the doorway to her room, looking angry, but these gradually receded as her image of herself as courageous and independent increased.[6] As her self-respect grew, so did her ability to face the abusiveness of her husband. This finally triggered her bereavement, not for the loss of her husband, but a deep grief for the years he had taken from her.

Antonia also gradually started to share her life story with her children and grandchildren, although this was very difficult for all of them. Her children began to see her as resilient and even 'heroic' rather than as the frightened victim of their father. They stopped trying to control her future (as their father had) and listened to what she wanted for herself. Antonia dreamed about getting a flat of her own with flowers on the balcony, buying herself new dresses for the first time in years and going to church again.

Antonia was enthusiastic about counselling and the opportunity to finally tell her story, and to begin to challenge her assumptions about life. It is interesting that once Antonia began to talk about her life with the counsellor, she was gradually able to share these details with her children. This seems to support the view that as an approximation of the social world, counselling can act as a 'rehearsal' for re-negotiating significant relationships in that world in a more honest and satisfying way. Theories about the 'bereavement process' and 'bereavement counselling' seemed less useful than staying close to Antonia's expressed needs and her gradual freedom from her own expectations of what bereavement should entail.

Antonia would have rated high on specific 'risk factors' and could have been the object of a well-intentioned plan of bereavement counselling or other intervention. The agendas usually presumed in such approaches may have hindered the unfolding of an entirely unpredictable process, directed by the client herself. It seems that working phenomenologically, without imposing the counsellor's preconceptions and in fact challenging the client's own preconceptions about what she should feel, provided an opening for her to engage in a comprehensive review of her life and her general way of being-in-the-world. We should remember that not every reaction to bereavement is grief and not every bond is a loving one.

Critical considerations

Paradoxically, critiques of an existential approach generally mirror what from another angle could be seen as its benefits. Bereavement counselling, like most 'specialisms' in counselling, is heavily imbued with a medical, 'treatment', approach to people. In this approach counsellors are considered experts in alleviating or curing another's distress. With scarce resources it is of course important that publicly funded counselling is as 'effective' as possible. But how is that defined?

An approach that offers treatment protocols, working assumptions of who is most 'at risk' and therefore prioritized for treatment, will be very attractive to funders. These approaches will also be seductive to counsellors who want to feel secure that they are being effective, and to clients in search of similar certainty. Such approaches, because they have a clear view of what is a positive outcome, are in a much better position to provide evidence for the efficacy of their approach. The phenomenological method is not compatible with attempts to develop counselling interventions based upon theoretical preconceptions. In fact, as was suggested earlier, a phenomenological counsellor will approach a bereaved client with the same openness as any other client, with no presumption regarding what should take place. This is difficult to sell in a marketplace where strictly delineated brief therapy is increasingly prescribed for bereavement.

Existential practitioners will need to acknowledge the interests of NHS institutions and publicly funded voluntary agencies if the approach is to achieve the significant impact it is capable of having in the area of bereavement counselling. In order to do this, existential therapists will need to engage in psychotherapy research.[7] This research could include studies based upon what bereaved clients themselves say about their counselling experiences, and research into what kinds of processes unfold and carry forward the client's experience as counselling continues. It may also be instructive to explore whether there really is such a thing as 'bereavement counselling' distinguishable from generic counselling in practice.

Notes

1 We will discuss later the work of Eugene Gendlin, who suggests that our bodies *are* constant body–environment interaction, the site of our *connection with* rather than *separation from* the world.
2 The same phenomenon can presumably occur with any bereaved person.
3 There is no neutral ground from which to compare human and animal behaviour – we cannot know an animal's world since we must perceive from within our own human worldview. The Norwegian philosopher Arne Naess uses the term 'maze epistemology' to refer to the experimenter who watches a rat in a maze and, without acknowledging it, projects his human motivations onto the rat to interpret the rat's behaviour.
4 Minna Pietila's study of support groups for family members bereaved by suicide suggests that sharing experiences with others in a group is enough to overcome

cultural expectations, specifically white middle-class 'stage and task' theories of grief and their 'coercive rules for normal grieving' (Pietila, 2002: 410). She emphasizes the sociological side of bereavement and the necessity of dealing with the person's world-interactions as much as with the hypothesized realm of 'individual inner psychology'.

5 Relationships which are not socially recognized may include, for example, gay relationships.

6 These visions clearly were not symbols of a positive continuing bond, nor were they signs of pathology, but rather indications of Antonia's self-construct at that time, and of her abusive marriage.

7 A recent volume of *Existential Analysis* (Vol. 15.1) includes a number of articles dealing with psychotherapy research from an existential perspective.

Further reading

Fraley, R. C. and Shaver, P. R. 'Loss and Bereavement: Attachment Theory and Recent Controversies Concerning "Grief Work" and the Nature of Detachment'. In J. Cassidy and P. R. Shaver (eds) *Handbook of Attachment: Theory, Research, and Clinical Applications.*

Gendlin, E. T. *Focusing – Oriented Psychotherapy: A Manual of the Experiential Method.*

Klass, D., Silverman, P. R. and Nickman, S. L. (eds) *Continuing Bonds: New Understandings of Grief.*

Parkes, C. M., Laungani, P. and Young, B. (eds) *Death and Bereavement Across Cultures.*

Walter, T. 'A New Model of Grief: Bereavement and Biography', *Mortality.*

Worden, J. W. *Grief Counselling and Grief Therapy: A Handbook for the Mental Health Practitioner.*

CHAPTER 23

Dreams

SARAH YOUNG

> In all of us, even in good men, there is a lawless wild beast nature which peers out in sleep.
>
> Plato, *Republic*

Introduction

Even before our existence became a concern for us and we were able to ask Heidegger's question 'What is the meaning of Being?', it is likely we were intrigued by our dreams. There is a long history of dream interpretation in all human cultures, but it was not until the beginning of the twentieth century, when Freud published his seminal work *The Interpretation of Dreams* (1900) that dreams were accepted by some as meaningful and their interpretation was given a measure of scientific credibility.

Freud believed that he had 'discovered the enigma of dreams', namely that dreams enabled the fulfillment of unacceptable wishes. He provided a highly elaborate theory of dream interpretation that involved unraveling the heavily disguised (as he believed it to be) dream material. His theory was embedded in a natural scientific, mechanistic framework and encompassed an intra-psychic model of the mind. As we know, for Freud our early experience is crucial in determining our adult experience, so invariably the wishes revealed in dreams originate from childhood. Because these wishes provoke anxiety they need to be hidden in manifest dreams. Hence Freud's idea that 'dreams are the guardians of sleep' – they allow wishes to be fulfilled without provoking anxiety that awakes the dreamer. Through psychoanalytic investigation and interpretation the latent dream wish can be revealed and the unconscious desires known.

Unconscious mechanisms such as 'condensation', 'displacement' and 'symbolism' are employed to disguise the unacceptable desires. Even the retelling of the dream adds to the disguise – the so-called 'secondary revision'. The procedure of analyzing the dream uncovers these mechanisms and allows access to unconscious 'primary process' thinking. Through free association the unconscious dream thoughts are revealed and the process by which the dream was formed is reconstructed (analysis by synthesis). We can see why Freud regarded his method of interpretation as the 'royal road to the unconscious' (Freud, 1900: 769).

Following Freud, Jung produced his own theory of dream analysis that made a move towards a more phenomenological understanding. He did not believe that dreams were disguised in the way Freud had described and he therefore showed a greater interest in the manifest content. At the same time his notion of archetypes and the collective unconscious led him away from the description of the phenomena of actual experience.

The Swiss psychiatrist Medard Boss, having studied both psychoanalysis and analytical psychology, went on to delineate Daseinsanalysis, a psychotherapy founded on Heidegger's ontology. Through his understanding of Heidegger's analysis of existence Boss was able to develop his unique understanding of the dreaming state. Like Freud, Boss accorded dreams great attention and published two books describing a phenomenological understanding of the dreaming state. In the first book *The Analysis of Dreams* (1957) he argued against the hypothetical constructs of 'depth psychology' and for a phenomenological understanding in which the dream phenomena are accepted for what they are in all their significance. His second book *I Dreamt Last Night…*(1977) provides us with a handbook for investigating dreams phenomenologically.

The existential-phenomenological perspective described here is for the most part derived from Boss's work. But in contrast to Boss (though following Heidegger) I do not accept it is possible to discover the 'essence' of a phenomenon – this difference will be discussed later. Moustakas (1994) and van Deurzen (2002a) have also discussed working with dreams from an existential perspective.

An existential perspective

> Everything is what it is, not something else. (Goethe: 1977)

The radical difference between existential phenomenology and depth psychology is particularly apparent in the area of dream analysis. The idea of an encapsulated psyche separate from the world is replaced by Heidegger's understanding of human existence as 'invisible, intangible capacities for receiving-perceiving what it encounters and what addresses it.... This new view of the basic constitution of human existence may be called Da-sein, or being-in-the-world' (Heidegger, 2001: 4). The psychoanalytic concepts described above are dispensed with, gone are theories of the unconscious and its mechanisms, the enclosed mind with its internal conflicts and with them all the elaborate disguises associated with dreams. Consciousness has moved out into the world and become relational; we are beings-in-the-world, a world that we cannot get out of any more than we can avoid being in relation with others.

Thus the emphasis is on our unity with our world – we carry our world with us, and when we die our world dies with us. Dasein as a being-there is a 'realm of world-openness', we are nothing other than a 'receptive, alert world disclosiveness' (Boss, 1963: 29). In other words we *are* our interactions with others and all our experience reveals our relatedness to everything we encounter. Consciousness is always consciousness of something and experience is always of or about something. Consciousness is relational and our interactions take place in the space between us and others, us and the phenomena of our world. This fundamental relatedness of human existence is revealed in dreaming life just as it is in waking life.

We exist no less in dreams than we do in waking life and we always exist in our relations with other people and things. Our experiences in dreams are as real as anything we experience in waking life. A dream dog is experienced as a dog and is as real as any dog encountered in waking life. In dreams our emotional responses are felt and experienced as they are in waking life. There are no images or symbols but rather in dreams we experience 'real psychical facts' – 'a thing is a real thing, an animal a real animal, a man is a real man, a ghost a real ghost' (Boss, 1957: 106). Dream phenomena do not refer to or stand for something else, they are what they are and are accepted in their own full meaning and content just as they are felt to be within the immediate experience of the dream.

We do not *have* dreams, they are not separate objects that happen upon us, rather 'we are our dreaming state' and we can realize our existence in dreams just as we can in waking life through the most varied relationships and attitudes. We are always connected with the meaning in whatever we encounter and this is as true of dreaming life as it is of waking life. Boss argues that meaning can be derived from what is present in the dream phenomena themselves, but as will be discussed later I believe the meaning of a phenomenon requires the dreamer's experience of that phenomenon to be taken into account. Boss is concerned with this to the extent that the dreamer's interaction with a phenomenon will reveal their 'world-openness'.

Dreams are an integral part of our everyday existence and we can explore them like any other phenomena. The dream phenomena require as much or as little interpretation as the phenomena of waking life. They should be allowed to show themselves in all their significance, they are openings to be attended to, not puzzles to be solved. Dream phenomena are adhered to in terms of their own nature without theoretical presuppositions so that meaning can emerge as the dreamer interacts with the dream phenomena.

What does this mean for the exploration of dreams in therapy? The therapist encourages the former dreamer to tell the dream as experienced without the logic and reactions of everyday thinking. The context of the dream needs to be fleshed out and by asking questions a fuller picture can be gained. The therapist will have in mind the tripartite question (Condrau, 1993): *Where* does the dream take place? *What* is encountered? *How* does the dreamer respond? The therapist is at all times concerned to stay with the dreamer and their experience, to gain with greater and greater precision a description of the dream phenomena. Despite the seeming simplicity of this task it is far more difficult than it first appears. There is an ever-present temptation to interpret dream phenomena and fall into the trap of 'this means that', rather than stay with the phenomena themselves. But there is a wealth of significance inherent in the dream phenomena and once revealed an understanding of the dreamer's way of being can be reached.

Dreaming and waking behaviour are seen as analogous. The dreamer's way of being can only be revealed once the dream phenomena have been penetrated for all their significance and once the context and the mood of the dream is clearly understood. When this has been achieved the dreamer can be asked, 'what does this dream tell you about your everyday existence?' For Boss the emphasis was on 'bearing' (how one bears oneself towards others, the world and life) and 'possibility' (as yet unlived possibilities). He believed that if dreams were understood they could have healing effects. Once the dreamer has gained an insight into their 'existential condition' as revealed in the dream, they then become aware of their as yet unlived possibilities. By not attending to our dreams we miss out on a wealth of self-knowledge, we remain only half awake to ourselves. If we neglect to develop this self-understanding our unlived possibilities will remain in the shadows.

Case illustration

> So if I dream I have you, I have you.
> For, all our joys are but fantastical.
>
> Donne, *Elegy X The Dream*

Sally, a twenty-seven-year-old psychiatric nurse lived with her partner of six years. They had recently become engaged and moved into a flat they purchased together. Sally wanted to extend her work as a psychiatric nurse so she embarked on a Diploma in Counselling, which required her to be in therapy (she had some previous telephone counselling and acknowledged she might have sought therapy even without the course requirement). She found the process of therapy extremely difficult, as she had always been a very private person and hated asking for help or support from anyone. The process became so intolerable for her that after three months she began attending sessions fortnightly. This arrangement continued for six months until Sally decided to return to weekly therapy. Despite still finding the process uncomfortable she recognized she was gaining in self-understanding and wanted to extend this further. She was also more able to tolerate being the focus of attention.

Sally described her early background as reasonably stable and materially comfortable. This became completely disrupted during her adolescence when her father left home for a period. He suffered a serious depression, was sectioned and also imprisoned. He was drinking heavily throughout this time and his business went into difficulties. Her parent's relationship looked in jeopardy and the family home had to be sold. Throughout this period Sally felt totally isolated. Her brother, to whom she was not close, had left home just prior to her father's illness. Her parents were completely caught up with their own concerns and Sally found herself unable to accept tentative offers of support from school friends and teachers. Her feelings of abandonment and anger have been explored in therapy and though she would now describe herself as close to her father she continues to feel resentment towards her mother.

Sally considered that her relationship with her partner was caring and supportive. Eventually they planned to marry and have children, and Sally described herself as feeling very 'broody'. The following dream was reported recently and was explored over two sessions.

> I am with my baby but I am aware this is weird because I have just told someone I want a baby. My mother has brought some clothes for the baby but they are the wrong colour, they are pink and the baby is a boy. I start to make a list of all the things I will have to buy, it gets longer and longer. I become aware that a nurse on my ward is the father of the baby, yet she is female and this isn't possible. I start to feed the baby and feel overwhelming love and great responsibility.

The process of exploration and clarification that is embarked upon is really no different from that which occurs in existential therapy generally. The client and therapist are in dialogue – they are concerned with a 'discourse' that 'lets something be seen' (Heidegger, 1962: 56). This phenomenological investigation involves broadening the context so that a fuller understanding of the phenomena can be reached, though, as mentioned earlier, there is no expectation of discovering the 'essence' of any phenomenon. The process is never completed, there are no final answers and aspects of any phenomenon remain concealed. Heidegger emphasized that a 'phenomenon is not only what immediately shows itself, that in fact whatever shows itself arises from something that remains concealed' (Cohn, 2002: 48).

Through this process of questioning and clarification an attempt was made to gain a fuller understanding of Sally's experience whilst dreaming. For example:

What was it like for you realizing you have told someone you want to have a baby yet you have one?

I felt embarrassed, it didn't make sense.

Embarrassed in what way?

I can't really say, I felt ashamed – *ashamed?* – I think I felt stupid really.

Who was it you told? Were they present in the dream?

No, its like a memory, in fact that day I had actually been telling one of the doctors on the ward that I wanted to have a baby.

You said your mother brought the wrong clothes – what was it for you that she had done that? Was she there? Do you know where you were?

I've just remembered there was a red T-shirt. I felt annoyed and worried. She wasn't there, there was no one else in the dream but I did have a sort of awareness of my partner being somewhere in the flat.

What was worrying/annoying?

I would have to buy the right clothes and there might not be enough money.

We continued to explore the dream in this way in order to try and establish the full context of the dream. What was encountered, how did she respond to

what was encountered, what was her mood? For the most part we stayed with
the dream experience though at times it was hard to resist the temptation to
digress into an exploration of aspects extraneous to the dreaming state – for
example her waking relationship with those who entered the dream. To some
extent I followed Boss's suggestion of answering the 'tripartite question'
before broadening the exploration but this was not something I stuck to
rigidly, though my questions or reflections would have it in mind. Having
gained some understanding of the dreaming state we then went on to explore
in what ways this state was analogous to her waking experience. Frequently
Sally made her own connections to her waking experience and on occasions
I tentatively suggested possible links. For example:

> *At the beginning of the dream you both have a baby and are aware that you have*
> *just told someone you want one. Does this reflect your feelings of ambivalence*
> *about having a baby?*

Yes that's it, I really thought I wanted to have a baby but now I realize the
huge responsibility of it.

> *You describe being aware of your partner but not being in direct communication*
> *with him – this sounds similar to your description of your waking experience.*

Yes, it's so often like that, we seem to live side by side but are never really
together.

> *Your mother buys clothes for the baby but they are wrong – that too sounds*
> *familiar.*

That's so typical, she hasn't a clue about me and even if she does try to do
something it's never what's needed.

> *You seem to be saying that your overall feeling during the dream was one of*
> *fear and overwhelming responsibility. How does that resonate with your*
> *waking experience?*

It is not possible in such a brief account to give a full picture of what
emerged during our exploration of this question but I will highlight some of
the themes. Sally realized her desire to get things 'right', her perfectionism
and her horror of appearing stupid were apparent in various ways. She felt
humiliated that the doctor, with whom she had a mutually respectful relationship,
should be a witness to her mistake. Her desire to make everything 'perfect' for
the baby was revealed when we explored the list she was making. Her troubled
relationship with her mother was exemplified in terms of her getting it
'wrong' – ever since the family troubles Sally had felt let down by her mother.
That her colleague at work should be the father of the baby was extremely
puzzling – during an exploration of this relationship Sally realized she felt
unsafe with this colleague, she never knew 'where she was coming from' and
she could not trust her.

Her preoccupation with money worries was revealed when exploring her
feeling that the clothes were 'wrong', 'there may not be enough money to get
the best things'.

Sally recognized that ever since the change in the family finances she had
worried about not having enough money. In her present situation with her

partner it was she who put a constraint on their spending. She was struck by the fact that during the dream she was aware of her partner but he was not actually visible. It came home to her how much they had both been concentrating on their careers and sorting out the flat and how little time they had given to their relationship.

During our exploration Sally found it difficult to expand on her experience of various emotions. This was a recurring theme, at times she found it almost impossible to describe what she experienced and she expressed a desire to be 'more in touch with her feelings'. She believed that during the time of her father's difficulties 'she closed herself off from others and her own feelings'. As we explored this dream, contrary to her usual experience, Sally became quite emotional. Her overall feeling was one of fear: she was frightened of appearing stupid; fearful about shortage of money; but most profoundly of all fearful of the responsibility of having a baby. She realized how overwhelmed she felt by all her commitments (running the ward, studying for the course, taking on the flat) and despite 'being swept along with the desire to have a child I'm not ready for it'. Her awareness of her tendency to say 'yes', to put others first and to ignore her own needs also emerged in our exploration. The family lore of 'Sally will be alright' once again featured in our discussion.

As a result of this exploration Sally recognized the importance of attending to her relationship with her partner. She acknowledged her tendency to be independent and not show any vulnerability – it was interesting that no one else, aside from the baby, was actually present in the dream. She resolved 'to be more open with her partner to allow him in and let him see her vulnerability'. The extent to which she felt anxious and overburdened came home to her forcefully and she realized she needed to make some changes. She decided that she certainly did not want to have a baby yet, at the same time she was struck by the intensity of her desire to eventually become a mother. Sally was dimly aware of most of what was revealed in this exploration but she was surprised by the strength of her feelings and recognized there was much that needed to be resolved between her and her partner before any decisions could be made about the future.

Critical considerations

> Nothing belongs to you more intimately than your dreams! They alone are your own work. (Nietzsche: 1957)

Boss accused Freud and Jung of producing theories of dream interpretation that allowed for a large measure of arbitrariness. It was the analyst who unravelled the elaborate disguises of dream-work or the archetypal material and arrived at the final interpretation. The interpreter's insight and understanding took precedence over that of the dreamer.

Despite Boss's awareness of this danger and his insistence on staying with the dream phenomena this very insistence provokes its own measure of arbitrariness. Boss argued that in our technological age we have lost sight of the full meaning and richness inherent in the phenomena we encounter. He believed that the *essence* of a phenomenon was there to be discovered if we take the time and this essence was universal, something we could all agree on. We can therefore arrive at a *correct* interpretation of a dream. Boss believed that absolute knowledge of any phenomenon was achievable – here his allegiance appears to be more with Husserl than with Heidegger. Is it possible for us to ever know the full meaning of any phenomenon? Surely a phenomenon cannot be torn from its context as if it stands alone outside its situation. Earlier I touched on Heidegger's idea of 'hiddenness' and 'concealment': something may be revealed and in that process there is a covering over – we can never fully know, all our explorations are partial.

Boss's colleague Condrau (1994) made it abundantly clear that it is *not* for the dreamer (or the analyst) to decide the meaning of a dream but 'it is the dream itself that tells us its meaning'. This is all right in so far as it goes but I believe Boss fell into the same type of arbitrary behaviour of which he accused Freud and Jung. Frequently in his descriptions it seems it is Boss who is the arbiter of the dream's meaning and his values shine through. For a further discussion of these criticisms, see Scott (1977), Young (1993) and Condrau (1994).

Earlier I mentioned the importance given to dream analysis within psychoanalysis and Daseinsanalysis. But is there any justification for treating dreams as different from any other phenomena that our clients describe in therapy? Surely the dream phenomena described deserve the same kind of investigation and clarification as anything else. As we have seen we can learn about our ways of relating, our values and beliefs and, our fundamental stance in the world from dream phenomena just as from waking phenomena. Exploration of our dreams can give us an insight into our 'existential condition' and provide us with information we have in some way passed over. If we want to understand ourselves better and find new ways of realizing our possibilities then we had best not ignore our dreams.

I am arguing for an exploration of dreams, which does not necessarily place them in a special position but leaves them alongside any other phenomena discussed in therapy. I stand by my view that 'ultimately, it must be the dreamer to decide the meaning of their dream' (Young, 1993).

Further reading

Boss, M. *I Dreamt Last Night....*
Boss, M. *The Analysis of Dreams.*
Boss, M. and Kenny, B. 'Phenomenological or Daseinsanalytic Approach'. In J. L. Fosshage and C. A. Loew (eds) *Dream Interpretation: A Comparative Study.*
Condrau, G. 'Dream Analysis: Do We Need the Unconscious?', *Existential Analysis.*
Scott, C. E. (ed.) *On Dreaming: An Encounter with Medard Boss.*

PART V
SPIRITUAL DIMENSION

CHAPTER 24

Introduction to the Spiritual Dimension

EMMY VAN DEURZEN AND CLAIRE ARNOLD-BAKER

There is no question that a spiritual dimension is the most controversial level of human experience. Some people would strongly deny that it exists when few people would ever deny that there is a physical or a social dimension. Nevertheless it is obvious that all of us have particular points of view about things. We may start out copying other people's views about things or believe what we are told to believe, but sooner or later we discover that our own opinions differ from those of the people around us. We can therefore learn to be aware of the different layers of our beliefs, our values, our assumptions, our purpose and our aspirations. This dimension is really about how we make sense of the world and how we create meaning. This is something we can do either implicitly or explicitly. It is also about our relationship to the unknown or the metaphysical level of existence, and how we understand it or make sense of it for ourselves. We do not have to be religious to have ideals and a particular perspective on life. Existential therapy aims to enhance a person's capacity for being reflective about their perspective on the world.

1. All of us grow up with a given worldview. The outlook of our culture, our society, our particular time in history defines who we are to some extent.

2. We immediately begin finding out that there are other ways of understanding life and the universe from meeting new people, watching television and films, reading books, newspapers, and so on. We gradually discover that we have definite convictions that we may feel quite passionate about, and in this way we refine our own ideology.

3. Sooner or later we encounter opposition to our views and prejudice. We can then discover the drawbacks of dogmatism. We may of course already have experienced the pressure of dogmatism by having been told what to do and what to believe in by people with narrow minds, or with a particularly positive focus. A good way to expand our vision is to find out how people around the world live by different values and how these often clash with each other and may even lead to violence and war.

4. People may discover that they have a political conscience and are able to judge other people's actions good or bad when they begin to think for themselves during adolescence about the sort of world they would like to live in. Clients have often squashed this kind of discourse in their own minds and re-engaging with some form of political thinking can be very refreshing and liberating.

5. Quite frequently people in therapy realize that the beliefs they hold about everyday things have been programmed into them through instinct and education or through the sheer power of absorption from those around them. Reaching out for more than what is self-evident and near is scary but very energizing.

6. Finding that the overall worldview we conduct our lives from can be changed and adjusted through educating ourselves and learning to reflect about the world is often exhilarating to people in therapy. Of course this raises all sorts of practical questions and exposes us to new problems and dilemmas.

7. We can learn to use our intuitions to reach out to the dimensions of existence that go beyond what is obvious and immediately visible or tangible. Many people experiment with this, some through drug use, others through an interest in the occult, many more refuse to pay attention to their hunches and intuitions. Therapy may be a place to disclose and explore these kinds of taboo experiences without fear.

8. Having special or religious experiences and feeling initiated into a special secret about life that perhaps not everyone knows about can be a dangerous but also a potentially invigorating place to start living to the full. Not everyone wants to go as far as this, but those who do should not be condemned to being treated as crazy.

9. Clarifying values and beliefs can lead to finding ways of harmonizing our expectations about the world and life with the way in which we would like to be able to affect the world ourselves. Learning that we can have an impact on the way things are through our own attitude, beliefs and conduct can change our lives very much for the better.

10. On the whole it is probably important to ensure that there are all sorts of people in our lives, including people who can agree and disagree with our views about the world, so as to find both enough certainty and enough challenge to remain lively and vital in our appraisal of what is.

11. Our journey through the spiritual dimension will inevitably lead us to discover about good and evil and learn about the existence of both in ourselves and in those we love. Finding ways to encompass and accept them, and perhaps tame them both for everyone's benefit could be an interesting challenge.

12. Clients almost always do some learning about how their beliefs and values mould their lives and make it meaningful. They will gradually understand better how they become stuck in certain ways of living because they have avoided examining the values and beliefs underpinning their lives.

13. Not infrequently, clients discover that certain life events make us re-evaluate our beliefs and challenge our views of the world and others and

most of all of who we think we are. Even though those events may be traumatic at the time, it is often the case that they lead to more insight, understanding or even to wisdom. Such wisdom seems hard to come by without pain and conflict.

The spiritual dimension thus concerns our understanding of the world, human living and ourselves. This idea of understanding is a central tenet of phenomenology and important to consider when working with clients from an existential perspective. Chapter 25 focuses on understanding and shows how the existential approach moves away from interpreting and explanation and moves towards greater clarity and understanding of the client's world.

Another important aspect of the spiritual dimension, and of existential philosophy, is the concept of time. Do we perceive time in a linear or circular fashion? How do we live in time? How does time make us purposeful and active or paralysed and frozen? How do we conceive of our past, present and future and how does this impact on the way we live our lives? These questions will be considered in the chapter on time and purpose (Chapter 26).

A discussion of the spiritual dimension would not be complete without reference to values and beliefs. Our values and beliefs are the foundations on which we build our life, although for the most part we are either unaware of our values and beliefs or do not reflect on how they are influencing our decisions and choices in life. The chapter on values and beliefs (Chapter 27) will examine these aspects and demonstrate how useful an exploration of values and beliefs can be in existential therapy.

Our values and beliefs will also inform our political and ideological ideas. How do we see the world, or rather what kind of world would we like to see? What is important for us? Do environmental, political and humanitarian issues matter to us? How do these issues influence the way we live our lives? These issues will be considered in the chapter on political and ideological issues (Chapter 28), the chapter will highlight how these issues run through many facets of our lives, some of which we are unaware of.

Of course what really matters to us is what we find or make meaningful and this is central to the spiritual dimension. Our task in life is to make sense of a seemingly senseless world and to create meaning. Rather than searching for the elusive, the meaning of life, we should seek what is meaningful to our lives in a personal way. The chapter on meaning and transformation (Chapter 29) demonstrates the transforming nature of meaning, when clients are able to grapple with their lives and make sense of it. Of course this is not always so easy as there are many things that occur by chance that we have no control over, which can have devastating as well as positive implications. But even the suffering we experience can be transformed through making it meaningful.

The final chapter of this section, 'A New Ideology' (Chapter 30), points towards what clients can achieve through existential therapy. Through the process of living and grappling with the difficulties and pleasures of life we can come to formulate our own way of living. By examining and exploring in an open and reflective manner on the way we live life we will come to a new ideology, which is our own. It is only by questioning ourselves with the help of others that we are able to gain insight into our lives and ourselves. This final chapter offers a new way of thinking about existential psychotherapy and brings together the issues discussed in this book.

CHAPTER 25

Interpretation: Explanation or Understanding?

Hans W. Cohn

> In interpretation, understanding does not become something different. It becomes itself. Such interpretation is grounded existentially in understanding; the latter does not arise from the former. Nor is interpretation the acquiring of information about what is understood; it is rather the working-out of possibilities projected in understanding.
>
> Heidegger, *Being and Time*: 188–189

Introduction

Most psychotherapists who use interpretation as a means of helping troubled clients to explore their threatened lives have only a very restricted view of what the German theologian and philosopher Friedrich Schleiermacher (1769–1834) called 'Hermeneutik' and defined as 'the art of avoiding misunderstandings'. The term 'hermeneutics' is derived from the Greek verb 'hermeneuein' (to interpret), and it is important that it refers us to Hermes, the divine messenger god of the ancient Greeks. In the act of understanding we are confronted with a message, a phenomenon which addresses us, asking for our response. Already for Schleiermacher, as for existential thinkers afterwards, interpretation was fundamentally about the process of understanding.

For Schleiermacher, the 'message' to be understood was originally a Biblical text, but eventually it included anything expressed in written or spoken language. If we wish to understand it, a message needs to have an aspect that is familiar so that we can engage with it. But it also has an aspect which needs to be explored, 'interpreted' – 'for every utterance is surrounded by its entire living context' (Critchley and Schroeder, 1998: 418). This is of course inexhaustible, and here Schleiermacher touches on something that existential writers emphasize: all understanding is partial; misunderstandings can never be completely avoided. Something always remains un-understood. 'In hermeneutics every solution always again appears as an approach' (ibid., 419–420).

We can see that Schleiermacher's view of interpretation as 'understanding' gives the concept a range of meaning considerably wider than when used by most psychotherapists. Psychodynamic interpretation is, as a rule, the discovery of the 'latent' meaning behind the 'manifest' content of an utterance or 'symptom' whereby what 'appears' is considered only a disguise for what is 'real'.

The difference between the two approaches becomes clearer when we turn to the ideas of the German philosopher Wilhelm Dilthey (1833–1911) who was not only Schleiermacher's biographer but also influenced Martin Heidegger's views on interpretation.

For an existential view of interpretation, Dilthey's distinction between 'explanation' and 'understanding' is particularly illuminating. This distinction which arose from Dilthey's consideration of the difference between the natural and the human sciences has been lucidly characterized by Rudolph A. Makkreel in the *Cambridge Dictionary of Philosophy*:

> The distinction between the natural and human sciences is . . . related to the methodological difference between explanation and understanding. The natural sciences seek causal explanations of nature – connecting the discreet representations of outer experience through hypothetical generalizations. The human sciences aim at an understanding . . . that articulates the typical structures of life given in lived experience. (Makkreel, 1995: 203)

Later Makkreel continues with the following important assessment of Dilthey's position: 'Whereas the natural sciences aim at ever broader generalizations the human sciences place equal weight in understanding individuality and universality. Dilthey regarded individuals as points of intersection of the social and cultural systems in which they participate' (ibid., 203). This conception of the individual points clearly in the direction of Heidegger's 'Being-in-the-world', though Heidegger never talks of individuality but always of Dasein (Being-there).

Under the influence of psychoanalysis, which regards itself as a natural science in Dilthey's sense, a great deal of psychotherapy concerns itself with explanation rather than understanding. The ruling question is 'Why?' rather than 'How?' The origin of a phenomenon seems more important than how it is experienced at present. Such an approach favours answers of an apparent finality.

Understanding, on the other hand, is the slow process of exploring and clarifying the many-stranded tangle of a life situation that can never be complete and does not lead to final answers. It seems to me like an opening of new doors rather than the closing of one that no longer works.

An existential perspective

Heidegger sees human beings as concerned with their own Being both ontologically – in their given 'existentiality', say their mortality or their being-with-others – and ontically – in their so-being, in specific situations in their history.

It is this concern ('Sorge' in German, not very happily translated as 'care'), this questioning of their own Being which Heidegger calls interpretation (the German word 'Auslegung' means something like 'laying bare'). The human way of being is thus self-interpretation. By self-interpretation Heidegger does *not* mean 'introspection'. He means 'understanding' (i.e. 'standing in the midst of') our involvement with the world which we both co-create and inhabit. We can see that the meaning of interpretation is here clearly 'understanding' rather than 'explanation'. It is this approach which is usually implied when existential thinkers talk of 'hermeneutics'.

In *Being and Time* Heidegger develops at some length his view of interpretation as understanding. This is, of course, long before he had concerned himself with psychotherapy: for him the hermeneutic way was the human way of making sense of human Being. This has remained the view of other existential thinkers, particularly that of Heidegger's pupil Hans-Georg Gadamer: it is at the core of Gadamer's whole philosophical work.

I shall outline the most important aspects of Heidegger's considerations. I am indebted to Dreyfus' more extensive comments in his book *Being-in-the-world* (Dreyfus, 1991: 30ff.) which are lucid and helpful. I shall then proceed to show how such a concept of interpretation can be used within the context of therapy.

What we are trying to interpret and understand is a phenomenon. Heidegger defines phenomenology as the attempt 'to let that which shows itself be seen from itself in the very way in which it shows itself' (Heidegger, 1962: 58). This can be easily misunderstood as advocating that we should stay with whatever reveals itself at first sight. Heidegger, however, points at the importance of that part of a phenomenon which at first remains concealed: '...something lies hidden...but at the same time it is something that belongs to it so essentially as to constitute its meaning and its ground' (ibid., 59). As Dreyfus puts it: 'The subject of phenomenology must be something that does not show itself but can be made to show itself' (Dreyfus, 1991: 32).

What is it that 'can be made to show itself'? Heidegger describes it as the 'being of beings, its sense, its modifications and derivatives' (Heidegger, 1962: 60).

But, as Dreyfus puts it, 'our understanding of being is so pervasive in everything we can never arrive at a clear presentation of it' (Dreyfus, 1991: 32). Thus our understanding will always remain incomplete, and something will always remain concealed.

Dreyfus, like most writers on Heidegger's existential phenomenology, stresses the difference between Heidegger's views and Husserl's views: 'Heidegger takes Husserl's phenomenology and turns it around. We are to investigate not consciousness but Dasein' (ibid., 33). And Dasein is 'being-there' – in the world. The world is always included, and nothing in it can be 'suspended' in the way Husserl seemed to suggest.

On the contrary, part of the phenomenon is concealed. There are two kinds of hiddenness. This is what Heidegger says about it:

> In the first place, a phenomenon can be covered up in the sense that it is still quite undiscovered. It is neither known nor unknown. Moreover, a phenomenon can be

buried over (verschüttet). This means that it has at some time been discovered but has deteriorated, to the point of getting covered up again. (Heidegger, 1962: 60)[1]

Dreyfus' comment on the second of these two concealments is helpful: 'Our understanding of being is distorted. Since everyday Dasein does not want to face up to its own interpretive activity and the consequent unsettledness of human being, it uses its everyday understanding to conceal the truth about itself' (Dreyfus, 1991: 35).

At this point Heidegger's view of a 'revealed' and a 'concealed' aspect of the phenomenon comes very close to the aim of interpretation as seen by most forms of psychotherapy – the restoration of an unlived dimension of life, whether this is described as forgotten, denied, repressed or abandoned.

We might be tempted to equate the search for the 'concealed' aspect of the phenomenon with the Freudian recovery of the 'repressed' trauma from a secret psychic location, an 'Unconscious'. We need, however, to remember that the process of revealing the unknown part of a phenomenon does not replace a deceptive manifest utterance or symptom with the reality of a true meaning which invalidates what we have seen so far. On the contrary, the perceived phenomenon gains clarity, richness and meaningfulness whenever a new aspect of its totality is discovered. The concern is always with amplification and exploration rather than explanation.

Case illustration: interpretation in existential practice

Having seen how for existential thinking interpretation is a way towards understanding the lived experience of 'Being-in-the-world-with-others', the question arises, to what extent interpretation can also, in a narrower sense, play a part in existential practice. My suggestion is that such an interpretation will have the character of understanding rather than that of explanation.

If we see existential exploration as a search for the gap in our lives, which announces the neglect or denial of our specific possibilities, the answer cannot be universal and applicable to all of us, but needs to arise from a consideration of the many specific strands that characterize the history of each of us. Instead of narrowing our enquiry down to one or a cluster of past traumas, which are seen as setting off a string of misunderstandings and distortions, we need to broaden the context so that such a trauma can acquire a new meaning in a wider field.

At this point we shall say something about some of the ways in which I try to help my clients to create a wider context for their experience. We have seen that this process has two crucial characteristics – it is unique for each person, each having a unique history and it has no final conclusion – each stage illuminates all the others, and we never reach a final stage.

I find myself incapable of showing this in the usual short excerpts from 'case histories', as I think such an excerpt cannot illustrate these qualities of uniqueness and incompleteness. Instead I shall outline a familiar life situation and try to illustrate how the creation of a wider context can open up new meanings.

Let us assume a man in his forties wants to see me because he feels unable to have successful relationships with women. Perhaps he will tell me that his parents split up when he was nine, and that he did not get on with his mother who was irritable and dominating. He may also offer a more or less definite connection between these facts, making his earlier difficulties an explanation for his later ones. Whether he mentions this only in passing or returns to it in many sessions, it is important that I do not follow him in this, even in my thoughts. At the same time, it is important that I respect his views and do not oppose them. It is very likely that there *is* some connection between his childhood experience and his later difficulties, but neither he nor I can know what this connection is – he might well remember his earlier difficulties in the light of his later experience so that one can say that it is the present that affects the past. In order to understand what is going on we have to know much more about his life.

I would encourage my client to tell me as much as possible about his later relationships, and whether they were similar, or dissimilar, to what he remembered of the relation between his father and mother, or his own relation to them. We might come to see that he might find it easier to think of his 'failures' as brought about by difficulties of his parents than to explore what they are in themselves.

Let us further assume, as one possibility among others, that my client's profession implies a great deal of travelling abroad, say, as the representative of an individual concern or a musician moving from place to place – what influence might that have on his relationship with his partner? Did such a situation involve a choice, of which he had not been aware?

It is, of course, impossible to mention here all the potential conflicts and difficulties which might come to light in such a broadening of the context, all relevant to some extent, though not equally so. The question is: What therapeutic possibilities emerge from them?

At this point, the difference between explanation and understanding might become clearer. To think of his childhood experience as an explanation of his relational difficulty will give my client a definite, and to some extent final, answer to his question: Why do I have these difficulties? But it does not seem to offer new possibilities. On the other hand, to discover that a professional commitment to travelling abroad may pose problems to a close personal relationship (which can be met one way or another) opens the door to a new understanding. The fact that my client has gone through a painful childhood experience may play its part in his response to this new understanding, but it will not be its 'cause'.

It is, of course, possible that my client might come across yet another of those fundamental conflicts which are an aspect of human Being, that is being human. We might have found that his relational problems are a response to a denial of the physical dimension of our existence manifesting itself in his case as a difficulty in reconciling friendship and sexuality. This also cannot be a final answer, but it opens up yet different responses.

It is clear that this kind of interpretation needs time – existential time which is multidimensional and non-linear. This does, of course, not mean clock time, and mere duration. But it means that the exploration cannot be 'targeted', as therapist and client are on the way together towards an aim they still have to find.

Critical considerations

Such explorations are a fabric of partial answers and new questions. But as therapists we need to remind ourselves

- we cannot have answers to the client's questions;
- the aim of our questions is to help clients to ask their own questions about the way in which their actions and life events are variously connected; and
- there are no final answers – the degree of their helpfulness can only be decided by our clients themselves.

These limitations point to the difference between interpretation and understanding, if we use interpretation in the guise in which it has found a place in most kinds of psychodynamic therapies. There we are confronted by a 'text' where the 'true' or 'real' meaning is hidden or distorted by its manifestation as symbols and symptoms, and therefore needs to be 'interpreted'. The aim is a definite, usually explanatory answer to the question: What does it really mean?

Helping persons to 'understand' their difficulties aims at exploring as much of the web of their lives as is possible, focussing not on one particular 'line' but on the connections between as many lines as show themselves.

This is a task that cannot be completed and results in a number of meaningful answers; there is no final answer, but also no exclusion of any possible answer. Thus possibilities for change are opened up.

Editorial note

Sadly Dr Hans W. Cohn passed away on Thursday, 22 January 2004, before he had time to see his chapter in publication. We hope that this chapter will play a part in keeping his inspirational contribution to existential psychotherapy alive.

Note

1 'Disintegrated' is a more accurate translation of the German 'verfiel' than 'deteriorated', I think.

Further reading

Cohn, H. W. *Heidegger and the Roots of Existential Therapy.*
Critchley, S. Y. and Schroeder, W. R. (eds) *A Companion to Continental Philosophy: Part VII Hermeneutics.*
Madison, G. B. *The Hermeneutics of Postmodernity: Figures and Themes.*
Ormiston, G. L. and Schrift, A. D. (eds) *The Hermeneutic Tradition.*
Ricoeur, P. In D. Ihde (ed.) *The Conflict of Interpretations.*

CHAPTER 26

Time and Purpose

KAREN WEIXEL-DIXON AND FREDDIE STRASSER

> Dasein is an entity for which, in its Being, that Being is an issue.
> Heidegger, *Being and Time*: 236

Introduction

Human beings are such that they question the nature of existence. Their existence has significance for them, it is an 'issue' for them. 'What shall I live for?' 'What is the purpose of life, and what is the purpose of *my* life?' This kind of questioning illustrates the significance of purpose, and is manifest in literature, in all cultures and throughout history. It would seem that humans need purpose to make living comprehensible and worthwhile.

Time and purpose are aspects of life that have been addressed by both secular and religious perspectives, and by all known cultures in recorded history. Purpose is a concern to the beings that are aware of their existence, and time is of fundamental interest to beings that are mortal and finite. Furthermore, it would seem that these two notions are intricately bound.

'Purpose', in common usage as a noun, is '. . . the reason for which something is done or created or for which something exists . . .' As a verb with an object, the definition reveals another dimension: '. . . have as one's intention or objective . . .' (The New Oxford Dictionary of English, 1998). In conjunction, these definitions give a sense of something aspirational: 'purpose' as an expectation, and a rationale that includes an aspect that might be described as 'not-yet'. It is this aspirational, or *anticipatory*, characteristic of purpose that is of particular interest to those who appreciate the fundamental relevance of time and temporality for human existence.

An existential perspective

In the Continental philosophical tradition, Martin Heidegger was a foremost proponent of the proposal that Time is the single most significant aspect of existence for human beings. Heidegger set his study of human being firmly in relation to time: although philosophers for many centuries have considered time as a fundamental category, he singled it out as most significant because human existence is essentially temporal. It is his seminal work *Being and Time* (1927) that will be used as the foundation for this exposition.

Heidegger is also well known for his query: 'Why is there something instead of nothing?' If one reflects upon this question, it may become apparent that existence as we know it, including our own personal status, could all be otherwise, or could all be non-existent. This quality of the contingency of everything leaves us groundless: in an effort to bring order to this chaos and uncertainty, we create systems of meaning and value that support and reflect our purpose.

As suggested previously, purpose has a distinct temporal characteristic: the future. It may be proposed, then, that we are not essentially beings driven by biological factors, or motivated by historical antecedents: we are beings pulled or drawn forward towards a future that holds possibilities for us to realise, or fail to realise, our purpose. These potentialities stretch before us for the expanse of our mortal life.

This proposal certainly distinguishes the existential perspective from many other views in the human arts and sciences.

The considerations indicated in the type of questions posed in the opening of this chapter demonstrate a concern regarding the purpose of Being for those that exist in a particular manner in relation to time. For Heidegger, the notion of 'concern', or 'care', has a particular and fundamental relevance for Dasein, and it is a principle that is directly related to temporality. Furthermore, as a concept with a future-oriented aspect, purpose might be described as a component of this notion of 'care'. The correlation between these two elements will be considered subsequently.

Living in ec-stasies

> *Time must be brought to light – and genuinely conceived – as the horizon for all understanding of Being and for any way of interpreting it. In order for us to discern this*, time *needs to be* explicated primordially as the horizon for the understanding of Being, and in terms of temporality as the Being of Dasein, which understands Being. (Heidegger, 1962: 39)

To clarify the notion of temporality: 'Temporality is the name of the way in which Time exists in human existence' (Warnock, 1970: 62). In other words, temporality belongs to beings who have an involvement with time and who care about time. To even begin to appreciate or comprehend human existence, according to Heidegger, we must necessarily understand it in the context of temporality.

The three tenses of time – past, present and future – are what Heidegger refers to as *ec-stasies* (literally 'ways in which we stand out'). These *ec-stasies* are absolutely cohesive: to understand any one of these temporal dimensions, in fact to even consider any one of them, we must appreciate their relation to the others. Hence, the most apropos comment from Merleau-Ponty: '...each moment of time calls all the others to witness' (Merleau-Ponty, 1962: 69).

Furthermore, Heidegger labels the structure of existence with respect to temporality thus described by these *ec-stasies* as 'care'. What Heidegger describes here is the intrinsic connection between temporality and care: 'Temporality reveals itself as the meaning of authentic care' (Heidegger, 1962: 374).

Thus, concern, or care, is directly related to temporality. To say that we are temporal beings indicates that we have a relationship to time, or an engagement with it in a particular manner.

Hence, it becomes more apparent how temporality fundamentally qualifies our involvement with the world, indeed, with existence.

However, as Barrett (1958) and others suggest, Heidegger seems to assign a priority to one aspect of temporality: the future. A reflection on the concept of what is 'not yet', as it is the context for the utmost possibility and eventuality that awaits us all, may reveal the significance temporality has with reference to the notion of purpose: '...death is something distinctively impending. Its existential possibility is based on the fact that Dasein is essentially disclosed to itself, and disclosed, indeed, as ahead-of-itself. This item in the structure of care has its most primordial concretion in Being-towards-Death' (Heidegger, 1962: 294).

As implied above, we are never a 'finished' item, or a totalised entity in our lifetime: we are always ahead of ourselves in the process of becoming, until we become no more. We do not make our choices, or choose ourselves, once and for all: we are faced with choosing and re-choosing as we project ourselves towards our deaths. Furthermore, by virtue of the interconnectedness of the *ec-stasies*, every choice impacts on, and is affected by, all three dimensions of temporality.

The discussion of freedom and choice, and the interrelatedness of the proposed existential givens is beyond the scope of this brief chapter; it may suffice to say here that whether we *choose* our purpose in life or *find* it by virtue of injunction from a 'higher source' (although Heidegger would deny this possibility), it would seem that we still have some latitude in deciding how to engage with purpose.

It would seem then, that the questions regarding life and purpose represented early in this exposition are not simply rhetorical, or the subject of a purely academic enquiry: we answer them with our choices and in our actions.

An analysis of, or reflection upon, these actions and choices may reveal one's purpose(s). For example, an individual that is aggressive or violent may be engaging with the world in a manner that demonstrates their objectives in terms of power; a person that is involved in acts of charity or altruism may be manifesting their hopes and expectations of affecting the world for the better. In any case, purpose is always present, and may be both implicit and explicit.

Thus exemplified, it seems that purpose is a manifestation of care: it is a demonstration of our inherent connectedness to and with the world.

Death as the key to living

Heidegger often speaks of 'death' in *Being and Time*, and in different contexts throughout the text. Sometimes death may refer either to the actual demise of an individual, or to the many limitations inherent in human existence that preclude some options (sometimes referred to as 'factical' or given aspects of human living) or to mortality, which is '. . . the possibility of the impossibility of any existence at all . . .' (ibid., 1962: 307). In any case, what is noteworthy for this discussion is that humans, and all that comprises human existence, are finite: we are neither omnipotent nor immortal.

This element of temporality, directly related to finitude, and common to all existents, has been proposed here as the source of 'care'. In part, 'care' indicates an orientation towards the future, towards the ultimate eventuality and possibility of our demise, and engagement with our possibilities and limitations. Care is a pro-ject towards death.

'Care' is also comprised of 'facticity' and 'falling'. Facticity or 'thrownness' indicates that aspect of existence that is based in 'having been', that is, the past, and falling is manifest in 'being alongside', and may be described as the everyday mode of existing or the present.

Past, present and future: we are again reminded of the interrelatedness of temporal dimensions. Temporality and care qualify human existence: we are always in-the-world, as finite beings that have concern for and are engaged by existence.

Inherent in the tripartite structure of care lies the possibility of authentic living: when I accept how I 'find myself' (as thrown into the world, and as a being with a past), and acknowledge that I am bound to existence (I am involved in a world that matters to me), then I may, in anticipatory resoluteness, *choose* to *choose* how I will live. This choice, which is the basis of purpose as I create it and value it, is in reference to the limitations and conditions implied in both facticity and being-in-the-world. Additionally, this choice is open to re-evaluation, and may be re-chosen, or we may choose instead to distract ourselves with commonplace diversions, thereby avoiding the call to authentic existence.

And so, temporality and care qualify human existence: we are always in-the-world, reaching out to engage with what we encounter, because our existence matters to us. In sum, and with reference to the proposals and definitions presented, it would seem that 'purpose' serves as an adjunct to Heidegger's notion of 'care'. Whether chosen or found, purpose is an aspirational dynamic: it implies an orientation to the future, but can be realised in the philosophical present, and acknowledged as part of the lived past.

Applied existential concepts

We would like to sketch out a short framework of some other crucial existential concepts that will underpin the case vignette. This will provide an illustration of the linkage between the theory and the practice in existential therapy. At the same time, however, it needs to be noted that the two powerful existential and universally shared characteristics of human existence, 'purpose' and 'temporality', do not exist in isolation from other existential facts of life or of other 'givens'.

We will demonstrate that these 'givens' play a vital role in the exploration of clients' worldviews.

In order to understand the vignette in terms of an existential exploration, we need to keep in mind:

1. what we as existential therapists expect from the outcome of the therapy; and
2. what are those existential 'givens' that limit our choices and what are the possibilities within these boundaries that we can expect from the outcome of the therapy.

The guideline of existential therapy is that the therapist is able to create a condition for the therapeutic encounters, which is conducive for clients to express themselves without restraint in a trusting atmosphere. In this trusting 'interpersonal relationship', clients would have acquired self-confidence to reveal themselves as transparently as possible. Through this 'interconnected' relationship, clients would be able not only to become aware of their worldview, but also would be capable of challenging the ambiguities and vulnerabilities in relation to their worldview.

What is worldview?

Van Deurzen in her book *Existential Counselling and Psychotherapy in Practice* (van Deurzen, 2002a) explains that in 'examining the client's experience of the world it is useful to have a frame of reference . . .' She encompasses within this frame of reference those inevitable givens which limit human beings as well as provide them the freedom to choose within these constraints.

Van Deurzen beautifully describes this and underpins this view in her statement in her book *Everyday Mysteries*:

> Existential psychotherapy aims at full description of the essential givens and challenges of human living. Its objective is to help people to uncover the everyday mysteries in which they are enfolded and in which they may have become entangled. Careful attention is paid both to the universal and the particular aspects of a person's existence in order to understand the relationship and tension between them. (van Deurzen-Smith, 1997: 177)

There are many givens or natural limitations in our world that do not come within the scope of this chapter.

However, we cannot speak about 'worldview' without including the human tendency to create and, to varying degrees, fix our own value systems. Fixing our values can be viewed positively (sticking to one's principles) or negatively (being dogmatic or closed-minded). We stick to our values because these values have proven to be useful in navigating life and by conforming to our values, we are able to approve of ourselves and hopefully receive approval from others. This enhances our self-esteem and our sense of security. The cost, however, comes when events do not allow us to uphold our value system or when our values and those of others are at odds, leading to the disapproval of others.

Then we can feel rejected by others and perceive ourselves as failures. Values are interconnected with most of the other 'givens', which encompass and reveal our worldview. Our value system determines our aspirations and our purpose in life, which in turn shape our self-worth.

From our existential perspective, life choices are indeed limited by givens, but this still leaves plenty of scope for freedom and decision-making. Even in the most hopeless and desperate circumstances, we can always rely on a modicum of free will, if only in terms of choosing how we respond to our predicament. Even the 'sedimented' (fixed) value systems are prone to be shaken. Van Deurzen writes about limitations and choices: 'People will discover sooner or later that freedom is an intangible concept or even a fallacious one if it is not counterbalanced by the notion of obligation or necessity' (ibid., 12). Our choices as our aspirations are limited by the uncertainty and temporality of our existence, although there is most of the time an attitudinal freedom to choose from.

Case illustration

We will see, in the following vignette, how central these notions are, how they link with other existential givens (or facts of life) and the vital role they play in the formation of each individual's worldview.

Purpose – John (by Freddie Strasser)

John (32) came to therapy in order to eliminate his fear of leading seminars in his new job. The business which John had built up and expanded over five years had recently been bought out, although John had been retained as chief executive. In his new job, he was required to run seminars for large audiences and his life was being ruined by the terror he felt at this prospect. He could not escape from images of himself struck dumb with panic on the podium, with the audience looking on mockingly.

Each individual's experiences are unique in the value and meaning that have been attached to them. Our mode of working with clients involves getting as detailed a description of our clients' experiences as possible. The therapist began, therefore, to explore the details of John's fear by suggesting that he 'concretise' his predicament by describing an occasion when he felt this emotion acutely. He responded by relating a recent incident when he faced an audience of forty. He was so wound up with stress that he felt his legs trembling to the extent that he could not even reach the flip chart to note the timetable of the seminar. He fulfilled his task but rushed to conclude the seminar as soon as he could. Feeling that the whole experience had been a disaster, John decided there and then that he would never allow himself to be lured into such a situation again. The experience had shaken John profoundly, being at odds with his image as a very powerful, successful businessman, renowned in the city as a ruthless operator.

We used this episode as a prototype to discuss the intricacies of the fear that John felt and how it undermined his self-esteem and self-image. In so doing,

John became aware that the fear he felt derived from his sense of a threat of rejection. This short narration thus far has already revealed a part of John's worldview. His aspiration and the purpose of his being was vested so much in this idea of becoming a ruthless and powerful operator that the slightest threat to achieve this triggered off massive behaviour patterns to maintain this image. Not only his self-worth hinged on that image, but also all his survival efforts were focused to maintain this purpose.

On being prompted to unravel this fear of rejection further, John came to an unexpected conclusion. He was not afraid of being rejected on the grounds of demonstrating insufficient knowledge of his topic, nor was he worried about being judged as lacking lecturing experience. His deepest fear was that he would be rejected simply because of his physical appearance. This realisation was a revelation to John himself: he expressed it with the greatest astonishment and bewilderment.

Following this revelation, we proceeded to explore what physical appearance meant for him and through this he became aware of the family ethos out of which some of his ideas had emerged. The values and beliefs that our families and the environment instil in us might dramatically affect our worldview. The importance of physical strength, in John's perception, was as much of a 'given' for John as his awareness of the inevitability of death. Value systems can, however, be shaken and attitudes may be modified.

John's family ethos placed great value on strong males able to demonstrate their physical strength in sport, and their psychological power by dominating decision-making and exerting their control over all situations. While describing this, an important experience emerged which exemplified the adolescent John's plight in relation to his family. He narrated a story about an athletics competition after which his trainer told him that he was not built for the sport and that he should stop training. Just prior to this put-down, his peers, who had been bullying him for some time, had beaten him up. Gathering himself after both of these hurtful experiences, John described trudging towards home, consoling himself with thoughts of being held and comforted by his mother. Instead, he was severely reprimanded by his father who expected him to be first in all sport activities. Most hurtfully of all, John's mother not only concurred with his father, but further punished John by ridiculing him. John withdrew from all sporting activities, and condemned himself as a pathetic, fragile person who would only exhibit failure. This had the knock-on effect of making it difficult for him to create and sustain relationships as he always considered himself a feeble and frail outsider that nobody would love.

To avoid a repeat of the humiliation he had experienced when his peers, his trainer and his parents rejected him, John had learned to protect himself by using anger. He found that this provided him with a temporary feeling of being the strong, controlling, authoritative male that he wanted to be.

Expanding on these emerging connections, during one session the therapist asked John to compare his fear of being rejected because of his physical appearance with the real experience of being rejected by his athletics trainer. Unexpectedly, John stood up and started shouting about this 'shit of a trainer' that did not deserve even to be mentioned. It was clear to the therapist that the anger might not have been directed only at his memory of the trainer, but was equally aimed at the therapist.

On following this through, it transpired that during the early days of his business development, John had felt severely handicapped by his shyness and often found himself blushing in front of his employees. When I asked him how he had survived these nauseating experiences, he explained in an ashamed voice that he had become angry and found some reason to shout at his colleagues, which gave him a feeling of having regained control.

For all of us, much of our value system and purpose in life are being influenced by cultural attitudes and values imposed on us by our family and our social, ethnic and cultural contexts, and we as individuals are also capable of creating, recreating and reinventing our own individual culture. These templates we create may forge our ambitions and our sense of others and ourselves by placing greater or lesser importance on certain attributes and attitudes.

In John's case, we have seen that his worldview was inextricably bound up with the purpose that he has chosen in life. Values that his parents placed on beauty, strength, aspiring to perfection and amassing considerable material wealth were the guiding motives in John's life. Creating ideas such as these can be extremely beneficial in achieving material and social success but, as we have seen, they can also be the cause of considerable distortion and distress. Aspirations and values have a tendency to become sedimented, that is, they become so rigid and exaggerated that they lead to behaviour that is automatic and could almost be considered compulsive. We can be dogmatic or stuck to such an extent that we have become blind to other possible ways of viewing the world or conducting our lives.

This is exactly what had happened to John. Although he told his story casually, John's public-speaking anxiety was having a devastating impact on his self-image. With his worldview entirely centred on the physical world and his energies consumed with trying to live up to a mythical ideal, John was left with no space to explore or enjoy any of the other aspects of life. Reflecting upon his family ethos, as a metaphor only and not as causation in therapy, gave John the opportunity to challenge these acquired values and behaviour patterns in him and thus helped him to clarify and review his purpose.

Focusing on his life story and some of its metaphors, in a trusting therapeutic relationship, enabled John to challenge his attitude towards his own worldview and made him realise that he was not totally isolated from the world. Now that he understood better how his value-system formed and influenced his worldview in life, he began to see that he had the power to reassess these values and modify his aspirations, within the limits of the 'givens'. John came to recognise that while he could not entirely eliminate his anger, his anxiety about public performances or the fluctuation in his self-esteem, there was a great deal that he could do to lessen the impact. Becoming aware that his self-image was a movable and changeable state of being, and that others had their own built-in vulnerabilities, enabled John to feel connected in this respect with other human beings, rather than isolated and alone. Furthermore, he released himself from the assumption that an imperfect physique meant that he was good for nothing. He realised that his self-image need not be hooked exclusively onto one meaning, one dimension and one purpose in life. Perhaps most importantly of all, John learned that he could not always exercise mastery over his emotions and every event in his life, but that he may have a possibility to change his attitude. His life thus became more open to explore other meanings and purposes.

Critical considerations

An analysis of or reflection upon one's purpose in life can be a formidable undertaking: it requires an acknowledgement of one's responsibility in choosing how to live, and a confrontation with the finitude that is inherent in human existence. Such an endeavour can, in fact, provoke or exacerbate anxiety: where there is choice, there is risk.

Considering the choices one has already made can induce guilt and remorse: we may be forced to attend to our losses and note our fallibility. A consideration of the future may compel us to realise that what lies ahead is not only uncertain, but likely to bring more of the same kind of suffering, as well as the possibility of joy or happiness.

Finally, we are not allowed the luxury of making significant and difficult choices, like those concerning purpose in living, just once: we will have to reconsider and re-choose these possibilities again and again, if we are to live resolutely, creatively and authentically.

Such an enterprise is not for the faint-hearted, or for those unwilling or unable to appreciate the burdens and blessings that being an aware, responsible human being entails.

Further reading

Cohn, H. W. *Heidegger and the Roots of Existential Psychotherapy.*
Cooper, M. *Existential Therapies.*
Polt, R. *Heidegger: An Introduction.*
Strasser, F. and Strasser, A. *Existential Time-Limited Therapy: The Wheel of Existence.*
van Deurzen, E. *Everyday Mysteries: Existential Dimensions of Psychotherapy.*

CHAPTER 27

Values and Beliefs

BO JACOBSEN

> For the first time in history the physical survival of the human race depends on a radical change of the human heart.
>
> Erich Fromm, *To Have or To Be*: 19

Introduction

Values and beliefs are important aspects of every therapy. They are important within psychodynamic and cognitive therapy, but especially important within existential therapy. Whether the client suffers from anxiety, depression, eating disorders or something else, the client will act out of his or her values and beliefs, the therapist will do the same thing, and the two representations of values and beliefs in the consulting room will interact. You could even say that the most important dimensions of the therapeutic process and the therapeutic result consist of changes in the client's value structure and belief system.

Value is generally understood as our basic ideas and principles of what we consider good and evil in this life and in this world. Belief is understood as our basic thoughts on how this world and its human beings are constructed, including how we basically see ourselves.

It is not only existential therapists who think of values and beliefs as important in therapy. There is a long tradition in psychoanalysis for discussing these subjects. Since Freud's day it has been discussed as to whether therapy should be allowed to influence the values of the client. Some analysts maintain, for instance, that psychoanalysis can only take place in a society where individual and socio-cultural values are largely identical so that 'the neutrality required by analytic technique is not offensive to society' (Waelder, 1964: 247). Also, in the cognitive tradition values and beliefs play a central role. The cognitive theory of depression developed by Beck (1976) holds that depression is partly caused and maintained by 'false' (i.e. unrealistic) beliefs about reality and that it may be cured by the correction of these beliefs.

An existential perspective

In many ways existential therapists have a sharper focus on values than other schools. The reason is that existential therapy is not seen as a technical enterprise with the purpose of helping the client to 'function' better. Existential authors are critical of the contemporary trend of the Western societies to assume that we should all be top-performing and well-functioning: socially, sexually, intellectually and physically. If we are not, we are dismissed. The French existential philosopher Gabriel Marcel advocates more love, understanding and tolerance in human relationships and baptizes the individual of our time as 'the functional man' (Marcel, 1962: 1; Macquarrie, 1972: 176). Traditional therapy helps 'the functional man' to function still better, whereas existential therapy helps the individual to find his or her roots and define the value base of the life he or she chooses to live.

The most crucial questions regarding values and existential therapy are these: Is existential therapy value neutral? And: Are other therapies value neutral? The answer to both questions is: No. There are some values that are inherent to the therapeutic enterprise and some values that the therapist stands for and tries to convey to the client. It is important to be clear and open about these values.

The following are some of the values that existential therapists, according to my observations, often stand for:

- It is a good thing to listen openly and carefully to each other.
- It is valuable to treat each other with respect for the other person's autonomy and dignity.
- It is a good thing to communicate clearly and openly with each other.
- It is a good thing to show generosity and social conscience.
- It is a good thing to allow the other person to be different from oneself.
- It is a basic value to take every human life and every life question very seriously.

These values are built into the therapeutic enterprise, and they are hopefully imparted to the client during the therapeutic process. So, when doing existential therapy these values are transmitted and further distributed in our society. Other schools of therapy transmit and distribute other values. For instance, psychoanalysis transmits the idea that it is good to have a non-mutual social relationship and that it is helpful to make interpretations sitting behind the client. Cognitive-behavioural therapy seems to accept the idea that human development can be pre-programmed in the form of exercises and assessed in percentage figures.

But there are other values at play than the inherent therapeutic values. Every therapist has his or her personal values, which may or may not coincide with the personal values of the client. For instance, the therapist may be politically right-wing and the client left-wing. The therapist may be very religious and the client a devoted atheist. The therapist may believe in ecology and the client in unlimited consumption. Such constellations create certain challenges to the therapeutic process and we shall see some examples in the case section.

The job of the therapist here is of a double character: On the one hand, he or she must create and maintain a secure and close bond of affection between client and therapist, a relationship of therapeutic love. On the other hand, he or she must be able to handle and challenge the value differences between the two in a fruitful way. To hit this balance is one of the most crucial tasks for the therapist. In the Daseinsanalytic tradition of Boss (1994) and Condrau (1992) there is a magnificent word for this balance: 'seinlassen', letting be. The term 'seinlassen' can be traced back to Heidegger's key word 'Gelassenheit' that can be translated as 'living calmness', a non-intervening calmness that allows the client to find himself or herself (Condrau, 1992: 272). The ultimate art of the therapist is to be able to let the client be in order to set him or her free.

There follows some contributions from existential authors on the role of values and beliefs in therapy. Important contributions have been made by Gordon Allport, Erich Fromm, Viktor Frankl, Emmy van Deurzen, Ernesto Spinelli and Irvin Yalom. I will briefly consider these in turn.

Gordon Allport

What life values are to be found at all? Gordon Allport, the American humanistic psychologist, has made a catalogue of life values. Allport distinguishes six types of people, classified according to what the person lives for. The description is about pure types. In real life many people are combinations of more than one type.

1. The theoretical person lives to discover or uncover truth. The most important thing in life for the theoretician is to seek knowledge and insight, or in some way to show others the path to truth. Research and teaching are among the occupations in which this life goal can be accorded priority.
2. The economic person is oriented towards the utility of things. What counts for this person is the use to which something can be put and the monetary value that is placed on it. To create a profit, to see one's business or bank account grow is what matters. Occupations in the sphere of business offer opportunities to develop this orientation in life.
3. The aesthetic person is oriented towards the forms and harmonies of things. Beauty is what matters to this person. Life is seen as events and impressions that can be enjoyed for their own sake. Living for the sake of beauty can be realized in such occupations as those of the artist, architect, craftsman or designer.
4. The social person cultivates love for and affinity with other people as the life value that has highest priority. This person wants to mean something to other people and to help them. Occupations as care-persons and many other occupations in the health and social sectors offer opportunities to realize this life value.
5. The political person is interested in power. What counts for this person is the ability to place himself or herself in a position of power and to exercise influence over other people. An occupation as politician offers the opportunity to pursue this life value in a relatively pure form.

6. The religious person seeks unity with something that lies beyond the everyday world. This search can take the form of adhering to the practices of a particular religion or of aspiring to find some other form of spirituality that is less clearly defined. Occupations in the sphere of the church, such as that of priest, can offer an opportunity to realize this dimension of life (Allport, 1961: 294ff.).

Gordon Allport distinguishes the six types, placing them on an equal footing. He makes no judgement as to whether one type is more necessary or more valuable than another. But are these life values equally worthwhile? Is the task of making money just as worthwhile as that of seeking spiritual fulfilment? Is the search for beauty just as worthwhile as the search for love?

The viewpoint of neutrality is one approach to this question, according to which, a person, who espouses one life value, cannot set himself or herself up as the judge of another person who happens to have chosen differently.

Opposed to this is the viewpoint of necessity, according to which, certain life goals should be preferred insofar as they are needed by the world around us. Not all ways of life are equally worthwhile. Conditions in the world around us may be such that some ways of life should be accorded particular importance, while others should be seen as less fortunate choices.

Erich Fromm

This is the approach taken in the book *To Have or To Be?* by Fromm (1976). Fromm presents two fundamentally opposed modes of existence for our consideration, one oriented to having and owning, the other to being and living. He points out that a number of ordinary everyday activities (learning, remembering, conversing, etc.) change character, according to whether they are undertaken in one or the other of these modes. When the mode of having is dominant, love for others will tend to be expressed in the form of setting limits, seeking to control others, to own them and to have rights over them. Loving acts take a different form in accordance with the mode of being. They will in that case tend to seek the enjoyment of being together, of giving to each other and inspiring each other.

Fromm holds the view that there are excellent reasons for seeking to limit the influence of the 'having' mode of existence, while seeking to promote the 'being' mode. Unless people's habits can be weaned away from the mode of having to that of being, an environmental catastrophe threatens all of us on a global level. 'For the first time in history the physical survival of the human race depends on a radical change of the human heart', writes Fromm (1976: 19).

Let us return to the question of value priorities. Is one life value and life meaning just as good as the next? According to Allport, the answer would seem to be yes, they are. According to Fromm, however, the answer seems to be no, they are not.

Viktor Frankl

Different life values become important at different points in our lives. The Austrian existential psychiatrist Frankl (1973) has made an important contribution in regard to the relation between life values and life stages.

Frankl (1973: xiii) distinguishes three kinds of values. The first are termed creative values. They are realized in activities such as those of constructing and giving, and are pursued in the spheres of work and family life. These values have an expansive character, tending to enlarge as well as establish the person's world.

The second are termed experiential values. They are realized in the ability to open oneself to the world and to respond to nature, art and love. To realize such values is to lead a life that is rich in experience. These values have a receptive character, that of letting the world in.

The third are termed attitudinal values. They are realized in the ability to prepare oneself for the limitations of circumstance, the reality of suffering or perhaps the renunciation needed to cope with a harsh fate. These values come into play in the face of illness or approaching death. They are also called into play when we have to abandon some project we have striven to achieve. It then becomes a task in itself to be able to accept our fate and to find a meaning in that circumstance.

Frankl's three values sum up what people live for in our time. Each type of value is different in character and seems to correspond to a particular manner in which the human psyche functions. As Frankl understands it, each type tends to come into play in a given chronological order. The usual pattern is one whereby people try to realize the creative, expansive values while they are young, striving to form their existence through their work and by creating a family. Later in life, people tend to be more receptive to the values of experience as enjoyed in nature, art and the experience of loving. Towards the end of life, when fate is less kind, they are presented with the task of finding a meaning in their suffering. But for some people this order is reversed, for instance if they are hit by a serious accident or a serious somatic disease at a young age. Also some people nowadays seem to be receptive before they get expansive. The sequence of life stages is not so predetermined as it was some decades ago.

So far we have considered what kinds of values the therapist meets in a typical client (Allport's six types), what kinds of values are called for in our time (Fromm's two types) and in what typical or atypical rhythm the values show up during our life course (Frankl's three stages). Let us now briefly consider what the therapist can do in practice in order to work with and relate to the values and beliefs of the client.

Emmy van Deurzen

Emmy van Deurzen has formulated a practice of value clarification. She considers the process of 'taking stock of one's life' (van Deurzen-Smith, 1988: 103) as a basic task of existential therapy. An important aspect of this 'taking stock' is for the client to determine what values he or she lives for and especially which of these values really count upon closer reflection and which are going to count in the future. The core of this process is not so much to look critically at what you have been doing and what priorities you have happened to make in the past, as would be the case in the cognitive approach. In existential therapy the process is more to find out what you really live for and what you really want to live for, and through this exploration to get strength and energy to find your purpose (ibid., 116–117).

Ernesto Spinelli

Ernesto Spinelli has formulated an approach to help the client make personal changes out of the confrontation between a meeting with an unexpected reality on the one hand and the values and beliefs which the individual so far has connected with himself or herself on the other. When a client is confronted with some surprising reality (e.g. being sacked or finding that somebody unexpectedly cares for him or her), the client has two choices. Either he or she can deny the reality and maintain his or her beliefs or values up to now. Or the client can choose to accept the new aspect of reality which means that he or she must change beliefs about what kind of person he or she is. The second choice may be therapeutically very fruitful and can in turn lead to an amount of consequent changes in the relational network of the client (Spinelli, 1994: 353).

Irvin Yalom

Irvin Yalom has developed an approach to therapy that places a primordial emphasis on cultivating the special relationship between client and therapist. Value changes and other deep personal changes in the client take place through developing a special bond between client and therapist, namely a mutual recognition of a communality of fate between the two. The defining element of existential therapy according to Yalom is not the content, but the process (Yalom, 2002: xvii). The crucial element is the bond that develops gradually as client and therapist discover and experience that they are confronting the same fundamental issues in this life (ibid., 8ff.).

Case illustrations

I will describe three cases from my own practice. Together they illustrate the six existential theories and practices delineated above.

The couple who disagreed about orderliness in their home

A young married couple with two small children were having serious and constant quarrels about the degree of order and cleanliness in their home. He always scolded and grumbled about the mess. If one of the children spilt milk or food on the table or the floor he became very tough and unpleasant for a long time. She felt that all the pleasure and joy had been drawn out of their common life.

In such a case I always let one of the two give his or her version for an extended period of time with the other listening silently. I ask questions to get a deeper understanding of what the world looks like from the perspective of that person. Afterwards the other person is allowed a brief response and then the roles are reversed. In this case the wife started giving her version. Afterwards the husband presented his case. He explained how he found it horrible with all this mess and all these spots. He really wanted a nice home with beautiful and rather expensive furniture.

At this point I found it quite difficult to empathize with this man. I have always felt strongly that there should be life, spontaneity, love and joy in a home and that the children living there should have freedom to express themselves. I felt more on the wavelength of the woman. In order to try to understand the man and make the woman understand the man, I asked: 'Can you please explain what it means to you to have such a nice home with such fine furniture? What is it that makes it so desirable?' I saw the woman getting ready to listen eagerly.

'I love beautiful things', said the man. 'I think there should be nice and harmonious proportions between my pieces of furniture. Clean surfaces. I like colours that play together. I always dreamed of becoming an architect. I used to love drawing too.' Upon hearing this, the wife and I got a new understanding of what drove this man. She followed up by asking him whether there could be some way for him to unfold his creative wishes. Their interaction changed from fixed repetitive negative patterns into something more constructive and new.

What happened here was an example of three people belonging to each of Allport's value types and therefore they found it difficult to understand each other. Also, when the man started to articulate his basic values we saw a movement from Fromm's category of 'having' to his category of 'being'.

A young woman with hidden artistic values

A professional woman in her early thirties found that her life was one big misery. The work situation at her office was almost unbearable, she felt harassed and teased by all her colleagues and was unable to retort. Her friendships and relations with boyfriends had the same character. She was exhausted, without confidence and her spirits and hope were exceedingly low.

I was about to suggest to her to set herself the goal of developing more assertiveness in her social relations when I suddenly became aware of one kind of situation where she felt wholly different: as soon as she was doing any kind of arts and crafts she felt completely at ease with herself. It suddenly became apparent to both of us that actually she did not like her job very much. Nor did she like any conventional way of being together with friends. For a period, she gave priority to all kinds of arts and crafts and she decided to only relate to other people in the same genuine and authentic (non-role-playing) way as she related to her artistic material. Through this process she changed a lot and she described this change as becoming much more herself in her activities and in her being-with-others. After ten sessions she ended the therapy, fully confident in her future.

This is an example of van Deurzen's value clarification and of a person who has been living a life founded on values other than her own authentic ones. She finds her way forward through finding her values. It also represents an example of a client moving from one type of Frankl's values to another, from his first to his second value type.

The lady with HIV

A woman in her fifties had been suffering from massive tiredness and suddenly discovered that she had contracted an HIV infection. She was naturally shocked and was referred for medical treatment and to psychological crisis therapy. She was a single, professional woman with no stable boyfriend and she used to be a very lively, well-functioning woman who had much pleasure in her life. She was of course preoccupied by the perspective of developing AIDS, but she was more concerned about the prospect of being socially put into a category of sufferers. Most of all she grieved because she had, or so she felt, to say goodbye to all sexual life from now on. Sex had been a prime source of pleasure and satisfaction all her adult life, it had been a pivotal value in her self-esteem and life satisfaction. Now it was all over.

'I am unclean', she thought. 'Of course I cannot offer myself to any prospective boyfriend. Should I tell him at the bedside, or beforehand? No, it is impossible.' Staring directly at me, she added: 'I am sure a man like you wouldn't care to sleep with an unclean woman like me.'

In such a situation there is no time to think, you have to rely on your intuition. And my intuition told me to reply like this: 'Well, I am happily married so it is not relevant. But in the case that I had been looking for somebody, I would not think the way you presume. If I met an HIV-infected person that I really got along with well, I would calculate the risk if using a condom. Then I would probably conclude that the risk would be so minute that it could be compared to being run over in the traffic. So that wouldn't stop me.'

The woman became very silent and reflective and appeared somewhat shaken. Shortly after, she told me that she no longer considered herself unclean and that she no longer considered herself as defined by the disease. The disease was not important any more. A few weeks later she resumed a very satisfactory sexual life and blossomed again.

This is an example of how a Yalom-inspired personal contact leads to changes in the person's value system and beliefs. Looking at the case in terms of Spinelli's theory you could say that the confrontation with an unexpected reality (i.e. the therapist's reaction) leads to an immediate change in her self-concept and her value realization.

Critical considerations

The most obvious risk in working with your client's values and beliefs is one which unfortunately many therapists are drawn into: the therapist is not sufficiently conscious about his or her own values and beliefs as something special and subjective, but takes these values and beliefs to be natural and self-evident. Much harm is done to clients when this therapeutic error takes place. The therapeutic situation is extremely vulnerable to the event that the therapist in this way superimposes his or her own values and beliefs upon the client and thereby kills something that is unfolding within the client: the client's new self and the client's own core values. Here is an example of a mild case of this type of violation of life values: A woman in her fifties seeks therapeutic help because her husband has been unfaithful and behaves more and more in an egoistical and ruthless way. For the first time she fears that her thirty-year-long marriage may end up in divorce, something she considers catastrophic because of the children (who are now grown up) and because of her religious convictions and family tradition. The woman appears to be warm and loving, but very dependent on her husband. The therapist is a young independent woman. She thinks that her client certainly has to learn to stand on her own two feet. She urges her to find a lawyer to get clear about her rights and her economical situation in case of a divorce. The therapist challenges the client's value position with the question: What do you want yourself? What do you want? What requirements do you have for your own life? The client cannot answer these questions, because she does not think of herself as an 'I' but as a 'we'. Her primal value is to preserve her family. She feels that the therapist does not understand her at all and quits therapy unchanged after two sessions.

Further reading

Allport, G. W. *Pattern and Growth in Personality.*
Frankl, V. E. *The Doctor and the Soul.*
Fromm, E. *To Have or To Be?*
Spinelli, E. *Demystifying Therapy.*
van Deurzen, E. *Existential Counselling and Psychotherapy in Practice.*
Yalom, I. D. *The Gift of Therapy.*

CHAPTER 28

Political and Ideological Issues

MARTIN MILTON

> Psychotherapy concerns itself with applied philosophy or more specifically with
> applied ethics and personal politics ... subjective reality needs to be connected
> to the reality of the group and the culture.
>
> van Deurzen-Smith, *British Journal of Psychotherapy*: 464

Introduction

In his very comprehensive text, one of the first to address the relationship
between psychotherapy and politics, Samuels defines 'politics' as 'the concerted
arrangements and struggles within an institution, or in a single society, or
between the countries of the world for the organization and distribution of
resources and power, especially economic power' (Samuels, 1993: 3). On that
same page he goes on to note that

> 'On a more personal level; there is a second kind of politics. Here political power
> reflects struggles over agency, meaning the ability to choose freely whether to act
> and what action to take in a given situation [...] But politics also refers to a crucial
> interplay between these two dimensions, between the private and public dimensions
> of power. (Ibid., 3–4)

For the purposes of this chapter it is important to recognise that politics and
ideology are clearly related. Ideology relates to systems of thought that underlie
political actions and structures. People can of course see ideology as political
and political structures as ideological. Something that unites them is the
relationship they both have to power and how it is exercised.

The relationship of existential ideas and practice to the political and
ideological is interesting. An existential focus is by definition related to the
existence of the individual in the world. It is an aspect of individual activity; it
is our world in a microcosm. Politics, as noted above, is often thought of as
manifesting itself in the macrocosm, being more than the experiences of
individuals since it is about the global ways in which societies are organised.
However, existential thought addresses the fact that the individual always
exists in relation to others – whether that 'other' is an individual, a group of

known individuals or the collective. The task that faces existential thought therefore is – by its very nature a difficult one – to account for the experience of Dasein *as well as* recognising and understanding the political. Existential literature understands our experiences and the meanings we create as embedded in this world – politics is experienced individually and relationally. The political and ideological impact on Dasein by the impositions of the givens of particular existences, through the allowing (and disallowing) of certain experiences – can of course occur at all levels. For David,[1] vegetarianism was both an individual response to the given of nourishment and also a political stance to the world.

Environmentalism was for him a very personal issue of how he related to the natural world in his day-to-day actions – and it was also linked to keenly held political positions – such as how his decisions during the run-up to the general election were based on the environmental, agricultural and transport policies of the political parties. In this respect the limits of our existence and our situated freedom should be seen not only as physical and individual, but political too.

Having said this, on the whole, psychotherapy as a discipline and as a profession has struggled to integrate political and ideological issues into practice and this has often been due to an anxiety related to whether or not the inclusion of an external, political focus limits the psychotherapeutic project from being at all therapeutic (Milton and Legg, 2000). It may also be more personal than this. In effect, 'by avoiding the political domain we may be avoiding the impotence we experience in the face of major political developments/experiences' (ibid., 2000: 284; see also May, 1977).

Some psychotherapeutic approaches have a tendency to see the person as a 'self-contained individual' (Strawbridge, 1996) and this means that the political (and anything else 'external' to the individual) is almost an irrelevance for psychotherapy. An existential perspective is very different.

Being political: an existential perspective on political and ideological issues

Some argue that existential thought is irrelevant to political issues and Macquarrie notes that these

> would say that it is essentially an individualistic and personalistic philosophy, perhaps even in those forms where it seeks to develop an understanding of the interpersonal, and that when one has to consider nations, corporations, labour unions, political parties, and the like, existentialism is seen to be completely irrelevant. (Macquarrie, 1972: 235)

Indeed, the aim for an existential project 'is to elucidate the primary function whereby we bring into existence, for ourselves, or take a hold upon, space, the object or the instrument, and to describe the body as the place where this appropriation occurs' (Merleau-Ponty, 1962: 154). This means that the focus is on the individual, not on the context. Spinelli notes this when he states that 'Merleau-Ponty is not interested in the issues of male or female sexuality, sexual orientation or the socio-political dimensions of sexuality. His is an investigation aimed toward the clarification of sexuality as it is revealed in its intentional dimension' (Spinelli, 1997: 7, 2001: 82).

This stance may explain why explicit existential writing on political or ideological issues has been scant. Therefore, we must consider whether the critics are right in their evaluation of the literature. There are, however, other authors whose work has a great deal of relevance for the political.

Existential writers offer various different perspectives including attention to the political as a subject in its own right (see Szasz, 1961; van Deurzen-Smith, 1993, 1995; Foucault, 1995; du Plock, 2000a,b), those whose work is clearly embedded in political events of their time (de Beauvoir, 1960; Frankl, 1984) and those that draw upon their personal experiences of political events (see Strasser, 1999) or ideological tension (Cohn, 1997).

Existential philosophy is clearly not allied with any one political agenda or ideological view. Indeed we see

> a wide variety of political affiliations among those who may be called existentialists. Heidegger was for a brief time a Nazi, but Jaspers consistently opposed the Nazis. Sartre has been attracted to Marxism, but it would be hard to find more penetrating and damaging critiques of Marxism than have come from Berdyaev and Camus. (Macquarrie, 1972: 237)

Along with others (see Cohn, 1989; van Deurzen-Smith, 1997; du Plock, 2000a,b; Spinelli, 2001), du Plock's stance is that psychotherapy is inevitably political and this

> recognizes that changes our clients make in their lives impact on others and provide opportunities for the creation of new familial, work place, social and organisational relationships. More importantly, it recognizes that therapists inevitably play an active role in either supporting or challenging the way society is regulated. (du Plock, 2000b: 703)

Frankl conceptualises the political and suggests a stance towards it. He notes that 'fanaticism politicizes humans more and more; while actually politics should be humanized [...] the difference between fanatical and humanized politics is this: that the fanatic believes that the end justifies the means, whereas we know that there are means which desecrate even the most sacred ends' (Frankl, 1967: 116). These can be brought about in a myriad of ways, by the actual beating and killing of individuals – or more subtly by the pointing of a finger towards a death camp or the allocation of a number instead of a name (Frankl, 1984).

This of course highlights the point that 'power is, per se, neither good nor bad – what is important is what we do with power once we have become aware that we have it' (du Plock, 2000b: 704). As Frankl and others highlight, the ignoring of identity can be as difficult and personally and politically powerful as the enforcement of another identity. In an understated way Spinelli notes that 'it's odd to know that you exist but not to be recognized as existing' (Spinelli, 2001: 111). Considering Sartrean notions, Stavro-Pearce notes that 'in so far as self-identity requires the acknowledgement of the other, and since the gaze of the other is from the outset threatening, a struggle to the death ensues. Hence "self-identity" is not self-identical, but emerges out of conflictual and non-transparent relations' (Stavro-Pearce, 1999: 5).

As well as the work of those that identify as existentialists themselves, the work of a number of other authors enriches the writing and practice of existential psychotherapists. Szasz is an example of one such author. Van Deurzen notes:

> Szasz says that psychotherapy ought to be classified as a form of applied politics and ethics and I couldn't agree more. It seems to me that it is self-evident that the therapists are totally engaged in a political and ethical enterprise and as such the dialogue they have with their clients or patients is often about converting the other perspective to one's own particular political or ethical position. (van Deurzen-Smith, 1995: 107)

Foucault is another important author whose work resonates with existential themes and who draws our attention to the fact that psychotherapy is a political and ideological activity creating identities and particular practices that regulate such aspects of existence as gender, sexuality and power (Foucault, 1995). Spinelli (2001) has recently taken up this challenge and called for existential therapists to reflect with their clients on the impact of their way of being on those around them. Some might conceptualise this as reflecting on our ethical responsibilities as beings in a shared world (and therefore undoubtedly part of psychotherapy) – others will argue that this takes the existential therapist out of their legitimate domain (du Plock, 2000a; Spinelli, 2001).

All of these writings are relevant to the practising therapist as they illuminate the difficulties that people experience as political beings in the world, as well as highlighting how a clarification of political/ideological issues in the therapeutic encounter can deepen psychotherapeutic practice. Only by thinking in this way are we able to 'ask questions about how we can be political in our relationship with our clients' (du Plock, 2000b: 705).

At this point, attention shifts from an account of the issues to an illustration of how an existential-phenomenological approach to psychotherapy can be used in practice in a political context.

Fighting inertia: an ongoing struggle in psychotherapy

While some argue that the notion of technique is counter to existential practice, is it not true that the same way that action (doing) is a part of Being, agreed-professional practices (technique) can be a part of encounter? Without technique, encounter threatens to be solely an empty, purposeless (potentially self-serving and confining) form of engagement. Without an open encounter of course, technique becomes a dehumanising technological exercise – prone to political use in the modification of people to fit a norm.

In terms of the existential practices, it is important to consider some of the few principles underlying technique. For both research and practice, existential literature frequently draws upon the 'phenomenological method' (Spinelli, 1989).

> The phenomenological method requires the therapist to encourage descriptive statements, the withholding of significance and the holding back of theory (Spinelli, 1989). These steps aim for a clear description of the client's realities to be developed outside of implicit or formal theories of reality so that the client might experience the multiple meanings that any phenomenon might hold. (Milton and Legg, 2000: 286)

The therapist therefore encourages the client to look beyond the habitual and limiting meanings available to us and encourages a richer, more critical reflection on the meaning of an issue and whether those meanings are really adequate. In doing so the therapist may engage with a range of political 'issues' such as the meaning of masculinity in the life of a young adolescent considering the 'type' of man he wants to be, or the issues of gender and sexuality in the life of the trans-gendered person – both of which may well take us out of our sedimented binary conceptualisations of gender and sexuality. A concern of course is that the change may lead us into alternative 'herds' (du Plock, 1997a; Goldenberg, 2000; Spinelli, 2001).

Case illustration

I recently met with a client who professionals had great difficulty speaking and writing about. Genetically, this person had been born male but experienced himself as female. Professional communications reflected this difficulty in that the letters and reports were littered with such statements as 'Mr X feels that he/she ...' or 'Ms Y also said that he ...'. Mr X's preference to be known as Ms Y was acknowledged, but somehow professionals felt inhibited in granting this client this form of self-identification. This struggle seemed to be the way in which this client was known, regardless of the fact that for Ms Y the experience of gender reassignment was not (as she saw it) central to her difficulty – nor was it an area that she felt required an explicit focus. She wanted to think about her impulsivity, her depression and her vulnerability.

At this point it was clear that as a therapist I was faced with a choice. Do I immerse myself in the meaning structure of this client? Or do I stay safely within the meaning structure of the psychological and psychiatric professions? Do I understand the client in the manner that she wants to be understood – and save myself the discomfort of being 'accused' of ignorance about the 'pathological presentation'? Do I avoid the pain of being seen to 'act out' with the client and be accused of depriving the client the chance to reflect on their 'obvious self deceit' and 'hatred' which some views see as being core to this type of experience of self? To take this tack would mean that I could work with colleagues and not try to challenge the generally held views about rigidity of gender. However, that tack threatened to lead me from a stance where I was able to attend to the spirit of 'horizontalisation' – waiting for a meaning to emerge out of this client's experience. It also meant that, like the Nazi soldiers who refuse to hear or use the names of the inmates, I was at risk of denying this client their particular existence or at best paying lip service to it.

My limited way through this difficulty was to reflect on this dilemma and to 'own up' to the fact that I had limited power to challenge this system – and to try to work within it. My client and I reflected on the fact that as in the 'world out there', mental health services struggle to engage with aspects of experience that are not mainstream. The system has the power to regulate experience (as well as the expression of experience) and this can be impossible to overcome in the short term. While it does not immediately assist this client, this experience led to a research project to explore attitudes and practices to sexual minority clients in this Trust.

As an existentially oriented practitioner I have often wondered about the notion of freedom and whether this can lead us unreasonably to urge our clients to resist a call to bad faith. All being equal in a utopian world this challenge to self-determination may be appropriate. However, 'wanting freedom for clients and wanting them to become more capable of understanding free action in the world, may be as prescriptive as wanting their internment or their adjustment to the status quo' (van Deurzen-Smith, 1995: 105).

This is certainly one of the difficulties raised by engaging with Ms Y – and I have to think that the awareness of an existential conceptualisation did nothing to ease this client's access to psychotherapy. One comfort is that while Ms Y remained somewhat vulnerable, alone and afraid, perhaps she had been spared further overt attacks on herself that may have occurred if I had been successful in providing her an entry to a mental health service that clung onto rigidly dichotomous views of gender and sexuality. In addition, our brief contact benefited from an existential perspective, as this allowed us to acknowledge the givens of existence – thereby offering the client the opportunity to reflect not only on her Being-in-the-world but Being-in-THIS-world.

Critical considerations

As there is no one existential view or set of techniques, a particular responsibility falls upon the existential psychotherapist. As well as attending to the conflicting perspectives of others and our field, we must also be prepared to question our own deeply held beliefs, because 'nothing is gained if the existential approach purely incites a one-sided idealistic engagement in some course. Blind fanaticism, however satisfying it may be, is not preferable to blind fatalism. The reverse is of course, equally true' (van Deurzen-Smith, 1988: 195). While being a creative and satisfying challenge in some respects, it can also be a very unsettling experience. One example is the discussion of Heidegger's political allegiance. Cohn asks whether 'I can be guided in my work as a psychotherapist by the thinking of a philosopher, who saw in a political movement unsurpassed in its destructiveness and disregard for human values, a potential answer to questions that arose from his own explorations of human existence' (Cohn, 1997: 96).

A number of other authors have also addressed this issue (van Deurzen-Smith, 1997; Strasser, 1999; Spinelli, 2001). In this way it is important that existential practitioners continue to take up the challenge, not only to deal with 'the political' *out there*, but to attend to the political implications of being a psychotherapist (see e.g. Farias, 1991; Rockmore and Margolis, 1992).

Research-active, existential-phenomenological therapists are in a good position to contribute to a developing understanding of how political and ideological aspects affect Dasein. Phenomenological research illuminates the experiences of individuals, groups and communities in a way that larger-scale, quantitative, positivist approaches are not able to do. The dehumanising approaches to research (which are useful in for example confirming the safety of particular medical procedures or the prevalence of illness in a community) can be complemented by a personalising approach to the experience of Being. It would be useful to see phenomenological research that explored the experience of, for instance, 'Being a Refugee', 'Being on a waiting list', 'Being an environmental protester' or 'Being a survivor of the Holocaust'.

Conclusions

In some respects the proponents of an existential approach still have some work to do if its usefulness is to be made more accessible to people. Refuting the accusations of the critics, Macquarrie states that existentialists

> are not individualists in the sense of being indifferent to social and political arrangements, but they remain free to criticize every political movement that needlessly restricts human freedom and diminishes human dignity, every system that sets the abstraction of the system itself above the concrete well-being of the persons whom the system is supposed to serve. (Macquarrie, 1972: 238).

Like a social-constructionist view, the fact that existential thought challenges so much certainty rather than provide it may be its particular contribution. Again, Macquarrie notes that it does not 'generate an ideology of its own. Indeed, the very idea of an ideology would suggest a form of heteronomy or bad faith' (ibid., 238). This is of course useful, but the same way that the 'critics of Foucault maintain that his analysis of power is simply a dead end that disallows any possibility of political action' (Fillingham, 1993: 151), as existentially oriented practitioners we must carefully reflect on whether we just assist our clients to deconstruct their worlds or whether we assist them in the generation of alternative meanings that allow them to find as satisfactory a way to live in the world as possible. That in itself seems a political endeavour and until we rise to the challenge that this poses we will be limited to the uncertain response that active inertia brings.

Note

1 When referring to clients, steps have been taken to ensure anonymity and maintain confidentiality.

Further reading

Foucault, M. *Madness and Civilization: A History in the Age of Reason.*
Frankl, V. *Psychotherapy and Existentialism: Selected Papers on Logotherapy.*
Samuels, A. *The Political Psyche.*
Spinelli, E. *The Mirror and the Hammer: Challenges to Therapeutic Orthodoxy.*
Strasser, F. *Emotions: Experiences in Existential Psychotherapy and Life.*

CHAPTER 29

Meaning and Transformation

MYRTLE HEERY AND JAMES F. T. BUGENTAL

> The most beautiful experience we can have is the mysterious.
>
> Einstein: *Ideas and Opinions*

Introduction

This chapter will address meaning and transformation in existential-humanistic psychotherapy. We present these mysterious processes as they apply to the client, therapist, and supervisor. Our orientation is existential. This means that we ask ourselves and our clients to look at how we are each meeting this basic fact and mystery of our existence. Mystery is infinite, not finite. Mystery is the latent meaning always awaiting our discovery, and it is always more than our knowing in the objective world. Mystery points to the subjective world where implicit meanings are waiting to be *transformed* into explicit meanings in living experience.

Our *value system* is humanistic, meaning that we regard all humans as valuable and as having the potential for experiencing greater meaning in their lives. Through the processes of inner searching, we can access the human potential inherent in our being. The open spectrum of possibilities is a powerful encouragement for us – client, therapist, and supervisor – to reconceive the familiar, to attempt the new, and to explore with innocence of perception. Existential-humanistic psychotherapy is a lengthy, in-depth searching process, not a few visits to the doctor's office for a quick answer to a client's objective concerns (Bugental, 1999).

One of the great gifts of being human is the capacity to search and particularly to search for meaning. In *Man's Search for Meaning* (1984), Victor Frankl, an existential pioneer on this topic of meaning and psychotherapy, proposes that answering the question, 'What is the meaning of life?', is essential for each individual in the psychotherapy process. It is not an 'out there' search for an objective answer to a problem, a dream, or a symbol, but rather an 'in here' search for one's full life potential with all its paradoxes and complexities. This inner search for meaning weaves individual experiences into a tapestry of meaning from inside. The individual is transformed from inside. Searching is

253

a process of transformation from inside, facilitating transition and psychological shifts inwardly by which the individual moves the process of living from one stage of life to the next, forming patterns of beginnings and endings. These patterns become conscious and choiceful to the individual through the searching process lived in existential psychotherapy.

In-depth, long-term existential-humanistic psychotherapy focuses on the search for meaning and transformation by accessing and using implicit meanings and capabilities. This chapter first establishes the importance of the distinction between subjective versus objective and then defines the core psychotherapeutic work, *searching* and *resistance* – that is, how the searching stops. We explore the vitality of the actual moment and the components necessary to support inner searching in existential-humanistic psychotherapy. We elaborate on meaning and transformation through a case, *Inside a Cage of Diagnosis* and end with what we feel we are offering new to the process of meaning and transformation in existential-humanistic psychotherapy.

An existential perspective

Objective verses subjective: explicit verses implicit

In this moment, we the authors are writing. The objective reality of writing involves our fingers touching letters on the keyboard of a computer and in a broader view of the objective reality it is a spring day in California in the year 2002. The subjective realities of the two authors include searching their inner truths about meaning and transformation and then finding words to match these truths. We sit in silence to see if there is a match, feeling, and being with our world from inside concerning these subjects. We share this immediate focus with you the reader to bring you into our actual moment as we write. As you read these words, part of your objective reality is that you are holding a book and reading. Part of your subjective reality is that what you are reading is stirring feelings, impressions, images, and other unknown dimensions of your subjective world.

The inner world of each person is immense, perhaps larger than will ever be consciously known to yourself or to others. This vast unknown territory is the landscape through which we accompany our clients on their psychotherapeutic journeys.

What can be said about a client is always at least in some measure an abstraction, an objectification, and a distortion. To talk *about* a client is to make that person an *object* – of observation, of speculation, or of report. Human objects are not to be confused with human *subjects*. The very fact of human subjectivity is the most distinguishing and salient feature of human life (Bugental, 1999).

We have the paradox of the human as simultaneously being both subject and object. This paradoxical distinction is crucial and is at the root of existential-humanistic psychotherapy. Thus this recognition of limitation – which we are now writing and you are now reading – applies to what we are saying right now.

Existential-humanistic psychotherapy provides a safe place for clients to face their inner worlds and to take responsibility for their human existences. We are here concerned with the uniqueness and irreducibility of human experience. This puts a strong focus on the psychotherapist and any therapist's supervisor to recognize the uniqueness of each client and to respond to it with a unique and particularized adaptation of the therapist's knowledge, skill, intuitions, and sensitivities. The supervisor shares this focus with the therapist by attending to what is subjectively stirred in the therapist presenting the case.

The core work – searching and resistance

What we are here calling 'searching' is simply one way of tapping into our native endowment – our inner world. Freud's 'basic rule' of free association is another (Freud, 1997), as are Martin Buber's (Buber, 1978) and John Welwood's 'unfolding' (Welwood, 1983) and Gendlin's 'focusing' (Gendlin, 1996). Our instinctive searching powers are called into play whenever we need something (e.g. food, companionship, intellectual stimulation, physical activity, and rest). The same is true when we search for meaning. The inner search for meaning is usually activated by difficult or challenging life experiences such as loss of a job, an unhappy relationship, or difficulty with children. These are all concerns boldly or hesitantly brought into the psychotherapy room. These external concerns often bring the individual into searching for meaning not only for this external concern, but for the *intention* of their living, the driving force behind being here with purpose plus awareness of our limited time here. 'It is this changing or moving the concern which points to the fullness of the client's capacity for living' (Heery and Bugental, 1999: 25). The question of meaning moves into involvement of living with choices and responsibilities for one's life. The existential-humanistic approach not only invites inward searching but also moves forward with choices and responsibility in living. In order to access choices, this approach adds a very distinctive perspective to the process inhibiting choice, *resistance*.

In spite of the therapist's good intentions and the client's good intentions, this search encounters many *resistances*. When we become fully engaged in searching in psychotherapy, we discover difficulties in letting our thoughts and feelings range widely and meaningfully. These are the *resistances* and in a very real way, they are necessary and sometimes predictable.

The resistances, which we encounter while searching, have three profound implications. First, we experience them as interfering with our capacity to search. It is like paddling a canoe down a river and at times we slow down or even stop because of an object that temporarily blocks our movement. The slowing of our movement in the canoe and in searching is a very natural part of our lives. Resistances give form and range to our thinking. They are essential to rational thought and meaningful discourses.

Second, resistances are integral to how we organize our world; they are central to the ways we define who and what we are and what is possible in our reality. Resistances are at the core of our construct of self-and-world; the ways we implicitly define ourselves and our conception of the nature of the world within which we live. They are knit into our ways of being in our world. Resistances are the patterns of thoughts or behaviour, which each person develops to protect his or her conception of nature of the world and reality and to guard the person's speech and behaviour in the world.

Finally, depth psychotherapy raises the question of how the resistance is serving or not serving the individual. Resistances are not to be thrown away for they are essential for human life. Just as our skin holds our physical body together, resistance is necessary to hold our subjective world together. The question is whether the resistance is truly *serving* the individual. The answer to this question is likely to be disclosed through 'the inner searching of the client rather than the opinion of the psychotherapist or the supervisor of the psychotherapist'.

Transformation and meaning in a client's life involves *experiencing* resistance in the here and now, not there and then. It is not in talking about meaning or transformation but in actually experiencing what is stopping the individual in the moment in psychotherapy. This process opens the client to actualizing choices and responsibility in living, a major cornerstone of existential-humanistic psychotherapy.

The actual in psychotherapy

The client, therapist, and supervisor are never static. The therapist's impression of a client in the first ten minutes of a session may differ from the last ten minutes. This constant change points to the fluidity of living. 'Life is incessant movement, always going forward into the next moment. Bodies change, thoughts change, emotions flow – there is no final form of any aspect of life. Without flow, an organism is dead. Psychological reality is always the present, the ever-moving, never-repeatable present' (Heery and Bugental, 1999: 25).

Change, constant change, movement, growth, decline, expansion, contraction – such is the nature of life. Clients tell stories and the therapist listens. Therapists tell stories to supervisors and the supervisors listen. What do the therapist and supervisor listen for? Our work does not focus on content of the story but rather *how* the story is told, whether by client or supervisee. The *how* can include pauses between the words, repeated physical gestures, or varied information, emphasis, gestures, and focuses. The following demonstrates focusing the *how* of a client's story. The therapist seeks to take it all, to assess it, and to recognize if his or her input will be effective.

Cl: 'Well, Mom is about the same this week. She does not seem to be getting better or worse, same old, same old response to her chemotherapy treatments' (said with a big grin).

Th 1: 'John, tell me more about the chemotherapy treatments?'

Th 2: 'John, are you aware you smile when you speak about your mother's chemotherapy?'

Cl: 'Gee, I didn't know I was smiling. I am sorry. I will try not to do that.'
Th: 'John, I'm not passing a judgment on your smile, and I'm not asking you to stop smiling, I am noticing your smile when you talk about your mother's chemotherapy and I want to bring it to your awareness.'

In this brief vignette we see two different responses from two therapists. The first therapist is following the content of the story and collecting more facts with her response. The second therapist is attending to the actual moment by bringing the client's smile into his awareness. We are not talking about the content of his mother's illness, but actually bringing into awareness aspects of John's resistance; John being the good client, and avoiding deeper feelings of the possible loss of his mother. By pointing to the actual, these resistances become alive in the moment. In listening to clients' concerns, beginning therapists will often slip into the content of the story and miss the *actuality*. Death and dying concerns are givens of being human, which are often not explored in training a psychotherapist (Heidegger, 1927; Jaspers, 1951; Yalom, 1985). Of course, there will be resistances alive in a therapist or supervisor who attends to the content of death and dying and not to the lived moment of the therapy. These resistances need to be monitored by the therapist through consistent supervision and confronted with questions such as, 'What is happening in you right now as you talk about John's mother's chemotherapy?' This question brings into the therapist's awareness how she or he is being emotionally touched or not touched by John's concern, his dying mother. Allowing the client's concern to touch the therapist can become the touchstone of transformation for both the client and the therapist. Certainly, this perspective does not *exclude* the content of the client's story but it shifts the focus from content to *process in the moment inside the client and the therapist*. The process of meaning and transformation is happening in the moment and pointing to responsibilities and present choices taken or not taken. These processes will never be the same with the same client on different occasions or with a different client voicing a similar concern. We are each unique and the meanings we search for regarding our concerns are unique as well.

Necessary components for therapeutic support

The five necessary components of therapeutic support are presence, holding, caring, challenging, and confirming. These components blend into one other, working together to support the vitality of the client's searching process.

Presence is that aspect of the therapist's subjective being which shows up physically, emotionally, and spiritually and engages with the client. It is a full response to the client in the moment. Presence is allowing the client to matter to the therapist (Yalom, 2002). 'Presence is accompanied by heightened self-awareness on the part of both therapist and client' (Heery, 2001: 437).

In *holding* we are not referring to a physical act but rather a subtle way of being with a client. *Holding* is how the therapist provides a client with a secure and dependable framework within which to experience and explore a wide range of feelings and impulses. Holding may include accepting socially disapproved feelings and impulses from the client, but it does not imply acting on them.

Caring is the therapist accepting to be engaged with a client's suffering. 'Caring is an experience shared between therapist and client; at times it is satisfying to both, and at other times, it is exhausting to both' (Heery, 1989: 438). The state of caring allows the experience of empathy: as if you are this person suffering and at the same time separate from this person.

Challenging brings the therapist into authenticity with the client, with a commitment to speak the truth to the client. Challenge supports the client's innate ability to become more than what the client experiences himself or herself to be in the therapeutic hour.

Confirmation provides a stable, accepting, and understanding accompaniment to a client's inner search, particularly to a client's struggles and experiences of psychological pain and/or anxiety. Confirmation is not 'hand holding', rather, it is a part of the container of the therapeutic alliance, providing support for inner searching.

Case illustration: inside a cage of diagnosis

Allen[1] is a tall, thirty-eight-year-old single man. In his first session, Allen paces the room and announces in a very matter-of-fact tone, 'I'm schizophrenic. I've been diagnosed several times over the past twenty years by several reputable psychiatrists and I want you to know that I'm schizophrenic. I take my meds regularly. I live at a meditation centre and the directors of the centre have told me that I have to get a job. I cannot get a job as I am schizophrenic and no one hires schizophrenics. The directors of the meditation centre gave me your name and said you could help me sort out this problem. I don't know how you could do such a thing but maybe you could, I'm not sure. Do you think you can help me?'

I am caught by the fact that Allen has not sat down this whole time; he is still pacing as he waits for my response. I am drawn into his physical presence, which in turn draws me deeper into the inner Allen. With curiosity and careful pacing, I invite Allen to sit down and he responds. 'No thank you, I prefer to stand and walk.'

I leave the invitation and his response but hold my invitation and his response as the beginning of our therapeutic alliance. I have accepted him exactly where he is and he not only knows this but also has experienced it. He seems to be in a cage. He can only walk so far and no further. He expresses himself quickly and succinctly, as if he is coming up against the invisible bars of the cage that holds him back. He feels determined, which manifests in his determined walk. Each step seems clearly measured. His determination is a window to his inner world and what it is to live with this diagnosis of schizophrenia. My supervision with Dr Bugental this week is filled with Allen's presence.

'"Let yourself walk his walk, be him as much as you can." Dr Bugental leans forward in his chair full of the curiosity that I have grown to know so well.'

By walking in Allen's shoes, allowing myself to be this client as much as possible, I begin the real work. This role-play is what I refer to as a sacred entrance into the client's world. Yes, I walk Allen's walk over and over, many sessions, many times. I begin the journey of a man diagnosed as schizophrenic. He is a brilliant man who has never worked in the world. He has been supported financially by his father and lived a sheltered life at a meditation centre. Now he is being asked to get a job in a world that he does not know. It is a world that does not know him or want to hire him. He has been labelled and he bears all the consequences of this label. Employment is the external challenge for Allen, but our work is cut out for us from the inside.

Knowing, not knowing

What does it mean to be schizophrenic? What is the meaning of this man's life from inside? How can I really walk in his shoes? How can my supervisor help me to help him? This is a journey of existential-humanistic psychotherapy taken by three people: the client (Allen), the therapist (Dr Heery), and the supervisor (Dr Bugental, referred to as Jim hereafter). This is a journey of meaning and transformation for the three of us out of a cage of diagnosis into unknown possibilities. The vehicle is our common humanity. Several psychiatrists had given Allen a diagnosis but the real Allen is unknown to Jim and me. The analysts knew Allen was schizophrenic and now Allen knows himself as schizophrenic.

As I imagined being in Allen's shoes, I knew I did not know what it is to be labelled schizophrenic. My experience opened me to the *not-knowing*. Beginning to look at Allen's inner world from not-knowing awakened a persistent sense of curiosity and awe in me – behind this objective diagnosis lives a person who has yet to be seen by himself, Jim, or me. We are actively engaging in presence, holding, caring, and challenging, and confirmation is *being with* Allen from the *inside* of our existence. We use our inner experiences of Allen and ourselves being Allen to move forward in our search for meaning.

Diagnosed and searching for meaning

My sense of curiosity and awe brought up many questions for Jim and me. How does this diagnosis of schizophrenia impact Allen's inherent capacity to search? Is he searching for more than a job and if so, for what? Allen is still pacing during his sessions as he answers these questions.

'I'm not here to look for a job; that is my father's concern, not mine. My concern is enlightenment. If getting a job can help me reach my goal, so be it.'

Allen is searching. He is searching for enlightenment, even if the route to it lies *out there* in a job. Allen has been living at a meditation centre for fifteen years in search of enlightenment, accompanied by his diagnosis of schizophrenia. Soon after his diagnosis, he entered this meditation centre to find meaning in what he described as a 'meaningless life'. He is well read in the literature in every Eastern and Western spiritual tradition available to him.

Part of Allen's diagnosis includes hearing voices, yet these voices are not harmful to him or others; he describes them as helping him to reach God. His experience confirms my research that hearing voices can be helpful as long as they are not instructing harm to self or others (Heery, 1989). Allen is determined to reach enlightenment as he continues to pace the floor of my office. But he has not reached his goal and here he is in my office, pacing. He comes two, sometimes three, times a week to my office (Heery). An objective reality, which intensifies his search for meaning and transformation.

My weekly supervision continues. We individually and collectively begin to experience Allen from inside. I actually pace during some of my supervision sessions. In pacing, I experience determination accompanied by hesitation, as if I was a caged bird, able to fly but stopped by invisible bars of the invisible cage formed by a diagnosis. Because this work involves fluctuating states of curiosity and awe extending beyond the individual, there is blurring of the identities of the client, therapist, and supervisor. Perhaps, this blurring can be defined as *loss of boundaries*. We are not referring to physical boundaries in this blurring process but rather inner experiences lived by the client, therapist, and supervisor. It is an experience of *being apart of* and at the same time *a part from*. By walking Allen's walk I can feel into his state, as if I am Allen, yet separate from Allen. Of course, I hesitate.

'Jim, his continued pacing is concerning me.'

'What is happening inside you right now?' Jim asks me.

'I feel impatient. He knows he can sit down. I am moving away from the present moment and into the future with fear. What if he never sits down?'

'So.'

'I feel so deeply moved by him (tears come). I feel so alone when I feel into his inner world. I need to stay where he actually is in the moment. I need to slow down.'

'Yes, continue your pacing.'

I move slower and experience a felt sense of Allen's inner world. I call Allen's pace the *sacred pace*, as it allows me to enter Allen's inner world without judgement of good or bad, right or wrong, but rather with deep awareness of what is. I continue to pace during some of my supervision hours and Allen continues pacing for roughly a month during his therapy hours. Accepting his pace is sacred to him, to me, and to Jim. Sacred in the sense of embodying Allen's world as it actually is in the moment.

'I'm going to sit down today. I can see you and the tree outside much better that way.' Allen makes this announcement in a very matter-of-fact manner accompanied by clear determination as he sits in the chair, looks at me clearly and then at the tree outside the window.

In trusting this sacred pace, we have all entered a sacred relationship. I never verbally tell Allen that I had walked his pace but he knows that I have entered into his inner world. Client, therapist, and supervisor share this unspoken knowing. Allen trusts me now. He acknowledges his changed relationship with me and also his relationship to the world by wanting to see me and the tree clearer. We are now in the beginning stages of a new relationship, which points to the very intricate and delicate work of weaving meaning into Allen's world.

There are many aspects of Allen's work we could share over the next four years of twice, sometimes three times, a week therapy; yet time and space do not permit such an in-depth discussion. In accepting these present limitations, we are reminded of Allen's acceptance of his limitations.

In a very real sense, Allen's search for meaning came through the acceptance of his actual life. Transformations are processes of embracing the actual. Allen could lower his dosage of medication but could not function without his medication. With the assistance of a psychiatrist, he tried briefly to stop his medication but experienced his self-demeaning voices as unbearable. The medication helped control the volume of the voices. There was never any full meaning to the causes of his various voices. Searching for causes was not the focus of our work, rather accessing Allen's potential, making choices and taking responsibility for his life, which is what existential-humanistic psychotherapy offers to this journey of meaning and transformation. Within Allen's limitations, we challenge him over and over to live *his* full potential.

His passion for enlightenment was channelled into his love for spiritual literature and sharing that love with others. After many failed attempts at employment, Allen volunteered at a bookstore to organize their spiritual books. After a few months, he became like a mentor to seekers frequenting the bookstore. In time, he became an employee at the bookstore with a limited income but an income. These outer changes matched his inner departure from the caged diagnosis. Our mysterious and awesome journey together was coming to a close with some meanings and no meanings, a paradox of being human. One significant meaning for Allen is he found his voice of spirituality could be heard and accepted by a significant other, his therapist. This therapeutic acceptance was critical to his self-acceptance and his ability to function in the world simultaneously hearing voices. It was through this fundamental therapeutic relationship that Allen could move into the larger world with a sense of worth. His work at the bookstore mirrored the positive aspects of his inner world. Certainly, at times his mysterious voices of the mystical realm of life made no sense to him, yet he found other kindred souls to discuss these paradoxes of walking the earth with mystical feet.

Allen went through a process of transformation and woke up to what was actual in the moment. Enlightenment moved from a wished-for mystical state of being in the future to an embodiment of the here and now within himself, between us, and in his relationships to others in the world. This change from the imagined future to the actual present moment certainly did not stop his dreams of the future but placed more focus on how his future was forming now. In the later phase of his therapy a pivotal experience occurred with his estranged father who had played the role of an emotionally absent father most of Allen's life. According to Allen, his father was a very successful man professionally and Allen's unusual experiences such as hearing voices and his diagnosis of schizophrenia had been shameful to his father's self and world image. They had spoken very little over the years with his father's main contact being a check once a month for Allen's living expenses. During the four years of therapy Allen began to correspond with his father who lived on the opposite side of the country. Their physical distance mirrored their emotional distance. Slowly their relationship began to open with their correspondence.

'I got a letter from Dad today and he wants to come here and attend one of my therapy sessions.'

'Is that something you want Allen?'

'Well, it seems ok with me, I do not know what would happen but I do know what has happened in the past.'

'And in this moment, what is your wanting?'

'It is all mixed up. I am scared and hopeful at the same time.'

'I am too.'

The authenticity between Allen and myself is palpable. During Allen's searching, he explores our relationship and how his father's physical presence could change our relationship. He decides to say yes to his father attending a session, feeling the positive far outweighed the negative. I join his decision and know I will review this decision with Jim in supervision.

'Allen's father is coming to Allen's session in about a week. I feel scared.'

'So?'

'It is as if I am going to be observed and reviewed by a parent. Am I doing a good enough job with Allen and if not, what? And what if I am doing a good job? I do not like the judgement.'

'Who is judging right now?'

'I am.'

'So?'

'I am so harsh on myself. My ever-faithful critic is raising her head up and attempting to destroy what we have done and what could be done. Allen also shared a similar concern. Ah, it is good to feel my critic's power and take her power into the session, not the judgement.'

In my office a week later, a tall, distinguished man accompanies Allen into my office. A gentle smile immediately widens his mouth as he shakes my hand

and says, 'Thank you. I wanted to personally come here to thank you for accepting Allen. Something which I have had a great deal of difficulty in doing myself.'

Humility fills me. As Benoit so beautifully said regarding transformation, 'The only task, incumbent upon us is to understand reality and to let ourselves be transformed by it' (Benoit, 1990: 242).

This brave father continues and apologizes to Allen. They speak openly for an hour. There are bumps in their communication as there are in all human communications and at the same time their hearts remain open to each other. Simultaneously, in a very precious, unique way, my heart is also opened to myself as a therapist.

The depth of becoming fully human is confirmed in Allen's search for meaning and transformation and actualizing these meanings in his personal relationships. Through our presence, holding, caring, and challenging, Allen and all of us are confirmed in being here and now. The present moment is confirmed once again in existential-humanistic psychotherapy.

Concluding thoughts

We have not seen or heard from Allen in over twenty years but we visited him through watching a movie, in 2002. Jim and I along with our spouses saw *A Beautiful Mind*, a story of a brilliant schizophrenic's healing process. I found myself riveted to my chair at the end, weeping as the memory of Allen and our work together once again moved me. Will the memory of Allen ever not move me? I looked over to find Jim and our spouses also weeping. Each moved in their unique way. My journey with Allen transformed me into a therapist who deeply trusts the client to do his or her work and to trust myself in *accompanying* their work in the moment. For Jim, he had the great delight in being a part of my transformation, experiencing the work from inside myself. When we slow down, we have the opportunity to become aware of the actual moment, should we turn our attention to it – whether as client, therapist, or supervisor? Meanings and transformations are found in the actual moment. When we allow ourselves to experience the moment, we open to the gifts and challenges inherent in searching for meaning and transformation. The job of being and becoming fully human is awesome and mysterious and to accompany an individual on this journey is a great honour.

Critique – a new perspective offered and revisited

It is a new century accompanied by many new beginnings for individuals and the world we live in the aftermath of the historic destruction of the World Trade buildings in New York by terrorists is imprinted on everyone's consciousness. As psychotherapists we bring this present world reality into our sessions and are continually challenged with helping our clients' search for meaning in their individual lives within the context of an increasingly unpredictable world. This unpredictable quality of living is an old backdrop to the stage of living, as we as psychotherapists and supervisors well know. Perhaps it is at this juncture in time that our profession needs to look back to critical incidents in history and re-examine the lessons learned. Frankl (1984), a pioneer existentialist in meaning and transformation in psychotherapy, continued to hope for a truly humanistic psychology within a fascist state that was mobilizing in Germany. Perhaps the truth he saw and experienced in humans in concentration camps was akin to the truth seen in the couple holding hands as they jumped from the World Trade building on 9/11.

We each project a different meaning onto this couple dying together and this critical incident speaks to each of us. What choice will we make when we face the end of our lives? Do we hold the hand of a stranger or of someone we know by our bedside if we were so lucky? What *do* we hold when our lives are threatened? What is the meaning of each of our lives? How do we make these meanings and take on the awesome responsibility of living? What do we hold to be true as we pass through great hardships? These questions and more are critical to psychotherapy today in these heightened unpredictable moments. We are offering not only to look to history of what psychology offered in critical times but what we have to offer in this present moment. Our offering is the present moment of psychotherapy in all its richness and human capacity to be. Existential philosophy has offered this reality for a very long time. In these heightened unpredictable times, we are again offering an ancient and timely perspective to psychotherapy, the actual moment with all its richness pointing to the choices we have, the process of relinquishment and the responsibility to live the choices we make. We do not diagnose the couple holding hands and poignantly meeting their death. We accept their final choice with awe; the courage to meet the unknown by holding hands is mysterious and beautifully moving. This image is imprinted on many minds, pointing to a very real existential moment. We invite you to remember this moment as you practice psychotherapy as a supervisor, therapist, or client. We are holding each other's hands in most challenging times. We are stepping out of diagnosis and into the full potential of the human being in this moment in time. Do we dare to jump as clinicians into this unknown moment with our clients? In a very deep way we are in this business of living together, holding hands through the mystery of being. It is our invitation to each of you, to dare to explore the mystery of being here and now, to make a choice for this present moment.

Note

1   For confidentiality the name and identity of the client has been disguised.

Further reading

Bugental, J. *Psychotherapy Isn't What You Think.*
Yalom, I. *The Gift of Therapy.*
Yalom, I. D. *Existential Psychotherapy.*

CHAPTER 30

A New Ideology

EMMY VAN DEURZEN

> If a man hasn't discovered something that he would die for, he isn't fit to live.
> King, 'Speech at the Great march on Detroit, 23 June 1963'

Introduction

As we have seen throughout this book, human beings are always embedded in a context. This context influences our view of the world. This worldview determines the way in which we interpret our physical, social and psychological existence. The filter of our personal beliefs colours the way we feel about our lives. The interaction between worldview, beliefs and feelings is often a passive, reactive process. We seem at the mercy of the beliefs and values we pick up from our surroundings. As the later Sartre (1960) and Merleau-Ponty (1964b, 1968) have shown we are the product of the ideology that we absorb from the epoch and cultural environment we live in. Nevertheless it is always possible to bring this ideology into our awareness and to begin to question it. Sedimented or mineralized beliefs can be challenged and recycled. New ideas can be created and projected into the future. As human beings we continuously transform our outlook on the world and in the process we remodel our world. We are not only products of our socio-cultural environment, we also produce it. We act on what we believe is the state of play of the world and our actions create the framework for our future experiences. As Arendt (1958) has pointed out in her book *The Human Condition*, people are just as much defined by the unexpected new beginnings they are capable of initiating as by their confrontation with endings and limitations. The chapters in this book have shown some of the ways in which our physical universe directs our everyday preoccupations about survival, how the social influences in our environment engage our attention in relation to others and how we struggle as individuals to create a personal life for ourselves out of the givens of our temperament, character and past experience. At the same time the wider angle of the spiritual dimension influences the way in which we experience everything else in our lives. Our ideology colours our existence and determines the way in which we direct our lives. There are many

265

sorts of ideologies that influence us unknowingly: some are imbibed from our culture, others from our family, from our religion, our class, our race or our specific age group or other group of reference. We can distinguish longitudinal ideologies that influence us all because of the historical era we live in, from the latitudinal ideologies which are determined by the circles we move in, from the altitudinal ideologies which are constituted by the depth at which we think about the issues at stake. Our beliefs will vary in strength according to the level at which we plumb the depths of human existence. Some people merely brush over the surface of life and remain largely trapped in the mores and expectations of the cultural values around them. Most of us these days are guilty of such unthinking, unknowing ways of existing and we are more likely to pick up our ideas and judgements from newspapers, television or the Internet than from our own thinking. In this sense the multi-layered media, with their interwoven reports of fact and fiction currently influence us more than established religions. This means that many of us are likely to be a little bit fickle and change our minds in accordance with the latest fashions. Soap operas provide the forum for emotional and moral debate and celebrity culture provides the role models of our lives. The advantage of this state of affairs may be that we are given specific ways of thinking about our own lives. All we have to do is live by imitation and fit into the world. We are presented with a variety of narratives and we can pick and choose our adherence to different representations of human living according to what suits us best at any particular time. This means there is some flexibility and that we can change and adapt rapidly when necessary, since we encounter many different ideas and beliefs in a short period of time. The downside is that we may just copy the beliefs and actions of real or imaginary authorities on our screens and that our lives become modelled on a mediocre blueprint, which provides us with a middle of the road common-sense approach to issues, but not with a sense of critical evaluation. The questions we then ask ourselves are no longer who we are, what we are able to do and what we can contribute to the world, but rather what is sensible, profitable and desirable. We will play it safe and stick to what we perceive as normal. In the Western world, radicalism of any sort has become an undesirable threat. Even psychotherapy and counselling can easily become a part of this normalizing tendency, when interventions are geared to help fit people back into the established ideology. The existential approach, however, challenges this state of affairs and calls people to wake up, claim their freedom and rethink their own ideology.

Foucault in his books *The Order of Things* (1966) and *The Archaeology of Knowledge* (1969) showed that there are limits to our understanding of the world, since we cannot distance ourselves very much from the ideology of our particular time. He described the unconscious belief systems that underlie and structure our modes of thinking. Our knowledge and understanding of the world advances in spurts and bounds, providing us with the so-called 'epistemes', which are like lenses through which we perceive and know the world. Foucault recognized that the Middle Ages was the age of *exclusion*, where everything needed to be separated out between good and bad and where the bad was then discarded outside of society. The Renaissance or Seventeenth century was the epoch of *resemblance*, where the emphasis was on trying to be in God's image. The Classical Age during the eighteenth century was the epoch of *representation*, where it became possible and necessary to make distinctions, splitting the subject and the object, the mind and the body. The Modern Age, during the nineteenth and early twentieth centuries, was the age of *self-reference*, where science and humanism triumphed and anthropocentrism reigned. People thought themselves capable of becoming like God and began to set the standards for everything and everyone. Then in the Post-modern Age, which is the post-nuclear age where we discover that mankind has the means to destroy itself and the planet, we enter the age of the *death of the self* and the death of truth. I have proposed elsewhere (van Deurzen, 2000) that we have to move on into a further era with the arrival of computer technology and a global world structure, which has brought us the age of *virtuality*. This is an era where things are virtually determined and where much can be imagined and explored electronically if not in reality. It is an age where we have acquired the technical means to widely access information of all sorts. We can welcome and appreciate difference and variety. Hopefully then it can become an age of inclusion rather than one of exclusion. It is an age where we have the means to personally reflect on the world, so that we can make our own decisions about right and wrong, creating a new kind of virtue in the process.

An existential perspective

An existential outlook on life demands of us that we think and look for ourselves and do not jump to conclusions too quickly. As Heidegger suggested (Heidegger, 1966, 1977) existential thinking calls us to attention. It requires us to have a new clarity and to become aware of the way in which life guides our choices and dilemmas, our good and bad intentions, our purposes and objectives, and our happiness and sadness. The process of sharpening up our ideology is not about falling into a new and prefabricated outlook on the world, from which we can interpret everything with ease, but rather to reflect on life whilst living it and think afresh about what we are learning. This will by itself transform the way of our experiencing and living. We will have to think about the values we appear to adhere to and reproduce continuously. We may have to revalue these values, as Nietzsche suggested (Nietzsche, 1882, 1883, 1887) and sometimes even invent entirely new ones, from scratch. Nietzsche pointed out that God was no longer credible in an era of science and humanism and that this introduced the necessity of thinking again about the things we had thus far taken for granted. We have to start asking questions about the human condition again. Why do we live? How should we live? The answers this time have to come from us rather than from a God or a dogma. Camus (1942) focussed this idea further by stating that the only philosophical question worth addressing was that of suicide, in other words whether life was worth living or whether it was absurd. His conclusion was that it was absurd and yet worth living, providing we were willing to put ourselves on the line. 'All that remains is a fate whose outcome alone is fatal. Outside of that single fatality of death, everything, joy or happiness, is liberty. A world remains of which man is the sole master' (Camus, 1942: 106).

If we have to create our own meanings and values, how are we to create the parameters to guide our search? Various authors throughout this book have sketched out aspects of this new type of living and most would agree that it will involve some of the following.

- To reflect on life but without a set theory to interpret our findings.
- To have an open and receptive attitude and allow ourselves curiosity and wonder about all that is, keeping an open mind about what we can be ourselves.
- To be flexible and remain available for constant transformation and new information.
- To live with the tension that is indispensable for life. This also means to accept that death is part of life, in that it is the ultimate release that we will all experience eventually.
- To see that life is larger when we can take its multiple challenges, tensions, opposites and contradictions into our stride. Life's polarities are the limits of our own reality. To stretch the entire range of life is to come fully into our own.
- To accept that values are the coinage of life and to realize that human living involves a constant exchange of energies and therefore a continuous process of discrimination and judgement about which things are worthwhile and which are worthless.
- An acknowledgement that morality in a post-modern world has got to be rebuilt on a new basis since established and stagnant values can be dismantled and deconstructed.
- Enabling people to become aware of their own capacity for a radical new kind of moral thinking, or morability, as I have called it elsewhere (van Deurzen, 2005). This is the ability to trace antecedents and consequences to events and to make choices accordingly. It is an ability that grows, as we understand more about the world.

The process of becoming morally reflective and active is in the first instance a philosophical one. To make this process practical and relevant to an individual's quest for a better life a therapeutic intervention may be relevant. Existential counsellors and therapists enable people to think about the world, their position in it and the ideology they want to live by. Instead of teaching people to obey a new dogma or an old religious order they enable them to begin to think for themselves and come to their own conclusions. This is not really anything new, since it is precisely what philosophy in the early Greek days was meant to do, but it is certainly something that we have forgotten about for many centuries in-between (Savater, 2002; Hadot, 1995).

Morability requires us to be transparent to ourselves and to inquire into the way things really are, learning to see the manner in which everything is related and connected. If we become morable rather than just moralistic, moral or immoral we think through moral issues, rather than acting according to set ideas and principles. To make a decision with morability is to decide on the basis of creativity. Rather than making decisions motivated by self-interest or habit, we discover that we can make decisions on the basis of wanting to make a contribution to the creation of the kind of world we believe to be most valuable. If I want a world where people can rely on each other I will be loyal. If I want a world where freedom is paramount I will keep my choices open. If I want a world where determination reigns I will submit to the predictions of the past. If I want a world of pleasant illusions I will hide from reality. It is taking the categorical imperative one step further. But of course it is not so easy to think through consequences, for these are inevitably complex and multiple. Most often moral situations are composed of a variety of elements, all of which have to be taken into account (de Beauvoir, 1948). It is not so much a matter of favouring one objective, as to set one objective in relation to another and decide which is more important. According values to things is about deciding what a thing is worth in relation to another. It is about establishing the exchange value of things. So to make a decision with morability is to be clear about my part in the world I create with others (Buber, 1929). If it matters more to me to be seen as dominant rather than to be dominant then I will assert myself no matter what, even if I may be in the wrong. If it matters to me more to be truly dominant than to be meek, I will speak up and stand up for myself, but only if I know what I am talking about. If it matters more to be fair than to be dominant then I will only speak up if I can speak up for a good cause. If it matters more to be cooperative than to be fair, I will work with the other in order to achieve a joint goal rather than the goal of domination or even a good cause. If I want to be loved more than be cooperative, I might pretend to believe what you do even when I do not, rather than speak up for myself. Every person in this way makes decisions about how to act in the world on a daily basis, but often without thinking. We vote with our feet, our attitudes and our actions, mostly without much reflection. We do it impeccably; accurately opting for the choices closest to what we believe, creating the kind of world we are looking for or expect to find. Unfortunately those choices are more often than not choices we arrive at by default. They are literally arrived at by following our default settings. Of course these settings are frequently determined by family, society or influenced by current ways of thinking, which may not actually be our own at all. The question is often: At what cost are we prepared to continue following the path of least resistance and make choices in this default-based way? There are, sooner or later, moments when we know that suddenly the automatic way to proceed is no longer the right way. We see all at once that our fate requires a different move. We find ourselves awoken by circumstances and come to our senses with the realization that only deliberate decisions will be acceptable and satisfactory. This is often the case when a person has arrived in a crisis. Perhaps morability requires us to start living at all times as if we are in crisis. The crisis is that of the shortness of our existence. Time is running out. We have to get our priorities straight. We have to buckle down and ask pertinent questions about what it is that we really want.

There are no absolute answers to any question. Psychotherapy is a process of learning to explore the possibilities and limitations that we are dealing with. We need, in other words, to learn to practise our ability to think about our actions and their impact on our own and other people's lives, rather than live according to someone else's plan for us. To help people think through their own motivations and projects and to be clear about what kind of person they want to be, rather than teach them what they should be, is the objective of existential psychotherapy.

This way of doing psychotherapy is never about applying formulae, recipes or set bits of doctrine. It is about learning to be nimble in our thinking and elucidating other people's thinking about themselves and about their lives in a way that enables them to be wise in their lives.

It may help though to bear in mind the following points.

1. This way of working does not depend on skill but on philosophical method, helping people to ask the right questions, rather than give them answers.
2. It opts for being direct rather than indirect and it values mutuality in exploration.
3. It is neither directive nor non-directive but aims to help people find their own direction.
4. It teaches people to situate themselves within the human condition, rather than to see themselves purely as a self with a personality or character that has been formed by parents.
5. It helps people to become aware of their role as product/producer of meaning, rather than see themselves as helpless and passive recipients of conditioning or upbringing.
6. It enables people to start seeing how they are constantly self-deceiving, since their truths are invariably based on short-sightedness and partial vision.
7. It shows how we can face up to the limits of life and our own limitations as human beings.
8. It encourages people to start thinking in a meditative manner, rather than be caught up in reactive emotionality or in abstract reasoning.
9. It uses lots of descriptions, clarifications and verifications, elucidations of what is aimed for and what is desirable.
10. It seeks truth in a global, universal sense, but never contents itself with half-truth, false truths or lies.
11. It seeks to relate through resonance and reciprocity. Cooperation and communication are considered the prime mover of human relationships.
12. The adventure of being human and getting caught up in all sorts of complex situations, conundrums, paradoxes, dilemmas and impasses that we have to learn to negotiate is the starting point for the engagement.
13. Time and its need for recollection of the past, intense awareness of the present and clear projects for the future is one of the guidelines for the work.
14. Crisis is seen as a necessary transition point from which transformation becomes possible.

15. To be in touch with both finite and infinite dimensions of human experience allows people to find a balance or at least to make up their mind about where they want to be in relation to the universe.
16. Coming to terms with life and death, isolation and togetherness, possibility and necessity, and good and bad is a good starting point for a well-lived life.
17. Helping a person to question and reflect and sometimes to dare and do what is difficult is to challenge them to be real.
18. This is about human living in an artful way and within the givens of the human condition. It is not about being great or good but rather about becoming masterful at life.
19. Evolving truth and renewal of understanding is the key to the process of clarification in therapy.
20. We reveal and see what is hidden. We come to terms with the unspeakable and we may even hide again, in order to live.
21. We feel, we understand, we articulate, we communicate, we clarify, we verify. We think again. We do all this with undivided attention in the spirit of a search for a truth, which we know is ultimately unknowable.
22. The only questions worth asking in the end are: Who are we? How are we to live? The answers we get will be many and our view on the world and ourselves will change over time as we see life from different perspectives.
23. Only by listening to our own and other people's answers over the years and by gathering as many of the facets of living as we can, will we come closer to truth and yet it will continue to elude us till we die and others define the facts of our life.

Values on all dimensions

Since this book has used the model of the four dimensions of existence it seems consistent and logical to conclude by asking what sort of moral questions have to be addressed on each of these dimensions.

On the *Physical dimension*: we find ourselves having to struggle with the extremes of life and death and their corollaries of health and illness, wealth and poverty, and strength and weakness. To do so in a balanced manner that does not exclude either side of the equation, nor ends up in a constrained middle leads to what I like to think of as *vitality*.

On the *Social dimension*: we find ourselves having to struggle with love and hate and their corollaries of dominance and submission, inclusion and exclusion. When we manage these challenges fully and gain some kind of mastery over them we do so from the principle of *reciprocity*, where both sides are done justice and there is give and take, generosity and equity in both directions.

On the *Personal dimension*: we find ourselves struggling with the contradictory needs for identity and freedom, having to assert ourselves and having to let go. The principle that allows us to check our own continued flexibility and fairness is that of *integrity*. This means that we find a way to not exclude too many influences from our self, neither to go under in them and become taken over by them: we are capable of being both free and yet assertive, affirmative of who we want to be.

On the *Spiritual dimension*: we struggle to deal with the opposing forces of good and evil, and meaning and meaninglessness, often feeling lost between these extremes. The principle of *transparency*, which consists of openness towards all that is, can guide our search for truth. This means that we no longer see ourselves as the centre of the universe, but situate ourselves as part of a greater complexity to which we remain open to find out about.

The following table summarizes what has been said and can provide us with a minimalist framework of the existential territory in which we have to find our bearings. It can guide our understanding of our position in the world but it does not dictate any particular solutions or correct behaviour.

	DESIRES	FEARS	VALUES
PHYSICAL	life	death	vitality
SOCIAL	love	hate	reciprocity
PERSONAL	identity	freedom	integrity
SPIRITUAL	good	evil	transparency

On all dimensions it is useful to check whether our understanding has *universal* value. The objective is to be in tune with what actually is. Truth, though it is never to be known for sure is always aimed for. True knowledge or wisdom may be out of reach, but trying to understand is still the right objective. In addition we aim for *excellence*. Virtue becomes just that: *V*itality, *I*ntegrity, *R*eciprocity, *T*ransparency, *U*niversality and *E*xcellence.

Case illustration

Tom was forty-five years old, dark, handsome in a classic way, well groomed and stylish. He was on the brink of his second divorce and had just filed for bankruptcy. He felt that his way of life had come to grief and having ended in disaster had been shown to be corrupt and defective. He wanted to find out where he had gone wrong and how he should live in future, if living was what he would continue to do, despite his desire to put a halt to it all.

Tom had taken risks all his life and had just lost most of his assets through what had seemed like a sure-fire investment, but had turned out to be a bad gamble on the stock market. He had concurrently discovered that his second wife was having an affair with his business colleague and that she had decided to leave him. Tom was quite cynical about the whole thing, saying it was simply a matter of money. He could see a certain wry justice in the situation when I pointed it out to him. Lydia was a trophy wife and she belonged to those who were successful.

Tom presented himself to me as tough, detached and inclined to sarcasm, often at his own expense. One minute he spoke of shooting himself, the next he was building new castles in the air. I remarked to him that the common denominator between the two was that he seemed determined, one way or another to put this phase of his life behind him. He agreed wholeheartedly, passionately, as if I had hit the nail on the head. Yes, this was his credo. He had to be tough and real. His life the way it was had not worked. He had failed. He was going to be a good loser and learn from his mistakes. He became quite bullish when helped to see that these were basic principles of life for him: to be strong, to learn from mistakes, to move on rapidly and make new plans, take new actions. He already had some ideas about the new projects he might embark on but he realized that he was scared and worried about getting it wrong again in the future. He was not used to doubting himself in this way and was very annoyed with himself for showing such weakness. He was keen to ascertain that I would not talk to anyone about his cowardice, but there was still a tone of defiance, as if he had to cheat fate by pretending that he was not really frightened at all. He relaxed a little bit when it became clear to him that I was more interested in hearing about the things that were frightening him than in his pretence to be immune to fear. It came as a pleasant surprise to him that I wanted to hear more about the things that were hurting him, than about the wonderful things he had achieved and would achieve again. As he dropped the macho pretence, he finally began to talk in a different tone.

He was bereft over the children he had had in his first marriage, for they had turned against him. They had taken sides with their mother, his first wife Ann, whom he had left for Lydia, his second, much younger, wife. It really riled him that the things he had left his family for, that is, unlimited business success and a beautiful new woman, had now both turned out to be ephemeral, since he had lost them both. He wondered whether he had made the wrong choice after all? I asked him if they would have seemed the right choice if he had been able to hold on to them. In other words, was he judging these things bad and wrong, simply because they had failed him? This brought him up short, as he had to start thinking about life and what he wanted to make it. He realized that what he had gone for was success and the unlimited enjoyment of the good things in life. I asked him if there was a negative side to that and he said it did seem like a policy of grabbing what you can grab, while the going is good. He thought he had perhaps taken the Thatcher yuppie era too seriously. Perhaps he had made some wrong judgements in the process. I thought he was rather harsh on himself and perhaps a bit rash to make these judgements. He countered that it was clear to him now that Lydia was a good-time girl and that he had opted for her because he wanted to have a good time himself. He had been just like her, but now he had changed, because his circumstances had opened his eyes. Perhaps the things he had gambled on were not worth having in the long run because they were bound to come to an end. I asked him if he would want Lydia and his large bank balance back if he could reinstate his former life? He thought he would not, because he would not now gamble on what had turned out to be unreliable and temperamental. He claimed he had discovered the truth about 'live by the sword and you will die by the sword' and since he had no intention of dying again, he was not keen to live by the sword again either. We looked at what he wanted to replace his old values with and he felt strongly that loyalty, durability and commitment were some of the values he wanted to reinstate in his life. He was going to be a humanitarian from now on, with a job that would afford him a social conscience. He might even get his kids' respect back, he said with self-mocking laughter. I remained unconvinced that Tom was truly looking at his life. It rather seemed to me that he was applying the old values of wanting to be tough, successful and active again. Within weeks he had it all worked out and he was planning a career in business consultancy. There was a one-year course he could get on for free, because the guy who set it up was an old pal of his and wanted him to go into business with him. It was hard to get Tom to think he might be racing into another risky venture, or that he might be better off taking the time to ponder before forgetting to think about his life once more. He seemed unstoppable, unwilling to take stock. Our sessions dragged on in a kind of manic state of self-improvement for a couple of weeks. Then fate struck once more and he stayed away for a week, because he had started having serious problems with his liver. This led to a series of medical investigations, which showed up that he had a mild form of cirrhosis of the liver, something he had already been vaguely aware of, but had tried to forget. His doctor told him categorically that he had to give up alcohol. I had not even been aware that Tom had abused alcohol. It was something he had never mentioned in therapy. Now we talked about his self-deception and his avoidance of the realities of his existence and also about his failure to come clean in the therapy. He accepted the challenge. He wanted to confess everything. It emerged that Tom had been addicted to strong painkillers, as well as nursing a 'modest' but regular cocaine habit. He claimed that his addictive lifestyle was based on his desire to fit in with those around him. This was, he then discovered, because he was terrified of being found out. His fear of failure was overwhelming. We spoke for many weeks of the reality of failure and where it left him. He realized he had often just rushed around 'like a headless chicken', trying not to think too much, because he had assumed that thinking was dangerous and that it was best to fit in and be a smashing success. 'What is success when you do not even let yourself feel you are alive?', I asked him one day and he said, after thinking for a long time, that he was just afraid to feel the pain of being alive. When I asked him to tell me about the pain of life, for the first time the front of machismo collapsed and I saw a human being who was as full of doubts, fears and weakness as the next person.

Now the work could begin in earnest. He recognized himself that there was a new seriousness in his desire to create a better lifestyle for himself. Perhaps, I queried, it was not so much a change of lifestyle he was looking for at this stage but a rethink about what his values and priorities were? This was the beginning of Tom's philosophical crusade to discover new principles to live by, weighing up the old ones against potential new ways of living and often finding all of it 'wrong-footed', until he was able to work out what he actually really valued, in the light of the possibility of him dying of liver failure, and what was worth fighting for. Tom's struggle with himself lasted for a couple of years and required his full attention, but it led to him creating a much sounder basis for his life and feeling what he termed 'a better man'. Throughout this work I had to be careful to avoid falling into the trap of imposing my own values on his life, always verifying that his principles worked for him and were chosen deliberately with morability rather than moralism. Interestingly, Tom admitted that his early 'conversion to humanism' had been inspired by the values he had at the time assumed I held. We had a good laugh about this together, but it was a salutary lesson for me to realize that clients are constantly guessing at what their therapists believe. It was good to be able to be direct in response and to say to him that I did not believe in self-development for the sake of self-development and that I thought that his switches from one lifestyle to another were a bit too quick to be very profound. Speaking my mind with Tom invariably led to him thinking more carefully. I invited him to argue with me until he had uncovered his own meanings rather than aping his friends or me. It was his opening up to reflection that allowed him to lay the basis for a true new beginning in his life. It led to reconciliation with his kids, a new friendship with his ex-wife and to a business life infused with enthusiasm. Tom continued to have problems with addiction for which he sought help in other ways, but mercifully his physical condition forced him to keep chipping away at this until it became manageable. The existential therapy helped him to stay clear about his own motivations and aspirations, every step of the way. He continued to see me, for occasional consultancy, long after his life was back on the rails.

Critical considerations

Existential priorities vary from person to person and yet there are many universal factors that underpin every human being's life. It is often difficult to know when to tackle a person's problems as a case of universal existential problem and when to see it as a personal predicament. My rule of thumb is that it is usually both and that I need to look for the universal angle and the personal one at the same time. It is always tempting to invent new theories that can explain everything to everyone and to invent rules that people have to follow if they are to turn their lives around. Existential thinking can just as easily fall into the old traps of dogma and prescriptiveness which other therapeutic or ideological frameworks present us with. As long as we remain aware of these traps and counteract them by continuing to explore different avenues of understanding and continue with multiple descriptions of human living there is a chance that our thinking remains true to life. If we settle for deadening truisms and prefabricated ideas and ideals, the chances are that our efforts to aim for truth turn to dust. The only way to continuously verify what we believe is to keep comparing notes with each other, trying to state as simply and clearly what our own experiences and those of our clients are. To be called back by truth is to remain open to contradiction, paradox and ambiguity as much as by the doubt and wonder about what we see inside and around us. Wisdom is not to know for sure but to always continue questioning and trust that somehow, somewhere, sometime, what seems incomprehensible will start to make sense as opposites meet and contradictions come together.

Conclusion

Working with spiritual principles and values and beliefs is a risky business. It requires therapists to have some philosophical training and some expertise in thinking about life and death. There have been many remarks throughout this book about the need for more thorough and serious existential research. Nowhere is this truer than when we deal with the level of ideology. The existential patterns of thinking can give rise to elucidation and inspiration, providing we are rigorous in our explorations and careful in how we articulate our findings.

We need to base our work on philosophical research of a pragmatic nature. What is invaluable for the training of therapists is not just to read philosophy, but to inform therapeutic work with research into what makes human beings tick and what makes the difference between a life well lived and a life wasted or regretted (Baumeister, 1991; Guignon, 1999; Curnow, 2001). Out of such explorations we may begin to sketch our understanding of the different sorts of beliefs and values that human beings hold. We can also get a better understanding of where different paths lead and how people go wrong. If we can draw up a better map of the many and various routes that people can take through their lives, we will be in a better position to help them find their own direction. Putting such a map together will require quite a lot more concerted effort on the part of all those who work with people and who have intimate knowledge of what makes human beings tick. Since existential therapists are particularly interested in the study of human living, they will have an important role to play in this.

Further reading

Jaspers, K. *The Way to Wisdom.*
Mace, C. *Heart and Soul: The Therapeutic Face of Philosophy.*
Merleau-Ponty, M. *Sense and Non-Sense.*
Nagel, T. *What Does it All Mean? A Very Short Introduction to Philosophy.*
van Deurzen, E. *Psychotherapy and the Quest for Happiness: Hoping for Utopia.*

Conclusion: Therapeutic Work on Four Dimensions

EMMY VAN DEURZEN

> To lead a philosophical life means also to take seriously our experience of men, of happiness and hurt, of success and failure, of the obscure and the confused. It means not to forget but to possess ourselves inwardly of our experience, not to let ourselves be distracted but to think problems through, not to take things for granted but to elucidate them.
>
> Jaspers, *Philosophy*: 122

Introduction

Existential therapy is about understanding life as our clients experience it, enabling them to take charge of their own existence and become more self- and world-possessed. Therapy rarely concerns one single dimension of existence. The issues discussed in this book are seldom found in isolation. Clients are usually preoccupied with many aspects of the world they live in. Human life is complex and varied. Personal predicaments are generally an intricate mixture of interwoven dynamics at different levels. Assorted elements of human living cannot be neatly stored away in separate compartments. The various dimensions of human experience are intertwined and wind together in unpredictable patterns and shapes. What clients bring to their therapists is usually a mass of tangled experiences, snarled up in knots. Existential therapists find a way to clarify this complexity, by looking for the underlying unifying concerns. They shed light on priorities, assist people in sorting out what seems confused and messy and they help to unravel the whole jumbled mass of twisted strands of reality, sometimes cutting through the Gordian knots of apparent contradictions and impossibilities. It may take quite a bit of training in living to get confident enough to intervene in human existence in this manner, but when therapists can muster the wisdom to let life lead the way, clients reap the benefits.

What follows is the description of a fragment of therapeutic work with one client demonstrating the interlinked nature of the four dimensions of human existence as well as the relevance of addressing each during the course of the therapeutic work. It will show the usefulness of keeping the different realms of existence separately in mind whilst considering how they are structured and interrelated in the client's life. We do not have to address the different dimensions as if they are separate entities. By drawing our clients' attention to their particular mode of engagement with each realm of existence, they can become more aware of the inevitable tensions at each of these levels and learn to handle these better than before. The framework works best when it remains invisible, used as a transparent map of human existence, which provides a background frame for the investigation of the client's particular predicament.

Case illustration

The client and her preoccupations

Molly was a young woman in her early thirties who came to see me because she despaired of herself and everything in her life. She was certain that she would never be 'happy like other people'. Molly was of medium height, with long sleek brown hair that was parted in the middle. She had grey eyes. She dressed casually in jeans and sweater and she liked putting her legs underneath her, huddling in the chair, looking apprehensive and a little bit lost. She felt quite unable to cope adequately with her life. She was single and she had become embroiled in an ambivalent relationship with a man twelve years older than herself. Six months previously she had dropped out of university, where she had been a mature student, trying to complete an MBA. Although she was obviously bright and described herself as fairly ambitious, she had felt over-whelmed by the demands of the course. She thought she had floundered because she had found it exhausting to do the programme whilst trying to hold down a secretarial job. She was not stupid, she said, but her personal problems had got the better of her. She then specified that these problems were 'eating problems'. When asked to describe these, she said she was obsessed with keeping her weight under control. This was far from obvious, since she looked an average weight for her medium height. She explained that she regularly made herself sick after binge eating, in order not to go above eleven stone, which was the absolute upper limit she had set herself. There had also been times in the past when she had gone below eight stone, becoming frail and feeling weak. This made me more aware of her drawn and tired features, and I got the impression that if she was not nurturing herself very well, she did not look as if she were enjoying much sleep either. This impression was confirmed as Molly complained of insomnia and depression. Soon after this it emerged that she was also self-harming and was in the habit of cutting her abdomen and upper arms with shards of glass. She claimed it was the best way of dealing with her frequent panic attacks. These occurred mostly when going out with Greg, the man who was dating her, but they had also happened when going to university lectures. The panic attacks were severe and incapacitating. The student counsellor she had seen for a one-off emergency session had told her that panic attacks were imaginary and could not lead to fainting. Yet, she had passed out several times in public.

She was afraid of 'being hysterical', as her sister Ellen had suggested, and had therefore read up on hysteria on the Internet. This had led her to ICD-10

(International Classification of Diseases) and she knew the histrionic personality disorder characteristics by heart. She told me in a calm and collected manner that she was often accused of self-dramatization and exaggeration and that she was easily suggestible. She also told me confidently that she was desperate for approval by others and that she was terribly preoccupied with her (lack of) physical attractiveness. She was also often self-indulgent (as when binge-eating or dropping out of her course). When I gently pointed out the apparent contradictions between her calm, confident and organized manner and what she was telling me, she smiled wryly and informed me that this was just an example of her manipulativeness. She claimed, almost triumphantly, but nevertheless rather sadly, that she had most of the symptoms of histrionic personality disorder and proceeded to make a convincing case for her own psychopathology. It was quite overwhelming to be faced with someone who seemed so intent on having all these symptoms and who presented herself to me as a rather hopeless case, throwing herself at my mercy. It was a surprisingly seductive appeal to my usually rather well suppressed desire to be an omniscient psychologist. I found myself thinking about alternative diagnoses and started wondering whether she may have borderline personality disorder instead. Then I realized that I was letting myself be sucked into her negative self-characterization and that it was imperative for me to clear my mind and start thinking in a much more open but also much more incisive and systematic way about Molly's predicament. Neither Molly's nor my own biased views of who she was were a good starting point. We needed to look a little more carefully at her actual experience.

Life world

Molly and I agreed that we would together, over the first few sessions, try to get a better picture of Molly's life world. I had been struck from the start by Molly's moral self-flagellation. She seemed particularly expert at putting herself down and very good at demeaning herself. This reminded me of her self-harming and I remembered that she had told me she did this in order to cope with her panic. When I asked her if she felt more real whenever she described herself in a negative and demeaning manner, she sat up and took notice. It was as if my observation called her out of her habitual self-debasement and made her realize that there might be another way. 'What are you afraid will happen if you do not put yourself down in this way?', I said gently and the answer came very swiftly: 'that other people will do it instead'. 'Who?' 'Well, you, for instance, or Greg', she said. Her relationship with Greg was a fundamental and rather threatening aspect of Molly's current life world.

Greg, her boyfriend, was forty five, well off and divorced, with no children. He had initially seemed a godsend, when she met him in a club and he had wanted her for more than just the usual one-night stand. She had found him quite attractive and had felt flattered by his advances. Now she had grown afraid that she would not be able to respond properly to his demands and she was certain that she would inexorably lose him. He wanted her to move in with him, but she could not contemplate this idea. She felt it was not an option for her for the moment to commit to the relationship, but she thought he would not have the patience to continue to wait for her. She wished he would just content himself with being friends. She needed his support badly and had valued it greatly over the past year and a half.

There were all sorts of obstacles to her being more intimate with Greg. For starters she did not feel comfortable having sex at the moment. She also thought that Greg could not love her for what she really was. He was in love with an image she had projected, not with the weak person she was underneath. He would reject her when he found out what she was really like. For instance, she did not think she could stay with him unless she was able to finish her degree, for he was the one who had pushed her into doing the MBA in the first place and he was insistent that she should complete it. He was a company director and he wanted her to achieve a lot more than continuing to be a secretary. His ex-wife had been a barrister. When I asked her if finishing the MBA was what she wanted herself as well, her answer was hesitant. She was not really able to formulate any plans for herself at this stage. She was aware that she usually just conformed to other people's expectations. She had serious doubts about her ability to finish her degree course and knew that she would not be able to complete it if she did not return to her studies before the start of the next academic year. Her financial situation was not very good, since she had only worked part-time whilst doing the course and had been off sick for six months now. At the very least she needed to get back to work if not to her studies, but she felt she could not face either. Her job made her ill because she worked in a high-pressure environment where most people treated her like a bimbo. Greg was not keen on her going back to her job. She thought it would indeed be better if she could get a managerial job, as Greg kept telling her, but that was only achievable if she finished her degree, which she did not feel she had the stamina to do. It seemed to her that she was caught in a vicious circle. Her physical state undermined her ability to work; her work upset her physical balance. When she had told Greg of her despair over ever resolving the work/study situation, he had said to her that she could give it all up and marry him instead. She felt that was not an option either for if she married him she would flounder even further and now she felt under even more pressure from Greg. She was certain that if she gave up on her job and her studies she would never do anything with her life. She thought that Greg quite liked the idea of her giving up, marrying him and staying at home to have and raise his children. He constantly offered to help her out with money. She panicked every time he did. I remarked that she seemed to give Greg the power to block every possible avenue she could go down and that she seemed to have forgotten which way she wanted to go herself. She agreed with this wholeheartedly and gladly, as if she was relieved that I understood the essence of her problem. She said she was just weak. I said she clearly felt weak, but could not be as weak as she feared since she had coped with some very difficult things in her life. She thought that might be true, but that she always felt weak anyhow because of what had gone wrong in her childhood. She just did not have the confidence to find her own way.

Molly told me that her relationship with both her parents had been problematic. She had not felt close to either of them and had often imagined that she was a disappointment to them. Her four-year-older sister, Ellen, had always been the favourite child and Molly had soon realized that she could not give her parents anything that Ellen had not already provided them with. Ellen was a solicitor, and she was married to another solicitor with whom she had four children. Though Molly adored her nieces and nephews, she did not like to visit Ellen because she felt that Ellen bossed her around and had always done so. Their mother had died of breast cancer when Molly and Ellen were teenagers, and their elderly father was now in a psychiatric institution with dementia. This was Molly's prompt for telling me that she herself had had two brief spells in a psychiatric unit, something she had not disclosed in her initial interview.

The first episode was in her early twenties, when as an undergraduate student she had become increasingly socially isolated and anorexic. She had eventually broken down completely and was hospitalized after she had slit her wrists. She had been so unwell that they had kept her in for several months and she had been unable to finish her degree. After her first hospitalization she had stayed with her sister for quite a number of years and she had looked after Ellen's young children while Ellen worked with her husband in their law practice. They had given her board and lodging as well as a small 'allowance'. Molly had felt confused during this time, for she enjoyed and loved the children and got on very well with them, but she felt that her sister looked down on her and treated her disdainfully. She did not get on with her sister's husband John either. It was a time when she began to self-harm in secret and she started to binge eat at teatime, whilst feeding the children before Ellen and John arrived home. Then had followed a period when their father, who lived next door, had fallen ill and Molly had looked after him, since Ellen's kids were now in school most of the day.

During this time she had felt more useful and she had coped better than before, because dad had been appreciative and she had felt as if she could redeem herself at least in his eyes, showing herself to be grown up and good.

When doing dad's shopping she had struck up a relationship with Mark, a young man her own age who lived nearby and who was a shop assistant in a local chain store. Ellen had ridiculed Molly's interest in Mark, whom she had judged below par for the family. This was the first time that Molly had felt rebellious in her life and in spite of Ellen's judgement, or perhaps in order to spite her, Molly had eventually moved in with Mark. He had seemed caring and loving with her, by comparison to the way in which her sister had treated her. She had constantly struggled with the guilt of abandoning her father and with the shame of disappointing her sister, even though she had tried her best to continue looking after dad in the daytime. Ellen had blamed it on Molly when their father had to be placed in a home shortly after, saying that Molly had caused the worsening of their father's condition. Molly had become very anxious, doubting her own decision to live with Mark. She got herself a job in Mark's store but felt unable to cope with the work since she had panic attacks every time she was asked to do a new task. She had worried that Mark would leave her if he found out how vulnerable she was. She had not been surprised when she caught him out having an affair with a colleague at work. It was a traumatic event that involved her seeing them kissing in the storeroom and feeling as if her entire world collapsed in front of her eyes. The upheaval of the end of the relationship led to her having to move into a bedsit. She had felt unable to continue in the job and she became so anxious and depressed that she had made several suicide attempts, which had gone unnoticed. Then she had stopped eating and lost a lot of weight. Ellen had finally spotted her deteriorating state and had wanted her to move back in with her, but Molly had by now realized how much Ellen bullied her and had felt unwilling to move back. She saw no way forward on her own though and she grew increasingly desperate. Eventually she was hospitalized for the second time after a serious suicide attempt. This had happened four years previously and she had remained in hospital for several months and from then on had taken anti-depressants until quite recently. She had also had eight sessions of cognitive-behavioural therapy, which she had found useful. It had helped her to start thinking more positively about her life.

Her mental health team had been very good altogether. She had had a social worker, who had helped her apply for financial support to finish her degree, and a community mental health nurse who had been really supportive. A very helpful tutor at university had practically coached her through her final year and her exams. Although she minimized her success, she was really quite proud of her achievement. Because she attributed it mostly to other people's determination on her behalf, she had always doubted whether she could sustain this level of functioning. She did grudgingly accept my remark that all these people had helped her because they had confidence in her and that the effort had been hers, not theirs. She said that at the time she just felt pleased that they were so kind to her. The social worker had also helped her to get her first administrative job and had arranged for her to continue living in a protected environment. It made her feel a bit feeble, though she had felt good about earning her own living. Soon she had made new friends and had started occasionally going out with them.

This is how she had eventually met Greg. Of course, she had not told him her history and he had no idea of her struggles. Greg had expected her to do all sorts of things she was not ready for, she said. She had more or less felt obliged to go along with it, for fear of losing his respect. Even now she had not told him much about her past and she did not want him to know how poorly she was at times and how frightened of the world around her. When he urged her to enrol on the MBA she had protested as much as she could, but she could not resist his considerable pressure. She just knew it meant that she 'had bitten off more than she could chew'. Now, as she could have predicted, the plan had backfired and she had lost all her self-confidence. She was sure that Greg was very disappointed in her and that he would turn out to be as unreliable and rejecting as Mark. This was why she dare not commit herself to the relationship. Greg was very generous but often impatient with her. He was paying for her therapy and she felt that he only did so because he wanted her to get better so that she could become what he wanted her to be. I pointed out that though she often seemed to experience other people as knowing better than herself what was good for her, she nevertheless had a good sense of what she could and could not manage and was determined to find her own way and keep Greg at bay. She seemed quite definite about her abilities and limitations and had clear views about what went wrong for her in certain situations. Had she not just clearly told me what had happened to her and how at each step she had been able to predict whether or not she would be successful? Molly was a bit surprised at this, but she could see with some glee that there was truth in it. Each time she made her own decisions and took steps to create her own life, she felt a bit better and more confident and each time she let others take over from her, she plunged back into a state of confusion and weakness. She agreed this was an important realization and one she needed to hang on to and build on. I suggested she better take charge of the therapy as well in that case.

We then discussed what role she wanted me to play in her life. She agreed that she had been mistrustful of me at first, expecting me to be in alliance with Greg, who paid the bills. She thought that her previous therapist had similarly 'just wanted her to get better and get on with it'. 'And that wasn't enough?' 'No, it wasn't. I never really found out what it's all about. I never stopped panicking and hurting myself. Look what a mess I have made of it all.' 'Because you have not taken charge of your life?' She had to think about that for a long time, then corrected my formulation decisively: 'Because I don't know yet what I am about or what I am capable of.' 'And you want to find out?' 'Yeah, if I can', she said in a measured but rather eager manner. Then she went on to tell me about her self-doubts and she explained why she often thought she was not fit to live. As I let her speak her mind she became again very self-dismissive and self-destructive. I called her attention to the general drift and direction of her remarks and asked her if she could see how quick she was to denigrate herself. She was only vaguely aware of her habit of putting herself down. 'It isn't really surprising that you end up feeling low in self-esteem, if you systematically undermine yourself, is it?' 'I just didn't realize I was doing that', she said. We tried to tentatively formulate a hypothesis about her reasons for keeping herself small. She thought everyone had always wanted her to be incompetent (except dad after he fell ill). Even Greg wanted to be able to keep the upper hand. I remarked how determined and clear she sounded the moment she started reflecting on herself rather than drifting down the familiar path towards self-destruction. Over the next weeks I would keep drawing her attention to this radical change in her when she took charge of the process of thinking about herself. We observed that these positive strands of self-determination were often annihilated by moments of raw anxiety, self-doubt and despair. I floated the idea that the problems she had been wrestling with were all a consequence of a fundamental lack of confidence. It seemed to me that she basically doubted that she had a right to take up her own place in the world. This remark had a surprising and shattering effect on

Molly, well beyond what I had expected. She cried profusely for a long time, using most of the tissues in my box, and acknowledged that I had touched a very sore spot. That was exactly how she felt: that there was no point in her existence and that other people did not want her there, because she had really nothing to contribute. She had no place in the world. She told me tearfully that this was the reason she could not tell people how she really felt, for if they knew her true weakness, they would never even consider giving her a chance.

I proposed to Molly that our work together should initially focus on helping her find her place in the world. She liked this idea and she agreed that she had not really ever had a chance of doing so. She liked the notion that I would not do anything to direct her, but that my task would be to assist her in staying on track and finding her own direction. She wanted me to let her feel her weakness, whilst helping her to think of ways in which she could get stronger. She badly did want to find a way to keep herself safe and find her place in the world. She could easily see how she let her troubles sap her energy. She wanted to learn to build up her energy instead.

Start of therapy: the physical dimension

Molly expressed a desperate craving for the therapy from the outset and yet she feared it too. In the session after we had made the agreement to work together, she said she would be 'dedicated to a positive outcome', although she 'could not promise that she would be able to get better'. Although I was struck with the reserved quality of this statement, I resonated with her underlying terror of being a disappointment to me and I told her that it seemed to me that her statement was a positive affirmation of her being in charge of her own therapy and a warning to me not to push her too hard. This disarmed her and made her laugh and in this new atmosphere of confidence she proceeded to show me the scars on her abdomen and lower arms with a mixture of pride and self-loathing. She also told me that she had started depriving herself of food again. She felt that anorexia was preferable to bulimia and anyway, she did not really have an appetite anymore. Her bulimia had lasted for a year and a half. I noted it had also been a year and a half that she had been with Greg. She smiled sadly and agreed there was a direct connection. She said she had had to eat a lot when she went out with Greg. He was of Mediterranean origin and attached great importance to food. He liked to wine and dine her. He hated it when she refused to eat. He got offended if she did not eat with gusto and so did his family, who had invited her for dinner regularly. She said she had had to learn to eat large amounts and discreetly vomit afterwards. She made it sound as if this was the most natural thing in the world, as if it were a rather clever strategy, a ploy she had devised for her own well-being. I did not bring in any cautionary note, bracketing judgement and parental prescription from my interventions. This allowed her to tell me she was quite pleased that it was not necessary to continue bingeing and regurgitating food, since now that she was having a breakdown everyone would have to accept that she could not eat in the state she was in. I thought she sounded quite pleased about this.

She acknowledged this and also admitted that she got great satisfaction from having started losing weight. She felt much better since she had stopped eating. She felt as if she was getting her own body back. I asked her when she had stopped eating and she told me it was after Greg had asked her to marry him. She said that this had made her very anxious and panicky and she simply lost her appetite. She was vaguely pleased that she would be able to get her body back to a size ten now and she imagined this would be good for the relationship too. We looked at her two statements that she would get her own body back and that she would get it back to a ten. This led to us considering the contradictions in all this. On the one hand, it felt good and important to keep the world at bay and retrieve her compact form. She loved the idea of not eating for a while, making herself thin and pure. On the other hand, she spoke of her body as a thing that she could use and abuse and change at will. Was depriving her body of food a good way to treat it? Did she even recognize she was depriving herself? This made her thoughtful and she said she did not want to punish or hurt herself. She believed that her body was her best friend. 'And yet you seem to treat it more like an enemy sometimes', I observed, 'you starve it, you deprive it and sometimes you cut it'. She cried for a bit, blew her nose a few times and said tentatively: 'Not the way you should treat a friend, is it?' 'It doesn't seem a very kind or caring way to treat it, does it?', I said. 'Kindness only makes you weak', she countered. She explained then that her body had to be tough, so she could not be too nice to it. 'Tough, for what?' 'Just to cope with people', she said. I reminded her she had told me before that she cut herself so that others would not hurt her. She now told me it was better to be the master over her own body and be the one hurting it, because this meant that she was in charge of it and other people could not take it over. It was an interesting turn of phrase in the light of our agreement that it would be good for her to take charge of herself. I ventured that it seemed as if Molly believed that being in charge might mean 'hurting' rather than 'looking after'. She was not sure, for although she could see in an objective sort of way that it was not a nice thing to hurt herself, internally she felt compelled to deprive herself for that was the way to keep others out. Being in charge of her body meant tightening its boundaries. Also, when she hurt her body or deprived it of food she felt very much herself. She could oversee what it was that was her and keep others at bay.

The exploration of her physical way of being-in-the-world took up lots of time. She was fascinated with the life of her own body. We kept coming back to it, alongside other things, and Molly would definitely seem closer and more vulnerable whenever she did talk about her body. She seemed to relax when I paid close attention to her sensations and she was gratified to discuss her bodily experience. By being able to talk about her body rather than just feeling trapped in it, she grew increasingly familiar with her ambiguity towards her embodied existence. Sometimes she felt like disappearing because the world seemed too dangerous for her to thrive in. Those were the times when she did not want to nurture herself. She recognized that she was playing with death at those times. At other times, when she felt that her bodily reality was getting lost, she felt panic. Those were the times she resorted to cutting. Cutting was not about dying; more about reminding herself she was alive. Where in all of this was her care for her body? Her body was her best friend, maybe even her only true friend, but she was hesitant to be a good friend to it. Were there kind things she might do for her body, instead of cutting it, when her body felt anguished? She agonized about this and eventually decided to try and stop hurting herself, out of compassion for herself and her body. She learnt to rub lotion into her body instead of cutting it when she felt dreadful and disembodied. This seemed to work and she valued the notion of being more in harmony with her skin and treating it well, after all she would not take a knife to her nice new shoes, but she would enjoy putting shoe-cream on them and making them shine. Her thoughtfulness about physical actions and their consequences made her begin to feel a little better in herself. She allowed her body to let her know what it needed from her. She came to articulate very clearly and graphically how she was in a physical way. In her body she experienced everything with great intensity. When she fainted she knew she could not cope with the world around her, when she vomited she knew she wanted to empty herself of what others had wanted her to absorb, when she cut herself she felt she could determine her own fate and make herself feel pain and bleed at will. To know such intensity was important. The trick was to find less destructive ways of feeling it.

She explained to me over the first weeks that it felt really much safer to be physically unwell, for then Greg could not pressurize her into anything anymore. He could not force her to eat lots. He could not expect her to go back to work or finish her degree. He would even have to wait for her to accept to marry him until she was better. She appeared to have developed a whole raft of strategies to keep Greg at a distance and was avoiding sex with him whenever she could. At first this was apparently because when she had cut herself, she did not want him to see the wounds, until they had healed. Actually it was simply because she could not tolerate anyone that near her. Once she acknowledged that, it became easier to stop the cutting, for she could see that the cutting was a way of giving herself an excuse to keep others away from her. As she became more able to talk to me about other people's invasiveness, she realized that she experienced others as encroaching on her physical space. Memories began to emerge of her sister Ellen making her eat forcibly after mother had died and Molly had wanted to fast. Then earlier memories filtered through of mother and Ellen making fun of her for not having an appetite and being thin. She had learnt that she could keep others away by warding them off and refusing their nurturance. It had seemed necessary for her to keep others out. She simply knew no other way of doing so than by using her own body. She perceived mother and Ellen as having been against her. They had always been a team, mother and Ellen, and they had imposed their rules on Molly. She had never felt comfortable in their company, always dreading their demands, which she felt she could not meet. Mother's death had given all of this a terrible finality. Molly had felt deeply betrayed by mom's death. From then on she had felt quite alone in the world. She had felt ill-equipped to cope with this. Starving herself had been a way of surviving on very little. It had worked for her then, though she recognized that it did not work for her now.

We spent a lot of time talking about all of this before she could really feel for her own body and see that she was paradoxically doing it the harm that she reproached others for having done to her. She was not in tune with her body and did not really respect it much. She certainly did not provide it with all it needed. She used her body as a kind of armour to hide away in and keep herself safe. She also turned against it as if it were not part of her, as if it was not her. Her sexual experience, unsurprisingly, had always been disappointing. She had only slept with Mark and Greg, but with neither man had she felt really at ease with sex and she had never experienced an orgasm. She was able to climax on her own, but was cagey about this at first. Later it transpired she only allowed herself to pleasure herself when she had a period. This was not a very satisfactory arrangement, especially since she had been amenorrhoeic for quite a while at times. To link sexual stimulation to absent periods was another way in which she deprived herself and hurt herself. It took a long time before she began to allow herself to feel pleasure on her own and start to even contemplate the possibility of learning to enjoy sex with Greg.

There were many other strands to our work at the physical dimension. This is often the case when people have been deprived or abused in their early years. They need to learn to master the relationship to the natural world and to their own body since they have never had a chance to find themselves at ease on this level. The first year of the therapy was, for instance, marked by regular fainting spells, which was no wonder for Molly was hardly eating at all. I began drawing her attention to the way in which she inhabited a body that she was not servicing. I remarked that even if she wanted her body to be an object, she still had to tend to it. A story she had told me about going on an outing with Greg in his vintage car and running out of petrol so that they had to walk two miles to a garage became a useful metaphor for her relationship to her own body. What she was doing to herself was like driving a car without putting petrol in it. She had not even considered that the fainting spells and the weakness were a consequence of her alienating herself from her physical needs. We discussed hypoglycaemia. She bought a book on physiology and began to acquaint herself with her own bodily and dietary needs. She soon became an expert and explained to me how her body had not been able to cope because she had wilfully neglected it. She understood how feeling faint had been the origin of her panic. In other words she had interpreted as psychopathology something that was essentially the consequence of her starving herself. Her pathologizing herself had led to self-loathing, which in turn was the origin of her hurting herself.

She could see how the whole sequence was generated by her self-imposed weakness. It was all connected and it all started with her neglecting herself. Once she could see this cycle we worked on helping her recognize it in action. We were not setting any targets and I often reminded her not to expect too much of herself, but to just keep observing and describing her experience. She saw it as a game and did it quite readily, getting very familiar with her own experience and much more respectful of it. She felt as if she could liberate herself from her self-condemnation and she decided that she was going to try and break the cycle. She increasingly wondered about ways in which to be constructive and kind to herself, but this remained difficult. She was not just in the habit of treating her body badly, she also relied on doing so to shield her from others. Being nice to it had never really been an option. Her body had always spoken for her, expressing her distress and her self-loathing. How could she be good to it? It was too challenging a question, which she would come back to repeatedly over the following months without being able to answer it. It was only really when we formulated the notion that being good to her body meant speaking up for it that things got going. She took to the idea of articulating what she had previously expected her body to express on her behalf. She soon realized that this meant that she had to think about what she was feeling in her body and then find a way to say it in words instead. Practising saying in words what her physical state was and what this said about her state of mind was a regular part of the therapy sessions for a long time. As Molly became more explicit about the implicit language of her physical experience, her life began to change. It was almost as if a new relationship was established: since her body was helping her to express herself, she could also look after it a bit better. She did simple things like going to a hairdresser to have a more flattering haircut and taking daily instead of fortnightly baths. She even learnt to drive. These practical, physical things had far-reaching effects. Then she began to take an interest in her own shape and she started working out what kind of clothes would look good on her when previously she had been uninterested in what she wore. It became a pleasure to her to show new clothes off to me in the sessions. Only later did she begin to wear them in public as well. Now she also started paying attention to symptoms she had long taken for granted. We worked quite actively on her insomnia, seeking to locate the things that kept her awake. It was not too difficult: she drank lots of sugary coffee (to give her energy and overcome the panic attacks, of course in fact setting them off!) and she slept in a noisy, over-lit room. After we discussed these things in a very practical manner, knowing of her interest in Internet research, I encouraged her to investigate research data on sleep disturbance. She did so and promptly decided to stop drinking coffee and to put thick curtains up in her bedroom. She also made an effort of going to bed at the same time every night, and getting up at the same time rather than sleeping in. She stopped napping or getting up at night when she awoke. If she really had to, she did not turn a light on anymore. She soon re-established a healthy sleeping pattern. It made her feel physically better. This was proof to her that she had indeed neglected herself in the past and that it was possible to do something about it. She felt gratified at having such a positive impact on her body. As we progressed with the work it became possible to reinforce the idea that it was not just her body she was affecting, but that it was herself she was taking care of.

Molly only then became aware of the way in which she had always separated her body from herself and treated her body not as what she was but as something she owned and could treat any way she chose. An integration of herself as a body slowly began to take place. As she became more truly embodied, less inclined to separate herself out from her body, the urgency to feed herself properly became greater. She started seriously studying up on diets and different food groups and she became acutely aware that she had done everything completely wrong. She had often had an intake of pure carbohydrates, rejecting protein and fat in particular. She continued to find fat a problem, but began to supplement her diet with more protein. This had an almost equally strong effect on her well-being as the re-establishment of sleep had had. For a long time, she could only feed herself properly when she was alone, whereas she continued to find it easier to feed on cakes, chocolates and soft drinks when with others. If she went out with Greg she would sometimes still overeat and disgust herself. She continued to throw up on these occasions, but not in a deliberate way. We agreed that she would need to learn to talk to Greg rather than comply with him. Learning to be more decisive and expressive with others was another important strand of our therapeutic work.

Being with others: the social dimension

If the physical dimension of Molly's experience was rich, complicated and multi-faceted, the social dimension was even more of a maze. As Molly came to think systematically and explicitly about her world experience, she became aware that it was always in relation to others that she felt most distressed. Whenever she ended up hiding in her body, hurting it or depriving it of food, she could be sure that someone had been, might be or actually was threatening her. Unfortunately in Molly's experience this was most of the time, for she lived her life as if other people were a constant danger to her. Interestingly she kept referring to herself as a single girl. It was as if she was trying to affirm her separateness. Yet she was, she knew, deep into the relationship with Greg and had to make up her mind about him. In the beginning she felt torn between letting herself fantasize about how he might bail her out and look after her on the one hand, and wanting to keep him away from her on the other hand. We soon came to reformulate her experience as one of dreading intimacy and closeness and yet craving it more than anything. It was not very hard for Molly to trace the history of her relations with others and to notice how she had generally run in fear from oppressive relationships like her relationship with her mother and her sister. Alternatively, in relation to people who were kind but rather distant from her, she always ended up feeling let down and abandoned, as she had in relation to her father and Mark. With Greg it was oppression she most feared. In relation to me she feared both possibilities: I might either oppress and denigrate her, or distance myself from her and abandon her. But Molly was not keen on discussing any of these relationships at first, especially not her relationship with me. She was far more preoccupied with her past relationship with Mark, the boyfriend who had cheated on her. She found it too painful to talk about her parents and her sister, and too challenging to think through her relationship with Greg. It was as if she knew that she had a real chance of sorting out what had gone wrong with Mark. It was something her previous therapy had neglected to look at.

As soon as we started talking more about her relationship with Mark the tears started to flow abundantly. Mark had seemed quite needy of her at first and he had been desperate for a sexual relationship with her. Molly had soon given in to this, even though she had been a virgin and wary of her first time. Sex had felt dangerous and invasive, but it had also made her feel wanted and needed. Mark had seemed safe and she thought he was really fond of her, even loved her. With hindsight she realized she might have mistaken his sexual need for care. She thought he had looked up to her because she had been a student, whereas he had left school at sixteen. After a while though, she had become 'over attached' to him, wanting more from him than he wanted from her. He had begun ridiculing her background, claiming she was not tough enough and had been over-protected. He had become annoyed with her for not working and spending too much time looking after her dad. He had called her a snob for having been to university and having a sister who was a solicitor. He had begun to get the upper hand. It was then that she had become obsessed with Mark's faithfulness, fearing he might prefer someone else to her. Somehow she knew that he would betray her and that she did not matter as much to him as he did to her. He had become annoyed about this as well and later he had claimed he had started the relationship with the other woman because he might as well do what she seemed to expect him to do anyway. Molly concurred with this view and she believed she had driven him to it. She also believed that she must have been a disappointment to him in many ways, for being so weak and helpless and for not being very sexually liberated. Mark had been her first boyfriend and she had been quite shy with him. It was obvious that Molly misunderstood a lot of the interactions that had happened between them, always expecting rejection and eventually getting it. She underestimated her own attractiveness and the contribution she might be able to make to a loving relationship. Mother and Ellen had told her so often that she was second best (compared to Ellen) that she truly believed it. She had always thought that the one thing she had on offer was her kindness and devotion to others, but in the past years Ellen had chided her for it. Now Mark had as well. If Ellen and Mark agreed about her uselessness, they must be right about her. When I enquired about the ways in which Ellen had belittled her, Molly became quite emotional. A huge amount of past frustration and distress came spilling out.

Ellen had always made her feel bad about herself. She had even made it sound as if Ellen had done her sister a favour letting her look after the children. Molly felt that this was very unfair, since she had given Ellen several years of her life, allowing her to pursue her career while Molly looked after the little ones for her. She now regretted having done it and felt an outraged but impotent resentment at her sister's put-down. With some difficulty she was able to recognize this as anger and to treat it as a very intense reminder of her newfound desire to establish that she was worthy of respect by others. She really liked it when I said that it felt to her as if Ellen had undervalued and disrespected her contribution to the family. This was exactly it, Molly said, for she had intended to be good and help her sister and her children and now she had been treated as if she had in fact been selfish in doing so. Reformulating her anger as an expression of her lost value helped Molly to locate her own stance in relation to others. She did want some respect. She did want some recognition. She wanted people to see that she had a contribution to make. She was not the lame duck some people made her out to be. From this new more affirmative perspective we were able to retrieve lots of positives from her past experience that Ellen had not been able to rob her of. For instance, Molly came to remember that she had in the process of looking after Ellen's children, learnt a lot about childcare, made a wonderful relationship with her nephews and nieces (who all continued to be extremely fond of her) and had also had a chance of finding out about the dynamics between herself and her sister. This had been a necessary experience, in the same way in which her relationship with Mark had taught her some fundamental facts about love or the lack of it. Molly could see very clearly that she had been passive and dependent in both relationships, whereas now she wanted to pull her weight and assert herself much more.

Could she do this with Greg? She was not sure, but from then on that was the new target she was trying for in her relationship with Greg. She agreed with the principle of taking time in the therapy to go over her relationships, past and present, and work out a better way of being with others in the future. Molly learnt quickly how to evaluate bad experiences in a more positive light and distil principles and a new understanding from them. She agreed about some of the good things she had already acquired, such as having a knack for being on the same wavelength as children, being vulnerable with others and wanting to be close. She also knew she was good at caring for others, when they were frightened or in need. She thought this had worked best with the children, although it worked with dad as well when he became confused. She knew how to calm people down when they were scared, because she knew what fear was. She could give kids the comfort she herself craved. It was a crucial insight that moved her forward. She began to wonder whether she might want to become a carer or a teacher instead of a secretary or a manager. Then in a surprising and sudden flash of assertion, she acted on this insight. She applied for a teacher-training course starting a few months later and was offered a place. She even organized finance for herself and this resolved both the problem of her sick leave from work and the question of her finishing her MBA. She had made a decision and was dropping both and starting a new life. Molly took me as much by surprise as everyone else around her. I sensed that it was important to back her decision, though it was tempting to sound cautious or question her motivations. Molly felt very relieved when I expressed respect for her decisiveness and determination and suddenly she could allow herself to be proud of her resolve in making these moves. She was then able to stand up for herself when Ellen and Greg questioned her decision. She knew she was taking a risk, but felt she was doing what she wanted to: making room for herself to be in the world in a new way. She remained afraid of other people's judgements though and the period between her bold decision and the start of the course was fraught with difficulties and doubts.

So we decided she needed to work out why and how she had always let other people undermine her so much. She realized, going over her female friendships, that her submissive attitude was a pattern across the board. The only time she had ever been really confident in her relationship with another adult was when she looked after her dad. He had needed her totally and she had not worried about having to prove herself to him, for he had become rather childlike. He was not judgemental anymore, in other words. She found him reassuring in his childlike state and she was aware that he had initially been quite grateful to her for being kind to him. Tragically he now seemed too out of touch to know she was there. Even when she had looked after dad, or after her nieces and nephews, Ellen usually found a way to diminish her achievements, for she knew she would never be able to prove herself worthy of Ellen's high standards and Ellen had always found fault with what she did. She had never been a match for Ellen and had let her undermine her confidence.

I pointed out to her that this was only possible because she had believed Ellen. This remark amazed her. How could she not believe Ellen? I countered that there was no reason why she should believe Ellen rather than her own observations. She thought about this for ages and it proved another hinge around which she turned things around for herself. Now she was ready to focus more on the personal dimension.

Taking a place in the world: the personal dimension

Proving herself worthy was a remarkably important value for Molly. She had started thinking of herself as unworthy from as far back as she could remember. She remembered how as a child she had always felt put-down by mother in relation to Ellen. She had picked up the notion that of the two daughters in the family Ellen was all strong and accomplished and she, Molly, was all weak and incompetent. At the same time she had felt a sense of injustice in this. She had often used the phrase 'it isn't fair' as a child and Ellen used to imitate her saying it and belittled her for it. All her life she had tried to do what Ellen would do, in order to make the grade, and all her life she had failed. Finally semi-certitude had formed in her mind that she was a failure. She would never be able to make the grade. She had bought into Ellen's dismissive attitude towards her and she held the same dismissive attitude towards herself. It was actually so deeply engrained that it was difficult to uproot. She thought of herself as unworthy. Unworthy of what? Of being loved by mom. Of being equal to her sister. Of being a worthy person in her own right. The worst thing was that she had not had a chance to grow up and prove herself worthy to mom. Mom had died and was gone before she had even had a chance to become herself. When mom was ill she had always asked for Ellen to be around and not Molly. This had left an indelible mark of deficiency on Molly's mind. She saw mom and Ellen as a real team, far superior to Molly. Molly was like dad and dad had always been rather silly and incompetent. He had become pre-senile soon after mom died. All this had left Molly quite simply feeling pretty rotten about herself. Caring for her dad may have been good, but it was still a confirmation of her inferior status. He was losing it and then so had she. She was really not worthy of achieving either a higher social status or a secure and loving relationship. That had been her growing conviction. Being rejected by Mark, who had already been judged inferior by Ellen, was the final confirmation. She was an inferior person and she deserved all she got. Molly soon accepted that she had applied other people's dismissive and offensive attitudes to herself and that she had not really given herself a chance to grow up and develop into the worthy person she knew deep inside that she could be. Molly protested at first when I said she was good or strong or determined, and I had to accept that her sense of self-worth was buried too deeply to be accessible in a direct way.

It was only really through the slow work we did on her relationship to her body that Molly started to think of herself as capable of much more. She also gained some self-respect from understanding her own predicament. She built confidence by starting to experiment with new ways of being and achieving small successes. It was much easier for her to do so in relation to her physical universe than to her social universe. It did help her to discover that she could make sense of what had happened between her and others and that she could alter the dynamics between herself and others as well. With Molly it was almost as if she had to develop a solid sense of whom she was from scratch. Previously her self-reflective style had been almost exclusively negative, leading to a lack of positive self-concepts. Making her pay attention to who she was for her nieces and nephews made a big difference, since her relationships with these four children were mostly positive and highly dynamic. She began to be able to evaluate her own actions in relation to them and note that she was patient or understanding, or a little irritable for example when one of them attacked a brother or sister. She came to see herself much more clearly, or maybe really for the first time. Her self-esteem improved drastically as she made progress in the physical realm. She could see her own determination, her inventiveness, her courage for overcoming some very debilitating habits. I found that it paid off to focus on the positives with Molly. When she spoke of her body with self-loathing I was at first often tempted to contradict her loudly. I discovered that the intervention that worked best on these occasions was instead to softly enquire whether she really thought this about herself or felt obliged to say it (so that others would not do it for her).

She began to trust that I could see through her 'symptoms' and her self-dismissive strategies and that I was truly interested in finding out, together with her, what on earth made her act so destructively. Moreover she started to see that I was truly interested in helping her uncover her own vitality and ability to become all that she was capable of being. I had to remember to not be taken in by her negativity but not to counter it with too positive an attitude. I had to open up space for her to see herself in a different light, from a different perspective. Then she would soon start to sound more positive about herself as well or come up with actions in the world that confirmed her ability rather than her infirmity. She would be really pleased when telling me about these successes, for instance in relation to her nieces and nephews or later on when she had started her teacher-training course. She was keen on positive confirmation and she quickly learnt that she could get it for herself. As we got better at understanding each other, if she did come up with a negative statement about herself, I only needed to say something like 'really?' or even just look at her inquiringly for her to stop going on a self-deprecating crusade.

There was no doubt that her experience of being the younger of two daughters, with Ellen being 'the clever, pretty one', had played a large part in her restricting her outlook on the world. Mother had often commented negatively on Molly's 'ugly duckling' looks and she had encouraged Ellen's preening and success with the boys. Molly was able to appreciate that since mom had died before Molly's adolescence there had not been a chance to get mother's confirmation that the ugly duckling was growing into a swan. It had not occurred to her that by calling her an ugly duckling mom had implied that she was expecting her to grow beautiful later on. It was a touching new thought, almost as if mom was suddenly able to encourage her from beyond the grave. It allowed her to question her previous assumptions that she was ugly and useless. She saw now that there had not really been anyone to help her grow into a woman. After mom died Ellen had soon left home and she had married young, hiding away in her own family, not seeing Molly's distress. It sounded, I once mused, as if Ellen may have used Molly's sense of inferiority to make herself feel better. It was as if she had shored herself up by keeping her younger sister down and under her control.

Molly felt quite shocked at the notion that her sister may have had reasons to keep her down. Yet it felt eerily real, as if I had suddenly exposed a trace of truth. It certainly explained why she had such a hard time with Ellen, always. It also allowed her to reappraise her own role in the family. It occurred to her now that she might have seemed a threat to Ellen rather than just a feeble victim. This was an astonishing and revolutionary thought to her. She reasoned that if she had kept herself away from other people because she thought she was unworthy, this might have been a waste of time if it was based on an error to start with. While she had thought herself incompetent and pathetic, she had just been going along with other people's convenience in disposing of her. Perhaps she was not a lame duck after all. It certainly made sense of why Ellen had criticized her more when she became important to the children. Could Ellen really have envied her growing closeness to them? It was a strange but liberating idea.

The issue of identity became important for a while after this, for she now had to answer the question over who she was. She came to see that the special identities of anorexia and hysteria that she had assigned to herself were weapons in her fight with Ellen. When Ellen had called her stupid and weak and lazy and pathetic, Molly had inwardly replied with 'you don't know me, I have histrionic personality disorder, I am suicidal, or I am anorexic'. It had made Molly feel superior to Ellen to put medical labels to the same concepts. Her hospitalizations had similarly conveyed a certain kind of status on her, even though she could see that status was a potentially negative one. Having brought all this to mind, Molly soon began to realize that there were better ways to rethink her identity, not just in terms of Ellen's image of her, but rather in terms of what she might be capable of being herself. The notion of freedom became a catalyst for Molly at this stage. At first Molly just wanted to claim freedom from Ellen's judgements and from Greg's demands. Later she was ready to explore her freedom to start determining her own life and developing as the person she wanted to be. With a bit of encouragement she began to wonder about the positive capacities she had, for instance in relation to her nieces and nephews. She was able to consider the hypothesis that her abilities with the children might have significantly contributed to their development and as such might even represent a threat to Ellen. She went to visit her nieces and nephews on several occasions and thought Ellen's envy of her ease with the kids was a likely explanation for her sister's behaviour in relation to her. Ellen tried to stop her having special moments with her children and in particular with Alicia, the littlest one, who had taken Molly into her confidence in relation to something she could not talk to her mom about. Molly began to see that she was a person in her own right and that she affected other people more than she knew. As her post-graduate training course unfolded her faith in her own educational insights grew and this made it even easier to be with Ellen's children. She felt a new sense of excitement about her life and about her potential for development. For the first time she started thinking of herself as someone worthy and with some good things to offer to the world. Perhaps she was a good person and she might be able to really contribute something to others. It became very much easier to help Molly develop a sense of who she was, what she was capable of and where she wanted to go in life once she had started engaging with the world in this way. It meant that we could work more intensely on her actual relationships with others as well, since she began to find other people far less threatening once she had a more accurate conception of her own abilities. She learnt to become a bit more assertive and outspoken with Ellen first, especially in relation to educational issues, on which she soon felt she had real expertise. She just had to keep remembering to hang on to her own sense of what she knew about things and learnt to convey what she felt and thought. In this Molly was much helped by a growing reliance on her ability to know what was right and wrong.

Learning to be human: the spiritual dimension

Right from the start Molly had been interested in her values and beliefs. We often progressed most when she could locate something that meant a lot to her and use it as the starting point for change. Molly's values and assumptions about the world proved to be very powerful for her. Whilst her physical universe had been squashed and constricted, her social world distorted, and her personal world had long remained underdeveloped, Molly had a very personal line on morality from the start. She had always valued her own secret world and her private thoughts more than anything. She knew much about creating an intimate place of sacred worship. Food deprivation and self-mutilation had played a part in this. Since other people were a danger to her, she had had to learn to make herself at home with herself and with an ultimate reality no one else could take from her. She had always read a lot and she loved to sit in a safe corner, curled-up, dreaming up romantic stories, without ever imagining that she could achieve very much in real life. Now that she was revising her own view of herself and reclaiming her bodily existence as well as her place in the world with others, she had to revisit her beliefs about the sacred rituals and aspirations as well. As she gained confidence in her therapeutic journey, she began to value her own astuteness in making sense of things. She was a person for whom the meaning of life was very significant. When she had believed the world to be an unfair and depressing place, the meaning of life was to isolate herself from it as much as possible. Being able to hide had been a valued commodity. As the world was turning out to be a place in which you had to play your own part in creating fairness (both for yourself and others) then the values of learning and teaching became paramount. One day, as we were reflecting on her past opinions of herself as a hysterical and weak person, she admitted that she had been looking, even then, for a kind of special martyrdom, a holy mission, a distinctive mark of her merit. Being mentally ill in some form or shape had seemed her best bet, for it gave her some protection and yet marked her out as someone for whom the world was a terrifying and bad place. Now she did not need to turn to such desperate tactics. She did not need to hide or martyr herself. She could concentrate on being the best of what she was capable of being instead. This was what she wanted to do. Not just for her sake, but also for the sake of the children (meaning both Ellen's and the children in her school classes as well).

Up to now she had always believed that she needed to suffer in silence and keep her own council. God and the universe demanded this of her. It was her role in life to carry her martyrdom uncomplainingly. Now she thought she needed to let as many people as possible know what had been wrong with that kind of attitude. She was a bit zealous about this at first and started to preach at Greg about good childcare. When I confronted Molly with the question of whether she actually knew what Greg thought about these matters and whether she had let him know where her thoughts came from, she began to see that her new-found energy required a new reciprocity as well. We could begin to work on her actual relationships in the real world at a new level. Greg needed to be told a lot of what Molly had continued to keep secret from him, keeping him out of the loop. He needed to understand that Molly had long been a disappointment to herself and that she had protected herself as best she could from becoming a disappointment to others. These things were hard for her to own up to and discuss with Greg. She wanted to hang on to the religious experience of the therapy and to her belief that she had to be the lone wolf crying in the wilderness. Now, the test of the reality of the changes in her was to integrate what she had learnt with the rest of her life and with the people who mattered to her. It took a long time for Molly to feel secure enough of the changes she had made to start confiding in Greg, who had patiently hung on for her throughout several years of slow progress in their relationship. She respected him for having been true to her and eventually decided to make a go of the relationship. She finally came clean about the self-harm and anorexia. She fully expected rejection and in fact got quite a bit more understanding than she had bargained for. It paid off immediately in terms of her relief at being able to be more herself with Greg. Now she did not need to be evasive about her reasons for not having wanted to do the MBA, nor did she need to sound holier than thou when talking about child rearing. She experimented with transparency in relation to Greg, though not with Ellen, and let the distance between Greg and her become less. She discovered that she had contributed a lot of her own suspiciousness to her human relations and had judged Greg unfairly in the past. He turned out to be a rather loving man who was able to respond generously when she opened up to him.

It became increasingly obvious that a lot of her narrow worldview could be expanded. It was going to have to involve revising her views of Ellen as well. This turned out to be the greatest difficulty, since her new educational zeal was clearly about competing with Ellen and getting her own back. She was in effect punishing Ellen for having bullied her. This needed a little time to sink in. She was not ready to reconcile with Ellen. It was easier to work on Molly's positive values and pay attention to the way she attributed meaning to life. We were of course still working with her embodied experience, her conflicts with others and her growing self-esteem, but she was constantly focusing on her purpose and where she wanted to get in the long run. In terms of what made life worthwhile Molly had always believed in love as the central value. She had been raised a Christian and had believed in Christian values, all giving love and charity until she had lost her faith after losing Mark. Even now she believed that love was the only thing worth living for, but she had not believed it was achievable. When her heart had been broken, love had seemed a dangerous thing to live for. She had sworn never to be so innocent as to pursue love blindly again. Originally she did not think that what she had with Greg could possibly be love. She feared that he was the sort of man who might use women. She was certain that she was the sort of woman too weak to stand up to him. The only reason she had stayed with him was that she felt she might redeem him. I questioned her notion that she was able to redeem another person in this way. We had long discussions about the nature of love. It was possible by now to directly contradict Molly when necessary and call her bluff or point out errors of logic that she seemed to be making. She was able to stand up to me and hold her own. As her confidence in her own understanding of important life issues increased, she became capable of standing up to Greg as well. She enjoyed the discovery that she was good at thinking through her fears and her opinions. She respected herself for becoming more clear and consistent in her thinking. The reality of her relationship with Greg was changed. She learnt, for instance, that it was not feasible to remain on the moral high ground with him and that in loving relationships we are never beyond making mistakes of judgement in relation to each other. She came to understand that people learn to love each other gradually as they give and receive each other's respect and trust.

As she became stronger, she could also afford greater humility and generosity. She began to listen to Greg and let him know when and why she agreed or disagreed. Their relationship began to flourish. She was able to reveal more and more about herself without lapsing into neediness. She grew able to listen to him without prejudice in return. She soon realized she had over-estimated him and that he needed her love more than she could ever have imagined. Greg turned out to be less of a macho company director and more of a rather desperate person who craved for a special closeness with her. In the later stages of the therapy we often talked about the couple's interactions. Molly was moving forward at the speed of light once she trusted in the fundamental possibility of being real with Greg and expecting him to be real in return. On the strength of this they decided to move in together. Their sexual relationship remained precarious at first, but got better as Molly learnt to trust Greg more and as she became more physically confident and playful.

The conclusion of the therapy

I saw Molly for about two and a half years and at the end of this period she considered herself to be capable of living her life well enough to meet any new difficulties that might arise. The issue for her, she said, was no longer whether or not she could be happy, but rather that she had learnt to live in a way that was satisfactory and that seemed to lead somewhere. The point was that she had discovered that the world was not such a bad place, if you did your best to make it better. The therapy with Molly involved reminding her almost continuously of her own ability to handle the pressures of her initially precarious existence. She learnt to deal with the apparent contradictions, paradoxes, dilemmas and conflicts by applying her considerable personal strengths to the task. She became really rather good at thinking and talking things through, first with me, then with herself and later with Greg. Being in dialogue was a pleasure for Molly and she gained in self-assurance as she noticed that this was something she was good at. She very quickly cottoned on to the notion that she could reshape her life and her own experience of living. She had already known but had not articulated for herself that she was engaged in some very counter-productive ways of being that she did not want to continue with. Much of the work was about learning to make herself safe at a physical level. In terms of her social world, the work on her relationship with Greg was a lynchpin to recovery. She had to overcome her fear of being bullied like she had been by Ellen. She did this on the back of establishing herself in a job she had chosen to suit her own abilities in education. Once she knew she could shape her own world, she became less scared of the influence of other people on her. Moving our therapeutic relationship from initially very supportive to increasingly challenging encouraged her to recognize that she was stronger than she thought and had nothing to fear from being outspoken in relation to others. In her personal world she developed a new way of knowing herself. First she came to see how she was often inclined to please me and accept my views. Then, as she became bolder, she recognized that she never actually accepted anything I said at face value and that she tended to check it out and often rejected it in order to think about it for herself. Molly had in fact quite a rebellious and self-reliant streak. She learnt to trust that she could take or leave my remarks and that it was important for her to come to her own formulations about herself and her life. She took pride in finding her own direction. This helped her in asserting herself in relation to Greg in the same way. Owning up to her self-harm and her anorexia with Greg was a big step towards being real as a person. Doing so was an important breakthrough towards honesty in relationships as well. Unfortunately she was unable to extend this principle to her relationship with her sister, who she continued to avoid.

Molly came to respect herself for all the hardship she had been through and for her willingness to deal with it. It was a breakthrough for her to see the self-harm as more of a source of self-esteem than of self-loathing, because she had been able to break away from it. In the final analysis claiming her own traumatic experience as formative rather than as destructive was what made her able to turn over a new leaf. Learning to expect a bit more respect from others for her position in the world was a desirable step, which took a little bit longer. She managed this very well in relation to children, then in relation to Greg and a number of other people. She gradually felt able to take up more space in the world.

Coda

Molly ended the therapy when she had re-established a worthwhile life for herself. We agreed to meet a year later for a follow-up session, and it was obvious when she came that she was continuing to develop and learn. She looked quite different, more mature and grown up somehow. Her hair was dyed auburn and her clothes were elegant. There had been plenty of problems during the year, which she had dealt with successfully. Her father had suddenly died in the intervening period and this had grieved her deeply, but Greg had supported her through it and this, she said, had allowed them to get even closer. She was enjoying her first year of teaching but also spoke of the stresses this was bringing. There had been times when she had had problems in maintaining order in the classroom. She had enlisted the help of her nieces and nephews to tell her how to handle this and it had worked. She sounded quite proud of herself. She was much more realistic about children and what could be expected of a daily job. She and Greg were planning to get married and have children of their own and while she was a bit anxious about this, she also greatly looked forward to it. She could see that there were many difficulties ahead in trying to juggle a complicated new lifestyle. She felt confident that this was what she wanted and that she was capable of managing it all. She was trying to eat sensibly, she said, though she looked rather slender to me. She and Greg cooked together every evening, since he wanted to make sure they would eat something they both liked. They were also sorting out dad's estate, because Ellen was going through a bout of depression and had not coped too well with the aftermath of dad's death. When I expressed some surprise at this, since Ellen was the solicitor in the family, Molly admitted that she and Greg had insisted on doing their bit and this had led to a row with Ellen and John. Relations with Ellen and John were still rather remote, since Greg was suspicious of the bad influence Ellen had had on Molly. This highlighted both the fact that Greg was now unconditionally supportive to Molly and that Molly's relationship with Ellen was unresolved. She had avoided Ellen as much as possible in the past year and knew that this was something that needed sorting out. She said she wanted to find the courage to move forward towards having things out with Ellen eventually, but felt she needed to concentrate on her career and her forthcoming marriage first. Although I was a little worried about the way in which Molly and Greg were forming a little world of their own, away from the rest of the family, I accepted that this was how they had chosen to manage their lives at the moment. It was not for me to challenge that plan, since Molly was doing as well as could have been expected. When I alluded to her original agenda for the therapy, a smile broke out across her face: she had long since set aside her negative thoughts about her own personality. The labels had never been very credible and she did not attach any further credence to them. We recalled the objective we had set at the outset of Molly's time in therapy, which was to find a place for herself in the world. She beamed as she reminded herself of how much she had achieved. She had in fact created a way of life that was satisfactory and that had integrity and she was continuing to develop this in a manner which made her feel efficient and in charge of the process. Both her work in the school and her relationship with Greg were sources of much satisfaction and ongoing adventures and challenges. In spite of some remaining threads that might have been unravelled further, especially in relation to her sister, Molly was enthusiastically engaged with her new existence and demonstrably brimming with a new zest for life. I expressed my conviction that she was flourishing and doing well. Perfectionism is not an objective of existential therapy.

What are man's truths ultimately? Merely his *irrefutable* errors.

Nietzsche

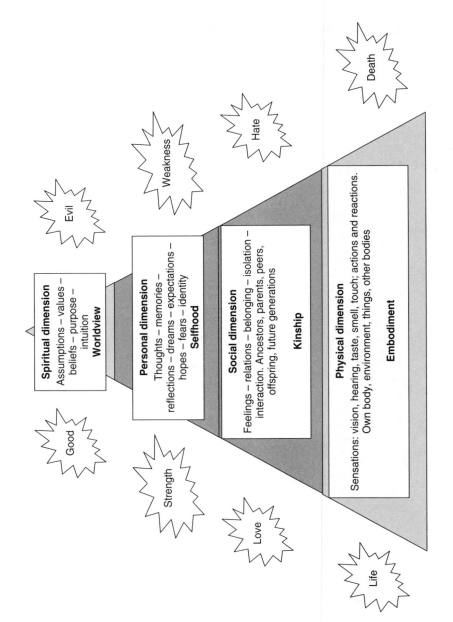

Figure 1   Four dimensions of human experience

Bibliography

Anon. 'Toward the Differentiation of a Self in One's Own Family'. In J. L. Framo (ed.) *Family Interaction: A Dialogue Between Family Researchers and Family Therapists* (New York: Springer, 1972), pp. 111–173.

Abram, D. *The Spell of the Sensuous* (New York: Vintage, 1997).

Ackroyd, P. *London: The Biography* (London: Chatto & Windus, 2000).

Adams, M. C. 'Practising Phenomenology: Some Thoughts and Considerations', *Existential Analysis*, 12(1) (2001) 65–84.

Adorno, T. *The Jargon of Authenticity* (London: Routledge, 2002).

Alanen, Y. *Schizophrenia: Its Origins and Need-Adapted Treatment* (London: Karnac Books, 1997).

Allport, G. W. *Pattern and Growth in Personality* (New York: Holt, Rinehart & Winston, 1961).

American Psychiatric Association *Diagnostic and Statistical Manual of Mental Disorders: DSM IV* (Washington, DC: American Psychiatric Association, 1997) 1994.

Arendt, H. *The Human Condition* (Chicago: University of Chicago Press, 1958).

Arnett, R. *Communication and Community* (Carbondale: Southern Illinois University Press, 1986).

Arnold-Baker, C. *Life Crisis or Crisis of the Self? An Existential View of Motherhood* (University of Sheffield: MA Dissertation, 2000).

Artal, M. and Sherman, C. 'Exercise Against Depression', *The Physician and Sports Medicine*, 26(10) (1998).

Austen, J. *Pride and Prejudice* (Oxford and New York: Oxford University Press, 1990) 1813.

Baker, A. (ed.) *Serious Shopping: Psychotherapy and Consumerism* (London: Free Association Press, 2000).

Bakhtin, M. 'Discourse in the Novel'. In M. Holquist (ed.) *The Dialogic Imagination* (Austin: University of Texas Press, 1981), pp. 259–422.

Barnes, H. 'Sartre's Concept of the Self', *Sartre and Psychology: Review of Existential Psychology and Psychiatry*, Special Issue (Seattle, WA: Boadella 1990).

Barrett, W. *Irrational Man* (London, Melbourne: Heinemann, 1958).

Bass, B. M. 'Does the Transactional-Transformational Leadership Paradigm Transcend Organizational and National Boundaries?', *American Psychologist*, 52 (1997) 130–139.

Bass, B. M. and Steidlmeier, P. 'Ethics, Character, and Authentic Transformational Leadership Behavior', *The Leadership Quarterly*, 10 (1999) 181–217.

Batchelor, S. *Buddhism Without Beliefs: A Contemporary Guide to Awakening* (London: Bloomsbury, 1983).

Bateson, G., Jackson, D. D., Haley, J. and Weakland, J. H. 'Toward a Theory of Schizophrenia', *Behavioral Science*, 1(4) (October 1956) 251–264.

Baumeister, R. F. *Meanings of Life* (London: Guilford Press, 1991).

Baumeister, R. F. and Leary, M. R. 'The Need to Belong: Desire for Interpersonal Attachments as a Fundamental Human Motivation', *Psychological Bulletin*, 117 (1995) 497–529.

303

Beck, A. T. *Cognitive Therapy and the Emotional Disorders* (New York: New American Library, 1976).

——. *Cognitive Therapy and the Emotional Disorders* (Harmondsworth: Penguin, 1991).

Becker, E. *The Denial of Death* (New York: Free Press Paperbacks, 1973).

Bell, N. W. 'Terms of a Comprehensive Theory of Family Psychopathology Relationships'. In G. H. Zuk and I. Boszormenyi-Nagy (eds) *Family Therapy and Disturbed Families* (Palo Alto, CA: Science & Behavior Books, 1967), pp. 2–10.

Benoit, H. *Zen and the Psychology of Transformation* (Rochester, Vermont: Inner Traditions International, 1990).

Berger, M. M. (ed.) *Beyond the Double Bind: Communication and Family Systems, Theories, and Techniques with Schizophrenics* (New York: Brunner/Mazel, 1978).

Binswanger, L. *Grundformen und Erkenntnis menschlichen Daseins* (Zurich: Max Niehans, 1942).

——. 'The Existential Analysis School of Thought'. In R. May et al. (eds) *Existence* (New York: Basic Books, 1946).

——. (ed.) 'Der Fall Jürg Zünd', *Schizophrenie* (Pfullingen: Günther Neske, 1957), pp. 189–288 (1957 [1946–47]).

——. 'The Case of Ellen West'. In R. May, E. Angel and H. F. Ellenberger (eds) *Existence: A New Dimension in Psychiatry and Psychology* (New York: Basic Books, 1958), pp. 237–364 (1958 [1944–45]).

——. *Being-in-the-World*. Trans. J. Needleman (New York: Basic Books, 1963).

Bion, W. *Experiences in Groups* (London: Tavistock, 1961).

——. 'Elements of Psychoanalysis'. In R. Emmanuel (ed.) *Ideas in Psychoanalysis* (Cambridge, UK: Icon, 1963).

Bohm, D. *David Bohm: On Dialogue* (Ojai, CA: David Bohm Seminars, 1990).

Boss, M. *The Analysis of Dreams* (London: Rider, 1957).

——. 'Anxiety, Guilt and Psychotherapeutic Liberation', *Review of Existential Psychology and Psychiatry*, 11(3) (September 1962).

——. *Psychoanalysis and Daseinsanalysis* (New York: Basic Books, 1963) 1957.

——. *I Dreamt Last Night . . . .* Trans. S. Conway (New York: John Wiley & Sons, Inc., 1977).

——. *Existential Foundations of Medicine and Psychology*. Trans. S. Conway and A. Cleaves (Northvale, NJ: Jason Aronson Inc., 1979).

——. 'Martin Heidegger's Zollikon Seminars'. In K. Hoeller (ed.) *Review of Existential Psychology and Psychiatry*, 16 (1988), 7–20.

——. *Existential Foundations of Medicine and Psychology* (New York and London: Jason Aronson, 1994) 1971, 1983.

Boss, M. and Kenny, B. 'Phenomenological or Daseinsanalytic Approach'. In J. L. Fosshage and C. A. Loew (eds) *Dream Interpretation: A Comparative Study* (New York: PMA, 1987).

Bowen, M. 'A Family Concept of Schizophrenia'. In D. D. Jackson (ed.) *The Etiology of Schizophrenia* (New York: Basic Books, 1960), pp. 346–372.

Bowlby, J. *Attachment and Loss*. Vols 1–3 (New York: Basic Books, 1969–80).

Brandes, G. *Creative Spirits of the Nineteenth Century* (New York: Thomas Y. Crowell, 1923) 1882.

Briod, M. 'A Phenomenological Approach to Child Development'. In R. S. Valle and S. Halling (eds) *Existential-Phenomenological Perspectives in Psychology* (London: Plenum Press, 1989).

Brontë, C. *Jane Eyre* (London: Thomas Nelson, n.d. [1847]).

Brown, G. W. and Harris, T. O. *Social Origins of Depression: A Study of Psychiatric Disorder in Women* (London: Tavistock, 1978).

Brown, G. W., Harris, T. O. and Peto, J. 'Life Events and Psychiatric Disorders. Part 2: Nature of Causal Link', *Psychological Medicine*, 3 (1973) 159–176.

Brown, S., Lumley, J., Small, R. and Astbury, J. *Missing Voices: The Experience of Motherhood* (Melbourne: Oxford University Press, 1994).

Buber, M. *I and Thou*. Trans. W. Kaufmann (Edinburgh: T&T Clark, 1923).

——. *Between Man and Man*. Trans. R. G. Smith (London: Kegan Paul, 1929).

——. *I and Thou*. Trans. W. Kaufmann (New York: Scribner, 1970).

——. *I and Thou* (Farmington Hills, Michigan: Gale Group, 1978).

——. *I and Thou* (A New Translation, with a Prologue and Notes) (New York: Touchstone, 2003).

Bugental, J. F. T. *Psychotherapy and Process: The Fundamentals of an Existential-Humanistic Approach* (Boston, MA: McGraw-Hill, 1978).

——. *The Search for Authenticity: An Existential-Analytic Approach to Psychotherapy*, Exp. edn (New York: Irvington, 1981).

——. *Psychotherapy Isn't What You Think: Bringing the Psychotherapeutic Engagement in the Living Moment* (Phoenix, AZ: Zeig, Tucker & Co., Inc., 1999).

Camus, A. *The Myth of Sisyphus* (Harmondsworth: Penguin, 1942).

——. *The Myth of Sisyphus*. Trans. J. O'Brien (London: Penguin, 1955).

Canetti, E. *Crowds and Power* (New York: Continuum, 1981).

Cannon, B. *Sartre and Psychoanalysis: An Existentialist Challenge to Clinical Metatheory* (Lawrence, KN: University Press of Kansas, 1991).

Caplan, P. J. *Don't Blame Mother: Mending the Mother Daughter Relationship* (New York: Harper & Row, 1989).

The Chambers Dictionary (Microsoft Bookshelf: British Reference Collection, 1994).

Chomsky, N. *Aspects of the Theory of Syntax* (Cambridge: MIT Press, 1968).

Clulow, C. *To Have and To Hold, Marriage, The First Baby and Preparing Couples for Parenthood* (Aberdeen: Aberdeen University Press, 1989).

Cohn, H. W. 'The Place of the Actual in Psychotherapy', *Free Associations*, 18 (1989) 49–61.

——. *Existential Thought and Therapeutic Practice: An Introduction to Existential Psychotherapy* (London: Sage, 1997).

——. 'Mother', *With All Five Senses* (London: Menard Press, 1999).

——. *Heidegger and the Roots of Existential Therapy* (London: Continuum, 2002).

Collins, J. *Heidegger and the Nazis* (Cambridge: Icon Books, 2000).

Condrau, G. *Sigmund Freud und Martin Heidegger* (Bern: Huber, 1992).

——. 'Dream Analysis: Do We Need the Unconscious?', *Existential Analysis*, 4 (1993) 1–12.

——. 'Letter', *Existential Analysis*, 5 (1994) 45–47.

——. *Martin Heidegger's Impact on Psychotherapy* (Dublin, New York, Vienna: Mosaic, 1998).

Cooper, D. E. *Existentialism* (Oxford: Blackwell Publishers Ltd, 1999).

Cooper, M. 'The Genetic Given: Towards an Existential Understanding of Inherited "Personality Traits"', *Existential Analysis*, 12(1) (2001) 2–12.

——. *Existential Therapies* (London: Sage, 2003).

Cooper, R., Friedman, J., Gans, S., Heaton, J. M., Oakley, C., Oakley, H., et al. (eds) *Thresholds Between Philosophy and Psychoanalysis* (London: Free Association Books, 1989).

Critchley, S. Y. and Schroeder, W. R. (eds) *A Companion to Continental Philosophy: Part VII Hermeneutics* (Oxford: Blackwell, 1998).

Crossley, N. *Intersubjectivity: The Fabric of Social Becoming* (London: Sage Publications, 1996).

Curnow, T. *Thinking Through Dialogue: Essays on Philosophical Practice* (Oxted: Practical Philosophy Press, 2001).

d'Agustino, F. *Public Justification* (http://plato.stanford.edu/entries/justification-public/Fred D'Agostino fdagosti@metz.une.edu.au, On-line, 1997).

Dally, A. *Inventing Motherhood: The Consequences of an Ideal* (London: Burnett Books, 1982).

Damasio, A. *The Feeling of What Happens: Body, Emotion and the Making of Consciousness* (London: Random House, 1999).

Davies, J. B. *The Myth of Addiction: An Application of the Physiological Theory of Attribution to Illicit Drug Use* (London: Harwood Academic Press, 1997).

Dawkins, R. *The Selfish Gene* (Oxford: Oxford Paperbacks, 1989).

de Beauvoir, S. *The Ethics of Ambiguity*. Trans. B. Fechtman (New York: Philosophical Library, 1948).

——. *The Second Sex* (London: Vintage Classics, 1953).

——. *The Second Sex* (London: Jonathan Cape, 1960).

——. *The Second Sex* (New York: Vintage Books, 1989).

DeCasper, A. J. and Fifer, W. P. 'Of Human Bonding: Newborns Prefer their Mother's Voices', *Science*, 208 (1980) 1174–1176.

de Mare, P. *Koinonia: From Hate Through Dialogue, to Culture in the Large Group* (London: Karnac Books, 1991).

De Rivera, J. *A Structural Theory of the Emotions* (New York: International University Press, 1977).

Derlega, V. J., Hendrick, S. S., Winstead, B. A. and Berg, J. H. 'Psychotherapy as a Personal Relationship: A Social Psychological Perspective', *Psychotherapy*, 29 (1992) 331–335.

Diamond, N. 'Embodiment', *Existential Analysis*, 7 (1996) 129–133.

Donaghy, M. *Postnatal Depression: An Existential Crisis?* (University of Sheffield: MA Dissertation, 2001).

Donne, J. 'Elegy X The Dream', *Divine Poems* (Oxford: Oxford University Press, 1982).

Drew, L. R. H. 'Facts We Don't Want to Face', *Drug and Alcohol Review*, 9 (1990) 207–210.

Dreyfus, H. L. *Being-in-the-World: A Commentary on Heidegger's Being and Time, Division 1* (Cambridge: MIT Press, 1991).

Dunnewold, A. *Evaluation and Treatment of Postpartum Emotional Disorders* (Florida, USA: Professional Resource Press, Sarasota, 1997).

du Plock, S. 'Sexual Misconceptions: A Critique of Gay Affirmative Psychotherapy and Some Thoughts on an Existential-Phenomenological Theory of Sexual Orientation', *Existential Analysis*, 8(2) (1997a) 56–71.

——. (ed.) *Case Studies in Existential Psychotherapy and Counselling* (Chichester: John Wiley, 1997b).

——. 'Social Context'. In C. Feltham and I. Horton (eds) *Handbook of Counselling and Psychotherapy* (London: Sage, 2000a).

——. 'Counselling, Psychotherapy and Politics'. In C. Feltham and I. Horton (eds) *Handbook of Counselling and Psychotherapy* (London: Sage, 2000b).

Edwards, P. *Heidegger on Death: A Critical Evaluation* (La Salle, IL: Hegeler Institute, 1979).

Ehrlich, E., Ehrlich, E. and Pepper, G. *Karl Jaspers: Basic Philosophical Writings, Selections* (Athens, Ohio: Ohio University Press, 1986).

Einstein, A. *Ideas and Opinions* (New York, NY: Crown Publishers, 1982).

Ekman, P. and Davidson, R. J. *The Nature of Emotion* (Oxford: Oxford University Press, 1994).

Ellis, A. *Overcoming Destructive Beliefs, Feelings and Behaviors: New Directions for Rational Emotive Behavior Therapy* (USA: Prometheus Books, 2001).

Emmanuel, R. *Ideas in Psychoanalysis: Anxiety* (Cambridge, UK: Icon, 2000).

Erikson, E. H. *Childhood & Society* (London: Vintage, 1995).

Esser, J. K. 'Alive and Well after 25 Years: A Review of Groupthink Research', *Organizational Behavior and Human Decision Processes*, 73 (1998) 116–141.

Esterson, A. *The Leaves of Spring: A Study in the Dialectics of Madness* (London: Tavistock, 1970).

——. 'Families, Breakdown and Psychiatry: Towards a Science of Persons', *The New Universities Quarterly*, 30(3) (Summer 1976) 285–312.

Fabry, J. *The Pursuit of Meaning: Viktor Frankl, Logotherapy and Life*, rev. edn (San Fransisco: Harper & Row, 1980).

Farber, L. H. 'O Death, Where is Thy Sting-a-ling-ling?'. In R. Boyers and A. Farber (eds) *The Ways of the Will*, Exp. edn (New York: Basic Books, 2000).

Farias, V. *Heidegger and Nazism* (Temple University Press, 1991).

Feifel, H. (ed.) 'Attitudes Towards Death in Some Normal and Mentally Ill Populations', *The Meaning of Death* (New York: McGraw-Hill, 1959).

Figes, K. *Life After Birth* (Harmondsworth: Penguin Books, 1998).

Fillingham, L. A. *Foucault for Beginners* (New York: Writers & Readers Publishing Inc., 1993).

Fingarette, H. *Heavy Drinking* (London: University of California Press, 1988).

Firestone, R. W. 'Psychological Defenses Against Death Anxiety'. In R. A. Neimeyer (ed.) *Death Anxiety Handbook: Research, Instrumentation and Application* (New York: Taylor & Francis, 1994), pp. 217–241.

Fischer, F. 'Raum-Zeit-Struktur und Denkstörung in der Schizophrenie'. II., *Zeitschrift für die gesamte Neurologie und Psychiatrie*, 124 (1930) 241–256.

Fleck, S. 'A General Systems View of Families of Schizophrenics'. In J. Jørstad and E. Ugelstad (eds) *Schizophrenia 75: Psychotherapy, Family Studies, Research*. Proceedings of the Vth International Symposium on the Psychotherapy of Schizophrenia (13–17 August 1975) (Oslo: Univeritetsforlaget, 1976), pp. 211–228.

Flores, P. *Group Psychotherapy with Addictive Populations* (New York: Haworth Press, 1996) 1997.

Flynn, T. *Sartre and Marxist Existentialism* (Chicago: University of Chicago Press, 1984).

Foucault, M. *The Order of Things: An Archaeology of the Order of Science*. Trans. A. Sheridan (London: Tavistock, 1966).

——. *The Archaeology of Knowledge*. Trans. A. Sheridan (London: Tavistock, 1969).

——. *The History of Sexuality, Vol. 1: An Introduction* (London: Penguin, 1990).

——. *Madness and Civilization: A History of Insanity in the Age of Reason* (London: Routledge, 1995).

Foulkes, S. H. *Therapeutic Group Analysis* (London: George Allen & Unwin, 1964).

——. *Group-Analytic Psychotherapy: Methods and Principles* (London: Gordon and Breach, 1975).

Fraley, R. C. and Shaver, P. R. 'Loss and Bereavement: Attachment Theory and Recent Controversies Concerning "Grief Work" and the Nature of Detachment'. In J. Cassidy and P. R. Shaver (eds) *Handbook of Attachment: Theory, Research, and Clinical Applications* (New York: Guilford Press, 1999), pp. 735–759.

Framo, J. L. (ed.) *Family Interaction: A Dialogue Between Family Researchers and Family Therapists* (New York: Springer, 1972).

Frankl, V. E. *The Doctor and the Soul* (Harmondsworth: Penguin Books, 1955).

——. *Psychotherapy and Existentialism: Selected Papers on Logotherapy* (Harmondsworth, Middlesex: Penguin Books, 1967).

——. *Man's Search for Meaning* (New York: Washington Square Press, 1984).

——. *The Doctor and the Soul: From Psychotherapy to Logotherapy.* Trans. R. Winston and C. Winston (New York: Vintage Books, 1986) 1973.

Freud, S. *The Interpretation of Dreams*, Vol. 4. In A. Richards (ed.) (Harmondsworth: Penguin, 1900).

——. *Standard Edition*, Vol. XV (London: Hogarth Press, 1917).

——. *The Standard Edition of the Complete Psychological Works of Sigmund Freud.* Vols 1–24 (London: Hogarth Press and The Institute of Psycho-Analysis, 1953–74) (Freud *SE*).

——. *Introductory Lectures on Psychoanalysis* (London: Hogarth Press, 1963).

——. *General Psychological Theory* (New York, NY: Simon & Schuster, 1997).

——. *Beyond the Pleasure Principle and Other Works* (London: Vintage, 2001).

Friedman, M. *The Worlds of Existentialism: A Critical Reader* (New Jersey: Humanities Press, 1996).

Frijda, N. *The Emotions* (New York: Cambridge University Press, 1986).

Fromm, E. *To Have or To Be?* (London: Abacus, 1976).

——. *The Art of Loving* (New York: Harper Collins, 2000).

Gadamer, H. G. *Truth and Method.* Trans. J. Weinsheimer and D. G. Marshall (New York: Continuum, 2000).

Gendlin, E. T. 'Existentialism and Experiential Psychotherapy'. In C. Moustakas (ed.) *Existential Child Psychotherapy* (New York: Basic Books Publishers Inc., 1966).

——. 'Befindlichkeit: Heidegger and the Philosophy of Psychology'. In K. Hoeller (ed.) 'Heidegger and Psychology', *Review of Existential Psychology and Psychiatry* (Seattle: Humanities Press, 1988).

——. *Focusing-Oriented Psychotherapy: A Manual of the Experiential Method* (New York: Guilford Press, 1996).

——. *A Process Model* (Unpublished Manuscript, available from www.focusing.org, 1997).

Goethe. In Boss, M. *I Dreamt Last Night. . . .* Trans. S. Conway (New York: John Wiley & Sons, Inc., 1977).

Goldenberg, H. 'A Response to Martin Milton', *Existential Analysis*, 11(1) (2000) 103–105.

Goldstein, M. J. and Doane, J. A. 'Interventions with Families and the Course of Schizophrenia, followed by general discussion'. In M. Alpert (ed.) *Controversies in Schizophrenia* (New York and London: Guilford Press, 1985), pp. 381–407.

Golomb, J. *In Search of Authenticity: From Kierkegaard to Camus* (London: Routledge, 1995).

Gossop, M. 'Drug and Alcohol Problems: Investigation'. In S. J. E. Lindsay and G. E. Powell (eds) *The Handbook of Clinical Adult Psychology* (London: Routledge, 1994).

Gray, J. G. 'The Problem of Death in Modern Philosophy'. In N. A. Scott Jr (ed.) *The Modern Vision of Death* (Richmond, VA: John Knox Press, 1967).

Greenberg, M. *The Birth of a Father* (New York: Avon Books, 1985).

Guignon, C. B. 'Authenticity, Moral Values, and Psychotherapy'. In C. B. Guignon (ed.) *The Cambridge Companion to Heidegger* (Cambridge: Cambridge University Press, 1993).

——. *The Good Life* (Indianapolis: Hackett Publishing Co., 1999).

Gullone, E. 'The Development of Normal Fear: A Century of Research', *Clinical Psychology Review*, 20 (2000) 429–451.

Guttman, D. *Logotherapy for the Helping Professional: Meaningful Social Work* (New York: Springer Publishing Company, 1996).

Hadot, P. *Philosophy as a Way of Life* (Oxford: Blackwell Publishers, 1995).

Haley, J. 'Toward a Theory of Pathological Systems'. In G. H. Zuk and I. Boszormenyi-Nagy (eds) *Family Therapy and Disturbed Families* (Palo Alto, CA: Science & Behavior Books, 1967), pp. 11–27.

Haley, J. and Hofmann, L. *Techniques of Family Therapy* (New York and London: Basic Books, 1967).

Halling, S. and Nill, J. D. 'A Brief History of Existential-Phenomenological Psychiatry and Psychology', *Journal of Phenomenological Psychology*, 26(1) (1995) 1–45.

Handel, G. (ed.) *The Psychosocial Interior of the Family: A Sourcebook for the Study of Whole Families* (London: George Allen & Unwin, 1968).

Heather, N. and Roberston, I. *Problem Drinking* (Oxford: Oxford University Press, 1989).

Heery, M. 'Inner Voices: A Review of 30 Subjects Experience of Hearing Voices', *Journal of Transpersonal Psychology*, 21(1) (1989) 68–83.

——. 'A Humanistic Perspective on Bereavement'. In K. Schnieder, F. Pierson and J. F. T. Bugental (eds) *The Handbook of Humanistic Psychology* (Thousand Oaks, CA: Sage, 2001), pp. 433–446.

Heery, M. and Bugental, J. F. T. 'Unearthing the Moment', *Self and Society*, 27(3) (1999) 25–27.

Hegel, G. *Phenomenology of Spirit* (Oxford: Oxford University Press, 1979).

Heidegger, M. *Introduction to Metaphysics* (Garden City, NY: Anchor Books, Doubleday, 1961) 1953.

——. *Being and Time*. Trans. J. Macquarrie and E. S. Robinson (New York: Harper & Row, 1962) 1927.

——. *Being and Time*. Trans. J. Macquarrie and E. S. Robinson (Oxford: Blackwell, 1962).

——. *Discourse on Thinking* (New York: Harper & Row books, 1966).

——. *Poetry, Language, Thought* (New York, Evanston, San Francisco, London: Harper & Row, 1971).

——. (ed.) 'Language', *Poetry, Language, Thought* (New York, Evanston, San Francisco, London: Harper & Row, 1971a), pp. 187–210 (1959).

——. *What is Called Thinking?* Trans. J. Scanlon (The Hague: Martinus Nijhoff, 1977).

——. (ed.) 'The Question Concerning Technology', *The Question Concerning Technology and Other Essays* (New York: Harper & Row, 1977a), pp. 3–35 (1954).

——. *The Question Concerning Technology and Other Essays* (New York: Harper & Row, 1977b).

——. *What is Called Thinking?* (New York: Harper & Row, 1982).

——. (ed.) 'A Dialogue on Language Between a Japanese and an Inquirer', *On the Way to Language* (New York: Harper & Row, 1982a), pp. 1–54 (1959).

——. (ed.) 'Language in the Poem: A Discussion on Georg Trakl's Poetic Work', In M. Heidegger (ed.) *On the Way to Language* (New York: Harper & Row, 1982b), pp. 159–198 (1959).

——. *Gesamtausgabe Vol. 65: Beitrage zur Philosophie (Vom Ereignis)*. In F. W. von Herrmann (ed.) (Frankfurt: Klostermann, 1989).

——. 'The way to Language'. In D. F. Krell (ed.) *Basic Writings* (London: Routledge, 1994).

——. *Being and Time*. Trans. J. Stambaugh (New York: State University of New York Press, 1996).

——. *Pathmarks* (Cambridge: Cambridge University Press, 1998).

——. (ed.) 'Letter on "Humanism"', *Pathmarks* (Cambridge: Cambridge University Press, 1998a), pp. 239–276 (1947).

——. *Elucidations of Hölderlin's Poetry* (Amherst, NY: Promethus Books, 2000) 1981.

——. *Zollikon Seminars: Protocols – Conversations – Letters*. M. Boss (ed.) (Evanston, IL: Northwestern University Press, 2001) 1987.

Heraclitus *Ancilla to the Pre-Socratic Philosophers*. Trans. K. Freeman (Oxford: Basil Blackwell, 1962).

Hopkins, J. *Talking to a Stranger: Four Television Plays* (Harmondsworth, Middlesex: Penguin, 1967).

Howard, A. *Philosophy for Counselling and Psychotherapy: Pythagoras to Post-modernism* (London: Macmillan Press, 2000).

Hume, D. *A Treatise of Human Nature*, 2nd edn (Oxford: Clarendon Press, 1978).

Husserl, E. *Phenomenological Psychology*. Trans. J. Scanlon (The Hague: Nijhoff, 1925).

——. *Cartesian Meditations* (The Hague: Nijhoff, 1929).

Hycner, R. *Between Person and Person: Towards a Dialogical Psychotherapy* (Highland, NY: Gestalt Journal Press, 1991).

Ibsen, H. *Peer Gynt*. Trans. J. Fillinger (Oxford: Oxford Paperbacks, 1998).

Inwood, M. *Heidegger* (Oxford: Oxford University Press, 1997).

Irigary, L. *Thinking the Difference* (London: Athlone Press, 1994).

Izard, C. E. *Human Emotions* (New York: Plenum, 1977).

Jackson, D. D. (ed.) 'The Question of Family Homeostasis', *Communication, Family, and Marriage* (Palo Alto, CA: Science & Behavior Books, 1968a), pp. 1–11 (1957).

——. *Communication, Family, and Marriage* (Palo Alto, CA: Science & Behavior Books, 1968b).

Jackson, D. D. and Satir, V. M. 'A Review of Psychiatric Developments in Family Diagnosis and Family Therapy'. In D. D. Jackson (ed.) *Therapy, Communication, and Change* (Palo Alto, CA: Science & Behavior Books, 1961), pp. 249–270.

Jackson, D. D., Riskin, J. and Satir, V. M. 'A Method of Analysis of a Family Interview'. In D. D. Jackson (ed.) *Communication, Family, and Marriage* (Palo Alto, CA: Science & Behavior Books, 1968), pp. 230–250 (1961).

James, W. *Principles of Psychology* (New York: Dover Press, 1950).

——. *Pragmatism and Other Essays* (New York: Washington Square Press, 1963).

Jaspers, K. 'Boundary Situations'. Trans. E. B. Ashton. In *Philosophy*, Vol. 2 (Chicago: University of Chicago Press, 1932).

——. *The Way to Wisdom*. Trans. R. Manheim (New Haven and London: Yale University Press, 1951).

——. 'On My Philosophy'. In W. Kaufmann (ed.) *Existentialism from Dostoevsky to Sartre* (Cleveland: World Publishing Company, 1956), pp. 131–158.

——. *Philosophy* (3 Vols). Trans. E. B. Ashton (Chicago and London: University of Chicago Press, 1969).

——. *Philosophy of Existence*. Trans. R. F. Greban (Philadelphia: University of Pennsylvania Press, 1971).

——. *General Psychopathology*, Vol. 1. Trans. J. Hoening and M. W. Hamilton (Baltimore and London: John Hopkins University Press, 1997) 1913.

Jonathan, A. 'Unhappy Success: A Mid-Life Crisis; The Case of Janet M'. In S. du Plock (ed.) *Case Studies in Existential Counselling and Psychotherapy* (Chichester, UK: John Wiley & Sons, 1997), pp. 126–140.

Joyce, J. *Ulysses* (London: Penguin Books, 1992).

Judge, A. *Time-sharing System in Meetings: Centralized Planning vs Free-Market Economy?* (http://www.uia.org/uiadocs/time.htm, On-line, 1994).

Jung, C. G. *Collected Works*. Trans. R. Hull (London: Routledge & Kegan Paul).

Kaplan, A. 'Eating Disorder Services'. In C. Fairburn and K. Brownell (eds) *Handbook of Eating Disorders: Theory, Treatment and Research* (New York: Guildford Press, 2002).

Kaufmann, W. *Existentialism, Religion and Death: Thirteen Essays* (New York: New American Library, 1978).

Keenan, B. *An Evil Cradling* (New York: Vintage, 1993).

Kierkegaard, S. *The Concept of Dread*. Trans. W. Lowrie (Princeton, NJ: Princeton University Press, 1844).

——. *That Single Individual* (http://libnt2.lib.tcu.edu/staff/bellinger/untruth.htm, On-line, 1846).

——. *Works of Love*. Trans. H. Hong and E. Hong (Princeton, NJ: Princeton University Press, 1847).

——. *The Point of View for my Work as an Author*. Trans. W. Lowrie (New York: Harper Torch Books, 1851).

——. *The Concept of Irony* (Bloomington: Indiana University Press, 1965).

——. *Concluding Unscientific Postscript*. Trans. D. F. Swenson and W. Lowrie (Princeton: Princeton University Press, 1968).

——. *The Concept of Anxiety*. Trans. R. Thomte (Princeton, NJ: Princeton University Press, 1980a).

——. *The Sickness unto Death*. Trans. H. Hong and E. Hong (Princeton, NJ: Princeton University Press, 1980b).

——. *Fear & Trembling*. Trans. and Intro. A. Hannay (Harmondsworth: Penguin Books, 1985).

——. *Stages on Life's Way: Studies by Various Persons* (Princeton, NJ: Princeton University Press, 1988) 1845.

——. *Either/Or: A Fragment of Life*. Trans. and Intro. A. Hannay (Harmondsworth: Penguin Books, 1992).

——. *The Soul of Kierkegaard: Selections from his Journal* (New York: Dover Press, 2003).

King, M. L. 'Speech at the Great march on Detroit, 23 June 1963' (The Estate of Martin Luther King The King Centre, Atlanta, Georgia: 1963) (http://www.stanford.edu/group/king/publications/speeches_at_the_great_march_on_detroit.html).

Klass, D., Silverman, P. R. and Nickman, S. L. (eds) *Continuing Bonds: New Understandings of Grief* (Philadelphia, PA, USA: Taylor & Francis, 1996).

Klein, M. *Love, Guilt and Reparation: And Other Works 1921–1945* (London: Virago Press, 1988).

Klingberg, H., Jr. 'Tracing Logotherapy to its Roots', *Journal des Viktor-Frankl-Instituts*, 1 (1995) 9–20.

Klinger, E. *Meaning and Void: Inner Experience and the Incentives in People's Lives* (Minneapolis: University of Minneapolis Press, 1977).

Koestenbaum, P. *The Vitality of Death: Essays in Existential Psychology and Philosophy* (New York: Greenwood Publishing Company, 1971).

Kruckman, L. D. 'Rituals and Support: An Anthropological View of Postpartum Depression'. In J. A. Hamilton and P. Peel (eds) *Postpartum Psychiatric Illness a Picture Puzzle* (USA: University of Pennsylvania Press, 1992).

Kubler-Ross, E. *On Death and Dying* (New York: Macmillan, 1969).

Lacan, J. *Speech and Language in Psychoanalysis* (Baltimore and London: John Hopkins University Press, 1989).

——. *Ecrits* (London: Routledge, 2001).

Laing, R. D. *The Divided Self* (London: Penguin, 1960).

——. 'Series and Nexus in the Family', *New Left Review*, 15 (May–June 1962) 7–14.

——. *The Divided Self: An Existential Study in Sanity and Madness* (Harmondsworth: Penguin, 1965).

——. *The Politics of Experience and the Bird of Paradise* (Harmondsworth: Penguin, 1967).

——. *Self and Others* (London: Penguin Books, 1969) 1961.

——. *The Politics of the Family and Other Essays* (Harmondsworth: Penguin Books, 1971).

——. *The Voice of Experience: Experience, Science and Psychiatry* (London: Allen Lane, 1982).

——. *Wisdom, Madness and Folly: The Making of a Psychiatrist 1927–1957* (London: Macmillan, 1985).

Laing, R. D. and Cooper, D. G. *Reason and Violence: A Decade of Sartre's Philosophy* (London: Tavistock, 1964).

Laing, R. D. and Esterson, A. *Sanity, Madness and the Family: Families of Schizophrenics* (Harmondsworth: Penguin, 1970) 1964.

Längle, A. 'Old Age from an Existential-Analytical Perspective', *Psychological Reports*, 89 (2001) 211–215.

Layard, J. *The Lady of the Hare: Being a Study in the Healing Power of Dreams* (London: Faber & Faber, 1944).

Leavis, F. R. 'Anna Karenina: Thought and Significance in a Great Creative Work', *The Cambridge Quarterly*, 1(1) (Winter 1965–66).

LeBon, T. *Wise Therapy: Philosophy for Counsellors* (London: Continuum, 2001).

Lemma, A. *Introduction to Psychopathology* (London: Sage, 1996).

Lemma-Wright, A. *Starving to Live: The Paradox of Anorexia* (London: Central Books, 1994).

Levin, D. M. (ed.) *Language Beyond Postmodernism: Saying and Thinking in Gendlin's Philosophy* (Illinois: Northwestern Universities Press, 1997).

Levinas, E. *Time and the Other*. Trans. R. A. Cohen (Duquesne: Duquesne University Press, 1987).

Levinson, D. J. *The Seasons of a Man's Life* (New York: Alfred A. Knopf, Inc., 1979).

Lidz, T., Fleck, S. and Cornelison, A. K. *Schizophrenia and the Family* (New York: International Universities Press, 1965).

Lieberman, M. A., Yalom, I. and Miles, M. B. *Encounter Groups: First Facts* (New York: Basic Books, 1973).

Lukas, E. 'The Four Steps of Logotherapy'. In J. B. Fabry, R. Bulka and W. S. Sahakian (eds) *Logotherapy in Action* (New York: Jason Aronson, 1979).

Macann, C. 'Who is Dasein? Towards an Ethics of Authenticity'. In C. Macann (ed.) *Martin Heidegger: Critical Assessments, Volume IV Reverberations* (London: Routledge, 1992).

Mace, C. (ed.) *Heart and Soul: The Therapeutic Face of Philosophy* (London: Routledge, 1999).

Macquarrie, J. *Existentialism: An Introduction, Guide and Assessment* (Harmondsworth: Penguin Books, 1972).

——. *An Existential Theology* (Harmondsworth: Penguin, 1975).

Madison, G. 'Focusing, Intersubjectivity, and Therapeutic Intersubjectivity', *Review of Existential Psychology and Psychiatry*, XXVI(1) (2001) 3–16.

Madison, G. B. *The Hermeneutics of Postmodernity: Figures and Themes* (Bloomington: Indiana Press, 1990).

Mahler, M., Pine, F. and Bergman, A. *The Psychological Birth of the Human Infant: Symbiosis and Individuation* (New York: Basic Books, 2000).

Makkreel, R. In R. Audi (ed.) *The Cambridge Dictionary of Philosophy* (Cambridge: Cambridge University Press, 1995).

Malcolm, N. *Wittgensteinian Themes: Essays 1978–1989* (New York: Cornell University Press, 1995).

Mann, D. *Psychotherapy: An Erotic Relationship* (London: Routledge, 1997).

Marcel, G. *Man Against Mass Society* (Chigaco: Gateway, 1962).

Marx, K. and Engels, F. *Communist Manifesto* (USSR: Progress Publishers, 1969) 1848.

Maslow, A. *Towards a Psychology of Being*, 2nd edn (New York: D. van Nostrand Co., Inc., 1968).

May, R. *Love and Will* (New York: W. W. Norton and Co., Inc., 1969).

——. *The Meaning of Anxiety* (New York: W. W. Norton, 1977).

——. *Freedom and Destiny* (New York: W. W. Norton, 1981).

——. *The Discovery of Being: Writings in Existential Psychology* (New York: W. W. Norton, 1983).

——. 'Contributions of Existential Psychotherapy'. In R. May, E. Angel and H. F. Ellenberger (eds) *Existence* (New York: Basic Books, 1994) 1958.

——. 'Existential Psychology and the Problem of Death', *Review of Existential Psychology and Psychiatry*, 24 (1999) 40–48.

May, R., Angel, E. and Ellenberger, H. F. (eds) *Existence: A New Dimension in Psychiatry and Psychology* (New York: Basic Books, 1958).

——. *Existence* (Northvale, NJ: Jason Aronson Inc., 1994).

Merleau-Ponty, M. *The Phenomenology of Perception*. Trans. C. Smith (London: Routledge, 1962).

——. 'The Child's Relations With Others'. In *The Primacy of Perception*. Trans. C. W. Cobb (Evanston, IL: Northwestern University Press, 1964a).

——. *Sense and Non-Sense*. Trans. H. Dreyfus and P. Dreyfus (Evanston, IL: Northwestern University Press, 1964b).

——. *The Visible and the Invisible*. Trans. A. Lingis (Evanston, IL: Northwestern University Press, 1968).

Milton, M. and Legg, C. 'Politics in Psychotherapy: Therapists' Responses to Political Material', *Counselling Psychology Quarterly*, 13(3) (2000) 279–291.

Minkowski, E. *Lived Time* (Evanston, IL: Northwestern University Press, 1970) 1933.

——. 'Findings in a Case of Schizophrenic Depression'. In R. May, E. Angel and H. Ellenberger (eds) *Existence* (Northvale, NJ: Jason Aronson Inc., 1994).

Minuchin, S. *Families and Family Therapy* (London: Tavistock, 1974).

Moja-Strasser, L. 'Philosophy and Existential Psychotherapy Training', *Journal of the Universities Psychotherapy and Counselling Association*, 2 (2001) 31–40.

Moreno, J. L. *Psychodrama*, Vol. 1 (New York: Beacon House, 1946).

Moustakas, C. *Existential Psychotherapy and the Interpretation of Dreams* (Northvale, NJ: Jason Aronson, 1994).

Nagel, T. *What Does it All Mean? A Very Short Introduction to Philosophy* (New York: Oxford University Press, 1987).

Neimeyer, R. A. and Van Brunt, D. 'Death Anxiety'. In H. Wass and R. A. Neimeyer (eds) *Dying: Facing the Facts*, 3rd edn (New York: Taylor & Francis, 1997), pp. 49–88.

The New Oxford Dictionary of English. In J. Pearsall and P. Hanks (eds) (Oxford: Oxford University Press, 1998).

Nicolson, P. *Postnatal Depression: Psychology, Science and the Transition to Motherhood* (London: Routledge, 1998).

Nietzsche, F. *The Gay Science*. Trans. W. Kaufmann (New York: Random House, 1882).

——. *On the Geneology of Morals*. Trans. W. Kaufman and R. J. Hollingdale (New York: Vintage Books, 1887).

——. *Will to Power* (Stuttgart: Kroner Edition, 1910).

——. *The Viking Portable Nietzsche* (New York: Viking Press, 1954).

——. In Boss, M. *The Analysis of Dreams* (London: Rider, 1957), p. 47.

——. *Thus Spoke Zarathustra*. Trans. R. J. Hollingdale (Harmondsworth: Penguin, 1961) 1883.

——. *The Will to Power*. In W. Kaufman (ed.) (New York: Vintage Books, 1968).

——. *A Nietzsche Reader*. Trans. R. J. Hollingdale (Harmondsworth: Penguin, 1977).

——. *On the Geneology of Morality: A Polemic*. Trans. M. Clark and A. J. Swensen (Indianapolis, Cambridge: Hackett Publishing Company, 1998).

——. *The Gay Science* (Harmondsworth: Penguin, 2001).

Nolen-Hoeksema, S. *Sex Difference in Depression* (Stanford, CA: Stanford University Press, 1990).

Nussbaum, M. C. *The Therapy of Desire: Theory and Practice in Hellenistic Ethics* (Princeton: Princeton University Press, 1994).

——. *Upheavals of Thought: The Intelligence of Emotions* (Cambridge: Cambridge University Press, 2003).

Oakley, A. *Becoming a Mother* (Oxford: Martin Robertson and Company, 1979).

Oatley, K. *Best Laid Schemes: The Psychology of Emotions* (Cambridge: Cambridge University Press, 1992).

Olsen, T. *Tell Me a Riddle* (London: Virago, 1980) 1962.

Ormiston, G. L. and Schrift, A. D. (eds) *The Hermeneutic Tradition* (Albany: State University of New York, 1990).

Oxford Dictionary (Oxford: Oxford University Press, 1984).

Park, J. *New Ways of Loving* (Minneapolis, MN: Existential Books, 2002).

Parkes, C. M. *Bereavement: Studies of Grief in Adult Life* (New York: International University Press, 1972).

——. 'Bereavement as a Psychosocial Transition: Processes of Adaptation to Change'. In D. Dickenson and M. Johnson (eds) *Death, Dying, and Bereavement* (London: Open University Press, Sage Publications, 1993).

Parkes, C. M. and Weiss, R. *Recovery from Bereavement* (New York: Basic Books, 1983).

Parkes, C. M., Laungani, P. and Young, B. (eds) *Death and Bereavement Across Cultures* (London: Routledge, 1997).

Pattison, G. *The Later Heidegger* (London: Routledge, 2000).

Pearsall, J. (ed.) *The New Oxford Dictionary of English* (Oxford: Oxford University Press, 1998).

Penguin Dictionary of Psychology (Harmondsworth: Penguin, 1978).

Perls, F., Hefferline, R. F. and Goodman, P. *Gestalt Therapy: Excitement and Growth in the Human Personality* (New York: Julian Press, 1951).

Pescosolido, A. T. 'Emergent Leaders as Managers of Group Emotion', *The Leadership Quarterly*, 13 (2002) 583–599.

Piaget, T. *The Child's Conception of the World* (St Albans: Paladin, 1977).

Pictet, D. 'An Inquiry into Primordial Thinking: With Parmenides and Heidegger', *Existential Analysis*, 12(1) (2001) 33–47.

Pietila, M. 'Support Groups: A Psychological or Social Device for Suicide Bereavement?', *British Journal of Guidance and Counselling*, 30(4) (2002) 401–414.

Pines, M. 'The Coherency of Group Analysis', *Group Analysis* (2002).

Plato *Portrait of Socrates*. Trans. Sir R. W. Livingstone (Oxford: Clarendon Press, 1938).

——. *Republic*. Trans. R. Waterfield (Oxford: Oxford University Press, 1993).

Plutarch *Moralia*. I–XVII. Trans. F. C. Babbitt (Cambridge: Harvard University Press, 1967).

Polt, R. *Heidegger: An Introduction* (London: UCL Press, 1999).

Popper, M. and Mayseless, O. 'Back to Basics: Applying a Parenting Perspective to Transformational Leadership', *The Leadership Quarterly*, 14 (2003) 41–65.

Priel, B. and Besser, A. 'Bridging the Gap Between Attachment and Object Relations Theories: A Study of the Transition to Motherhood', *British Journal of Medical Psychology*, 74 (2001) 85–100.

Rank, O. *Beyond Psychology* (New York: Dover, 1941).

Raphael-Leff, J. *Pregnancy: The Inside Story* (London: Karnac Books, 2001).

Resnick, J. 'Jan Resnick'. In B. Mullan (ed.) *R. D. Laing: Creative Destroyer* (London: Cassel, 1997).

Ricoeur, P. In D. Ihde (ed.) *The Conflict of Interpretations* (Evanston, IL: Northwestern University Press, 1974).

Rochat, P. and Striano, T. 'Who's in the Mirror? Self–Other Discrimination in Specular Images by Four- and Nine-Month-Old Infants', *Child Development*, 73(1) (2002) 35–46.

Rockmore, T. and Margolis, J. *The Heideggar Case: On Philosophy and Politics* (Philadelphia: Temple University Press, 1992).

Rogers, C. R. *Client-Centred Therapy* (Boston: Houghton and Mifflin, 1951).

——. 'A Theory of Therapy, Personality and Interpersonal Relationships as Developed in the Client-Centred Framework'. In S. Koch (ed.) *Psychology: A Study of Science*, Vol. 3 (New York: McGraw-Hill, 1959), pp. 184–256.

Rossiter, A. *From Private to Public: A Feminist Exploration of Early Mothering* (Toronto: Women's Press, 1988).

Rowe, D. *Depression: The Way Out of Your Prison*, 2nd edn (London: Routledge, 1996).

Royzman, E. B. and Kumar, R. 'On the Relative Preponderance of Empathic Sorrow and its Relation to Commonsense Morality', *New Ideas in Psychology*, 19 (2001) 131–144.

Rudgley, R. *Wildest Dreams* (London: Little, Brown & Company, 1999).

Russell, B. 'Mathematical Logic as Based on the Theory of Types'. In B. Russell and R. C. Marsh (eds) *Logic and Knowledge: Essays 1901–1950* (London: George Allen & Unwin, 1956), pp. 57–102 (1908).

Rycroft, C. *Anxiety and Neurosis* (Harmondsworth: Penguin, 1968).

Sadler, W. A., Jr. *Existence and Love* (New York: Charles Scribner & Sons, 1969).

Safranski, R. *Martin Heidegger: Between Good and Evil* (New York: Harvard University Press, 1988).

Samuels, A. *The Political Psyche* (London: Routledge, 1993).

Sander, F. M. *Individual and Family Therapy: Toward an Integration* (New York and London: Jason Aronson, 1979).

Sartre, J. P. *Sketch for a Theory of the Emotions*. Trans. P. Mairet (London: Methuen, 1939).

——. *Being and Nothingness – An Essay on Phenomenological Ontology*. Trans. H. Barnes (New York: Philosophical Library, 1943).

——. *No Exit*. Trans. S. Gilbert (New York: Alfred A. Knopf, 1947).

——. *Anti-Semite and Jew* (New York: Schoken Books, 1948a).

——. *Existentialism and Humanism*. Trans. P. Mairet (London: Methuen, 1948b).

——. *Saint Genet, Actor & Martyr*. Trans. B. Frechtman (New York: Mentor Books, 1963).

——. *Nausea* (London: New Directions, 1964a).

——. *Saint Genet: Actor and Martyr* (London: W. H. Allen, 1964b) 1952.

——. *Search for a Method* (New York: Random House, Vintage Books, 1968) 1960.

——. *The Idiot of the Family*. Trans. C. Cosman (Chicago: University of Chicago Press, 1971) 1960.

——. 'Between Existentialism and Marxism'. Trans. J. Mathews. In *Situations*, Vols VII–IX (New York: Pantheon Books, 1974).

——. *Critique of Dialectical Reason*. Trans. A. Sheridan-Smith (London: Methuen and Co., 1976) 1960.

——. *Being and Nothingness: An Essay on Phenomenological Ontology*. Trans. H. Barnes (London: Routledge, 1996) 1958.

Savater, F. *The Questions of Life: An Invitation to Philosophy*. Trans. C. O. Arrowsmith (Cambridge: Polity Press, 2002).

Scheler, M. *The Nature of Sympathy* (London: Routledge & Kegan Paul, 1954).

Schneider, K. 'The Worship of Food: An Existential Perspective', *Psychotherapy*, 27(1) (1990) 95–97.

——. 'Guidelines for an Existential-Integrative Approach'. In K. Schneider and R. May (eds) *The Psychology of Existence: An Integrative, Clinical Perspective* (New York: McGraw-Hill, 1995).

——. *The Paradoxical Self: Toward an Understanding of Our Contradictory Nature*, 2nd edn (Amherst, NY: Humanity Books [imprint of Prometheus Books], 1999).

——. 'Existential-Humanistic Psychotherapies'. In A. S. Gurman and S. B. Messer (eds) *Essential Psychotherapies*, 2nd edn (New York: Guilford, 2003).

Scott, C. E. (ed.) *On Dreaming: An Encounter with Medard Boss* (California: Scholars Press, 1977).

Semyon, M. 'Mina Semyon'. In B. Mullan (ed.) *R. D. Laing: Creative Destroyer* (London: Cassell, 1997).

Shaffer, H. J. 'Denial, Ambivilance and Countertransferential Hate'. In J. Levin and R. Weiss (eds) *The Dynamics and Treatment of Alcoholism* (Northvale, NJ: Jason Aronson, 1994).

Sheehy, G. *Passages: Predictable Crisis of Adult Life* (Bantam: Doubleday Dell Publishing Group, 1976).

Sherif, M. 'Superordinate Goals in the Reduction of Intergroup Conflict'. In M. Hogg and D. Abrams (eds) *Intergroup Relations: Essential Readings; Key Readings in Social Psychology* (Philadelphia, PA: Psychology Press, 2001), pp. 64–70.

Shorter, E. *A History of Women's Bodies* (Harmondsworth: Pelican, 1984).

Smail, D. *Illusion and Reality: The Meaning of Anxiety* (London: Dent, 1984).

Sonnby-Borgstrom, M. 'The Facial Expression Says More than Words. Is Emotional "Contagion" via Facial Expression the First Step Toward Empathy?', *Lakartidningen*, 99 (2002) 1438–1442.

Sonne, J. C. 'Entropy and Family Therapy: Speculations on Psychic Energy, Thermodynamics, and Family Interpsychic Communication'. In G. H. Zuk and I. Boszormenyi-Nagy (eds) *Family Therapy and Disturbed Families* (Palo Alto, CA: Science & Behavior Books, 1967), pp. 85–95.

Sonnemann, U. *Existence and Therapy: An Introduction to Phenomenological Psychology and Existential Analysis* (Highland, NY: Gestalt Legacy Press, 1999) 1954.

Spiegelberg, H. *Phenomenology in Psychology and Psychiatry: A Historical Introduction* (Evanston, IL: Northwestern University Press, 1972).

Spinelli, E. *The Interpreted World: An Introduction to Phenomenological Psychology* (London: Sage, 1989).

——. 'Sex, Death, and the Whole Damned Thing: The Case of Stephen R', *Existential Analysis*, 3 (1992) 39–53.

——. *Demystifying Therapy* (London: Constable, 1994).

——. 'Some Hurried Notes Expressing Outline Ideas that Someone Someday Might Utilize Towards a Sketch of an Existential-Phenomenological Theory of Sexuality', *Existential Analysis*, 8(1) (1996) 2–20.

——. *Tales of Un-Knowing: Therapeutic Encounters from an Existential Perspective* (London: Duckworth, 1997).

——. *The Mirror and the Hammer: Challenges to Therapeutic Orthodoxy* (London: Continuum, 2001).

Spinoza, B. de, *Ethics*. Trans. R. Elwes (New York: Dover Publications, 1677).

Stadlen, A. 'Was Dora "ill"?'. In L. Spurling (ed.) *Freud: Critical Assessments*, Vol. 2 (London: Routledge, 1989), pp. 196–203 (1985).

——. 'Why Should Existential Therapists Study Freud?', *Hermeneutic Circular: Newsletter of the Society for Existential Analysis*, (April 2000) 20.

——. 'Rezension: Martin Heidegger'. In M. Boss (ed.) 'Zollikon Seminars: Protocols–Conversations–Letters', *Daseinsanalyse*, 18 (2002) 165–170.

——. 'Unknotting 1. Just How Interesting Psychoanalysis Really Is', *Are de Cercle*, 1(1) (2003a) 143–176.

——. 'Essay Review: Gion Condrau, Martin Heidegger's Impact on Psychotherapy', *Existential Analysis*, 14(1) (2003b) 162–178.

——. 'Heidegger's *Zollikon Seminars*: The "American" Translation', *Existential Analysis*, 14(2) (2003c).

Starck, P. L. 'Logotherapy: Applications to Nursing', *Journal des Viktor-Frankl-Instituts*, 1 (1993) 94–98.

Stavro-Pearce, E. 'Transgressing Sartre: Embodied Situated Subjects'. In 'The Second Sex', *Labyrinth*, 1 (1999) 1.

Steinbeck, J. *The Wayward Bus* (London: Heinemann, 1947).

Steiner, G. *Heidegger*, Fontana Modern Masters, 2nd edn (London: HarperCollins, 1992).

Stern, D. *The Interpersonal World of the Infant* (New York: Basic Books, 1985).

——. *The Motherhood Constellation: A Unified View of Parent Infant Psychotherapy* (New York: Basic Books, 1995).

Stern, P. J. 'Introduction to the English Translation'. In M. Boss (ed.) *Existential Foundations of Medicine and Psychology*, 2nd edn (New York and London: Jason Aronson, 1983), pp. ix–xxii.

Strasser, F. *Emotions: Experiences in Existential Psychotherapy and Life* (London: Duckworth, 1999).

Strasser, F. and Strasser, A. *Existential Time-Limited Therapy: The Wheel of Existence* (Chichester: John Wiley, 1997).

Strawbridge, S. *Myth of the Self-Contained Individual in Counselling Psychology* (Paper presented to the Conference of the BPS Division of Counselling Psychology, New York, 1996).

Stunkard, A. J. 'Obesity'. In S. Areti (ed.) *American Handbook of Psychiatry*, Vol. 7 (New York: Basic Books, 1981), pp. 445–476.

Szasz, T. S. *The Ethics of Psychoanalysis: The Theory and Method of Autonomous Psychotherapy* (New York: Basic Books, 1965).

——. *The Myth of Mental Illness* (New York: Harper & Row, 1974) 1961.

Szlezak, T. A. *Reading Plato*. Trans. G. Zanker (London: Routledge, 1993).

Tallis, F. *Changing Minds: The History of Psychotherapy as an Answer to Human Suffering* (London: Cassell, 1998).

Tantam, D. *Psychotherapy and Counselling in Practice: A Narrative Approach* (Cambridge: Cambridge University Press, 2002).

Tengan, A. *Search for Meaning as the Basic Human Motivation: A Critical Examination of Viktor Emil Frankl's Logotherapeutic Concept of Man*, Vol. 556 (Frankfurt am Main: Peter Lang, 1999).

Thomas, R. S. *Groping, Later Poems: A selection* (London: Macmillan Papermack, 1983).

Thompson, M. G. *The Truth About Freud's Technique: The Encounter with the Real* (New York: New York University Press, 1994).

Tillich, P. *Love, Power and Justice* (Oxford: Oxford University Press, 1954).

——. *The Courage to Be*, The Fontana Library (London: Collins, 1962).

——. 'The Eternal Now'. In N. A. Scott Jr (ed.) *The Modern Vision of Death* (Richmond, VA: John Knox Press, 1967).

——. *The Courage to Be* (New Haven: Yale University Press, 2000) 1952.

Tolstoy, L. *Anna Karenina* (Harmondsworth, Middlesex: Penguin, 1954) [1873–77].

Tompkins, M. A. 'Schizophrenia and the Family'. In S. Vinogradov (ed.) *Treating Schizophrenia* (San Francisco, CA: Jossey-Bass, 1995), pp. 319–349.

van Deurzen, E. *Paradox and Passion in Psychotherapy: An Existential Approach to Therapy and Counselling* (Chichester: John Wiley & Sons, 1998).

——. *The Good Life: Values for a New Millenium* (Dilemma website, www.Dilemmas.org, 2000).

——. *Existential Counselling and Psychotherapy in Practice*, 2nd edn (London: Sage, 2002a).

——. 'Heidegger's Challenge of Authenticity'. In *Further Existential Challenges to Psychotherapeutic Theory and Practice* (London: Society for Existential Analysis, 2002b).

——. *Psychotherapy and the Quest for Happiness: Hoping for Utopia* (London: Sage Publications, 2005).

van Deurzen-Smith, E. 'Existential Psychotherapy'. In W. Dryden (ed.) *Individual Therapy in Britain* (London: Harper & Row, 1984).

——. *Existential Counselling in Practice* (London: Sage, 1988).

——. 'Changing the World: Possibilities and Limitations', *Counselling, Journal of the British Association for Counselling* (May 1993) 120–123.

——. 'Dialogue as Therapy', *Existential Challenges to Psychotherapeutic Theory and Practice: Selected Papers from the Journal of the Society for Existential Analysis*, Vols 1–5 (1995a) 104–112.

——. *Existential Therapy* (London: Society for Existential Analysis, 1995b).

——. 'Psychotherapy: A Profession for Troubled Times', *British Journal of Psychotherapy*, 11 (1995c) 458–466.

——. *Everyday Mysteries: Existential Dimensions of Psychotherapy* (London: Routledge, 1997).

Vlastos, G. *Socrates: Ironist and Moral Philosopher* (Cambridge: Cambridge University Press, 1991).

von Uexküll, J. *Umwelt und Innenwelt der Tiere* (Berlin: J. Springer, 1921).

Wadden, J. A. and Stunkard, A. J. 'Controlled Trial of a Very Low Calorie Diet, Behaviour Therapy, and their Combination in the Treatment of Obesity', *Journal of Consulting and Clinical Psychology*, 54(4) (1986) 482–488.

Waelder, R. *Basic Theory of Psychoanalysis* (New York: Schocken, 1964).

Walter, T. 'A New Model of Grief: Bereavement and Biography', *Mortality*, 1(1) (1996) 7–25.

Walters, G. D. *The Addiction Concept: Working Hypothesis or Self-Fulfilling Prophesy?* (Needham Heights, MA: Allyn & Bacon, 1999).

Warnock, M. *Existentialism* (Oxford: Oxford University Press, 1970).

Waterfield, R. *Hidden Depths: The History of Hypnosis* (London: Pan, 2003).

Weichert, E. S. 'The Science and Typology of Family Systems. II. Further Theoretical and Practical Considerations', *Family Process*, 14(3) (September 1975) 285–309.

Welwood, J. *Awakening the Heart* (Boston, MA: Shambala Publishing, 1983).

Whitaker, C. (ed.) *Psychotherapy of Chronic Schizophrenic Patients* (Boston and Toronto: Little, Brown & Company, 1958).

Wiesenhütter, E. *Die Begegnung zwischen Philosophie und Tiefenpsychologie* (Darmstadt: Wissenschaftliche Gesellschaft, 1979).

Wilson, B. *Wittgenstein's Philosophical Investigations: A Guide* (Edinburgh: Edinburgh University Press, 1998).

Wilson, G. and Brownell, K. 'Behavioural Treatment and Obesity'. In C. Fairburns and K. Brownell (eds) *Handbook of Eating Disorders: Theory, Treatment and Research* (New York: Guildford, 2002).

Winnicott, D. W. *The Maturational Process and the Facilitating Environment* (London: Karnac Books, 1990).

Wittgenstein, L. *The Tractatus Logico – Philosophicus* (Oxford: Blackwell, 1922).

——. *Philosophical Investigations*, Vol. 2 (Oxford: Blackwell, 1997).

Wong, P. T. P., Reker, G. T. and Gesser, G. 'Death Attitude Profile-Revized: A Multi-dimensional Measure of Attitudes Towards Death'. In R. A. Neimeyer (ed.) *Death Anxiety Handbook: Research, Instrumentation and Application* (New York: Taylor & Francis, 1994), pp. 121–148.

Worden, J. W. *Grief Counselling and Grief Therapy: A Handbook for the Mental Health Practitioner* (New York: Springer, 1991).

Wurm, C. 'Deciding About Drinking: An Existential Approach to Alcohol Dependence'. In S. du Plock (ed.) *Case Studies in Existential Psychotherapy and Counselling* (Chichester: John Wiley, 1997).

Yalom, I. D. *Existential Psychotherapy* (New York: Basic Books, 1980).

——. *Love's Executioner and Other Tales of Psychotherapy* (London: Penguin Books, 1989).

——. 'Foreword'. In S. Vinogradov (ed.) *Treating Schizophrenia* (San Francisco, CA: Jossey-Bass, 1995a), pp. ix–xii.

——. *The Theory and Practice of Group Psychotherapy*, 4th edn (New York: Basic Books, 1995b).

——. *The Gift of Therapy: Reflections on Being a Therapist* (London: Piatkus, 2001).

——. *The Gift of Therapy* (New York: HarperCollins, 2002).

Yalom, I. D. and Elkin, G. *Every Day Gets a Little Closer: A Twice-told Therapy* (New York: Basic Books, 1974).

Yerkes, R. M. and Dodson, J. D. 'The Relation of Strength of Stimulus to Rapidity of Habit-Formation', *Journal of Comparative Neurology and Psychology*, 18 (1908) 459–482.

Young, S. '"Everything is What it is, not Something Else" A Response to Gion Condrau', *Existential Analysis*, 4 (1993) 13–18.

Zimmerman, M. E. *Eclipse of the Self: The Development of Heidegger's Concept of Authenticity* (Athens: Ohio University Press, 1981).

Index

A

absurd, 6, 267
aesthetic, 41, 162, 238
alienation, 6, 43, 45
alterity, 48, 51, 52, 53, 56, 147, 148
ambiguity, 41, 46, 51, 53, 108, 128, 137, 275, 285
anger, 46, 63, 64, 90, 97, 119, 194, 198, 211, 233, 234, 290, 291
anxiety, xvi, 6–7, 10, 12, 19, 23, 33, 34, 35, 36, 44, 46, 72, 73, 74, 76, 79, 80, 82, 85, 93, 99, 111, 113, 118, 122, 125, 146, 149, 150, 159, 161, 164, 166, 168, 172, 174, 175, 176, 180–9, 191, 193, 196, 198, 201, 207, 234, 235, 236, 246, 258, 283
aspirations, 62, 70, 168, 193, 217, 232, 234, 275, 296
attunement, 58, 94, 97, 112, 190, 191, 193
authenticity, 7, 12, 42, 43, 97, 123, 125, 128, 146, 159, 164, 170, 171–5, 177–9, 181, 258, 262
availability, 33
awareness, xix, xx, 7, 8, 14, 19, 20, 28, 34, 35, 41, 47, 54, 56, 57, 104, 121, 122, 123, 124, 157, 164, 173, 183, 188, 199, 201, 202, 211, 233, 250, 257, 260, 265, 270

B

bad faith, 7, 13, 139, 146, 165, 166, 172, 250, 251
Beauvoir, Simone de (1908–1986), 31, 34, 38, 126, 127, 247
becoming, xvi, 5, 7, 12, 35, 42, 46, 83, 125, 146, 160, 162, 164, 165, 166, 172, 174, 192, 229, 271
Befindlichkeit, 97, 112, 191
behaviour, xix, 42, 43, 45, 46, 50, 52, 54, 58, 59, 60, 61, 62, 63, 64, 65, 66, 70, 71, 72, 73, 75, 76, 79, 84, 96, 115, 118, 123, 129, 134, 137, 140, 144, 168, 176, 192, 197, 201, 204, 205, 210, 214, 233, 234, 256, 272, 295
being, xx, xxi, 7, 8, 12, 17, 19, 20, 21, 23, 28, 31, 32, 37, 38, 41, 42, 44, 45, 46, 48, 49, 50, 52, 53, 54, 59, 60, 62, 70, 71, 73, 74, 75, 79, 80, 81, 84, 85, 89, 91, 95, 96, 97, 98, 99, 100, 102, 103, 104, 105, 109, 112, 113, 121, 122, 123, 124, 125, 126, 128, 133, 135, 137, 145, 146, 151, 152, 154, 157, 158, 160, 161, 162, 163, 164, 165, 166, 168, 169, 170, 171, 172, 173, 174, 175, 178, 181, 182, 183, 184, 187, 190, 191, 196, 200, 201, 202, 207, 208, 210, 222, 223, 224, 225, 227, 228, 229, 230, 233, 234, 239, 242, 248, 250, 251, 253, 254, 255, 256, 257, 259, 260, 261, 263, 264, 270, 291, 293, 295, 298, 299
Being and Nothingness, x, 48, 51, 100
Being and Time, x, 52, 80, 85, 94, 98, 110, 188, 199, 221, 223, 227, 228, 229
being-for-itself, 81, 165
being-for-others, 81
being-in-the-world, xviii, xix, xxi, 16, 17, 27, 42, 44, 46, 48, 53, 59, 64, 67, 71, 74, 89, 94, 95, 109, 121, 135, 137, 150, 163, 164, 166, 174, 191, 199, 200, 204, 208, 222, 223, 224, 230, 248, 250, 285
being-there, 145, 170, 208, 222, 223
being-towards-death, 79, 80, 81, 85, 173, 229
being-with, xviii, xxi, 50, 59, 89, 104, 121, 128, 137, 164, 173, 174, 175, 199, 222, 224, 242, 254, 259, 289, 291
beliefs, xx, 7, 9, 10, 13, 22, 30, 37, 44, 58, 60, 62, 65, 70, 72, 75, 110, 132, 166, 169, 214, 217, 218, 219, 233, 236, 237, 238, 239, 240, 241, 243, 244, 250, 265, 266, 276, 295, 296, 302
Binswanger, Ludwig (1881–1966), xviii, xix, 15, 16, 21, 44, 59, 62, 63, 65, 113, 127, 135, 138, 192, 193
body, xix, 10, 11, 12, 27, 28, 33, 34, 35, 39, 42, 43, 44, 45, 48, 49, 50, 51, 52, 53, 55, 56, 59, 60, 62, 76, 95, 97, 98, 106, 109, 120, 137, 157, 160, 163, 190, 195, 200, 205, 246, 256, 267, 285, 286, 287, 288, 289, 293, 302

Boss, Medard (1904–1990), xv, 12, 16, 17, 22, 24, 113, 135, 136, 137, 138, 191, 192, 193, 196, 208, 209, 210, 212, 213, 214, 238

Brentano, Franz (1838–1917), 12

Buber, Martin (1878–1965), xix, 16, 104, 109, 127, 132, 137, 150, 151, 152, 165, 255, 269

Bugental, James, xii, xiv, 18, 19, 20, 253, 254, 255, 256, 258, 259, 264

C

call of conscience, 173–4

Camus, Albert (1913–1960), 6, 13, 81, 179, 247, 267, 268

care, 34, 40, 52, 76, 80, 90, 110, 118, 127, 163, 174, 175, 191, 197, 201, 223, 228, 229, 230, 241, 243, 286, 288, 290

causality, 133, 141

challenging, xi, 21, 22, 74, 75, 81, 82, 90, 94, 95, 101, 106, 107, 204, 231, 247, 255, 257, 258, 259

change, 3, 7, 8, 24, 30, 32, 35, 37, 63, 65, 71, 75, 90, 94, 127, 130, 131, 134, 143, 149, 150, 151, 159, 162, 163, 165, 173, 174, 177, 178, 179, 183, 185, 186, 190, 202, 212, 218, 226, 235, 236, 239, 241, 242, 243, 249, 256, 261, 262, 266, 271, 274, 283, 285, 288, 295

choice, 7, 17, 20, 32, 33, 35, 37, 41, 42, 45, 46, 60, 64, 69, 70, 74, 83, 84, 94, 97, 122, 124, 136, 145, 146, 165, 173, 174, 175, 181, 183, 194, 195, 199, 200, 202, 219, 225, 229, 230, 231, 232, 235, 239, 241, 249, 255, 256, 257, 261, 264, 267, 268, 269, 273

clarification, xi, xx, 3, 62, 70, 71, 75, 211, 214, 240, 243, 247, 248, 270, 271

client-centred psychotherapy, 15

cognitive-behavioural therapy, xiii, 10, 58, 65, 69, 71, 110, 180, 237, 282

Cohn, Hans W. (1916–2004), xii, 22, 180, 181, 184, 188, 192, 193, 196, 197, 211, 221, 226, 235, 247, 250

compulsive, 58, 61, 70, 71, 72, 74, 84, 193, 234

concealment, 74, 152, 214, 224

concept, xi, xv, xviii, xix, 20, 31, 40, 46, 67, 68, 69, 70, 72, 76, 94, 97, 98, 109, 120, 126, 134, 136, 137, 147, 159, 163, 166, 170, 171, 178, 182, 188, 198, 199, 202, 208, 219, 222, 223, 228, 229, 230, 232, 293, 294

Condrau, Gion, 17, 135, 209, 214, 238

confirmation, 258, 259, 293, 294

conflict, xii, xvi, 37, 40, 71, 72, 83, 107, 111, 139, 140, 151, 152, 160, 176, 183, 201, 219, 226

consciousness, 7, 37, 42–3, 48–53, 56, 72, 78, 120, 121, 164, 165, 172, 188, 208, 209, 223, 263

contradiction, xx, 24, 64, 96, 101, 103, 168, 268, 275, 277, 279, 285, 298

control, xix, 10, 29, 33, 34, 35, 36, 38, 59, 61, 62, 63, 64, 65, 70, 72, 75, 78, 80, 95, 112, 116, 130, 149, 172, 180, 185, 186, 187, 194, 199, 204, 219, 233, 234, 239, 261, 278, 294

Cooper, David (1931–1986), 21, 136, 137, 146

Courage to be, 36, 66, 113, 135, 166, 177, 179, 180, 182, 184, 188, 193

crowd, the, 126, 144–5, 148

curiosity, 76, 128, 258, 259, 260, 268

D

daimonic, 20

Dasein/Da-sein, xxi, 38, 52, 79, 121, 125, 128, 145, 150, 163–4, 170, 171, 172, 179, 181, 191, 201, 208, 222, 223, 224, 227, 228, 229, 246, 251

Daseinsanalysis, xiv, 12, 16–18, 23, 24, 137, 208, 214, 238

death, xx, 5, 12, 20, 27, 30, 32, 34, 36, 38, 44, 50, 59, 63, 64, 73, 74, 78–85, 112, 114, 115, 116, 123, 125, 137, 152, 159, 164, 166, 170, 173, 181, 182, 183, 190, 193, 197–203, 206, 229, 230, 233, 240, 247, 248, 257, 264, 267, 268, 271, 272, 276, 285, 286, 299, 302

death anxiety, 73, 74, 84, 85, 149

defences, psychological, 20, 73, 82, 84

desire, xix, 9, 10, 41, 51–2, 56, 90, 91, 94, 116, 118, 135, 175, 176, 183, 207, 272, 290

despair, 6, 12, 17, 23, 34, 35, 36, 40, 112, 114, 120, 128, 139, 140, 153, 161, 162, 168, 180, 189, 196, 280, 283

dialectic, 105, 127

dialectical, 11, 20, 48, 137, 145, 147

dialogue, xv, 9, 14, 18, 43, 54, 91, 100–9, 140, 142, 150–2, 162, 174, 202, 203, 211, 248, 298

disclosure and disclosedness, 94, 164, 202

discourse, 9, 94, 95, 103, 112, 154, 203, 211, 218, 255

disposition, 46, 112, 123, 132, 148

doubt, 40, 41, 46, 74, 113, 139, 162, 273, 274, 275, 280, 281, 282, 283, 292, 294

dreams, 17, 134, 159, 207–14, 261, 302

Dreyfus, Hubert, 182, 187, 223, 224
du Plock, Simon, xiii, 22, 67, 72, 247, 248, 249

E
ec-stasies, 228–9
Eigenwelt, xix, 44, 60, 62, 63, 135, 157
Either/Or, 47
embodied, 20, 27, 42, 48, 49, 50, 51, 52, 53, 57, 59, 62, 63, 64, 80, 96, 97, 165, 285, 286, 289, 297
emotions, xvi, 7, 9, 28, 64, 90, 91, 110–20, 121, 125, 143, 148, 149, 150, 153, 213, 235, 252, 256
encounter, xv, 14, 18, 19, 21, 23, 24, 50, 53, 54, 55, 56, 58, 71, 75, 93, 124, 133, 144, 165, 184, 188, 192, 208, 209, 214, 217, 230, 231, 248, 255, 266
engagement, 9, 11, 12, 14, 46, 51, 75, 99, 103, 109, 118, 153, 159, 180, 229, 230, 248, 250, 270, 278
engulfment, 20, 63, 113, 166
en-soi, 146
essence, 67, 70, 95, 99, 103, 124, 125, 161, 164, 171, 199, 208, 211, 214, 280
ethical, xv, xvi, 8, 9, 41, 42, 46, 76, 128, 129, 148, 162, 174, 175, 190
evil, 7, 8, 41, 144, 153, 179, 218, 236, 272, 302
existence, x, xi, xv, xviii, xix, xx, xxi, 3, 5, 6, 7, 8, 9, 12, 13, 14, 15, 16, 18, 19, 21, 23, 24, 30, 31, 32, 33, 36, 37, 41, 43, 44, 49, 50, 51, 52, 53, 56, 59, 62, 64, 65, 67, 73, 75, 77, 78, 80, 81, 82, 83, 84, 89, 91, 92, 112, 113, 121, 124, 126, 128, 131, 136, 146, 157, 159, 161, 162, 163, 164, 165, 171, 172, 173, 174, 176, 179, 181, 182, 183, 185, 189, 192, 196, 199, 201, 202, 207, 208, 209, 210, 217, 218, 225, 227, 228, 229, 230, 231, 232, 235, 239, 240, 245, 246, 248, 249, 250, 253, 255, 259, 265, 266, 269, 271, 274, 277, 278, 284, 285, 296, 298, 300
existence precedes essence, 124, 161, 164
existentiell, 128
explicit, 103, 106, 149, 229, 247, 249, 253, 254, 288, 289
extravagance, 62, 193

F
facticity, 50, 51, 54, 174, 183, 230
failure, 40, 46, 60, 95, 119, 140, 144, 174, 225, 232, 233, 274, 277, 292
fallen/fallenness, 7, 125, 128, 131, 181
falling, 145, 172, 178, 192, 230, 267, 275

fear, 6, 18, 20, 29, 32, 33, 34, 41, 45, 46, 54, 61, 62, 63, 65, 71, 74, 75, 80, 83, 90, 91, 96, 113, 115, 117, 118, 119, 120, 122, 123, 125, 130, 131, 150, 158, 166, 172, 176, 182, 183, 185, 186, 188, 192, 195, 212, 213, 218, 232, 233, 244, 260, 272, 273, 274, 280, 282, 284, 289, 291, 297, 298, 302
feelings, xix, 12, 17, 20, 32, 35, 36, 48, 62, 78, 82, 83, 84, 90, 107, 108, 110, 111, 113, 115, 116, 117, 118, 119, 120, 129, 139, 140, 146, 153, 154, 163, 175, 177, 189, 190, 193, 195, 196, 197, 211, 212, 213, 254, 255, 257, 258, 265, 302
finite, 9, 20, 60, 80, 81, 161, 162, 173, 182, 201, 202, 227, 230, 253, 271
focus, xix, xx, 3, 4, 9, 13, 16, 18, 23, 32, 33, 34, 36, 37, 40, 41, 43, 45, 49, 50, 51, 53, 54, 61, 63, 64, 69, 70, 71, 72, 75, 76, 80, 91, 94, 96, 102, 106, 119, 130, 131, 137, 138, 152, 159, 168, 172, 175, 181, 190, 193, 195, 200, 210, 217, 219, 233, 237, 245, 246, 249, 254, 255, 256, 257, 261, 267, 284, 292, 293
focusing, xiv, 13, 19, 31, 63, 112, 122, 206, 226, 234, 255, 256, 297
for-itself, 172
forgetting, 274
Foucault, Michel (1926–1984), 50, 51, 247, 248, 251, 252, 266
Foulkes, Sigmund Heinrich, 148, 151, 152, 154
Frankl, Viktor (1905–1997), 17–18, 24, 193, 202, 238, 240, 243, 244, 247, 252, 253, 264
free will, 193, 232
freedom, xi, xv, xx, 6, 11, 17, 20, 23, 33, 37, 42, 51, 52, 61, 64, 67, 70, 104, 119, 124, 125, 128, 129, 130, 132, 145, 146, 150, 158, 163, 164, 165, 166, 167, 168, 170, 171–3, 174, 177, 178, 181, 183, 186, 187, 193, 204, 229, 231, 232, 242, 246, 250, 251, 266, 269, 271, 272, 295
Freud, Sigmund (1856–1939), xv, xvi, 16, 17, 29, 39, 40, 41, 43, 68, 93, 94, 133, 134, 135, 138, 160, 181, 197, 207, 208, 213, 214, 224, 236, 255
future, 8, 12, 17, 23, 35, 40, 71, 73, 74, 81, 82, 83, 97, 125, 159, 161, 163, 164, 165, 168, 169, 173, 174, 176, 177, 183, 185, 186, 190, 192, 193, 195, 201, 202, 204, 213, 219, 228, 229, 230, 235, 241, 242, 260, 261, 265, 270, 272, 273, 291, 302

G

Gadamer, Hans-Georg (1900–2002), 101, 104, 223

Gendlin, Eugene, 19, 96, 97, 99, 112, 200, 202, 205, 206, 255

generosity, 13, 126, 128, 237, 271, 298

goals, 62, 176, 239

good, 3, 5, 8–9, 28, 29, 33, 39, 41, 58, 63, 68, 72, 80, 82, 91, 98, 105, 106, 107, 108, 113, 115, 119, 123, 129, 139, 140, 141, 148, 149, 152, 158, 159, 165, 166, 167, 185, 194, 203, 204, 207, 217, 218, 235, 236, 237, 239, 247, 251, 255, 257, 260, 262, 266, 267, 269, 271, 272, 273, 275, 279, 280, 281, 282, 283, 285, 286, 288, 291, 293, 295, 296, 297, 298, 302

Grundbefindlichkeit, 181

guilt, 23, 34, 39, 40, 60, 61, 96, 99, 113, 173, 174, 177, 181, 182, 189, 190, 192, 193, 194, 195, 196, 201, 235, 281

H

Heidegger, Martin (1889–1976), x, xii, xiv, xviii, xix, xx, xxi, 4, 5, 6, 7, 8, 12, 15, 16, 17, 21, 22, 35, 37, 38, 43, 48, 52, 61, 78, 79, 80, 81, 82, 83, 84, 85, 89, 93, 94–9, 103, 105, 110, 112, 113, 121, 122, 123, 124, 125, 128, 135, 136, 137, 141, 145, 146, 150, 151, 152, 157, 161, 163, 164, 166, 170, 172, 173, 174, 175, 178, 179, 181, 185, 187, 188, 190, 191, 199, 201, 207, 208, 211, 214, 222, 224, 227, 228, 229, 230, 235, 238, 247, 250, 257, 267

herd, the, 145, 172, 249

hermeneutics, 221, 223, 226

homeless, 125, 150

humanistic psychology, xii, xv, 4, 18–19, 66, 111, 169, 253, 254, 255, 259, 261, 263, 264

Husserl, Edmund (1859–1938), 12, 15, 48, 135, 137, 214, 223

I

identity, xii, xiv, xix, 6, 20, 27, 32, 33, 35, 37, 40, 48, 50, 64, 73, 85, 125, 127, 137, 157, 158, 159, 160, 167, 168, 169, 173, 174, 176, 192, 195, 247, 248, 264, 271, 272, 294, 295, 302

implicit, 41, 43, 46, 103, 149, 168, 175, 177, 202, 209, 217, 229, 249, 253, 254, 256, 288

implosion, 20, 113, 166

in-itself, 172

inauthenticity, 7, 12, 13, 42, 97, 146, 152, 164, 171–3, 174, 175, 177, 179, 182

indifference, 126

individual, the, 11, 33, 40, 41, 50, 59, 60, 61, 62, 72, 80, 99, 102, 123, 126, 128, 133, 134, 161, 171, 174, 178, 182, 185, 187, 189, 190, 199, 200, 201, 222, 237, 241, 245, 246, 253, 254, 255, 256, 260

infinite, 6, 9, 41, 79, 161, 162, 253, 271

insight, xi, xx, 4, 11, 17, 21, 54, 64, 65, 73, 84, 96, 102, 103, 104, 105, 112, 113, 133, 135, 138, 141, 157, 191, 195, 210, 213, 214, 219, 220, 238, 291, 295

intentionality, 7, 12, 49, 52, 465

interpretation, x, 8, 14, 22, 52, 65, 95, 96, 103, 108, 139, 175, 184, 187, 202, 207, 208, 209, 213, 214, 221–6, 237

intersubjectivity, 37, 42, 49, 50, 53, 127, 129, 137, 175, 199

intuition, 218, 243, 255, 302

ironist, 177–8

irony, 101, 109

isolation, 12, 20, 37, 40, 44, 59, 60, 61, 74, 91, 158, 172, 190, 198, 199, 230, 271, 277, 302

J

Jaspers, Karl (1883–1969), xix, 9, 13, 15, 35, 78, 79, 80, 82, 85, 121, 128, 166, 189, 190, 192, 247, 257, 276, 277

judgement, 8, 70, 75, 104, 106, 144, 146, 239, 260, 262, 266, 268, 273, 281, 284, 292, 295, 297

K

Kierkegaard, Søren (1813–1855), xix, 4, 6, 9, 11, 12, 19, 35, 41, 42, 43, 46, 47, 78, 109, 112, 120, 126, 127, 134, 137, 144, 145, 146, 153, 161, 162, 166, 170, 178, 179, 181, 183, 187, 188

knowing, 22, 50, 79, 101, 111, 131, 185, 199, 202, 253, 259, 261, 283, 288, 298

knowledge, 4, 18, 19, 22, 33, 80, 93, 96, 100, 101, 102, 105, 127, 135, 141, 191, 195, 210, 214, 233, 238, 266, 272, 276

L

Lacan, Jacques (1901–1981), 43, 98, 101, 109

lack, 5, 20, 29, 32, 46, 52, 58, 128, 131, 132, 140, 144, 191, 192, 201, 279, 283, 291, 293

Laing, Ronald D. (1927–1989), xv, 15, 20, 21, 22, 23, 24, 113, 132, 134, 135, 136, 137, 138, 142, 146, 166, 170, 190

Längle, Alfred, 17

language, xiv, xix, 4, 43, 44, 50, 52, 91, 93–9, 100, 104, 105, 106, 123, 136, 137, 138, 140, 146, 149, 158, 181, 188, 221, 288
leap of faith, 42, 46, 162
Lemma, Alessandra, 59, 60, 65, 189
Levinas, Emmanuel (1906–1995), 128, 129, 138
limit situations, 8–9
limitations, xx, 7, 13, 60, 61, 159, 164, 172, 184, 226, 230, 231, 232, 240, 261, 265, 270, 283
lived world, 22, 75, 76, 122
logos, 17, 104
logotherapy, 17–18, 23, 24, 252
look, the, 49
love, 9, 44, 45, 59, 61, 62, 69, 73, 89, 107, 108, 109, 116, 117, 118, 119, 120, 126, 127, 128, 132, 134, 141, 148, 176, 199, 201, 211, 218, 233, 237, 238, 239, 240, 242, 261, 269, 271, 272, 280, 281, 291, 297, 298, 302

M
Macquarrie, John, 78, 80, 81, 91, 180, 181, 188, 237, 246, 247, 251
masochism, 126
master and slave, 51
May, Rollo (1909–1994), xv, xviii, xix, 10, 16, 18, 19, 20, 24, 59, 60, 65, 77, 80, 81, 82, 113, 120, 127, 132, 180, 181, 182, 183, 184, 185, 188, 193, 196, 246
meaning, x, xiv, xv, xx, 6, 9, 13, 17, 18, 22, 31, 35, 37, 43, 50, 60, 62, 63, 64, 67, 69, 70, 72, 74, 75, 76, 78, 81, 96, 98, 101, 103, 104, 105, 106, 117, 132, 141, 151, 173, 176, 178, 179, 180, 181, 183, 193, 195, 198, 201, 202, 207, 209, 214, 217, 219, 222, 223, 224, 226, 228, 229, 232, 235, 239, 240, 245, 246, 249, 251, 253–64, 268, 270, 272, 275, 279, 296, 297
meaninglessness, 6, 17, 20, 42, 50, 59, 73, 74, 122, 137, 182, 192, 193, 259, 272
Merleau-Ponty, Maurice (1908–1961), 33, 35, 42, 43, 44, 45, 47, 48, 49, 50, 51, 52, 53, 55, 56, 59, 137, 200, 228, 246, 265, 276
Minkowski, Eugène (1885–1972), 16, 136, 192, 196
Mitwelt, xix, xxi, 44, 59, 62, 63, 67, 89, 135, 138
mood, 7, 32, 54, 55, 56, 68, 97, 110, 111, 112, 119, 120, 132, 153, 189, 190, 191, 193, 195, 210, 212

mortality, 7, 33, 34, 36, 40, 44, 79, 80, 113, 164, 199, 201, 206, 222, 230
motivation, 36, 56, 65, 73, 121, 205, 270, 275, 291
mutuality, x, 126, 270

N
nausea, 6, 98, 125, 143
Nietzsche, Friedrich (1844–1900), 4, 8, 11, 19, 39, 42, 43, 47, 48, 58, 67, 93, 98, 112, 126, 144, 145, 146, 162, 163, 170, 213, 267, 301
not knowing, 101, 259
nothingness, 5–6, 13, 48, 51, 52, 70, 81, 100, 125, 126, 164
Nussbaum, Martha, 9, 112, 120

O
ontic, 3, 51, 54, 56, 59, 96, 112, 122, 123, 132, 137, 163, 181, 182, 185, 187
ontological, 3, 20, 48, 49, 50, 51, 52, 53, 54, 56, 59, 96, 99, 112, 122, 123, 130, 132, 163, 181, 182, 185, 187, 222
ontological insecurity, 20, 113
ontology, 48, 51, 52, 57, 122, 123, 124, 182, 208
Other, the, 43, 49, 51, 52, 53, 57, 75, 81, 90, 102, 104, 105, 126, 127, 128, 130, 131, 147, 151, 165, 175, 190, 228, 241, 242, 248, 269

P
panic, 36, 98, 175–7, 183, 184, 188, 232, 278, 279, 280, 281, 283, 285, 286, 287, 288
paradox, xii, xx, 11, 14, 22, 65, 132, 161, 168, 171, 179, 202, 253, 254, 261, 270, 275, 298
paradoxical intention, 18
passion, xii, 9, 10, 70, 72, 112, 113, 116, 132, 134, 144, 148, 179, 261
past, xiii, 4, 8, 12, 17, 22, 23, 55, 63, 73, 74, 119, 138, 140, 143, 145, 146, 164, 165, 168, 172, 174, 176, 177, 192, 193, 204, 219, 224, 225, 228, 230, 241, 258, 262, 265, 269, 270, 278, 280, 282, 288, 289, 290, 291, 296, 297, 300
perception, xviii, 34, 35, 42, 45, 47, 48, 49, 50, 51, 56, 124, 131, 134, 139, 140, 141, 169, 182, 191, 192, 233, 253
petrification, 20, 113, 166
phenomenological method, 190, 205, 249
phenomenology, xv, 12, 15, 24, 47, 48, 51, 52, 67, 75, 159, 190, 208, 219, 223

phenomenon, 50, 51, 52, 55, 124, 152, 181, 189, 205, 208, 209, 211, 214, 221, 222, 223, 224, 249

Plato (427–347 BC), 4, 9, 10, 95, 102, 105, 109, 207

possibility, 6, 7, 11, 12, 30, 34, 35, 42, 45, 54, 75, 76, 79, 80, 81, 84, 96, 104, 105, 109, 112, 126, 136, 161, 163, 164, 169, 172, 173, 176, 177, 181, 183, 193, 198, 202, 210, 225, 229, 230, 235, 251, 271, 274, 287, 298

praxis, 13, 137, 138, 147

presence, 19, 44, 53, 55, 69, 103, 107, 126, 198, 199, 257, 258, 259, 262, 263

primordial, 42, 52, 95, 164, 202, 229, 241

project, original, 7, 45, 47

psychoanalysis, xiv, 5, 24, 32, 59, 98, 208, 214, 222, 236, 237

psychopathology, 15, 96, 190, 279, 287

purpose, xii, xx, 3, 10, 13, 14, 17, 28, 35, 46, 72, 75, 79, 93, 127, 132, 144, 183, 217, 219, 227–35, 237, 241, 255, 267, 297, 302

R

rational emotive behaviour therapy, 10, 65

ready-to-hand, 164

reciprocity, x, 126, 147, 148, 154, 270, 271, 272, 296

relationship, x, xii, xiii, xviii, xix, 10, 20, 22, 23, 27, 28, 29, 32, 36, 37, 40, 48, 49, 50, 53, 54, 55, 56, 57, 62, 63, 64, 73, 74, 75, 80, 82, 83, 89, 90, 91, 92, 95, 98, 100, 101, 102, 103, 105, 106, 107, 109, 114, 115, 117, 118, 119, 121–32, 134, 135, 137, 138, 141, 145, 147, 148, 149, 150, 151, 157, 159, 160, 161, 162, 163, 165, 173, 175, 176, 177, 178, 184, 185, 187, 196, 197, 198, 199, 200, 201, 202, 203, 204, 206, 209, 210, 211, 212, 213, 217, 225, 229, 231, 233, 234, 237, 238, 241, 245, 247, 248, 255, 261, 262, 263, 270, 278, 279, 280, 281, 282, 285, 287, 288, 289, 290, 291, 292, 293, 295, 296, 297, 298, 299, 300

religious, 4, 41, 42, 44, 45, 46, 61, 144, 152, 217, 218, 227, 237, 239, 244, 268, 296

resistance, 19, 20, 139, 254, 255–6, 257, 269

resolute living, 113

resoluteness, 164, 230

resonance, 110, 148, 270

responsibility, xv, 6, 7, 23, 33, 34, 36, 60, 61, 63, 64, 82, 83, 84, 101, 117, 126, 127, 128, 130, 138, 140, 141, 145, 166, 170, 172, 173, 174, 175, 176, 177, 178, 181, 182, 187, 194, 200, 211, 212, 213, 235, 255, 256, 261, 264

Rogers, Carl (1902–1987), 15, 19

S

sadism, 126

Sartre, Jean-Paul (1905–1980), x, 4, 5, 6, 7, 9, 13, 24, 33, 35, 47, 48, 49, 50, 51, 52, 53, 56, 69, 70, 72, 81, 89, 98, 113, 120, 124, 125, 126, 132, 136, 137, 143, 145, 146, 147, 148, 149, 150, 161, 164, 165, 166, 168, 169, 170, 171, 172, 174, 247, 265

Schneider, Kirk, xv, 18, 19, 58, 60, 61, 62, 65, 66

searching, 14, 19, 219, 253, 254, 255, 256, 257, 258, 259, 261, 262, 263

seinlassen, 238

self, xiii, xiv, xv, xix, 6, 7, 10, 12, 13, 20, 22, 24, 35, 39, 40, 43, 44, 45, 46, 48, 53, 60, 63, 66, 70, 78, 126, 128, 132, 142, 150, 157, 159, 160–70, 172, 177, 178, 192, 193, 202, 256, 260, 262, 267, 270, 271

self-concept, 293

self deception, 8, 13, 21, 180, 274

separateness, 20, 81, 125, 198, 289

seriality, 145

sexuality, xvi, 29, 30, 48–57, 99, 178, 225, 246, 247, 248, 249, 250

shame, 40, 60, 64, 119, 145, 146, 153, 154, 158, 262, 281

Sickness unto Death, 112, 170

social construct, 31, 68

Socrates (470–399 BC), 4, 9, 10, 78, 100, 101, 102, 105

Socratic method, 100, 102

solicitude, 122, 175

solution-focused therapy, 76

Spinelli, Ernesto, 22, 23, 24, 70, 71, 73, 74, 75, 81, 99, 238, 241, 243, 244, 246, 247, 248, 249, 250, 252

Stadlen, Anthony, xv, 133, 134, 136, 137, 138

Stimmung, 112, 191

Strasser, Freddie, xvi, 22, 70, 193, 227, 232, 235, 247, 250, 252

stress, 43, 73, 180, 184, 189, 223, 232, 299

subjectivity, 12, 48, 49, 52, 126, 254

Szasz, Thomas, 134, 135, 137, 141, 190, 247, 248

T

Tantam, Digby, xvi, 7, 114, 121, 143

temporality, 192, 227, 228, 229, 230, 232

They, the, 79, 164, 181

throwness, 35, 36, 38, 61, 94, 172, 181, 191, 230

Tillich, Paul (1886–1965), xix, 8, 10, 13, 18, 34, 35, 60, 66, 79, 80, 113, 127, 166, 180, 181, 182, 183, 184, 185, 187, 188, 193

time, xiv, xvi, 8, 12, 16, 17, 22, 34, 35, 37, 52, 69, 73, 74, 80, 82, 85, 94, 95, 98, 99, 102, 103, 105, 110, 112, 136, 188, 191, 192, 195, 199, 217, 219, 221, 223, 225, 226, 227–35, 242, 247, 255, 261, 264, 266, 267, 269, 270, 271, 274, 275, 281, 285, 287, 291, 297, 300

transcendence, 60, 61, 62

transference, 22, 101

trust, 29, 30, 40, 46, 82, 83, 90, 102, 104, 106, 107, 114, 116, 138, 212, 231, 234, 250, 261, 263, 275, 293, 297, 298, 299

truth, xvi, 3, 8, 9, 14, 34, 53, 69, 93, 94, 95, 96, 101, 102, 104, 106, 131, 144, 145, 151, 152, 187, 224, 238, 254, 258, 264, 267, 270, 271, 272, 273, 275, 283, 294, 301

U

Überwelt, xix, 44, 60, 62

ultimate concerns, 8, 20, 35

Umwelt, xviii, xix, 27, 44, 59, 62, 135

uncertainty, 34, 41, 44, 46, 51, 59, 60, 61, 73, 74, 80, 174, 176, 177, 178, 186, 228, 232

understanding, xi, xvi, xx, 3, 4, 5, 9, 10, 11, 12, 13, 15, 22, 28, 30, 32, 35, 36, 46, 47, 50, 51, 52, 54, 56, 57, 62, 65, 66, 75, 90, 91, 94, 96, 97, 103, 105, 112, 117, 118, 119, 122, 127, 131, 132, 134, 138, 140, 141, 146, 151, 158, 159, 163, 166, 169, 172, 177, 178, 182, 183, 184, 186, 187, 188, 190, 195, 198, 200, 201, 206, 208, 210, 211, 212, 213, 217, 219, 221–7, 228, 237, 242, 246, 250, 251, 258, 266, 271, 275, 276, 277, 291, 293, 294, 297

unfolding, 47, 204, 244, 255

Unheimlichkeit, 125, 150, 181

unknowing, 22, 24, 266

V

values, xx, 7, 8, 10, 11, 12, 13, 22, 35, 36, 37, 42, 44, 45, 60, 62, 64, 67, 70, 75, 84, 102, 103, 104, 110, 112, 120, 131, 132, 150, 151, 168, 169, 174, 176, 177, 178, 179, 193, 202, 214, 217, 218, 219, 231, 232, 233, 234, 236–44, 250, 265, 266, 267, 268, 269, 270, 271, 272, 274, 275, 276, 295, 296, 297, 302

van Deurzen, Emmy, xi, xii, xviii, xix, xx, 3, 9, 13, 21, 22, 23, 24, 27, 32, 35, 44, 89, 100, 102, 110, 113, 121, 129, 132, 146, 157, 160, 166, 167, 179, 208, 217, 231, 235, 238, 240, 243, 244, 245, 247, 248, 250, 265, 267, 276, 277

W

West, Ellen, 16, 59, 77, 113, 135

wisdom, xi, xiv, 4, 9, 10, 15, 22, 101, 219, 272, 275, 276, 277

wish-world, 61, 63

Wittgenstein, Ludwig (1889–1951), xiv, 4, 94, 96, 97, 99

worldview, xix, 7, 13, 60, 62, 78, 96, 187, 195, 205, 217, 218, 231, 232, 233, 234, 265, 297, 302

worship, 58, 60, 61, 65, 199, 296

Y

Yalom, Irvin, 18, 19, 20, 24, 60, 73, 74, 79, 82, 83, 85, 113, 138, 144, 146, 154, 189, 201, 238, 241, 243, 244, 257, 264